RESIDENTIAL SALES COMPARISON

&

INCOME APPROACHES

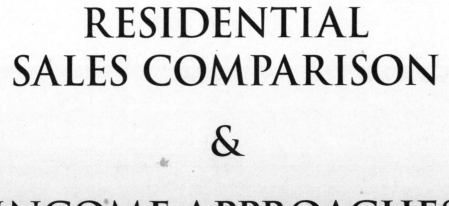

LEE R. HESS · GEORGE H. MILLER

This publication is designed to provide accurate and current information regarding the subject matter covered. The principles and conclusions presented are subject to local, state and federal laws and regulations, court cases and revisions of same. If legal advice or other expert assistance is required, the reader is urged to consult a competent professional in the field.

Director of Publishing &
Course Development
Lars Jentsch

Creative Editor/ Production Coordinator
Judy Hobbs

Real Estate Publisher
Leigh Conway

Graphic Design
Dria Kasunich, Assistant Manager
Susan Mackessy

Writer/Copyeditor
Sue Carlson

Technical Writer
Ben Hernandez

Senior Technical Writer
Judy Moyer

Copyeditor
Emily Rehkopf

Administrative Assistant
Stephanie Pratap

Published by
Ashley Crown Systems, Inc.
22952 Alcalde Drive
Laguna Hills, California 92653

Printed in the United States of America

ISBN: 978-0934772-02-0

TABLE OF CONTENTS

PREFACE

Residential Sales Comparison and Income Approaches covers all of the topics included in the 2008 pre-licensing appraisal course requirements established by The Appraiser Qualifications Board of the Appraisal Foundation. Although written for the beginning appraiser, anyone, including consumers and investors, will find detailed answers to his or her questions about the value and condition of property. This textbook will prepare the student to identify specific property, recognize factors affecting real estate, and to present analyzed facts in a coherent, organized format consistent with USPAP standards.

The entire real estate transaction evolves constantly. Therefore, the professional real estate appraiser must keep up with the changing marketplace. Although a large portion of the marketplace information is available through technology, it is important for an appraiser to know how to interpret and apply this data correctly. To obtain the competency required in real estate appraisal, basic knowledge of appraisal fundamentals is essential.

Each chapter in this textbook has been divided into topics. Topic content is reinforced through real-life examples, photographs, illustrations, charts, and tables. Important terms are highlighted in **bold type** in each chapter. Each chapter ends with a summary.

Review exercises have been designed for each chapter. The quiz exercises feature real estate terms and multiple-choice questions. The multiple-choice questions at the end of each chapter will help the student prepare for the real estate appraisal exam. These challenging questions were designed to test higher-level concepts and will often require the student to combine information he or she has learned in different chapters.

After completing a quiz exercise, students can check their answers by reviewing the Answer Key in the Appendix. Students are encouraged to review their work often to make sure they understand what they have read.

ABOUT THE AUTHORS

Lee R. Hess, Ph.D., C.G.A.

Dr. Hess brought many years of experience in real estate appraisal and education to the production of this textbook. He was a California Certified General Appraiser, and had considerable experience in commercial, industrial, single-family, and multiple-family residential real estate. Dr. Hess had a California real estate broker license, and testified in numerous court cases as an expert witness.

Dr. Hess first became involved with appraisal education in 1972 when he was Director of Education and Staff Development for American Appraisal Associates, Inc. Dr. Hess had considerable experience in appraising large numbers of properties. He was a nationally certified USPAP instructor by The Appraiser Qualifications Board. Dr. Hess taught at five universities and four colleges. He had a Ph.D. in Educational Psychology from Marquette University.

Dr. Hess wrote 18 books, numerous journal articles, a newspaper column and a monograph. He also wrote the article "Navigating USPAP" published in *Working Real Estate Magazine*.

George H. Miller, R.E.C.I., C.G.A.

George Miller brings a rich background in real estate appraisal and education to the creation and production of this book. He is a State of California Certified General Appraiser, and has more than 40 years experience in commercial, industrial, single-family, and multiple-family residential real estate. Mr. Miller has a California real estate sales license, is an expert witness in real estate values, and has testified in numerous court cases.

As Chairman of the Real Estate Department of West Valley Community College, Mr. Miller was responsible for the development and direction of a real estate program. Mr. Miller has 25 years of teaching experience, and has taught numerous courses in real estate and appraisal. He has a Bachelor of Arts degree in Business from California State University-Chico with a special Secondary Teaching credential.

Mr. Miller is the author of *Residential Real Estate Appraisal*, the co-author of *Residential Market Analysis & Highest and Best Use*, and is a well-known guest lecturer at the University of California-Berkeley, San Jose City College, Stanford University, and San Jose State University. He has also spoken at real estate boards and seminars on local real estate issues.

LAND

Land includes airspace, surface rights, and subsurface rights. Land refers not only to the surface of the earth, but also to everything attached to it by nature such as trees and lakes. Land also includes products of nature beneath the surface such as oil and limestone.

AIR RIGHTS

Airspace is considered real property to a reasonable height. An owner or developer of high-rise condominiums may sell the airspace as real property. Unrestricted ownership of air space, also known as air rights, has been modified significantly. Today, air rights are subject to commercial and military flights. At one time, landowners' rights extended into the skies above their land. Today, however, with virtually unrestricted air travel, no owner can practically claim the entire airspace above a piece of land.

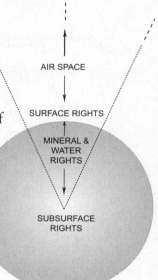

Land includes airspace, surface rights, and subsurface rights.

SURFACE RIGHTS

Surface rights are the rights to use the surface of land, including the right to drill or dig mineshafts through the surface when subsurface rights are involved. Surface rights also include water rights. The owner of property bordering a stream or river has **riparian rights** (a riparian owner). Riparian property owners have reasonable use of flowing water, providing it does not injure other riparian landowners. Owners of land bordering a lake (**littoral owners**) generally own to the average low water mark or the edge of the lake.

Riparian rights

Water rights that go with the land are considered real property. A person's water rights do not exceed the amount reasonably needed for one's own personal use. Because of the many disputes over the use of water, the law is very clear about the rights of owners. Water cannot be owned, nor can it be channeled or dammed for the benefit of one landowner to the detriment of other property owners. Under the **Doctrine of Correlative Use**, an owner may take only a reasonable share of underground waters (not to exclude adjoining owners). Most Western states use the **Doctrine of Prior Appropriation,** which gives the first person to use water from a water source the rights to it. If the first person does not use or consume all of the water, subsequent users can then use it.

SUBSURFACE RIGHTS

Subsurface rights are the rights to underground natural resources such as minerals, oil, and gas. **Minerals** are owned as real property unless they are fugitive substances, that is, non-solid, migratory minerals such as oil or gas. These may not be owned until taken from the ground and then they become the personal property of whoever removed them.

Visually, we can think of real property as an inverted, extended pyramid, with its apex at the center of the earth and its base somewhere in infinity. Through the years, Congress has limited the ownership of airspace.

> **Review – Land as Real Estate**
> - Airspace
> - Surface Rights (includes water rights)
> - Subsurface Rights (mineral rights, petroleum, gas)

PERSONAL PROPERTY

Personal property, as defined in USPAP, is identifiable tangible objects that are considered by the public as being personal. For example, furnishings, artwork, antiques, gems and jewelry, collectibles, machinery, and equipment are movable and tangible items. Tangible property that is not classified as real estate is personal property. Generally, it consists of items not securely attached to the real property. Personal property rights may also include non-tangible intellectual properties, which are a challenge to value.

My Life

Artwork is a movable and tangible item.

Personal property is also known as chattel. **Chattel** is derived from the word cattle, which was an early form of personal property. It is interesting to note that personal property and real estate can change according to circumstance.

> Example: A tree is real property until it is cut as timber; then it becomes the personal property of whoever cut it. If that timber is milled into lumber, sold, and used to build a house, it becomes real property. As the house ages, it deteriorates. When it is torn down, the scrap lumber that is hauled away is personal property.

Anything that may be owned and gained lawfully is known as property. Property can be real or personal. Anything that is not real property is personal property.

FIXTURES

Sometimes it is difficult for an appraiser to be sure if something tangible is personal property or real property. This applies most often to fixtures. A **fixture** is personal property that has become affixed to real estate. The problem is to determine if the attachment is permanent.

Disputes about real and personal property have caused the courts to adopt certain tests to help them decide ownership rights of disagreeing parties.

Tests of a Fixture

- **Method of Attachment.** How is the disputed item attached to the property? If it is permanently attached, it is considered real property. An item is personal property if it can be removed without causing defect to the real estate or itself. Using this test, for example, built-in bookshelves in a house are fixtures.

- **Adaptation.** Has the item been made especially for the property? Custom draperies could be removed but are considered fixtures because they are part of the decoration package and were made to fit those particular windows. Is the stove

Built-in bookcases are an example of a fixture.

built into the counter? If so, it has become a fixture and has lost its status as personal property.

- **Relationship of the Parties.** In a dispute about fixtures, when there is no convincing evidence of the right of one party, courts consider whether the parties are landlord-tenant, lender-borrower, or buyer-seller. The court then makes a decision based on the relationship of the parties. Usually, the court favors the tenant over the landlord, the lender over the borrower, and the buyer over the seller.

- **Intention of the Parties.** If apparent, either in writing or by the actions of either party involved, this is considered the most important test of a fixture. A fixture may remain personal property if all parties are informed. Intention should always be put in writing.

    Example: A tenant wired special cosmetic lights into the bathroom wall, but told the landlord he intended the lights to remain his personal property. He said he would repair the wall when he moved and would take the lights with him. This was a clear case of a tenant's intention to keep the lights as his personal property.

- **Agreement of the Parties.** One way a court will determine whether a fixture exists is to see if the parties have made a clear agreement concerning fixtures. Agreements should be in writing.

> **Review – Five Tests of a Fixture**
> **Mnemonic = MARIA**
>   **M**ethod of attachment
>   **A**daptation
>   **R**elationship of the parties
>   **I**ntention
>   **A**greement of the parties

TRADE FIXTURES

Though fixtures are considered real estate, trade fixtures are not. **Trade fixtures** are items of personal property used to conduct business, such as shelves, a cash register, room partitions, or a wall mirror. This is important to business appraisers and those who appraise specialty properties. Trade fixtures are also referred to as **chattel fixtures**. The key aspect of trade fixtures is that they are attached to a building by a tenant in order to conduct business. Tenants retain ownership of these items as personal property when they vacate the premises, but are responsible for repairing any damage that results from replacing the trade fixtures.

Trade fixtures may include fitness equipment in a health club or church pews in a rented church space. Industrial examples include special piping and machinery attached to the floor, or items installed for human comfort such as plumbing, lighting, heating, and air conditioning.

Patents, trademarks, and design rights are sometimes collectively known as **industrial property**, as they are typically created and used for industrial or commercial purposes. However, ideas and information, which are the product of the mind or the intellect, are known as intellectual property.

Health club fitness equipment is an example of trade fixtures.

INTELLECTUAL PROPERTY

In legal terms, **intellectual property** (IP) is a general term for various legal rights, which attach to certain types of information, ideas, or other intangibles. The holder of this legal entitlement is generally entitled to exercise various exclusive rights in relation to the subject matter of the IP. The term intellectual property reflects the idea that this subject matter is the product of the mind or the intellect, and that IP rights may be protected by law in the same way as any other form of property. However, the use of the term and the concepts it embodies are the subject of some controversy.

Intellectual property laws vary from jurisdiction to jurisdiction, such that the acquisition, registration, or enforcement of IP rights must be pursued or obtained separately in each territory of interest. Intellectual property laws confer a bundle of rights in relation to the particular form or manner in which ideas or information is expressed. It is important to note that the term intellectual property denotes the specific legal rights that authors, inventors, and other IP holders have, and not the intellectual work itself.

The appraisal implications of valuing intellectual property and other intangible property requires expertise in subjects such as copyrights, patents, trademarks, industrial design rights, and trade secrets. This is coupled with the valuation of goodwill and other aspects of a going concern.

In sports, an appraiser may be asked to value the goodwill that is associated with a key player. How much is Kobe Bryant worth to the Los Angeles Lakers in terms of the goodwill he brings to the team? How much was Mickey Mantle worth to the New York Yankees? These are very interesting appraisal problems.

RESTRICTIONS ON USE OF PROPERTY

Fee ownership—the ownership of land and everything attached to it, lying under it, and extending over it—implies unrestricted ownership. However, real property is subject to government and private restrictions. A **restriction** is a limitation on the use of real property and may be placed by a private owner, a developer, or the government. It is usually placed on property to assure that land use is consistent and uniform within a certain area. Private restrictions are placed by a present or past owner and affect only a specific property or development, while public restrictions are an example of government restrictions that benefit the general public.

GOVERNMENT RESTRICTIONS

Government restrictions are used to promote public health or the general welfare of the public. The four necessary powers of government that have some claim on all private real estate in the United States are: (1) police power, (2) eminent domain, (3) taxation, and (4) escheat.

POLICE POWER

The definition and extent of police power may vary from state to state. **Police power** is generally defined as power of the state to enact laws within constitutional limits to promote the order, safety, health, morals, and general welfare of our society. It includes enacting and enforcing building codes, building setback lines, zoning, installing traffic signals and controls, implementing sanitary and storm drainage requirements, and many other necessary controls.

Under the 10th Amendment to the United States Constitution, the powers prohibited from or not delegated to the Federal Government are reserved to the states or to the people. Police power belongs to the state unless there is some federal restriction. Police power is restricted by state constitutions.

Police power is generally defined as power of the state to enact laws within constitutional limits.

A law that operates upon all persons and property similarly situated, is not obnoxious to the constitutional provisions guaranteeing equal protection of the law to all persons and classes of persons, or guaranteeing persons' freedom of contract, or guaranteeing that no person shall be deprived of life, liberty, or property without due process of law.

Because the Congress has limited powers granted in the Constitution, the federal government does not have a general police power, as the states do. The exceptions are laws regarding federal property and the military. However, the federal government does have some police power over interstate commerce.

In condemnation under police power, the public body generally allows a reasonable time for the private property owner to correct any deficiencies of a property. Enforcement of local police power as they affect private property may not be capricious, arbitrary, or with prejudice. All deficient properties must be treated the same. The legislature may not impose onerous, unreasonable, or unnecessary burdens upon persons, property, or business.

Reasonable Uses of Police Power
- Zoning in cities so that neighborhoods may be kept free of objectionable businesses
- Limitation of districts in which cemeteries, slaughterhouses, factories and the like may be located
- Controls for speeding and other careless driving on the highways
- Prohibiting adulteration or selling of impure goods
- Garbage disposal
- Vaccination of school children
- Regulation or prohibition of liquor, prostitution, and gambling
- Requiring safety devices at places of employment

EMINENT DOMAIN

Many public and quasi-public agencies have the power of eminent domain. **Eminent domain** is the right of the government to take private property from an owner, for the public good, paying fair market value. In doing so, they must show a need for the property. This necessary power is exercised to purchase land for freeways, roads, schools, parks, airports, power lines, reservoirs, and military bases.

The Takings Clause of the Fifth Amendment to the Federal Constitution seems clear about the public use restrictions on the power of eminent domain. Recently, cities, counties, and states have been extending the power of eminent domain to take private property, not for public use, but to benefit private groups. Instead of building a highway or school, they take the private property and sell it to private developers to build shopping centers, luxury residences, and factories.

> Example: In June 2005, the United States Supreme Court decided the case of *Kelo v. City of New London.* The court heard from a group of New London, Connecticut homeowners who did not want their homes razed in order to allow the building of a hotel, health club, and offices. The city wanted to build these new structures to complement a multi-million dollar research facility, recently built by Pfizer, the corporation. The court decided 5–4 to allow the neighborhood to be razed for the new structures. The majority opinion stated that the city had carefully planned for the economic development, which is not limited to new jobs and increased tax revenue. The minority opinion stated that the decision effectively deleted the words, "for public use" from the Takings Clause of the Fifth Amendment.

The power of eminent domain is also called the **power of condemnation**, a term not to be confused with a city using condemnation on a property that is unsafe. **Condemnation** is the process by which the government acquires private property for public use, under its right of eminent domain. The latter type of condemnation is a police power.

The major difference between condemnation under the power of eminent domain and condemnation under police power is that in the former, the public (or condemnor) must pay fair market value for the property that is to be acquired for public use. There is no payment involved in condemnation under police power.

TAXATION

Most private real property in most states is subject to real estate taxation. Exempt properties may include those of certain religious, charitable, educational, and non-profit organizations. Real property taxes are assessed by the local taxing body to provide revenues for city and county governments; school districts; welfare, flood control, and sanitary districts; road bonds; junior college districts; and many other local government and education functions.

States without property taxation use other means for generating the necessary income to operate and administer state government and programs.

For example, Nevada relies on its gaming industry to offset government costs. Several states rely on sales taxes to fund their programs.

Real estate licensees and appraisers should be aware of local real estate tax implications on properties with which they are involved.

Nevada is a state without property taxation that relies on its gaming industry to offset government costs.

ESCHEAT

Escheat is a legal process in which property reverts to the state because the deceased left no will and has no legal heirs. For example, a state's statute might provide that when some- one dies without a will, and is not survived by a spouse, descendants, or parents, the person's estate would escheat to the state.

> **Review – Legal Considerations in Appraisal Mnemonic = PETE**
>
> Police power
>
> Eminent domain
>
> Taxation
>
> Escheat

PRIVATE RESTRICTIONS

Private restrictions are created in the deed at the time of sale or in the general plan of a subdivision by the developer. For example, a developer may use a height restriction to ensure views from each parcel in a subdivision.

Additionally, property located in common interest developments may have additional restrictions. These restrictions are commonly known as conditions, covenants, and restrictions. **Conditions, covenants, & restrictions (CC&Rs)**

are recorded deed restrictions that run with the land, usually initiated by the original subdivider. The CC&Rs for a new subdivision are listed in a recorded **Declaration of Restrictions**, which gives each owner the right to enforce the CC&Rs.

CC&Rs must be disclosed prior to the final sale of a home. Sometimes the CC&Rs make the difference whether a home is purchased. CC&Rs set forth particular rules that must be followed by the purchaser as well as existing homeowners. If a property owner fails to comply with CC&Rs, the homeowners' association (HOA) can issue warnings, fines, and possible legal actions against the homeowner. As part of the purchase agreement, the buyer agrees to follow all CC&Rs.

Some HOAs pride themselves on structural appearance that does not detract from the environment in which the homes are located. For example, homes that are supposed to blend into the surroundings and appear natural cannot be painted using colors that are inconsistent with the HOA's aesthetics. Materials used for building or remodeling may likewise be dictated by CC&Rs. Homeowners' associations may restrict additions to a house or limit additions to specific requirements.

In addition to the basic governmental restrictions on privately owned real estate, private restrictions imposed by previous owners can limit the full enjoyment of real estate by a present or future owner. An appraiser should be aware that CC&Rs could affect the valuation of a property, since it may impose restrictions such as minimum lot size or minimum house size. These tract restrictions are usually on file in the local county recorder's office. Generally, the existence of such restrictions can be determined by a title search. These types of restrictions are usually mentioned in a preliminary title report.

In most cases, when there is a conflict between a public (governmental) restriction on the construction or development of a home or lot and a private deed restriction on such construction or development, the one that is the most restrictive holds.

> Example: If the public minimum lot size as determined by police power is stated to be 6,000 square feet, but the private deed restriction states 8,000 square feet, then the one that is most restrictive must be met. In this case, a lot would have to have at least 8,000 square feet in order to build a home on the lot.

Appraisers need to consider possible violations of CC&Rs for properties that do not appear to conform to the other properties in a subdivision. Garage conversions, certain other additions, and unusual paint colors may be in violation of CC&Rs and could affect valuation.

WHAT IS VALUE?

According to USPAP, **value** is "the monetary relationship between properties and those who buy, sell, or use those properties." Another aspect of this is to see value as the monetary worth of a property, goods, or service to buyers and sellers at a given time.

Value expresses an economic concept. As such, it is never a fact but always an opinion of worth at a given time using a specific definition of value. In appraisal practice, value must always be qualified.

As defined in USPAP, **price** is the amount asked, offered, or paid for a property. Once stated, price is a fact—whether it is publicly disclosed or retained in private. Because of the financial capabilities, motivations, or special interests of a given buyer or seller, the price paid for a property may or may not be related to the value that might be ascribed to that property by others.

Cost is the expense in money, labor, material, or sacrifices in acquiring or producing something. Cost is either a fact or an estimate of fact.

A statement of the value sought and defined must be a part of every appraisal report. Value is always considered in terms of the property interest. For example, real estate valuation is the fee simple interest, the leased fee estate, the leasehold estate—or all three.

Value always has to be expressed in terms of cash, terms equivalent to cash, or some other precisely revealed terms. For an appraiser, value is not a fact—it is a qualified opinion.

ELEMENTS TO CREATE VALUE

There are four elements of value, all of which must be present for a property to have market value. They are demand, utility, scarcity, and transferability.

Demand is the desire to buy or obtain a commodity. **Effective demand** is desire coupled with purchasing power. Demand and purchasing power available will affect the value of a property. **Utility** is the ability of a property to satisfy a need or desire, such as shelter, income, or amenities. **Functional utility** is concerned with both the desirability and usefulness of a property because they affect its marketability. **Scarcity** is a lack of supply of some type of real property resulting in increased value when demand exceeds supply. It refers to the availability of a commodity in the marketplace. **Transferability** is the ability to transfer ownership of an item from one person or entity to another. It means that title to the property is unclouded and marketable.

> **Review – Four Elements of Value**
> **Mnemonic = DUST**
> **D**emand
> **U**tility
> **S**carcity
> **T**ransferability

Each by itself cannot create value. For example, something may be scarce—but if it has no utility, there is no demand for it. Air has utility and may be in great demand, but is so abundant that it has no commercial value.

The appraiser must decide if there is a demand for a property, such as a high-rise residential building or a low-cost housing project. Can it be used for the purpose it was intended, such as a family home or residential complex? How many similar projects are in the area? Is the title clear and can the seller grant ownership to a buyer? As you can see, all of these factors are important in assigning value to a property. An appraiser must hold each one up to the property in question to arrive at a correct estimate of value.

FACTORS AFFECTING VALUE

The value of all real property is constantly influenced by physical, economic, political, and social forces that motivate human behavior. There are also psychological factors. This is observed when markets are very active and there are bidding wars for specific properties.

PHYSICAL FACTORS

Many physical characteristics of land and property have a definite influence on value. Physical characteristics and environmental forces include the property's location, the surrounding climate, its topography and soil composition, the size and shape of the property, and the ease of navigation. These physical characteristics or environmental forces can exert major influence on values. Some of the physical characteristics can be changed, some can be worked around, and others are unchangeable. The expense of alteration must always be taken into consideration.

Location. Every appraiser has heard the phrase "location, location, location" as the three most important aspects of real estate. There are some interesting facts that go with this approach. Throughout the last 100 years, individuals who purchased a parcel of land adjacent to an ocean or lake at a relatively young age could often retire using the appreciation.

Size and shape of property. Land shape and topography have a big effect upon utility. The property utility is an important factor in valuation. Many appraisers make the mistake of adjusting land just from the size of the land without really considering how much of the land is usable.

View. View is a very important factor in determining property value. There

An example of an angled ocean view.

are obvious view premiums such as those associated with views of a body of water. However, the appraiser has a challenge when trying to determine how much a partial view is worth. If the property has a view of blue water that is on an angle and seen from only one room, is there much of a view premium? Or, is the view premium determined by the amount of blue water that can be seen?

A good way to find out how the market reacts to views is to talk to local real estate agents—ask them what their clients have been willing to pay for a particular view. One can also perform a regression analysis to determine the weight to assign to views as well as other property amenities.

Accessibility. One factor that is increasingly important to homeowners is commuting time. Whether the property has ready access to public transportation and major roads is an important factor in determining property values. One could argue that this is another aspect of location, but accessibility is important enough

A property located at the end of a bumpy dirt road is less valuable than a similar property with excellent roads.

to discuss as a special locational consideration. A property located at the end of a bumpy dirt road is going to be less valuable than a similar property with excellent roads.

Environmental factors. Environmental factors that affect value are natural as well as man-made. Environmental considerations include the typical conservation of natural resources such as wetlands, plant habitat, wildlife, timber, and threatened animal and plant species.

Appraisers who work raw land soon become familiar with varieties of birds on endangered lists, as well as certain types of plants that are decreasing. Kangaroo rats and birds, such as sandpipers, need a habitat. Wetlands have three-toed frogs and certain types of non-commercial fish.

Common Environmental Factors

- Climatic conditions including rainfall, snowfall, temperature, and humidity
- Soil conditions that can affect health certifications
- Topography that affects density and slope overlays
- Toxic contaminants such as oil and its derivatives, asbestos, or radon
- Primary transportation systems such as navigable waterways and man-made airports, public highways, railroads, and lakes
- Parks and recreational sources

Other Physical and Environmental Factors

- Drainage
- Privacy
- Availability of water and other utilities
- Underground mineral deposits and who owns them
- Soil composition that can affect types of foundations and footings a builder may use
- Located in flood or fire zone
- Located in an earthquake fault zone area
- Hurricane, tornado, or other storm influences
- Proximity to schools, shopping, and recreation areas
- Encroachments of fences or trees

ECONOMIC FACTORS

Cost and availability of mortgage credit. There is an inverse relationship between interest rates and the values of property. In the early 1980s when mortgage rates were in the 14-18% range, there was a decrease in property values as the high rates made effective demand low. The pendulum of supply and demand indicated a surplus of supply and the values of property went down.

In the period of 2000-2005, interest rates were at a historic low and property values increased dramatically across the U.S. Some areas of the country saw increases of over 20% per year. The wealth of individual property owners increased as the amount of equity they had in their properties went up dramatically.

Expansion or diminution of basic industry production. The U.S. has become a nation of service providers, and basic industry production in many areas has shifted to other countries. This is seen in Detroit, MI as the big three automakers have been shutting down plants and laying off large numbers of employees. Consequently, real estate values in the Detroit and surrounding areas have suffered.

Other industries that are related to computers and technology, for example, are flourishing. Corresponding real estate values follow suit. Many cities on the West Coast have this type of industrial base and have a solid real estate market.

Expansion or diminution of federal military contract. As the country tries to reduce the federal deficit, there is continuing pressure to close military bases. More and more services that used to be provided by the military are now provided by private contractors who have federal grants and/or contracts. Homeland security is an important issue and this has provided the impetus for many companies to get involved with protecting the country and other parts of the world. Having a secure homeland is very important for real estate values.

Real estate values are also positively affected by companies that make missiles, aircraft, radar systems, and other military hardware. Military contracts are the fuel that feeds the fires for these critical industries.

Wage levels. Another key economic factor affecting real estate values is wage levels. Each year, *Parade Magazine* publishes an article about what people earn

Real estate values reflect regional wage levels. A teacher in Alabama will not earn anywhere near the amount a movie star in Beverly Hills will earn.

in the United States. Wage levels vary from $15,000 to several million dollars as annual compensation. If you examine these reported wage levels in terms of where people reside and work, it is easy to see why real estate values are at a relatively low or high level as a function of how much people earn. Very often, it is regional. A teacher in Alabama does not earn anywhere near the amount a movie star in Beverly Hills earns. Real estate values reflect this.

Other economic forces. Other economic forces the appraiser has to consider include things like the economic base of the area, new developments under construction, rental rates, and occupancy rates. Also included are new construction planned in the near future, highway expansion, future supply and demand, industrial expansion, anticipated increases in purchasing power, and other specific local market conditions.

Effective demand is another economic consideration. **Effective demand** is demand coupled with purchasing power. There is a significant amount of demand for housing in the coastal areas of the United States, but the prices may be so high that the number of people who can afford the property is relatively small. For example, in Southern California, there is tremendous demand for housing, but only a small percentage of the population can afford to purchase existing properties.

POLITICAL FACTORS

Governmental policies, political changes, and legal rulings always affect property values. These can overshadow the natural market forces of supply and demand. Taxation policies are a prime example of governmental forces. Homeowners are now allowed to sell a residence that they have occupied two of the past five years and not pay taxes upon $250,000 to $500,000 of their capital gains. The larger amount is for married couples. It is governmental policy to allow property owners to sell one property and buy another using a tax-deferred exchange. Both of these tax benefits have a positive effect on property values.

Political changes can alter governmental policies. In some areas, local governmental policies allow the government to seize private property using eminent domain so that something more modern can be built which will generate higher property and income taxes. There are serious constitutional issues that are being considered, but these policies are affecting property values and urban renewal.

The government provides many necessary facilities and services that affect land use, but the courts react to lawsuits that sometimes change what can be done with the land use. It will be interesting to see how the eminent domain laws fare in the next several years. An appraiser has to diligently identify and examine how these and other factors affect property values.

Factors Affecting Property Value
- National, state, and local fiscal policies
- Federal guarantees in financing (FHA and VA guaranteed loans)
- Public services such as police and fire protection, utilities, refuse collection, and transportation networks
- Local zoning policies
- Local building code policies
- Local health code policies especially those that affect land use
- Federal housing and rent subsidies
- Expansion of federal, state, county, or city highway and public works programs (interstate and state improvements, dams, water projects, flood control projects, etc.)
- Environmental Protection Agency policies

- Environmental impact studies
- Endangered species designations
- Disabilities acts
- Local taxation and assessments
- Local regulations on business and industry
- Effect of Workers' Compensation laws

SOCIAL FACTORS

When appraisers consider social forces that affect property value, they usually consider population characteristics. Demographic composition can help an appraiser analyze the anticipated supply and demand as well as how much of the demand will be effective demand, as discussed above. Property values are not only affected by population changes, but also by the entire spectrum of human activity. Do soccer moms have an effect on property values? Does proximity to other sporting activities affect property values? What is the trend of marriages and couples forming households in other manners? Is there a trend toward household formation or is the trend toward people living alone?

Social Factors
- Reputation of area
- Attitudes of people toward owning property
- Population shifts
- Changes in size of families

Anyone concerned with the appraisal of real property must be constantly aware of these forces and their part in value determination.

> **Review – Four Main Factors Influencing Value**
> **Mnemonic = PEPS**
> Physical factors
> Economic factors
> Political factors
> Social factors

TYPES OF VALUE

Appraisers will encounter several types of value and it is important to understand that different types of value will produce different estimates. It is easy to see the problem of using the term value without a qualifying companion word. In this discussion, we primarily address the use of the term value as it relates to the more specific identification of market value, and to some other value terms and definitions common to appraisers.

COMMON TYPES OF VALUE

- Market Value
- Investment Value
- Going Concern Value
- Public Interest Value
- Insurable Value
- Assessed Value
- Partial Interest Value
- Leased Fee Value
- Leasehold Value
- Depreciated Value
- Economic Value
- Salvage Value
- Interim Use Value
- Nuisance Value
- As Is Value
- Book Value
- Hypothetical Value
- Evaluations
- Replacement Value
- Subsidized Housing Value
- Diminution In Value
- Real Property Collateral Value
- Exchange Value
- Historical Easement Value
- Easement Value
- Good Will Value
- Utility Value
- Value In Use
- Intrinsic Value
- AVM Value
- Front Foot Value
- Square Foot Value
- Discounted Cash Flow (DCF) Value
- Fractional Interest Value
- Segment Value
- Annuity Value
- Liquidation Value
- Intellectual Property Value
- Forecasted Value
- Aesthetic Value
- Military Value
- Excess Land Value
- Condemnation Value
- Life Estate Value
- Riparian Rights Value
- Prescriptive Easement Value

MARKET VALUE

The concept of market value is very important to the real estate and the business communities. Vast amounts of equity capital and various loans are committed each year in the form of real estate loans and investments. Market value is also known as **objective value** or **value in exchange**. The definition of market value used by appraisers and their clients must be clearly understood and communicated. Market value is created by the collective patterns in the marketplace.

The definition of market value can be controversial, due to continued debate that revolves around the issues of cash and non-cash equivalency, real estate versus real property rights, and most probable price versus highest price.

CASH VERSUS NON-CASH EQUIVALENTS

When the real estate market was relatively stable in the first half of the 20th century, appraisers used the concept of cash and cash equivalency in their definitions of market value, as financing terms were not as important. Mortgage rates remained fairly level and real estate values rose slowly.

In the second half of the 20th century, changes in real estate markets and financing created more complex property interests. Clients are interested in the value of property as affected by the mortgage instrument. It has become important for appraisers to understand the relationship between debt and equity interests.

Financing terms may or may not be equivalent to cash and they do affect value. Because they are created by the collective market, financing terms or leases can reflect market value. The problem for appraisers occurs when using comparable sales that are not affected in the same way by the financing and leases. There is controversy about exactly how appraisers should account for these differences in their definitions of market value.

This subject will be discussed in detail in Chapter 8.

REAL ESTATE VERSUS REAL PROPERTY RIGHTS

As stated earlier, many states consider real estate and real property to be synonymous. Is the appraisal of a fee simple property an appraisal of the real estate or of the bundle of rights associated with real property? Some see no difference, but traditional appraisal theory does make a distinction, which will be important when partial interest appraisals are discussed in Chapter 3.

MOST PROBABLE PRICE VERSUS HIGHEST PRICE

A viable market must have enough buyers, sellers, and real estate to provide competition. This competition develops both a high and low range of value. Many appraisers see the most probable price as a central price in this range of value. However, market value is defined legally as the highest price someone would pay in various civil codes for some purposes. An example is eminent domain. If an appraiser is valuing a property for eminent domain, he or she must use the highest price—not the most probable price a property would sell for on the open market. In which case, market value has to be considered as a function of the authority providing the definition.

MARKET VALUE AND USPAP

USPAP requires appraisers to identify the exact definition of market value, and its authority, applicable in each appraisal completed for the purpose of market value. USPAP defines **market value** as the kind of value a property should bring in a competitive and open market under all conditions requisite to a fair sale—the buyer and seller, each acting prudently, knowledgeably, and assuming the price is not affected by undue circumstances.

Implicit in this definition is the consummation of a sale as of a specified date and the passing of title from seller to buyer under conditions whereby:

- buyer and seller are typically motivated.
- both parties are well informed or well advised, and each acting in what he or she considers his or her own best interest.
- a reasonable time is allowed for exposure in the open market.
- payment is made in terms of cash in U.S. dollars or in terms of financial arrangements comparable thereto.
- the price represents the normal consideration for the property sold unaffected by special or creative financing or sales concessions granted by anyone associated with the sale.

An arm's-length transaction, such as a sale of property, is one in which all parties involved are acting in their own self-interest and are under no undue influence or pressure from other parties. The concept of an **arm's-length transaction** is a sale between unrelated parties.

The Four Conditions Requisite to an Arm's-Length Transaction

1. Neither the buyer nor the seller is acting under duress

2. The property has been offered for sale in an open market for a reasonable period of time, allowing that some properties are expected to take longer to sell than others

3. Buyer and seller are aware of the aspects of the property, including any adverse conditions or potential changes

4. No extraordinary circumstances, such as financing concessions, are involved

Adjustments to the comparable sales must be made for special or creative financing or sales concessions. No adjustments are necessary for those costs that are normally paid by sellers because of tradition or law in a market area—costs are readily identifiable since the seller pays these costs in virtually all sales transactions. Special or creative financing adjustments can be made to the comparable property by comparisons to financing terms offered by a third-party institutional lender that is not already involved in the property or transaction. Any adjustment should not be calculated on a mechanical dollar-for-dollar cost of the financing or concession, but the dollar amount of any adjustment should approximate the market's reaction to the financing or concessions based on the appraiser's judgment.

> **Review – Market Value**
> - Buyer and seller are operating in their own interest.
> - Buyer and seller are knowledgeable about the transaction and make careful decisions.
> - The property is available for a reasonable time on the open market.
> - The sale is for cash or trade, or is specifically financed.
> - Normal financing, available to qualified borrowers, if used.

INVESTMENT VALUE

Investment value represents the value of a specific property to a particular investor. As used in appraisal assignments, investment value is not market value, but is value to an individual. It is based upon the individual's investment requirements.

ASSESSMENT VALUE

Assessment value is the property value determined for ad valorem taxation by state and local tax agencies. **Ad valorem** is a Latin prefix meaning "according to value."

INSURABLE VALUE

Insurable value is the amount for which a property may be insured. This amount is generally a percentage of the market value at the time a policy is written or a calculation of future replacement cost, depending upon the type of policy and the insurer. It is important to realize that this definition does not include the land.

VALUE IN USE

Value in use is the value based on a specific use of a property, such as a manufacturing plant used to produce automobiles. It may be the highest and best use, or it may be some other use. Some legislatures have enacted laws to preserve farmland, timberland, or open space in urban areas. There are many other examples of value in use such as parkland and habitat.

Value in use is based on a specific use of a property. It may be an industrial plant, farmland, parkland, or habitat.

GOING CONCERN VALUE

Going concern value is the value existing in an established business property compared with the value of selling the real estate and other assets of a concern whose business is not yet established. The term takes into account the goodwill and earning capacity of a business. It includes the incremental value related to the business concern, which is distinct from the real estate.

CASE STUDY

AIR SPACE

Donald Trump, a well-known business tycoon, is worth billions of dollars and seems to succeed in whatever endeavor he undertakes. Early in his career, he wanted to build in New York City. He chose the site but had a problem—the owners of the property Trump wanted refused to sell at any price. Trump attacked the problem from many angles, but to no avail.

Finally, he was able to purchase the airspace above the existing building. No one could see why he did this—as the building that he could not buy was still in place. Trump approached neighboring property owners and was able to negotiate easements on their properties. These easements allowed Trump to establish footings and provide ingress and egress.

Trump went on to build a remarkable building using his airspace. He built over the existing building, and except for the footings and the means for access, he had a skyscraper almost entirely in airspace.

There are other examples of this in various parts of the country. There are highway bridges built above existing properties using the airspace only. Some developers have built platforms in airspace with the goal of building elevated commercial centers.

A highway bridge built above existing properties using only the airspace.

SUMMARY

Property is anything that is capable of being owned and gained lawfully. Property is often described in terms of whether it is personal or real. The Uniform Standards of Professional Appraisal Practice (USPAP) define **real estate** as an identified parcel or tract of land, including any improvements. **Real property** is defined in USPAP as the interests, benefits, and rights inherent in the ownership of real estate. Many states use these terms synonymously, but in this book, we differentiate between the two. **Personal property**, as defined in USPAP, is identifiable tangible objects that are considered by the general public as being personal. All that is not attached to the land is personal property.

According to USPAP, **value** is "the monetary relationship between properties and those who buy, sell, or use those properties." Value is the monetary worth of a property, goods, or service to buyers or sellers at a given time. **Market value** is the price a property would bring if freely offered on the open market, with both a willing buyer and a willing seller. Although market value has been defined by the courts, and more recently, by USPAP, it is often difficult to apply it precisely in practice.

The value of all real property is constantly influenced by physical, economic, political, social, and environmental factors. Government of all types has basic powers restricting the complete disposition and use of all private property by owners. These legal considerations are **police power**, **eminent domain**, **taxation**, **airspace**, **CC&Rs**, and **escheat**.

CHAPTER 1 REVIEW EXERCISES

MATCHING EXERCISE

Instructions: Write the letter of the matching term on the blank line before its definition. Answers are in Appendix A.

Terms

A. airspace
B. assessment value
C. bundle of rights
D. CC&Rs
E. chattel
F. demand
G. eminent domain
H. escheat
I. fee simple absolute

J. fixture
K. intellectual property
L. investment value
M. market value
N. personal property
O. police power
P. price
Q. property
R. real estate

S. real property
T. restriction
U. scarcity
V. subsurface rights
W. trade fixture
X. transferability
Y. utility
Z. value

Definitions

1. _____ Anything that is capable of being owned and gained lawfully

2. _____ The interests, benefits, and rights inherent in the ownership of real estate

3. _____ An ownership concept describing all the legal rights that attach to the ownership of real property

4. _____ An identified parcel or tract of land

5. _____ Real property to a reasonable height

6. _____ The rights to underground natural resources such as minerals, oil, and gas

7. _____ Identifiable tangible objects that are considered by the general public as being personal

8. _____ Another term for personal property

9. _____   Personal property that has become affixed to real estate

10. _____   An item of personal property used to conduct business

11. _____   General term for various legal rights, which attach to certain types of information, ideas, or other intangibles

12. _____   A limitation on the use of real property and may be placed by a private owner, a developer, or the government

13. _____   Power of the state to enact laws within constitutional limits to promote the order, safety, health, morals, and general welfare of our society

14. _____   The right of the government to take private property from an owner, for the public good, paying fair market value

15. _____   A legal process in which property reverts to the state because the deceased left no will and has no legal heirs

16. _____   Recorded deed restrictions that run with the land, usually initiated by the original subdivider

17. _____   The monetary relationship between properties and those who buy, sell, or use those properties

18. _____   The desire to buy or obtain a commodity

19. _____   The ability to transfer ownership of an item from one person or entity to another

20. _____   The most probable price property should bring in a competitive and open market under all conditions requisite to a fair sale

MULTIPLE CHOICE QUESTIONS

Instructions: Circle your response and go to Appendix A to read the complete explanation for each question.

1. Property is best defined as:
   a. real estate.
   b. real property.
   c. personal property.
   d. anything capable of being owned and gained lawfully.

2   Which of these is considered real property?

    a. Cut timber

    b. Airspace

    c. Trade fixtures

    d. Jewelry

3.   Which of the following is not one of the tests of a fixture?

    a. Method of attachment

    b. Time of attachment

    c. Adaptability of the item

    d. Relationship of the parties

4.   Tenant Bob installs a ceiling fan. Bob informs landlord Pat that he will re-install the old fixture when he moves. Of the five tests of a fixture, this is an example of:

    a. intention.

    b. attachment.

    c. relationship.

    d. adaptation.

5.   In legal terms,_____is a general term for various legal rights, which attach to certain types of information, ideas, or other intangibles.

    a. intellectual property

    b. industrial property

    c. chattel fixtures

    d. personal property

6.   The primary difference between condemnation through exercise of the power of eminent domain and condemnation through the exercise of police power is:

    a. there is no compensation necessary in the exercise of eminent domain.

    b. there is no payment involved in condemnation under police power.

    c. one is a power of the public body, and the other is not.

    d. there is no difference.

7.   In most cases, when there is a conflict between a public (governmental) restriction on a property and a private deed restriction, which one must be adhered to?

    a. The public or governmental restriction

    b. The private deed restriction

    c. The one that is most restrictive

    d. The one that is least restrictive

8. Privately owned real property in most states is subject to real estate taxation. Exempt properties may include:

    a. churches.
    b. schools.
    c. non-profit organizations.
    d. all of the above.

9. For an appraiser, value is:

    a. always a fact, never an opinion.
    b. not a fact, it is a qualified opinion.
    c. based on fact and is an unbiased opinion.
    d. neither a fact nor an opinion.

10. Price is the amount asked, offered, or paid for a property. Once stated, price:

    a. must be disclosed publicly.
    b. is relevant only to the buyer and seller.
    c. is a fact, whether it is publicly disclosed or retained in private.
    d. is not related to value.

11. The value of real property is best measured by:

    a. demand, depreciation, scarcity, and utility.
    b. cost, demand, transferability, and utility.
    c. cost, feasibility, utility, and scarcity.
    d. demand, utility, scarcity, and transferability.

12. The ultimate test of functional utility is:

    a. design.
    b. marketability.
    c. utility.
    d. maintenance costs.

13. According to the USPAP, the most probable price that a property should bring in a competitive and open market under all conditions requisite to a fair sale is known as:

    a. market value.
    b. marketability.
    c. market price.
    d. market stability.

14. A sale that is characterized as an arm's-length transaction is a sale:

   a. between related parties.
   b. in which all involved parties act in their own self-interest.
   c. in which either the buyer or seller is acting under duress.
   d. that includes creative financing or sales concessions.

15. As used in appraisal assignments, investment value is not market value, but is value to a(n):

   a. individual.
   b. appraiser.
   c. assessor.
   d. broker.

2
Chapter

INTRODUCTION

Basic economic principles apply to all aspects of the real estate industry. Appraisal is no exception. If we define **economics** as the science that studies the production, distribution, and consumption of wealth, we realize that the appraisal of real estate is simply interpreting what real property is worth to many potential buyers, each of whom is motivated differently. To understand their motivations, we must first understand the basic economic principles controlling value.

Although each principle discussed in this chapter has an individual application in the appraisal of real estate, the principles are often interdependent. Although they appear highly theoretical, they can be directly applied to determine reasonable valuations. The theories must be applied thoughtfully, as an appraiser is only as good as his or her ability to apply the proper theory at the proper time.

LEARNING OBJECTIVES

After reading this chapter, you will be able to:

- list the principles of valuation.
- describe how the principles are applied

FOUNDATIONS OF APPRAISAL

The foundation of appraisal is the valuation process. **Valuation** is the process of estimating market value for real property as of a specific time. Many valuation principles interact to determine the value of a parcel of real estate. Not every property exhibits each principle. However, an appraiser must know the following principles of valuation before assigning value to any property.

PRINCIPLE OF HIGHEST AND BEST USE

The **principle of highest and best use** is the use, from among reasonably probable and adequately supported alternative uses, that is physically possible, legally permitted, economically feasible, and maximally productive. This is the starting point for appraisal analysis.

Highest and best use may or may not conform to the current use. It is fundamental to real estate appraisal because it focuses market analysis on the subject property and the feasibility of alternative land uses. The appraiser's goal is to determine the property's optimum use in accordance with market conditions as of a certain date. The determination of highest and best use must be based upon careful consideration of current market conditions, the various trends that affect market conditions, and the current use of the subject property.

An appraiser must first look at highest and best use as the subject property being vacant. It takes a significant amount of analysis to determine the ideal improvement, if it is not its current use. If the improvements do not represent the highest and best use as if vacant, an interim use value may be estimated for the improvements. **Interim use** is a short-term and temporary use of a property until it is ready for a more productive highest and best use. This occurs when the highest and best use is expected to change.

The second part of the highest and best use determination is to look at the highest and best use as presently improved. An appraiser must consider the best use of the property with its current structures and improvements.

Example: There is a property that has eights units and an old dental office in the front. The neighborhood is residential and the dental office does not fit into the neighborhood. The appraiser has to determine if another commercial use is the highest and best use or if the dental office should be converted into a residential unit. There is also the possibility of converting the whole complex into condominiums. The highest and best use as improved can be different from the highest and best use as vacant.

In some instances, the appraiser is not able to come up with a value for the subject property as vacant. Before estimating a property's value, its most legally profitable and physically permitted use must be determined—that is, the use that will give the maximum overall return or benefit.

Consideration of feasible alternatives for land use, without the improvements, provides the basis for land valuation. Evaluating the contribution of improvements to the land provides a complete picture of property value.

Example: You are asked to appraise a level, vacant, square parcel of land on a corner of a busy intersection. The parcel is 250 by 250 feet. An old residence that had occupied the lot recently caught fire and burned to the ground. A recent city automobile traffic count indicates that 20,000 cars a day pass by the property.

Your first step would be to determine the reasonable probability of that land being used for some purpose that would result in a higher overall return to the land. The parcel could possibly be used for multiple-family residential units, professional offices, or even commercial buildings. In this event, the land alone would probably be worth more in the new use than the land and the old

Principle of Highest and Best Use:
Vacant property, interim use
(pumpkin patch), highest
and best use (new shopping
center under construction).

building together were worth as a single-family residence. Until you know which of these uses is most probable—presuming, of course, that the requisite zoning could be obtained—you cannot make an intelligent estimate of value.

It is important to note that existing or proposed zoning does not create value. However, it may significantly affect it. With zoning, the highest and best use of a property can be properly realized. Some properties today are zoned for a particular purpose, such as industrial or commercial. If there is no demand for that particular use, the property value may suffer or the owner may have to wait years for the area to grow or for demand to increase to the point that it becomes economically prudent to develop the property for this use.

> **USPAP requires that when necessary for credible assignment results in developing a market value opinion, an appraiser must identify and analyze the effect on use and value of existing land use regulations; and develop an opinion of the highest and best use of the real estate (See SR 1-3 in USPAP).**

CRITERIA THAT DETERMINE HIGHEST AND BEST USE

The two criteria that determine highest and best use are: (1) demand, either existing or imminent, and (2) police power approval (such as zoning, building site approval, and necessary permits).

The Four Tests to Explore the Criteria for Highest and Best Use

1. **Physically possible**. Is it feasible to build and maintain the intended structure on the property?

2. **Legally permitted**. Is it likely that the use is, or could be, legally permitted? If there has been no actual approval, the appraiser can weigh the probability of receiving this approval and apply it to the estimate of value. (In cases with a possibility of a zoning change, many properties are sold contingent on the buyer being able to obtain the necessary zoning.)

3. **Economically feasible**. Is the cost of establishing the use of the property economically sound?

4. **Maximally productive**. Will the use provide the highest present value?

The highest and best use of a property may change over time, depending on zoning changes and other factors. The use providing the maximum return on investment should be determined.

> ### Review – Highest and Best Use
> - An appraiser must first look at highest and best use as the subject property being vacant.
> - The second part of the determination is to look at the highest and best use as presently improved.

PRINCIPLE OF CONSISTENT USE

When properties are valued with an interim use, the principle of consistent use must be addressed. The **principle of consistent use** requires that land and improvements be appraised based on the same use. Improvements must contribute to the land value in order for them to have any value at all. Improvements that do not represent the land's highest and best use, but have a remaining physical life, may have an interim use that supports the land value. If the improvements do not support the highest and best use of the land, it can often have a negative effect on the value of the land.

This land has been rezoned for multi-family use.

It is common for appraisers to value properties that have an old single-family residence on it, but the zoning and general plan have changed to allow commercial uses. It is incorrect to value a residence as though it were zoned under a non-permitted use. According to the principle of consistent use, the improvements have to be valued in terms of the highest and best use of the site as if vacant.

If an improvement does not match the highest and best use of the land, it normally suffers from external obsolescence. **External obsolescence** is a type of depreciation occurring because of negative influences outside of the specific property site (i.e. an airport flight pattern). This is caused by existing buildings and other improvements that do not represent the highest and best use of their sites as though vacant.

An example of external obsolescence

Consider these examples: (1) a 20-year old house that sits on a lot that has a highest and best use of a modern, larger house and (2) a 15-year old apartment building that is located on a site that has a highest and best use of a modern apartment building with more amenities. Since the highest and best use is in the same category as the existing uses, there is no penalty for inappropriate use and there is no external obsolescence.

PRINCIPLE OF SUPPLY AND DEMAND

The **principle of supply and demand** states that market value is affected by the intersection of supply and demand forces in the market as of the appraisal date. Prices and rent levels tend to increase when demand is greater than supply, and tend to decrease when supply exceeds demand. Usually property values vary directly with changes in supply. This results in what are known as buyer's markets and seller's markets. A **buyer's market** is a market containing more supply than demand. A **seller's market** is a market condition in which demand exceeds supply. All private real estate transactions should involve a willing seller and a willing buyer, each with the ability to perform.

Real property has value as long as there is a desire for its use. Value increases as the supply of land decreases, as more and more people compete for the available land. The highest land values are found in the most populated cities, where small parcels of available land often bring very high prices.

Reduced to its simplest form, the principle of supply and demand must include an analysis of population growth, the buyer's ability to pay, and the relative scarcity of available land. If buyers with the ability to pay demand a scarce commodity, its value rises.

> Example: Within the city limits of San Francisco, where the supply of available land is fixed, the demand for land has become so great in most areas that single-family-home building is precluded. This is because the land can command much more money for use as a high-rise residential or commercial development. By this means, more people can be accommodated with the result of a greater monetary return to the land. The result is land values that are constantly rising, as demand grows for the available supply.

Review – Supply and Demand
- Increasing supply or decreasing demand will reduce the price in the market
- Decreasing supply or increasing demand will raise the price in the market

PRINCIPLE OF SUBSTITUTION

The **principle of substitution** affirms that the maximum value of a property tends to be set by the cost of acquiring an equally desirable and valuable substitute property, assuming no cost delay is encountered in making the substitution. When several similar or commensurate properties are available, the one with the lowest price attracts the greatest demand and widest distribution.

Principle of Substitution

Property values tend to be set by the price of substitute properties that have similar amenities. This principle not only governs amenity properties but also properties that are purchased for their income producing capabilities. Reasonably, a buyer will not pay more for a particular property than the cost of buying a similar property.

> Example: John is in the market for a new home and finds two that are suitable. The properties are for all practical purposes identical; however, one is priced $10,000 less. Therefore, John makes an offer on the lower priced property.

Another aspect of the principle of substitution is the cost to a buyer if purchasing a vacant lot and building a residence or income-producing property. If a buyer finds that it is possible to buy a lot and construct a home with all the attributes of an existing residence—for less than the cost of an existing residence—then the cost the buyer is willing to pay for an existing property will not be greater than the cost to construct a similar property. Of course, this principle is effective only if there is no unusual delay in the construction of the replacement property.

PRINCIPLE OF ANTICIPATION

The **principle of anticipation** states that value is created by the benefits to be derived in the future. According to this economic principle, the current value of a property is not normally based upon historical factors, such as the cost to create or historical prices. Rather, it is based on the buyer's perception of the future benefits and value of the acquisition. This is apparent even in residential properties, since the owner looks forward to future advantages, amenities, and enjoyment of ownership and occupancy.

Real property has value proportionate to the expected use of that property, whether it is a single-family residence or an income-producing property. In the case of an income-producing property, this anticipated return can be measured by the amount of money that is expected be realized over a given period. In the case of a single-family residence, the return can be measured by the anticipated enjoyment or amenities.

> Example: Most high-quality residential properties in exclusive areas sell at prices unrelated to any income-producing capabilities of those properties. Instead, the price reflects the buyer's desire to enjoy whatever future social or physical benefits the property may produce—whether the enjoyment is a quiet, natural setting in an area of large estates, or the social satisfaction of an exclusive address, or even the view of a picturesque coastline.

The principle of anticipation is most obvious and easy to measure in the case of income-producing property. Virtually all multiple residential, industrial, professional, and commercial properties are purchased with the vision of future economic returns. The buyer is interested in past and present production of income only because it suggests future earning capabilities of the property.

Buyers anticipate income from future property earnings.

The principle of anticipation applies not only to positive future benefits but to anticipated negative future influences as well.

> Example: A property might be located in a small town where the major employer indicated its operation would permanently close in the near future. In response to this news, property values would decrease due to anticipation. Similarly, a home in a presently quiet location could lose value if it is located next to a vacant field where a new extension of the interstate highway is to be built.

It is important that appraisers stay fully informed of local community affairs, as well as local economic trends, in order to analyze accurately the effect of anticipation in the subject property's market.

PRINCIPLE OF CHANGE

The **principle of change** holds that it is the future, not the past, which is of prime importance in estimating value. Real estate values are constantly changed by environmental, economic, political, and social forces. The value of real property is influenced by many variables—population shifts, changing economic conditions, increasing government controls, new routes of transportation, new shopping centers, new schools, urban growth and decay, changing social attitudes, changing political ideals, and changing cultural desires.

Although change is almost imperceptible to the resident who views an area from day to day, most people have only to go back to the area where they grew up to be struck by the changes that have taken place. Whether these changes reflect a growing, dynamic region or a decaying neighborhood, seldom does a neighborhood remain static for long.

In a dynamic, growing region, real estate appraisers, brokers, developers, and investors always take different routes as they move through the area to keep abreast of new developments.

Changing real estate values.

In this way, they are constantly informed about what is happening in the real estate industry in that area.

It is an appraiser's job to identify current and anticipated changes in the market that could affect property values. As change cannot be predicted with great accuracy, values that are date specific may only be valid for a limited time. In hot markets, it is easy to identify change. However, in normal markets it may be more difficult to discern. Abrupt changes can occur if a particular industry shuts down or experiences a large number of layoffs, if military bases close, or if there is a large amount of new construction.

A subtler example of change is to look at real estate preferences. In recent years, the idea has been bigger is better, and residences keep getting larger with more bedrooms and bathrooms. However, as the population ages, more and more consumers are interested in smaller homes and are often looking for single-story residences. Since real estate normally is not adaptable to change, it can suffer from obsolescence as preferences change. Homebuilders no longer construct houses with one bath and a one-car garage. Yet, if an appraiser were surveying homes that are 50-70 years old, he or she would find many examples of homes with one bathroom and a one-car garage.

FOUR STAGES IN THE LIFE CYCLE

All improved real property experiences a four-stage life cycle. The four stages, although not always distinct, can best be described as: (1) development, (2) stability, (3) decline, and (4) revitalization.

Life Cycle of a Single-Family Residential Neighborhood

1. **Development**. The first phase of the life cycle consists of initial construction of improvements on vacant land. Development begins with the filing of a subdivision map followed by the grading of lots, streets, and easements. Next, is the installation of off-site improvements, including all utilities, sanitary and storm drains, streets, curbs, gutters, sidewalks, and street lighting. Construction and sale of homes, including the installation of lawns, fencing, and landscaping, is also part of the development phase. The development phase is also referred to as integration.

Improvements in vacant land.

2. **Stability.** The second phase in the cycle of a neighborhood is marked by the stability of the existing buildings and occupants. Once the neighborhood has developed, there is a period when landscaping continues and the development reaches maturity. This phase generally lasts for many years. It is also referred to as equilibrium or maturity.

The stability phase is when the neighborhood
has developed and is reaching maturity.

3.   **Decline**. Delayed repairs and deterioration of buildings generally mark the third phase in the cycle of a neighborhood. When residents or occupants start delaying or neglecting repairs and maintenance, the overall upkeep of the neighborhood then becomes apparent, and the decline phase begins. The decline or decay of a neighborhood is also a result of wear and tear. **Wear and tear** is the depreciation of an asset due to ordinary usage. With these factors in place, the development declines into old age or its use changes. This is also known as disintegration.

A neighborhood is in decline when residents or occupants
start delaying or neglecting repairs and maintenance.

4.   **Revitalization**. The fourth and final phase in the cycle of a neighborhood occurs through the demolition, relocation, or major renovation of existing buildings. The revitalization phase, also known as the **renaissance**, can happen very quickly or quite slowly over a period of years. For example, a major event such as building a baseball park or football stadium can quickly revitalize an entire area. Conversely, some developments might take 60 years or more to experience the complete cycle. This is also referred to as gentrification.

Revitalization occurs when the neighborhood experiences demolition, relocation, or major renovation of existing buildings.

In fact, some residential areas in the U.S. are over 100 years old, yet they have not completed their life cycle. This is primarily due to continued demand caused by an absence of economic obsolescence—as well as good construction, maintenance levels, and appeal. Strong location and a healthy local economy can contribute significantly to extending the length of the life cycle.

Conversely, developments in some areas have gone through the first stages and are well into old age within a period of less than 30 years. Knowing these stages and how to analyze property located in an area of transition is important to anyone in the real estate industry.

PRINCIPLE OF CONFORMITY

A reasonable degree of conformity (homogeneity) results in maximum value. The **principle of conformity** states that maximum value results when properties in a neighborhood are relatively similar in size, style, quality, use, and/or type. Developers often use different elevations so that the same models have different external appearances.

Neighborhoods often have a general conformity of homes which are similar in price and size.

Homes of varying architectural styles are often located in one neighborhood, especially in an area of exclusive, individually designed homes. However, there is generally conformity in either the economic or the sociological sense in that the homes are of similar price and size, or are owned and occupied by people in similar economic circumstances.

> Example: The value of a 3,500 square-foot home, of good-quality construction, tastefully landscaped and appointed, will be maintained best when that home is located in an area of similar homes. Generally, the larger this area of similar homes, the less vulnerable the home is to outside influences that might depress its value.

As you will see in the next section, a lesser home in a good neighborhood will have its value enhanced by the value of the superior homes. However, if a superior home is built in a lesser neighborhood, then the superior home will have a tendency to be of less value than it would be in a different neighborhood. Wherever there are mixed types of homes, unstable real estate values may occur.

PRINCIPLE OF REGRESSION

The term regression has more than one meaning for the appraiser. The **principle of regression** states that higher-valued properties tend to suffer when placed in close proximity with lower-valued properties. It is seen as the opposite of progression.

Regression as used in Automated Valuation Models (AVMs) and other statistical models refers to determining the nature of the relationship between one or more independent variables and a dependent variable.

The principle of regression

Automated Valuation Models (AVMs) are computer software programs that analyze data using automated systems, such as regression analysis and/or so-called artificial intelligence. This technique is often called regression analysis. **Regression analysis** is a correlational technique that is very helpful to appraisers attempting to make predictions of value or determining how much weight to assign to various amenities.

Occasionally a large, custom-designed home is found in a neighborhood of homes less than half its size and of inferior construction. Appraisers refer to this as an over-improvement. An **over-improvement** is one which is not the highest and best use for the site on which it is placed by reason of excess size or cost—this is also called superadequacy.

> Example: A large custom home of 5,000 square feet in a neighborhood of similarly large, good-quality homes could be worth $1 million or more. However, in a neighborhood of homes of 1,600 square feet and moderate construction, it might be worth less than $600,000 depending upon what part of the country. The unit of higher value loses value when located in an area of lower value units. This is an example of regression.

PRINCIPLE OF PROGRESSION

The opposite case can be seen when the 1,600 square-foot home described above is located in an area of large, higher-quality residences. The effect of this turnabout would be a value increment to the smaller home. This is known as progression. The **principle of progression** states that the worth of a lesser-valued residence tends to be enhanced by association with higher-valued residences in the same area.

The principle of progression

> Example: Joe purchased a 20-year old condominium in excellent condition and in a neighborhood with strong demand. Not long after his purchase, developers put in a brand new high-end, high-rise condominium complex adjacent to his property. As a result, the value of Joe's property rose dramatically and immediately. In addition, having a brand-new, modern-styled structure in the area encouraged the various local neighborhood associations to revitalize their strip mall edifices and public streets, contributing to an overall better looking neighborhood. As a result, property values in the entire area rose.

The effect on value would be different from that discussed in the principle of regression. In the case of regression, there would be no practical way to salvage the apparent dollar loss brought about by an over-improvement. Seldom would a 1,600 square-foot home be built on a lot in an area of 5,000 square-foot homes. The cost of the land would not economically justify such a small home. What generally happens is that an older home might be located in a residential area where newer, larger homes are being built. The neighborhood is undergoing a change. Oftentimes, older homes are remodeled and enlarged as this change proceeds. The existing older houses that hold most of their value in the land see progression and an increase in value.

PRINCIPLE OF COMPETITION

Buyers and sellers of real estate operate in a competitive marketplace where each property competes with all other properties suitable for the same use in a particular market or area. The **principle of competition** states that real estate values are affected by supply and demand because of competition.

Typically, the principle of competition follows three steps: (1) market demand generates profits, (2) profits generate competition, and (3) competition stabilizes profits.

Most business ventures need to show a profit. Real estate is no exception. When demand is strong for homes of a certain quality, size, and price, a developer can realize a solid profit. As a result, other developers may be attracted to the area. With increasing competition, profits tend to decrease—sometimes to the point that profits no longer exist or are so marginal that they are not worthwhile. Moderate profits attract healthy competition. However, excessive profits can bring ruinous competition.

This can be seen when established residential areas must compete with new construction, or established downtown retail centers competing with new suburban centers.

Established downtown retail centers compete with new suburban centers.

Competition becomes very important for an appraiser using the income approach to value, for this approach stresses the present worth of future benefits. If competition keeps increasing, the value of future benefits can decrease.

PRINCIPLE OF CONTRIBUTION

Closely related to the principle of conformity, the **principle of contribution** calculates the worth of a particular component in terms of its contribution to the value of the whole property, or an item's worth is calculated as the amount that its absence would detract from the value of the whole. The value of an improvement to a property, whether to vacant land or an existing structure, is worth only what it adds to the property's market value, often less than the improvement's construction cost.

Every year, the National Associations of REALTORS® publishes a list of improvements that add the most to the value of a home. Two improvements rank near the top each year: (1) remodeling the kitchen and (2) adding another bathroom (especially if the house only has one existing bathroom).

Improvements that seem to contribute less to the value than the cost to add include swimming pools, which can add from zero to about half of the cost to construct, depending on the area of the country.

> Example: Although a home is worth more if it has a pool, the actual cost of adding a pool is higher than the expected increase in value. A swimming pool may cost $40,000 to install and yet add only $15,000 in incremental value. However, adding an extra bathroom or an additional bedroom may increase the value of the house by more than the construction costs.

The principle of contribution must be kept in mind by homeowners who want to add on or remodel. Before making any changes, the homeowner should try to determine if the changes would contribute enough to the property's value to justify the costs.

Appraisers must weigh only the actual contribution to value, not the cost of the improvement. For example, when evaluating a home with a pool, appraisers need to determine the amount that pools add to properties by using

market data. Common ways to do this include a matched pair analysis or a regression analysis. A **matched pair analysis** is a method of adjusting comparable sales in which two comparable properties with one differing feature are used to estimate an amount of adjustment for that feature.

Overall, the principle of contribution emphasizes that cost is not necessarily equal to value.

INCREASING AND DECREASING RETURNS

The **principle of increasing and decreasing returns** is based on the idea that income and other benefits available from real estate may be increased by adding capital improvements only up to the point of balance in the agents of production, beyond which the increase in value tends to be less than the increase in costs.

> Example: Suppose a contractor builds a house to sell competitively on the open market. It is a quality residence of 4,000 square feet in a residential community. To realize a profit, the builder may include a front lawn, minor landscaping, and a rear fence in the sale of the completed house. Carpeting, plantation shutters, a patio, and walkways may also be added to increase the salability of the house. However, there will be a point after which additional dollars spent for improvement will not yield a worthwhile return when the house is sold. This is the point of diminishing returns. A swimming pool, outdoor brick barbecue, screened patio, and even carpeting and shutters can be investments that may not show worthwhile return. People's attitudes, desires, and tastes differ so greatly that a builder generally does best by leaving as many personal touches as possible for buyers to install to suit themselves.

Another practical illustration is the addition of extra rooms and a bathroom. Assume you are asked to appraise an 8-year old house with such recent additions. You find that the original house was 1,600 square feet, in a neighborhood of comparably sized homes. The added construction contributes an additional 400 square feet, making the house a 2,000 square-foot residence. Although the addition increases the living area substantially, the resulting increase in value does not necessarily make the added investment profitable. Your appraisal should reflect whatever a willing and able buyer would pay for the total property, a value derived from market analysis of the prices new homes or other homes of 2,000 square feet in the area are bringing. Then, after a comparison of all the quality attributes, you can make a final estimate of the value of the home.

This home is too large for the lot size.

In addition to its application to improvements, the principle of increasing and decreasing returns can also be applied to lots that are oversized, either in total square footage or in added width or depth. Are buyers willing to pay the added cost proportionate to the increase in lot size for a lot that might be larger, longer, or wider than the standard lot in the neighborhood?

Review – Increasing and Decreasing Returns

- Increasing returns applies when additional investment in a property adds a reasonable return on that investment.
- At a certain point, maximum value will be reached. At this point, decreasing returns apply and continued investment will yield less and less return.

PRINCIPLE OF BALANCE AND SURPLUS PRODUCTIVITY

The **principle of balance** is used to determine the value of land based on the primary economic concept controlling all profit-making enterprises that affirms that all production is based on four agents or factors in production. **Surplus productivity** is the income generated by a project after the four agents of production have been paid. Each of the four agents of production has a specific cost associated with it. The real point of contention is whether management is compensated on a fixed basis or entitled to the entrepreneurial profit of the project. This analysis is useful in appraising future developments, commercial or residential, and calculating the total costs and potential profit associated with the development.

AGENTS OF PRODUCTION

The **agents of production** are labor, management, capital, and land. For any production—residential, agricultural, industrial, or commercial—to be profitable, four basic agents must be in proper proportion. Labor has first claim on returns from production, management is second, capital is third, and the last to be satisfied is land.

Labor

Labor includes wages and all payrolls except management. In addition, it includes all operating expenses (usually paid monthly), which generally represent a form of labor, maintenance, repairs, electricity, gas, water, rubbish removal, and supplies.

Management includes all charges for coordinating the enterprise. The

Management

entrepreneur who started the business manages smaller enterprises. In larger enterprises, salaried management personnel have replaced the entrepreneur.

Capital covers the costs of constructing the necessary buildings and providing equipment. It includes amortization of loans to pay for capital expenditures. Amortization, of course, includes return of money borrowed (principal) and return on money borrowed (interest). Capital also includes reserves for future depreciation of capital improvements. Fixed expenses of insurance and taxes also are included. Insurance is generally a protection against capital loss; the major tax assessments are against capital improvements (structure and fixed equipment). Taxes and insurance are usually payable either annually or semi-annually.

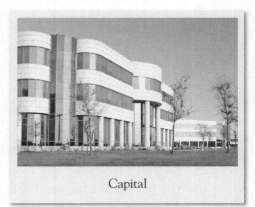

Capital

Whatever return is left after full satisfaction and payment of the other three agents in production is imputable to the **land**. This residual, if properly interpreted, can be used as a basis for determining the value of the land. This process occurs in the land-residual method of income approach to value and in the land-residual approach to site valuation, discussed in other chapters.

> **Review – Four Agents of Production**
> 1. Labor
> 2. Management
> 3. Capital
> 4. Land

Land

CONCEPT OF OPPORTUNITY COST

Opportunity cost occurs as a result of another kind of competition. The economic **principle of opportunity cost** recognizes competing investments, usually in different industries, that may have a greater return. This is the competition between different types of investment. If one invests in the stock market, he or she may have missed the opportunity to make money in real estate investments. Therefore, opportunity cost can be seen as the cost of opportunities not chosen.

Example: If $10,000 is invested in a real estate investment, that $10,000 is not available to be invested in the stock market. If the investor receives a return of 6% on the real estate investment, but could have received a return of 9% by investing in the stock market, the opportunity cost is the 3% (9% minus 6%) "lost."

Opportunity cost is the realizable dollar amount between various types of investments with differing rates of return. This concept applies to appraising income-producing property, in which the appraiser examines alternatives and selects a rate of return for the property, affecting the estimated value.

SUMMARY

For an appraiser to be effective, he or she not only needs the prerequisite skills, but also must understand appraisal theory and the factors that affect value. The basic principles controlling appraisal of real estate can be applied in varying degrees to all types of real estate. Although some of these principles overlap, the appraiser's basic understanding of each of them will be a good foundation for complete comprehension of the various appraisal concepts discussed in this text.

The foundation of appraisal is the valuation process. **Valuation** is the process of estimating market value for real property as of a specific time. An appraiser must know the following principles of valuation before assigning value to any property.

- **Highest and best use** is the use, from among reasonably probable and adequately supported alternative uses, that is physically possible, legally permitted, economically feasible, and maximally productive. This is the starting point for appraisal.

- **Principle of consistent use** requires that land and improvements be appraised based on the same use.

- **Principle of supply and demand** states that market value is affected by the intersection of supply and demand forces in the market as of the appraisal date.

- **Principle of substitution** affirms that the maximum value of a property tends to be set by the cost of acquiring an equally desirable and valuable substitute property, assuming no cost delay is encountered in making the substitution.

- **Principle of anticipation** states that value is created by the benefits to be derived in the future.

- **Principle of change** states that it is the future, not the past, which is of prime importance in estimating value. Real estate values are constantly changed by environmental, economic, political, and social forces.

- **Principle of conformity** states that maximum value results when properties in a neighborhood are relatively similar in size, style, quality, use, and/or type.

- **Principle of regression** states that higher-valued properties tend to suffer when placed in close proximity with lower-valued properties.

- **Principle of progression** states that the worth of a lesser-valued residence tends to be enhanced by association with higher-valued residences in the same area.

- **Principle of competition** states that real estate values are affected by supply and demand because of competition.

- **Principle of contribution** calculates the worth of a particular component in terms of its contribution to the value of the whole property, or an item's worth is calculated as the amount that its absence would detract from the value of the whole.

- **Principle of increasing and decreasing returns** is based on the idea that income and other benefits available from real estate may be increased by adding capital improvements only up to the point of balance in the agents of production, beyond which the increase in value tends to be less than the increase in costs.

- **Principle of balance** is used to determine the value of land based on the primary economic concept controlling all profit-making enterprises that affirms that all production is based on four agents or factors in production.

- **Principle of opportunity cost** recognizes competing investments, usually in different industries, that may have a greater return.

CHAPTER 2 REVIEW EXERCISES

MATCHING EXERCISE

Instructions: Write the letter of the matching term on the blank line before its definition. Answers are in Appendix A.

Terms

A. Automated Valuation Models (AVMs)
B. decline
C. development
D. four agents of production
E. interim use
F. matched pair analysis
G. obsolescence
H. over-improvement
I. principle of anticipation
J. principle of balance
K. principle of change
L. principle of competition
M. principle of conformity

N. principle of consistent use
O. principle of contribution
P. principle of highest and best use
Q. principle of opportunity cost
R. principle of progression
S. principle of regression
T. principle of substitution
U. principle of supply and demand
V. revitalization
W. stability
X. surplus productivity
Y. valuation
Z. wear and tear

Definitions

1. _____ The process of estimating market value for real property as of a specific time

2. _____ The use, from among reasonably probable and adequately supported alternative uses, that is physically possible, legally permitted, economically feasible, and maximally productive

3. _____ A short-term and temporary use of a property until it is ready for a more productive highest and best use

4. _____ Requires that land and improvements be appraised on the basis of the same use

5. _____ States that market value is affected by the intersection of supply and demand forces in the market as of the appraisal date

6. _____ States that it is the future, not the past, which is of prime importance in estimating value

7. _____ The first phase of the life cycle, which consists of initial construction of improvements on vacant land

8. _____ Delayed repairs and deterioration of buildings generally mark the third phase in the life cycle of a neighborhood

9. _____ The depreciation of an asset due to ordinary usage

10. _____ The fourth and final phase in the life cycle of a neighborhood that occurs through the demolition, relocation, or major renovation of existing buildings

11. _____ States that maximum value results when properties in a neighborhood are relatively similar in size, style, quality, use, and/or type

12. _____ States that higher-valued properties tend to suffer when placed in close proximity with lower-valued properties

13. _____ Computer software programs that analyze data using automated systems, such as regression analysis and/or so-called artificial intelligence

14. _____ States that the worth of a lesser-valued residence tends to be enhanced by association with higher-valued residences in the same area

15. _____ States that real estate values are affected by supply and demand because of competition

16. _____ Calculates the worth of a particular component in terms of its contribution to the value of the whole property

17. _____ Method of adjusting comparable sales in which two comparable properties with one differing feature are used to estimate an amount of adjustment for that feature

18. _____ The income generated by a project after the four agents of production have been paid

19. _____ Labor, management, capital, and land

20. _____ Recognizes competing investments, usually in different industries, that may have a greater return

MULTIPLE CHOICE QUESTIONS

Instructions: Circle your response and go to Appendix A to read the complete explanation for each question.

1.   Highest and best use can best be described as the use that will:
   a. be the most expensive to develop.
   b. result in the highest building.
   c. result in the maximum return on investment.
   d. result in the highest legal return.

2.   The principle of consistent use affirms that:
   a. all homes in an area should conform to one another.
   b. land and improvements should be valued based on the same use.
   c. all of the properties should be zoned the same.
   d. improvements are not taken into consideration.

3.   Which of the following statements is correct?
   a. If supply is high and demand is high, then value tends to be high
   b. If supply is low and demand is high, then value tends to be high
   c. If supply and demand are in equilibrium, then value tends to be high
   d. If supply is high and demand is low, then value tends to be high

4.   The principle of supply and demand must include an analysis of:
   a. population growth.
   b. the buyer's ability to pay.
   c. the relative scarcity of available land.
   d. all of the above.

5.   Reasonably, a buyer will not pay more for a particular property than the cost of buying a similar property. This is the underlying basis of which principle?
   a. Anticipation
   b. Conformity
   c. Change
   d. Substitution

6.   The principle of anticipation is easiest to measure in the case of:
   a. income-producing property.
   b. vacant land.
   c. high-rise condominiums.
   d. new construction.

7. What are the four stages of the neighborhood life cycle?

    a. Growth, stability, demand, and revitalization

    b. Regression, growth, stability, and decline

    c. Development, stability, decline, revitalization

    d. Scarcity, decline, revitalization, and growth

8. Sam purchased adjacent lots in a suburban area where the typical house is 3-bedroom/2-bath, under 2,000 square feet. Sam intends to combine the lots and build a 7-bedroom/5-bath, 6,000 square-foot Spanish-style mansion. Which principle of valuation is Sam disregarding?

    a. Progression

    b. Regression

    c. Conformity

    d. All of the above

9. The principle of _____ states that the worth of a lesser-valued residence tends to be enhanced by association with higher-valued residences in the same area.

    a. increasing and decreasing returns

    b. contribution

    c. regression

    d. progression

10. Typically, the principle of competition follows three steps. Which of the following is not one of the three steps?

    a. Market demand generates profits

    b. Profits generate competition

    c. Competition decreases profits

    d. Competition stabilizes profits

11. Ted and Gayle bought a cabin in the mountains for $145,000. They repaired the furnace, redecorated the interior, and repainted the exterior. All of this work totaled just over $9,000. When the couple tried to resell the cabin a few months later, their best offer was $148,500. Which principle of valuation does this scenario exemplify?

    a. Contribution

    b. Competition

    c. Highest and best use

    d. Opportunity cost

12. Overall, the principle of contribution emphasizes that cost:
    a. is equivalent to value.
    b. is not necessarily equal to value.
    c. adjusts according to value.
    d. is not a factor in value.

13. The principle of increasing and decreasing returns can best be applied when there is:
    a. an over-improvement on a parcel of land.
    b. an under-improvement on a parcel of land.
    c. a poorly designed home.
    d. minimal profit.

14. The income generated by a project after the four agents of production have been paid is known as:
    a. entrepreneurial profit.
    b. capital expenditures.
    c. opportunity cost.
    d. surplus productivity.

15. Joe is presented with Investment A and Investment B, both very attractive. He can only afford to invest in one and chooses Investment B. One year later, he learns that Investment A yielded 80% more profit than the investment he chose. Joe is a victim of:
    a. substitution.
    b. opportunity cost.
    c. unearned increment.
    d. regression.

Property Rights: Identification

3 Chapter

INTRODUCTION

Ownership is a basic element of real estate. Today, owning real estate is considered a fundamental right in our culture, but that right did not always exist. Our country's laws of property ownership began with English Common Law. At a time when all property was owned by an existing monarch or appointed noble, no one else was allowed to own property. Upset by their lack of rights, people set powerful forces of change in motion. Eventually, all people gained the right to own real property. In fact, ownership of real property is legally described in terms of these rights, and not in terms of what is owned.

Historically, the question has been, "Who owns this property, and what is that person's interest in it?" As an appraiser, you could be asked to value the fee simple interest in a property or group of properties held under group ownership with undivided interests. This requires identifying the property rights and type of interest conveyed. The appropriate appraisal methods are applied depending upon what class of property and what form of ownership are involved.

This chapter answers these questions about real property interests, partial interests, and types of estates, with information that will be used every time you are involved in the appraisal of real property.

LEARNING OBJECTIVES

After reading this chapter, you will be able to:

- define and describe the bundle of rights.
- identify freehold and leasehold estates.
- identify the various ownership interests.
- describe types of leases.
- define the types of ownership within common interest developments.

INTERESTS IN REAL PROPERTY

The property rights appraised are real property interests. As discussed in Chapter 1, real property as used here is not synonymous with real estate, but includes all of the interests, benefits, and rights inherent in the ownership of physical real estate. This is known as the bundle of rights.

BUNDLE OF RIGHTS

When buying real estate, you might think you are buying the property. What you are really buying are the rights to use that property. Property rights are commonly known as the bundle of rights. The **bundle of rights** is an ownership concept describing all the legal rights that attach to the ownership of real property. The bundle of rights includes the right to use, possess, transfer, encumber, and the quiet enjoyment of real property.

Bundle of Rights

An owner may choose to sell or give away one of the rights and keep the rest. For example, under a lease agreement, an owner may give away the right of use for a certain time to a tenant. A deed may also include a **quiet enjoyment** provision. This guarantees the buyer may enjoy possession of the property in peace and without disturbance due to other claims on the title by the seller or anyone else.

Review – Bundle of Rights
Mnemonic = UPTEE

Use: The right use of property, within the law in any way, or for any purpose

Possess: The right to live on the property and the right to keep others out

Transfer: The right to sell property, give it as a gift, or dispose of it in any way permitted by law

Encumber: The right to borrow money and use property as security for the loan

Enjoyment: The right to peace and quiet enjoyment without aggravation by others

The owner of the real estate has all of the above rights. The owner has the right to use his or her property in any way as long as it is a lawful purpose.

The owner has possession of the property and can refuse admittance to anyone. In plain English, it is the right to tell anyone to get off the property. In the United States, this means the owner may demand that anyone who does not have a court order of special circumstances must leave the property. This includes police, government officials, or just the person down the street. This very important right helps to provide the security that is part of real estate ownership.

TYPES OF ESTATES

An **estate** is the ownership interest or claim a person has in real property. The two types of estates that may be owned are freehold and leasehold. A **freehold estate** is an estate of indefinite duration and can be sold or inherited. The freehold estate is a real property estate of an owner, whose hold on the estate is free of anyone else's restrictions.

A **leasehold estate** is the tenant's interest in the leased property during the term of the lease. The tenant has temporary and limited right of use in a real property estate. The rights are described by a lease, which is personal property. This is also known as a **less-than-freehold estate** or **non-freehold estate**.

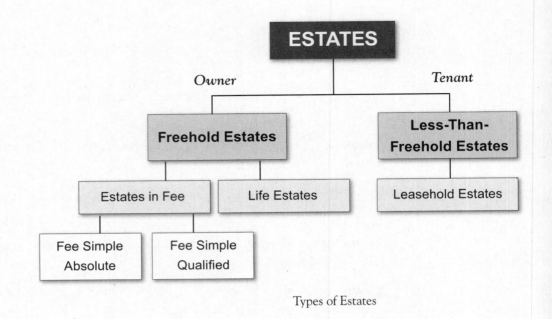

Types of Estates

The type of estate determines the extent of the claim. Each type of estate is described in terms of its duration and rights.

FREEHOLD ESTATES

Freehold estates are real property estates of ownership. Because this type of estate continues for an indefinite period, it sometimes is called an estate of inheritance. The two types of freehold estates are estates in fee and life estates.

ESTATES IN FEE

An **estate in fee**, also known as a **fee simple estate** or **fee simple absolute**, is the most complete form of ownership. Since an owner of an estate in fee may dispose of it in his or her lifetime or after death by will, it is also known as an **estate of inheritance** or a **perpetual estate**. This is the most common type of estate transferred in a normal real estate transaction.

A property owner may impose qualifications, conditions, or restrictions when transferring title to property. Property restrictions are created by deed or written agreement. If a seller imposes qualifications or conditions a buyer must do or not do, it is known as a **fee simple qualified** or **fee simple defeasible** estate. The conditions are classified as a condition subsequent or a condition precedent.

If a fee simple estate has a **condition subsequent**, there is something the owner must not do. If the owner breaks the condition, the property will go back to the former owner. This is also known as **reversion**.

> Example: A seller may require the property to be used for a specified purpose such as a church or a rehabilitation center. The owner sells the property with the condition this requirement be met. If the buyer breaches this condition subsequent after the sale, the seller may take possession of the property and regain title.

> In another example of a condition subsequent, the seller may place special limitations on the use of the property after the sale. A buyer may be denied the right to sell alcoholic beverages on the property or allow a board and care use. If either event occurs, ownership of the property reverts to the seller or his or her heirs.

The parties to a contract may also impose a restriction known as a **condition precedent**. In this case, something must occur before a transaction becomes absolute and final. For example, a sale may be contingent on the buyer obtaining financing or qualifying for a VA or FHA loan.

LIFE ESTATES

A **life estate** is one which is limited in duration to the life of its owner or the life of another designated person—also known as a **life tenant**. The term used to describe a life estate created on the life of a designated person is pur autre vie. The phrase **pur autre vie** means "for another's life."

Since a life estate is a type of freehold, or fee estate, the holder of a life estate has all the rights that go with fee ownership except disposing of the estate by will. Remember, the life estate is tied to a designated life, and when that party dies, the estate goes to either the person in reversion or the person in remainder, or his or her heirs.

Life estate holders must pay the taxes and maintain the property. They may collect all rents and keep all profits for the duration of the life estate. They may encumber the property or dispose of it in any way except by will. Any interest the life estate holders may create in the property—extending beyond the life of the person used to measure the estate—will become invalid when the designated person dies.

LEASEHOLD ESTATES

Freehold estates are the most complete form of ownership and include the most rights. The leasehold estate (also called a less-than-freehold estate) is owned by renters or tenants. Leasehold estates are also called **chattels real** because the lease is personal property (chattel) that concerns real property (real).

Remember, anything movable becomes personal property. The **lease** is a contract by which real estate is conveyed for life, for a term of years, or at will, usually for a specified rent.

The owner of the leasehold (tenant) has exclusive possession and use of real property for a fixed amount of time. This includes the right to the use and quiet enjoyment of the premises during the term of the lease. The tenant has the right to the exclusive use of the rented property, and the right to live quietly without privacy invasion. We will discuss appraising lease interests later in the chapter.

TYPES OF LEASEHOLD ESTATES

The duration of leasehold is known as a tenancy. Each type of leasehold is distinctive because of its duration.

1. Estate for years
2. Estate from period to period (periodic estate)
3. Estate at will
4. Estate at sufferance

ESTATE FOR YEARS

An **estate for years** has a fixed term. The lease does not have to be for only one year, but if a definite end date is stated, it is known as an estate for years. The lease of office space or a commercial center is commonly an estate for years. It is not automatically renewable and does not require notice to quit at the end of the lease (must be renegotiated). It is a less-than-freehold estate.

When an apartment lease mentions an end date, it is considered an estate for years. Increasingly, owners of residential income property (apartment buildings) are using this type of agreement to guarantee that a tenant will stay, at least until the lease expires.

The benefit of an estate for years to the landlord is that a desirable, long-term tenant may be attracted to the apartment or house. The benefit to the renter is assurance that the rent will remain the same over the period of the lease. At the expiration of the lease, the landlord and tenant must renegotiate the terms.

ESTATE FROM PERIOD TO PERIOD

Perhaps the most common type of lease or rental agreement for residential use is the **estate from period to period**, also known as periodic tenancy. This typical month-to-month tenancy requires 30-days notice to quit. It automatically renews itself unless terminated by the landlord or tenant.

ESTATE AT WILL

When there is no written agreement between the landlord and tenant, the tenancy is known as an estate or **tenancy at will**. The tenancy may be ended by the unilateral decision of either party. There is no agreed-upon termination date and either party must give 30-days notice before ending the tenancy.

ESTATE AT SUFFERANCE

An estate or **tenancy at sufferance** occurs if a tenant occupies the property without paying rent and without the permission of the landlord.

TYPES OF INTERESTS

An **interest** is the legal portion of the property and rights. Interests can describe the physical real estate, the property rights, or a combination of both. Again, a clear description of the interest owned is required in any appraisal.

An owner of real property may have a fee simple interest in the property or something less. **Fee simple** is ownership of all the rights to the property. An owner may purchase less than fee simple interest or have a limited or partial interest. A **partial interest** is an interest in real estate that represents less than the fee simple estate. Some examples of partial interests are ownership in common interest developments (such as condominium ownership) and leasehold interests.

Once the fee simple value of a property or group of properties is determined by an appraiser, the next step is to allocate the value between partial interest owners. In USPAP, STANDARDS RULE 1-2, the concepts of fractional interest, segment, and partial holding are discussed.

Partial interests refer to the bundle of rights owned by multiple owners of the property. A **fractional interest** is the land only or the improvements only. A **physical segment** could be the first floor of a high-rise or ten acres of a 30-acre parcel.

OWNERSHIP INTERESTS

When property is owned by two or more persons or entities at the same time, it is known as **concurrent ownership**, or co-ownership. Concurrent ownership has several forms such as tenancy in common, joint tenancy, community property, tenancy by the entirety, and tenancy in partnership.

Tenancy in common allows two or more people to hold unequal percentages. Each co-owner has an **undivided interest**, which means each owner has a certain equitable interest in the property, but has the right to use the whole property.

Types of Concurrent Ownership
- Tenancy in common
- Joint tenancy
- Community property
- Tenancy by the entirety
- Tenancy in partnership

Joint tenancy allows two or more people to hold equal percentages with the right of survivorship. In a **right of survivorship**, if one of the joint tenants dies, the surviving joint tenant automatically becomes sole owner of the property. In order to have a joint tenancy, four unities must be in existence: (1) time, (2) title, (3) interest, and (4) possession. If any one of the unities is missing, a tenancy in common is created.

Review – The Four Unities of Joint Tenancy
Mnemonic = T-TIP

Time	All parties must become joint tenants at the same time.
Title	All parties must take title on the same deed.
Interest	All parties must have an equal undivided interest in the property.
Possession	All parties have equal right of possession.

Tenancy by the entirety is a form of ownership by husband and wife in which each owns the entire property. If either one dies, the title is passed to the surviving spouse, who owns the property without probate. Both spouses have an equal, undivided interest in the whole property. If the marriage is dissolved, then the tenancy becomes a tenancy in common.

His   Hers

Community property is property acquired by a husband and wife during a valid marriage—except for certain separate property. Each spouse has an equal (50/50), undivided interest in the property. Nine states—Arizona, California, Idaho, Louisiana, Nevada, New Mexico, Texas, Washington, and Wisconsin—use the community property system to determine the interest of a husband and wife in property acquired during marriage.

LEASE INTERESTS

A **lease** is a contract between an owner (lessor or landlord) and a renter (lessee or tenant) giving the renter a tenancy. **Tenancy** is a mode or method of ownership or holding title to property. Normally, under a lease, the lessee takes possession and use of a property in return for rent payment. The lease is usually a written agreement, which transfers the right of exclusive possession and use of real estate for a definite time period. Another name for lease is **rental agreement**.

The **lessor** (landlord) owns the property and signs the lease to give possession and use to the **lessee** (tenant). The lessor keeps the right to retake possession of

A lease lists the rights and options of the lessor and the lessee.

the property after the lease term expires. The end of the lease period is also known as the **period of reversion** and the right of the lessor to reclaim the property is known as the **reversionary right**. The lessor's interest is called a **leased fee estate**. The lessee has the use, possession, and the right of quiet enjoyment of the property for the duration of the lease. The lessee's interest is a less-than-freehold estate in real property.

A lease can be described in any number of ways, as long as the names of the parties, description of the property, rent amount, and duration of lease are included. Sometimes the words to let or to **demise**, (another way to say, to rent), will be found in a rental agreement, but those words are optional.

CLASSIFICATIONS OF LEASES

There are many varieties of lease contracts. If a lessee and lessor agree on terms that differ from the law, both will be required to meet the terms of their written agreement. Leases are generally classified by the type of real estate, the length of term, or the method of payment.

TYPE OF REAL ESTATE

Leases based on type of real estate would include office leases, ground leases, proprietary leases, and residential leases. A **ground lease** is a lease for only the land. A **proprietary lease** is used in co-op apartment buildings. In which case, the lessee is also a stockholder in the corporation that owns the building. A **residential lease** is used for all residential property including single-family homes, duplexes, and multiple-family dwellings.

LENGTH OF TIME

Leases based on length of time would include short-term and long-term leases. An apartment lease is an example of a short-term lease. An example of a long-term lease is a major tenant in a shopping center that has multiple-renewal rights.

METHOD OF RENT PAYMENTS

Leases are also classified by method of rent payments, such as gross, net, and percentage leases.

Gross lease: A gross lease is also called a flat, fixed, or straight lease. The tenant pays an agreed-upon sum as rent and the landlord pays any other expenses such as taxes, maintenance, or insurance.

Net lease: In a net lease, the tenant pays an agreed-upon sum as rent, plus certain agreed-upon expenses per month (i.e., taxes, insurance, and repairs). The benefit of a net lease to the lessor is the increase in fixed income.

Percentage lease: A percentage lease is a lease in which the tenant pays a percentage of gross monthly receipts in addition to a base rent. Any extra rent paid in excess of the base rent is **overage rent**. Usually the higher the gross receipts, the lower the percentage rate. An example of a percentage lease is a commercial parking lot. It would typically pay the highest percentage in a percentage lease.

Review – Classifications of a Lease
- Type of real estate
- Length of term
- Method of payment

COMMON INTEREST DEVELOPMENTS

A **common interest development** (CID) combines the individual ownership of private dwellings with the shared ownership of common facilities of the entire project. The common facilities can range from roads and water systems to clubhouses, swimming pools, golf courses, and even stables and private airport facilities. The CID provides a system of self-governance through a community association, sometimes called a **homeowners' association (HOA)**. The HOA has the authority to enforce special rules called Covenants, Conditions, and Restrictions (CC&Rs) and to raise money through regular and special assessments. Restrictions on lots in a new development would be found in a recorded declaration of restrictions. Common interest developments vary in physical design and in legal form.

CONDOMINIUMS

The owner of a condominium does not own the entire real estate. He or she owns the airspace between the walls of the condominium and a partial interest in the common areas.

Generally, a **condominium** consists of a separate fee interest in a particular specific space (the unit), plus an undivided interest in all common or public areas of the development. All owners are allowed to use any of the facilities in the common area. Each unit owner has a deed, separate financing, and pays the property taxes for his or her unit. When appraising a condominium, an appraiser needs to consider and make note of both private and common areas. The appraiser needs to designate the location of the unit within the building and describe the overall upkeep of the building. Since most condominiums are

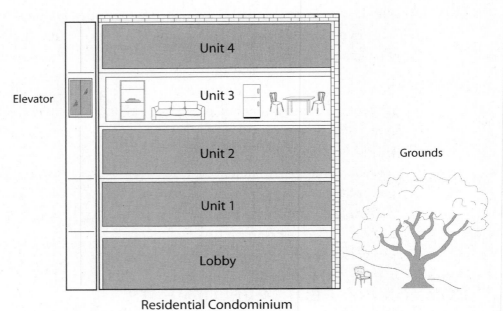

Residential Condominium

governed by an HOA, the monthly fees and common area amenities should also be included in the appraisal report.

Review – Condominiums

- Fee simple ownership to living unit
- Undivided interest in land and common areas
- Separate property tax bill, deed, deed of trust
- Operations controlled by elected governing board

PLANNED DEVELOPMENTS

A **planned development** (previously called planned unit development) is a planning and zoning term describing land not subject to conventional zoning requirements. It allows clustering of residences or other characteristics of the project that differ from normal zoning. In a planned development subdivision, the owner has title to the unit and land under it, together with membership in an HOA that owns the common areas.

Sometimes the owners of separate interests also have an undivided interest in the common area. In an **undivided interest**, the land itself is not

Individual Condominium Unit Appraisal Report
File #

The purpose of this summary appraisal report is to provide the lender/client with an accurate, and adequately supported, opinion of the market value of the subject property.

SUBJECT

Property Address		Unit #	City	State	Zip Code

Borrower   Owner of Public Record   County

Legal Description

Assessor's Parcel #   Tax Year   R.E. Taxes $

Project Name   Phase #   Map Reference   Census Tract

Occupant ☐ Owner ☐ Tenant ☐ Vacant   Special Assessments $ HOA $ ☐ per year ☐ per month

Property Rights Appraised ☐ Fee Simple ☐ Leasehold ☐ Other (describe)

Assignment Type ☐ Purchase Transaction ☐ Refinance Transaction ☐ Other (describe)

Lender/Client   Address

Is the subject property currently offered for sale or has it been offered for sale in the twelve months prior to the effective date of this appraisal? ☐ Yes ☐ No

Report data source(s) used, offering price(s), and date(s).

CONTRACT

I ☐ did ☐ did not analyze the contract for sale for the subject purchase transaction. Explain the results of the analysis of the contract for sale or why the analysis was not performed.

Contract Price $ Date of Contract   Is the property seller the owner of public record? ☐ Yes ☐ No   Data Source(s)

Is there any financial assistance (loan charges, sale concessions, gift or downpayment assistance, etc.) to be paid by any party on behalf of the borrower? ☐ Yes ☐ No
If Yes, report the total dollar amount and describe the items to be paid.

NEIGHBORHOOD

Note: Race and the racial composition of the neighborhood are not appraisal factors.

Neighborhood Characteristics			Condominium Unit Housing Trends			Condominium Housing		Present Land Use %	
Location ☐ Urban	☐ Suburban	☐ Rural	Property Values ☐ Increasing	☐ Stable	☐ Declining	PRICE	AGE	One-Unit	%
Built-Up ☐ Over 75%	☐ 25–75%	☐ Under 25%	Demand/Supply ☐ Shortage	☐ In Balance	☐ Over Supply	$ (000)	(yrs)	2-4 Unit	%
Growth ☐ Rapid	☐ Stable	☐ Slow	Marketing Time ☐ Under 3 mths	☐ 3–6 mths	☐ Over 6 mths	Low		Multi-Family	%
Neighborhood Boundaries						High		Commercial	%
						Pred.		Other	%

Neighborhood Description

Market Conditions (including support for the above conclusions)

PROJECT SITE

Topography   Size   Density   View

Specific Zoning Classification   Zoning Description

Zoning Compliance ☐ Legal ☐ Legal Nonconforming – Do the zoning regulations permit rebuilding to current density? ☐ Yes ☐ No
☐ No Zoning ☐ Illegal (describe)

Is the highest and best use of the subject property as improved (or as proposed per plans and specifications) the present use? ☐ Yes ☐ No   If No, describe

Utilities	Public	Other (describe)		Public	Other (describe)	Off-site Improvements—Type	Public	Private
Electricity	☐	☐	Water	☐	☐	Street	☐	☐
Gas	☐	☐	Sanitary Sewer	☐	☐	Alley	☐	☐

FEMA Special Flood Hazard Area ☐ Yes ☐ No   FEMA Flood Zone   FEMA Map #   FEMA Map Date

Are the utilities and off-site improvements typical for the market area? ☐ Yes ☐ No   If No, describe

Are there any adverse site conditions or external factors (easements, encroachments, environmental conditions, land uses, etc.)? ☐ Yes ☐ No   If Yes, describe

PROJECT INFORMATION

Data source(s) for project information

Project Description ☐ Detached ☐ Row or Townhouse ☐ Garden ☐ Mid-Rise ☐ High-Rise ☐ Other (describe)

General Description	General Description	Subject Phase	If Project Completed	If Project Incomplete
# of Stories	Exterior Walls	# of Units	# of Phases	# of Planned Phases
# of Elevators	Roof Surface	# of Units Completed	# of Units	# o f Planned Units
☐ Existing ☐ Proposed	Total # Parking	# of Units For Sale	# of Units for Sale	# of Units for Sale
☐ Under Construction	Ratio (spaces/units)	# of Units Sold	# of Units Sold	# of Units Sold
Year Built	Type	# of Units Rented	# of Units Rented	# of Units Rented
Effective Age	Guest Parking	# of Owner Occupied Units	# of Owner Occupied Units	# of Owner Occupied Units

Project Primary Occupancy ☐ Principle Residence ☐ Second Home or Recreational ☐ Tenant

Is the developer/builder in control of the Homeowners' Association (HOA)? ☐ Yes ☐ No

Management Group – ☐ Homeowners' Association ☐ Developer ☐ Management Agent – Provide name of management company.

Does any single entity (the same individual, investor group, corporation, etc.) own more than 10% of the total units in the project? ☐ Yes ☐ No   If Yes, describe

Was the project created by the conversion of an existing building(s) into a condominium? ☐ Yes ☐ No   If Yes, describe the original use and the date of conversion.

Are the units, common elements, and recreation facilities complete (including any planned rehabilitation for a condominium conversion)? ☐ Yes ☐ No   If No, describe

Is there any commercial space in the project? ☐ Yes ☐ No   If Yes, describe and indicate the overall percentage of the commercial space.

divided—just the ownership. The buyer receives an undivided interest in a parcel of land as a tenant in common with all the other owners. All owners have the nonexclusive right to use and occupy the property. Owners in a planned development have private ownership of their individual homes and lots but share the ownership of the common features. Shared facilities can include private roadways, water systems, septic systems, parks and open space, ponds and lakes, airport landing strips, trails, and ocean access. Some planned developments even share the ownership of forests and agricultural lands, which produce income for the community. A RV park with campground and other leisure-time amenities is an example of an undivided interest.

STOCK COOPERATIVES

A corporation formed for owning property is known as a **stock cooperative**. Each stockholder is given the use of a living unit and, through a proprietary lease, any amenities, and community recreational facilities. The building itself is owned by a corporation.

In a community apartment project, a buyer receives an undivided interest in the land coupled with the right of exclusive occupancy of one of the apartments in the project.

MANUFACTURED AND MOBILE HOMES

Due to the increased need for affordable housing and relatively low cost to build, manufactured housing has become a major source of the residential housing supply. The U.S. Census Bureau reports that manufactured homes make up 7% of the total housing stock.

What is the difference between a mobile home and a manufactured home? A **mobile home** is a factory-built home manufactured prior to June 15, 1976, constructed on a chassis and wheels, and designed for permanent or semi-attachment to land. In the past, mobile homes were known as trailers and were used mainly as a second, traveling home. **Manufactured homes** are homes built in a factory after June 15, 1976 and must conform to the U.S. government's Manufactured Home Construction and Safety Standards (HUD code).

The federal standards regulate manufactured housing design and construction, strength and durability, transportability, fire resistance, energy efficiency, and quality. The HUD Code also sets performance standards for the heating, plumbing, air conditioning, thermal, and electrical systems of the home. It is the only federally regulated national building code. Each home or segment of a home is labeled with a red tag that is the manufacturer's guarantee the home was built to conform to the HUD code (hence, the name "HUD-tag home").

Manufactured homes are built on a non-removable steel chassis and transported to the building site on their own wheels.

A mobile home

Financing of manufactured homes is available from the same sources as for fixed-foundation residences. Loans are available through government participation programs such as the FHA or VA. Special considerations when appraising mobile and manufactured homes is noting whether or not the residence is on leased land, as well as space rental fees and any HOA fees and amenities.

TIME-SHARE OWNERSHIP

A **time-share** is a real estate development in which a buyer can purchase the exclusive right to occupy a unit for a specified period each year. Time-share ownerships—also known as **interval ownerships**—are usually for one or two weeks per year. It can be a fixed week or a floating week. Time-share ownership is popular in resorts and other desirable areas where people like to vacation but do not need the right of possession the rest of the time. Time-shares might allow ownership, but sometimes they only grant a right to use for a limited time.

In addition to a one-time purchase price, time-share owners pay an annual fee for property management and maintenance. Time-shares are usu-

ally resort-type subdivisions created with the intention of selling them to people who want a retirement home or second vacation home.

The most common type of time-share is a resort condominium. This type of time-share can range from a studio with a partial kitchen to a five-bedroom unit with a full kitchen and luxury amenities. Less-common time-share accommodations include hotel rooms, houseboats, and even motor homes.

When appraising time-shares, an appraiser must strongly consider the type of amenities offered and the owner's assignment. Does the time-share owner have a fixed week or a floating week? Is the week during a peak period or off-season? Time-share units are often more valuable during holidays or peak seasons. For example, if a time-share owner has a ski resort unit in the Rocky Mountains, the unit would be more valuable during the winter months than the summer months. An appraiser must also consider the number of resale units available—as time-share units are frequently purchased and resold. This results in steeply discounted resale values.

FLOATING RESIDENCES

Before taking on a houseboat assignment, an appraiser must first determine if the value sought is for real or personal property. Some states allow certain floating structures (houseboats, barges, and floating houses) to be used as residences. Most states view the floating structures as boats. However, many states view

them as real property. It is not uncommon to find houseboats used as residences in Marin County, California and Miami, Florida.

A **houseboat** is essentially a barge designed and equipped for use as a dwelling. Initially, they were used as summer retreats, mostly for wealthy families. During the sixties, houseboats became lawless floating neighborhoods running along the west shore north of San Francisco, California. Today, houseboats permanently attached to city utilities are considered real property.

SUMMARY

The property rights appraised are real property interests. **Property rights** are the rights someone has in something and are known as the bundle of rights. The **bundle of rights** is an ownership concept describing all the legal rights that attach to the ownership of real property. The bundle of rights includes the right to use, possess, transfer, encumber, and the enjoyment of real property.

An **estate** is the ownership interest or claim a person has in real property. The two types of estates that may be owned are freehold and leasehold. A **freehold estate** is an estate of indefinite duration and can be sold or inherited. A **leasehold estate** is the tenant's interest in the leased property during the term of the lease. This is also known as a **less-than-freehold estate**.

An **interest** is the legal portion of the property and rights that are owned. Interests can describe the physical real estate, the property rights, or a combination of both. **Fee simple** is ownership of all the rights to the property. An owner may purchase less than fee simple interest or have an interest that is limited or partial. A **partial interest** is an interest in real estate that represents less than the fee simple estate. Examples of partial interests are ownership in common interest developments, such as **condominium** and **planned development** ownership, and leasehold interests. Condominiums and planned developments are located within a common interest development (CID). A **common interest development** (CID) combines the individual ownership of private dwellings with the shared ownership of common facilities of the entire project. The CID provides a system of self-governance through a community association, sometimes called a **homeowners' association** (HOA).

When property is owned by two or more persons or entities at the same time, it is known as **concurrent ownership**. Concurrent ownership has several forms such as tenancy in common, joint tenancy, community property, tenancy by the entirety, and tenancy in partnership.

A **lease** is a contract between an owner (lessor or landlord) and a renter (lessee or tenant) that gives the renter a tenancy. **Tenancy** is a mode or method of ownership or holding title to property. Leases are generally classified by the type of real estate, the length of term, or the method of payment.

CHAPTER 3 REVIEW EXERCISES

MATCHING EXERCISE

Instructions: Write the letter of the matching term on the blank line before its definition. Answers are in Appendix A.

Terms

A. bundle of rights

B. common interest development (CID)

C. concurrent ownership

D. condominium

E. estate

F. estate at sufferance

G. estate at will

H. estate for years

I. estate from period to period

J. estate in fee

K. estate of inheritance

L. fee simple

M. fee simple defeasible

N. freehold estate

O. interest

P. joint tenancy

Q. lease

R. leasehold estate

S. life estate

T. ownership

U. partial interest

V. planned development

W. quiet enjoyment

X. rental agreement

Y. tenancy

Z. time-share

Definitions

1. _____ Ownership concept describing all the legal rights that attach to the ownership of real property

2. _____ Ownership interest or claim a person has in real property

3. _____ An estate of indefinite duration and can be sold or inherited

4. _____ Tenant's interest in the leased property during the term of the lease

5. _____ The most complete form of ownership

6. _____ Limited in duration to the life of its owner or the life of another designated person

7. _____ A mode or method of ownership or holding title to property

8. _____ Lease with a definite end date

9. _____ Type of estate in which there is no written agreement between the landlord and tenant

10. _____ The legal portion of the property and rights that are owned

11. _____ Ownership of all the rights to the property

12. _____ An interest in real estate that represents less than the fee simple estate

13. _____ When property is owned by two or more persons or entities at the same time

14. _____ Allows two or more people to hold equal percentages with the right of survivorship

15. _____ A contract by which real estate is conveyed for life, for a term of years, or at will, usually for a specified rent

16. _____ Another name for lease

17. _____ Combines the individual ownership of private dwellings with the shared ownership of common facilities of the entire project

18. _____ Consists of a separate fee interest in a particular specific space (the unit), plus an undivided interest in all common or public areas of the development

19. _____ A planning and zoning term describing land not subject to conventional zoning requirements

20. _____ A real estate development in which a buyer can purchase the exclusive right to occupy a unit for a specified period each year

MULTIPLE CHOICE QUESTIONS

Instructions: Circle your response and go to Appendix A to read the complete explanation for each question.

1. The bundle of rights consists of all legal rights that are attached to the ownership of real property. These include the right to _____ the property.
    a. use and enjoy
    b. transfer
    c. possess
    d. all of the above

2. Which type of estate represents the most complete form of ownership?
    a. Leasehold estate
    b. Fee simple estate
    c. Estate in fee
    d. Both (b) and (c)

3. A property owner may impose qualifications, conditions, or restrictions when transferring title to property. If a seller imposes qualifications or conditions that the buyer must do or not do, this is known as a(n):
    a. perpetual estate.
    b. fee simple qualified estate.
    c. life estate.
    d. less-than-freehold estate.

4. Which of the following is a leasehold estate?
    a. Life estate
    b. Estate of inheritance
    c. Estate for years
    d. Estate in remainder

5. A month-to-month tenancy is typically an:
    a. estate from period to period.
    b. estate for years.
    c. estate at sufferance.
    d. estate in remainder.

6. A partial interest is best described as an interest in real estate that represents:
    a. a fractional interest only.
    b. less than the fee simple estate.
    c. the land or the improvements only.
    d. ownership of all rights to the property.

7. When property is owned by two or more persons or entities at the same time, it is known as concurrent ownership, or co-ownership. Which of the following is not a type of concurrent ownership?
    a. Joint tenancy
    b. Tenancy at sufferance
    c. Tenancy in common
    d. Community property

8. An uncle left his nephew 2/3 interest and left his nephew's wife 1/3 interest in real property jointly and without the right of survivorship. The couple will assume title to an estate that is classified as:
    a. leasehold.
    b. joint tenancy.
    c. tenancy in common.
    d. partnership.

9. The words time, title, interest, and possession are associated with:
    a. undivided interest.
    b. survivorship.
    c. tenancy.
    d. possession.

10. As used in real estate law, the term tenancy is best described as:
    a. the landlord-tenant relationship.
    b. the retention of rights.
    c. a tenant in a lease agreement.
    d. a mode or method of holding title to real property by a lessee or owner.

11. All of the following are classifications of a lease, except:
    a. amount of payment.
    b. type of real estate.
    c. length of term.
    d. method of payment.

12. The owner of a condominium has title to the unit and:
    a. the land under it.
    b. an undivided interest in the common areas.
    c. pays property taxes for his or her own unit.
    d. both (b) and (c).

13. In an undivided interest, the land itself is not divided—just the ownership. The buyer receives an undivided interest in a parcel of land as a _____ with all the other owners.
    a. tenant in common
    b. stockholder
    c. lessee
    d. tenant in partnership

14. What is the commonality between mobile homes and manufactured homes?
    a. Both are factory built
    b. Each must conform to HUD code
    c. Each is permanently attached to land
    d. They are primarily used as second homes

15. Time-share properties are primarily designed for buyers who want:
    a. income-producing real property.
    b. vacation property.
    c. a primary residence.
    d. agricultural property.

Chapter

INTRODUCTION

There are different types of property inspection. Inspections by contractors or property inspectors—generally conducted as part of a real estate sales contract—are to uncover defects or potential problems with the property. The second type of inspection is a property inspection conducted by an appraiser—which determines the components and characteristics of the subject property that can affect value in the marketplace. The importance of an appraiser's property inspection should not be underestimated, as it provides much of the primary data an appraiser uses in his or her valuation process.

After identifying the problem, the first step of data collection and analysis is to determine the highest and best use of the subject property. Closely related to this step is determining the value of the land or site, separately from the value of any improvements.

This chapter focuses on site value and analysis. The information presented here is applicable in assignments in which vacant land is being appraised, as well as situations in which the land has been developed and built upon—but the value of the land needs to be identified separately.

LEARNING OBJECTIVES

After reading this chapter, you will be able to:

- identify the considerations in site analysis.
- determine the importance of highest and best use in site analysis.
- describe a site and list physical features considered in a site inspection.

CONSIDERATIONS IN SITE ANALYSIS

Appraisers often need to determine the value of a site. There are many different reasons for this. Sometimes the subject property is a vacant lot. At other times, the subject property has improvements, but the appraiser needs to determine the land value separately in order to apply the cost approach or the income approach's building residual technique.

Every parcel of land and its location are unique. No two sites, no matter how similar, can be identical. Analysis and valuation of the site must sometimes be made separately from analysis of the improvements.

Reasons for Separate Site Valuation

- Local tax assessment
- Claim on federal income tax return for depreciation allowances on improvements
- Cost approach and certain income approaches of appraisal
- Insurance
- Eminent domain
- When the existing improvements do not represent the highest and best use of the land

Whatever the reason for separate valuation, the appraiser must keep in mind the factors that make one parcel of land more desirable than another parcel. These physical factors may all be combined into one word—utility. **Utility** takes many forms, but for our purposes, it relates to the ability of a property to satisfy a need or desire, such as for shelter or income.

A common saying in the real estate profession is "location, location, location." Although other physical attributes also contribute to value, location is certainly the most important factor. **Location** is the site, setting, or position of a property or object in relation to other properties or objects. Only one parcel of land in any area has the best location. From this one parcel or area, the value of every other parcel or area is measured. Since a parcel of land occupies only one fixed spot, it can be concluded that land translates to location.

Following this premise to its logical conclusion, location translates to use—since land in a certain location has a specific use—now and in the future. If demand is great enough and zoning and building permits are available, use translates to value—that translates to return. Return can be measured in terms of money. Reversing this simple progression, for land to be worth money, the land must have a return. To have a return, it must have value to someone. Value requires a use. The use of any parcel of real estate is a direct function of its location. Therefore, it can be said that location translates to money.

HIGHEST AND BEST USE

When appraising a property, an appraiser first has to determine highest and best use. Highest and best use is defined as the use, from among reasonably probable and adequately supported alternative uses, that meets four tests. An appraiser does this with a site analysis and by applying the four tests.

Four Tests of Highest and Best Use

1. Physically possible
2. Legally permitted
3. Economically feasible
4. Maximally productive

Appraisers cannot value land if they do not understand how the land is best used. An appraiser must apply the four tests when appraising vacant land and improved property. This also applies to appraising improved property as if it were vacant.

SITE DESCRIPTION

When an appraiser arrives at the subject property, he or she must be able to describe the site in the report based on its physical characteristics and any neighborhood characteristics that affect the site. There is some confusion with newer appraisers as it concerns the difference between a lot and a site.

A **lot** is a distinct parcel of land or plot of ground as described in a parcel or tract map recorded with the local government authority. A **site** is land that has been prepared for use with grading, utilities, and access.

An appraiser also considers a property's physical features.

USPAP permits the appraiser to value the site only—or the improvements only. This is discussed as a fractional interest in SR 1-2(e)(v). For a residential appraiser, this can occur when a client needs an appraisal for insurance purposes or if a client needs the value of improvements to assist in the depreciation process.

When appraisers consider the site as part of a property inspection, it is important to consider certain physical features.

Physical Features Considered in a Site Inspection

- Lot size, shape, and slope
- Access (ingress and egress)
- Excess land and amount usable
- Soil and topography
- Drainage/retention systems
- Grading
- Retaining walls
- Exposure to sun and weather
- View
- Off-site improvements
- Availability of utilities

- Deed restrictions, easements, and rights-of-way

- Availability of public transportation

- Proximity to natural hazard areas

- Proximity to nuclear waste, hazardous waste, or electromagnetic fields

The physical features listed relate differently to each specific parcel of land. Since parcels in one neighborhood vary in size, shape, slope, and so on, these variables and their definite influence on utility and, hence, value must be considered.

SIZE

The size of a site is a key factor in determining its value because the size influences how the site may be used. Utility is a function of size as well as a function of location. In some areas, a 3,000 SF lot is large enough to qualify as a single-family residential building site. In other areas, the minimum lot size is one acre or more.

A multiple-family residential site must have a certain number of square feet (SF) for the first unit and for each additional unit. Square foot requirements generally include off-street parking needs. For example, in many areas, each living unit requires parking for a car and a half.

When determining residential land value, it can usually be related to the price buyers pay per living unit. A site large enough to accommodate 20 units might be worth $50,000 per unit, or $1 million for the land. The values of multiple residential sites are usually proportionate to their size. As size increases measurably, value increases. This is assuming, of course, that the parcel does not have an unusual shape.

On the other hand, increases in the size of single-family residential sites do not necessarily create proportionate increases in value. For example, a single-family residential site of 6,000 SF in a neighborhood of 6,000 SF lots might be worth $20 per square foot or $120,000. It does not necessarily follow that a 10,000 SF lot in the same area would also be worth $20 per square foot or $200,000. The appraiser must carefully determine through market analysis what buyers are paying for lots larger than the standard for the area. In the case above, the 10,000 SF lot would probably not be worth more than $140,000 to $150,000. This is the economic concept of diminishing returns.

Appraisers can often find the size of the appraisal site in official legal documents. Acres or square feet make up the measurements for size in appraisal. Legal documents do not report the usable area of the site, which is more important than gross area. **Usable area** is the portion of the site that is suitable for building. Some areas of the site may not be usable because the soil or topography cannot support a structure. Usable areas can be limited also by zoning regulations such as setback requirements.

SHAPE

After estimating the size of a lot, the shape of it often comes into play. The typical buyer will often pay less for a lot that is long and narrow as compared to one that is nearly rectangular or even square. Lot dimensions and placement must be considered, and the appraiser has to use market data to determine if one configuration is preferable to another. Factors such as front yard, side yard, and rear yard setbacks are very important. These can affect lot utility and desirability, and

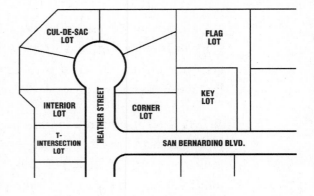

an appraiser has to determine if the type of lot affects market reaction. Lots may be described based on their shape and placement.

Cul-de-sac lots are situated at the end of a dead-end street that has a turn-around area. They generally have narrower frontage and a wide rear yard. In subdivisions, buyers usually pay a premium for a cul-de-sac location. Many families with young children prefer cul-de-sac lots because they offer more seclusion and safety than other lots. In a subdivision of moderately sized lots, a cul-de-sac lot generally has a greater number of square feet than other types of lots because of its shape. This results in comparable sales that are not on cul-de-sacs to receive an upward adjustment.

Corner lots are at the confluence or convergence of two streets. The developer of a subdivision may charge more for a corner lot—because it usually costs more in terms of off-site improvements, such as streets, sidewalks, and utilities. Because corner lots have the advantage of only having neighbors on two sides, this can be a positive or a negative depending upon traffic patterns and if the roads are busy. The appraiser's inspection will often occur during the day when there is little traffic. It is important to determine what the traffic patterns are at peak travel hours for the given area and how this affects value.

Most single-family residential lots are interior lots. An **interior lot** is surrounded by other lots on three sides, generally by no more than five lots. Advantages include having a larger backyard than front yard—affording more private play and entertainment area—and fewer offensive traffic noises. Interior lot value is usually the benchmark from which other lots are valued, primarily because most lots are interior lots. Interior lot prices can be estimated by using the market approach, if the lots are not developed with improvements.

The **flag lot** is located so that access can be had only at the side of another lot. It is named as such because its shape is similar to a flag on a staff. The staff portion generally includes the access road to the lot itself. Flag lots often provide additional privacy. Depending upon how much of the lot is used for ingress and egress, the flag portions can be perceived negatively. In general, flag lots tend to have less value because of the costs of extending a private road and utilities to serve the lot. If the flag lot enjoys a better view, due to being on a higher elevation than another lot, or if it is located below another lot and has better access to a lake, stream, or ocean frontage, then its value may increase. When making a site inspection, an appraiser must pay attention to the location of the house in relation to neighboring properties and whether the flag portion adds or detracts from the location.

The term key lot is somewhat misleading. A **key lot**, so named because it resembles a key fitting into a lock, is surrounded by the backyards of other lots. Many key lots were not originally incorporated into the plans of a development. It is the least desirable because of lack of privacy and visibility.

A **T-intersection lot** is an interior lot that is fronted head-on by a street. Therefore, the noise and glare from headlights detract from this type of lot for residences. In a well-planned subdivision, the house is positioned so that headlights of approaching cars do not bother people in the living area. In such cases, if any improvement were directly in the path of an errant automobile, it would most likely be the garage.

SLOPE

Slope refers to an incline or slant. Lots on hills are identified as uphill, down-hill, sidehill, top-of-hill, or bottom-of-hill. In some areas, depending on terrain and degree of slope, there is a marked difference in value between an uphill lot and a downhill lot. The skilled appraiser is aware of these differences and knows the reasons for them. Some hill lots do not precisely fit major classifications because of the virtually unlimited variances in the physical aspects of a particular lot.

As the slope of a lot increases, building costs also increase. It is more expensive to install streets and utilities and to carve out building sites in a hilly area. An appraiser can best determine the effect on lot value of varying degrees of slope by referring to recent sales prices of similarly sloped lots. The steeper the slope, the more pronounced are some problems.

The percentage or steepness of slope of a residential lot is very important in determining value.

Level to nearly level	0-3% slope
Gently sloping	3-10%
Moderately sloping or rolling	10-15%
Hilly	15-30%
Steep	30-45%
Very steep	Over 45%

ACCESS

A residential site must have access by some means, either a public or private road. The maintenance and repairs for a private road must be provided by the owners of the properties served by the road. Although a public road provides less privacy, maintenance costs are borne by the public body—city, county, or special district. Some property owners prefer to depend on their own initiative to keep access roads properly maintained, since the public body is not always responsive to road maintenance needs. On the other hand, in the case of private roads that serve more than one owner, disagreements among the private parties may cause road maintenance to suffer.

Security provided by public and private roads can vary greatly depending on their location, the patrolling activity of the local police or sheriff, and fencing and gates erected (for private access roads).

An appraiser should recognize that road engineering, including width, grade, drainage facilities, materials, and construction, could determine whether access to a site is adequate or inadequate. Value allowances should be made, for example, in the case of a road that may be virtually impassable during the winter because of rain, ice, or snow—or in the case of a road too narrow for fire equipment. In the latter case, a construction loan may be difficult to obtain since fire insurance to cover the loan may be nonexistent or exorbitant in cost. Local fire districts usually require a minimum paving of 20-feet wide, properly designed and engineered, if they are to provide fire protection to a residential site.

INGRESS AND EGRESS

Obviously, accessible land is more valuable than inaccessible land. As such, ease of ingress and egress is very important. An appraiser must note the **ingress** (access to the site or property) and **egress** (exit from the site or property) and how they contribute to the property's use. If an appraiser is valuing a view property that has a three-mile dirt road with no road maintenance agreement, this is much different from a similar property that has paved access.

It is important to determine the entity responsible for maintaining roads that are not public. How does the market react to this situation? Is it feasible for the homeowner to attempt to get all the neighbors together and write a road maintenance agreement?

SURPLUS LAND

Many appraisers mistake the market's reaction to surplus land. **Surplus land** is extra land that may or may not contribute additional value to the property. The additional land is atypical for a specific property in the area. The appraiser has to determine if the surplus land is usable or not. If it is not usable, there may be no adjustment required. If the surplus land provides additional privacy, even if it is not usable, the market may bear a slight premium. Surplus land cannot be sold off separately and does not have a separate value. Do not confuse surplus land with excess land.

Excess land can be divided from the property and sold off separately. In fact, it may even have a different highest and best use from the original property. Therefore, it will have to be treated differently and its value reported separately.

SOIL AND TOPOGRAPHY

The average appraiser cannot be an expert in all fields. Soil composition analysis should be done only by someone trained and equipped for the job. Professional soil engineers perform analysis on all types of land for a variety of uses. In addition, city and county agencies often employ soil analysts who determine, for example, the percolation ability (ability to absorb water) of soil in order to set minimum lot sizes in areas where sanitary sewers are not available, necessitating the installation of septic tanks with leaching lines.

Soil composition is of paramount importance in determining not only the percolation ability of soil but also the ability of the base material to support intended structures. Most level land poses no significant soil composition problems for residential development. For this reason, unless the base material is entirely unsatisfactory for percolation or support, the appraiser normally need not be concerned with soil composition of level or near-level land, provided adequate drainage is available.

TOPOGRAPHY

Topography is the nature of the surface of land. It is important as it affects view amenities, drainage, soil stability, and the amount of the lot that is usable. Topography also limits landscaping and the kinds of trees that will grow in a given area. Many hillside lots are graded to allow for a flat area on the top of the lot. This can create problems if compaction is not properly completed, as part of the land is normally fill. **Fill** is earth used to raise the existing ground level. In residential real estate, base material that is borrowed from another source is generally not as stable as a cut, for example. **Cut** refers to a level building site—or the space created in areas of sloping land when earth is removed. Unlike fill material, which can be unstable, a building site from a cut is generally a more solid base for structures. It is important for an appraiser to determine where the cut portion of the lot is, as well as the fill portion, if any.

DRAINAGE/RETENTION SYSTEMS

The adequacy or inadequacy of drainage facilities is one of the least understood physical aspects of site analysis and valuation. **Drainage** refers to the removal of excess surface water or groundwater from land by means of ditches or drains. Many residential lot buyers are extremely disappointed when they discover the need for spending additional money to provide adequate drainage and retention systems. Many lots have hills and banks and there may not be an adequate drainage system to keep the lot and structures from being damaged by heavy rains. Lots are sometimes graded improperly so that they slope toward the house. An appraiser needs to note these problems and determine if the house is adequately protected from potential water damage.

In some cases, a qualified appraiser can estimate the cost of providing these facilities. The opinion of an engineer or other drainage expert is often needed. The reasonable cost of providing adequate drainage is often discounted from the value of a site that compares in all ways except drainage to other sites in the area.

Lots with Possible Drainage Problems

- On a steep slope
- Located at or near the bottom of a hill
- Near a shallow watercourse

- Near a creek or watercourse's outfall into a lake, a bay, or the ocean
- At the bottom of a dead-end street
- On the lower side of a street
- In an area that lies below the high flood stage of a river
- In an area with unusually heavy rains that cause flooding

GRADING

Before structures of any variety are placed on a lot, the land must be prepared. This includes grading, followed by building retaining walls and foundations.

Grade is the slope of the surface of the ground expressed as a percentage. An example would be a 2% grade, where the slope climbs 2 feet for every 100 feet of horizontal distance. Sometimes the level or elevation of the ground has to be changed or altered using bladed machines that literally scrape the earth in a process known as **grading**.

Mountain grading is used to clear land for more homes.

Grading is important so that water runs away from the foundation and the structure itself. If the pitch or slope of the soil is toward the house, basements or crawlspaces may flood during storms, and damage to the foundation may occur over time.

RETAINING WALLS

Retaining walls hold back earth. They are usually found where elevation changes on a property and soil must be held back from falling down. Retaining walls come in many material types and have some type of reinforcement. There are numerous guidelines for their construction. They also should have drainage by means of spaces or holes in the face of the wall or drain tiles at its base.

EXPOSURE TO SUN AND WEATHER

Many people prefer a particular sun exposure for their home. Homeowners in the southern and western parts of the U.S. like to enjoy outdoor living as much of the year as possible. A backyard with a southerly exposure to the sun is most popular. Reason being, if the backyard faces south, homeowners can enjoy the sun on the patio or the porch throughout the cooler months, as well as during the summer. Residences with south-facing backyards suffer less sun

damage to the paint on the front of the structure. Since the front is usually more extensively decorated and more carefully maintained than the back, less maintenance means less expense.

Weather, such as high winds, is also a consideration. For example, in many parts of Texas, winds generally blow from the Northwest. If the backyard faces south, the house or apartment itself acts as a shield and adds to the outdoor living enjoyment.

It is important for appraisers to consider a home's exposure, as well as learning the desires of buyers—as many homebuyers insist on a particular exposure.

VIEW

The view of the surrounding area can be one of the most favorable physical characteristics for a property. Given a choice, most people prefer a site with a view toward the ocean, a lake or bay, the mountains, or a valley. As quality residential sites become scarcer and urban areas grow more crowded, the need for space becomes more acute.

In areas of exceptional scenic beauty, such as the Lake Tahoe region of the Sierra Nevada Mountains, residential view sites sometimes sell for twice the price of sites without a view. Even in suburban areas, it is usual for view sites to bring 50% more than non-view sites—all other features being equal. The adjustment for a premium view is the largest adjustment an appraiser will make.

Central Park and the Manhattan skyline in New York City

The precise location of the site determines whether it will have a view. Of course, it is also important that the house be designed and constructed to take full advantage of natural environmental features.

In most subdivisions, the view sites—even though priced higher—are usually the first to sell. As a rule of thumb, sites with a view sell for a premium. The same principle is true of multiple residential sites. Buildings erected on sites with views command considerably higher rents, as well. Good examples of such higher rents can be found in any urban area where view sites are available, such as New York City.

OFF-SITE FACTORS

The immobility of real estate means that the value of a given parcel of land is strongly affected by factors outside its boundaries. **Off-site factors** are those improvements not directly on the site that add to the site's utility. These factors include availability and quality of off-site improvements or infrastructure such as water, sewer, utility, and transportation systems.

Off-site improvement being
built in a new development.

Off-site improvements
in a rural area.

In exclusive areas, the only off-site improvement, other than utilities, is often a road. Residents of many such areas do not want sidewalks, curbs, gutters, or even streetlights—since these might detract from the rural atmosphere. Other areas may suffer from lack of these facilities.

> Example: Imagine an area recently annexed to an expanding city. A condition of the annexation is that a special assessment must be levied on all lots in the annexed area to provide sidewalks, street lighting, curbs, and gutters.

In this case, the amount of the special assessment would have to be considered as a value differential.

AVAILABILITY OF UTILITIES

Because utilities originate off-site, they are classified as an off-site factor. Utilities include water, electricity, natural gas, sewers, telephone, and sometimes cable television. Most residential areas now require underground installation of all utilities—primarily for aesthetic and safety reasons. Even though this adds to the cost of the site, the market value will usually increase to offset the cost.

In a well-planned and properly coordinated development, all facilities should be installed to minimize cost. As many services as possible (and as safe) should be installed in a single trench. If an appraiser's visual inspection does not reveal which utilities are present, he or she should interview the property owner to determine which utilities are present. The appraiser can also contact the city or municipality in which the property is located to confirm the utility services being used. Once the presence of utilities is verified, the appraiser should check to see what capacities are available for these utilities.

If an appraiser cannot see utilites, the property owner needs to be interviewed.

WATER

A residential site must have an ample supply of fresh water. An appraiser should determine if the site is supplied with water by a municipal water district or a private water company. He or she should know whether the water company or district has sufficient storage facilities to provide a continuing supply of fresh water for the near future. If the future supply of water is doubtful, for whatever reason—be it polluted water, low water table, or an ineffective or inefficient public or private water system—an appraiser must give this question prime consideration when appraising the residential site.

In remote areas where lots rely on individual wells for fresh water, an appraiser might gain some insight from a well-drilling or water expert. If the site does not have an adequate water system, appraisers should not try to foretell the future availability of water sources and supplies.

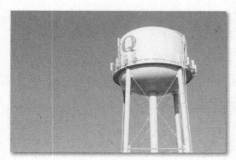

In hilly areas throughout much of the U.S.—even if existing private wells supply ample water for existing residential use—there is little guarantee that sufficient supplies will be available for additional users or that enough water will be available during dry years. In areas where there is greater rainfall, the problem is usually less acute, as there are more underground water supplies. With a typically less dense population, fewer people means less development and demand for water.

Where an abundant supply of quality fresh water is available now and for the near future, a site can realize maximum value, depending on other features.

ELECTRICITY

Electricity is generally available even in the most remote areas of the country. Private and public electrical utilities have supplied the U.S. with an electrical system second to none. The current supply of electric power provided by private companies from hydroelectric dams and power plants, steam-generating plants, nuclear power plants, and even some geothermal power plants, seems assured for the present. The cost of electrical power is continually rising because of increasing production costs. Additional power sources also may become a problem in the future.

For the most part, hydroelectric sources have been tapped. This places the main burden of future electrical power expansion on increased steam generation, which presently provides the major portion of electrical power, and on nuclear power (fission). Construction of additional nuclear (fission) reactors may be slowed by disagreement over safety and means of disposal of waste materials. Solar energy— an inexhaustible, clean, safe, and relatively inexpensive power source—will probably become more practical as the available supply of fossil fuel decreases.

Grand Coulee Dam, Washington

NATURAL GAS

Most urban areas of the country are supplied with efficient, low-cost natural gas, supplied from a network of private utility companies. For heating a home, natural gas is generally more economical than bottled gas or electricity. In outlying suburban areas, many homes are not served by natural gas because of the cost of pipeline installation. Many of these homes rely on manufactured bottled or tanked gas that is much more expensive than natural gas. At present, sites supplied with natural gas realize maximum value.

SANITARY SEWERS

Sanitary sewer hookups (not to be confused with storm sewers) provide the means for disposing waste material away from the site. Kitchen, laundry room, and bathroom facilities are directly connected to the sanitary sewer main located in the street. The cost of sanitary sewer facilities—including hookup, sewer main, pumping station, sewerage treatment plant, and all other attending facilities for sewerage disposal—may be borne by the local sanitary district and paid for by property taxes.

Suburban properties are often serviced for years by individual, relatively sophisticated septic tank systems. Properties located in more rural areas are often serviced by cesspools. As the city services of a nearby metropolitan area expand into suburban or rural areas, the residents agree to annex to the sanitary district to have the convenience and safety of sanitary sewer hookups. An assessment district is formed to extend the sanitary sewer main and other facilities to the remote areas. Each site is assessed a certain charge (usually based on the number of legal building sites per specific property), and the property assumes this indebtedness until it is paid.

SEPTIC TANK SYSTEM

If a site is not served by a sanitary sewer system, it must have facilities for waste and sewerage disposal on the site. This necessitates the installation of a septic tank system.

The disposal of waste material at the residential site poses several problems. First, will the local public body allow such a system? Under a police power, the local health department, building department, or in some cases, department of public works sets up health and safety requirements to be met by each residential site before it will issue building site approval.

Septic Tank System Requirement

- A sufficient supply of fresh water at the site

- The site must pass a percolation test

- That the installation of a septic tank system not endanger other water sources or supplies in the area

The determination of whether a septic tank installation may adversely affect neighboring water supplies is generally at the discretion of the local health, building, or public works department. A public or private water utility company operating in a particular area may either buy out the potentially hazardous properties, or insist on the installation of sanitary sewers before water service is supplied.

DEED RESTRICTIONS, EASEMENTS, AND RIGHTS-OF-WAY

Some sites, especially single-family residential sites, are encumbered with tract or deed restrictions that can affect a site's value. **Deed restrictions** are limitations that dictate certain uses that may or may not be made of the property. Even if the restrictions have only a minimal effect on value, the appraiser should consider these restrictions.

An **easement**, which is a non-possessory right to enter or use someone else's land for a specified purpose, may have a restrictive effect on site value.

> Example: Imagine a single-family residential site with a 25-foot wide underground storm sewer easement running diagonally across its backyard, prohibiting construction of a swimming pool or even a patio. Such a restriction would be difficult to value precisely because the value detriment might easily exceed 20% of the value of the lot.

A **right-of-way** is a right of passage on, over, or under another person's land—generally for a gas line, power line, roadway, railroad, or water line.

> Example: Suppose a road right-of-way is imposed along one side of a lot to provide access to a lot in the rear. The lot—100-feet wide by 200-feet deep—has a 20-foot right-of-way along one side. The negative effect of the right-of-way may be a 20% or more devaluation of the front site, not only because the right-of-way takes 20% of the land from the site, but also because of the added nuisance and inconvenience of automobiles and people using the road.

AVAILABILITY OF PUBLIC TRANSPORTATION

In some areas, the proximity of public transportation boosts the value of single-family and multiple-family residential sites. This is especially true in neighborhoods occupied predominantly by older people and by those who do not have private transportation. The close availability of public transportation can add 5-10% to the value of such residential sites.

PROXIMITY TO NATURAL HAZARD AREAS

Proximity to earthquake and flood zones, faults, or other potential natural disasters is of major concern to homebuyers, as well as to insurance companies and lenders. REALTORS® must disclose this proximity information to potential buyers. For example, close proximity to a fault line or zone may influence market prices in an area, and the appraiser must be careful to consider and document these factors. The paired sales technique for arriving at an adjustment value may be effective in this case, comparing sales located in the same or similar fault zones.

The **Federal Emergency Management Agency (FEMA)**, an arm of the Housing and Urban Development (HUD) Department, has established flood zones for the entire country. These zones must be disclosed to potential buyers. The flood zone map number and zone code, along with the date of the map consulted by the appraiser, are required for Fannie Mae and Freddie Mac appraisal reports.

Many of the area maps used by REALTORS® and appraisers show both earthquake and flood zones, but these zones are subject to change, as land and conditions change. These maps are updated from time to time, and appraisers should have access to current zone data.

PROXIMITY TO NUCLEAR FACILITIES OR HAZARDOUS WASTE SITES

The impact of close proximity to nuclear power plants or hazardous waste disposal sites is generally obvious by lack of sales in the area, coupled with extremely depressed sales of those properties that do sell. The government is grappling with how to clean up waste sites and how to minimize risk to the surrounding areas. Many nuclear power plants have been built in areas where sales history can be evaluated, which helps determine current value. However, the long-term effects on land and people have yet to be determined.

PROXIMITY TO ELECTRIC AND ELECTROMAGNETIC FIELDS

Public awareness of electric and electromagnetic field (EMF) emissions has created a volatile political environment in which contradictory scientific evidence abounds. Without definitive answers, it is difficult to assess the true impact of proximity to power towers and other EMF-emitting objects.

Buyers, in general, seem wary of the power towers and believe that close proximity to these towers has a negative influence, adversely affecting the price a buyer is willing to pay. Until conclusive scientific evidence is available, this issue will remain a gray area. Generally, aesthetic considerations reduce the value of properties located near such facilities.

SUMMARY

When appraising a property, an appraiser first has to determine its highest and best use. **Highest and best use** is defined as the use, from among reasonably probable and adequately supported alternative uses, that meets four tests. To qualify as the highest and best use, the use must be (1) physically possible, (2) legally permitted, (3) economically feasible, and (4) maximally productive.

It is important to remember the difference between a lot and a site. A **lot** is a distinct parcel of land or plot of ground. A **site** is land that has been prepared for use with grading, utilities, and access. The appraiser must keep in mind the factors that make one site more desirable than another parcel of land.

These physical factors are known as **utility**—the ability of a property to satisfy a need or desire, such as for shelter or income. **Location** is certainly the most important factor—although other physical attributes contribute significantly to value.

Before proper valuation can be determined on a site, an appraiser must consider not only the utility and location in the community but also the specific features of the lot. These include lot size, shape, slope, access, drainage, type of soil, exposure to sun and wind, view, availability of utilities, proximity to natural hazards and/or hazardous waste. These features will vary with every site, since no two parcels of land are precisely the same. The appraiser must always consider the use and presence of such physical features and relate each site to existing market demands.

CHAPTER 4 REVIEW EXERCISES

MATCHING EXERCISE

Instructions: Write the letter of the matching term on the blank line before its definition. Answers are in Appendix A.

Terms

A. corner lot	J. flag lot	S. off-site factors
B. cul-de-sac lot	K. grade	T. retaining wall
C. cut	L. grading	U. right-of-way
D. deed restrictions	M. highest and best use	V. site
E. drainage	N. ingress	W. slope
F. easement	O. interior lot	X. topography
G. egress	P. key lot	Y. T-intersection lot
H. excess land	Q. location	Z. utility
I. fill	R. lot	

Definitions

1. _____ Relates to the ability of a property to satisfy a need or desire, such as for shelter or income

2. _____ The site, setting, or position of a property or object in relation to other properties or objects

3. _____ A distinct parcel of land or plot of ground

4. _____ Land that has been prepared for use with grading, utilities, and access

5. _____ Situated at the end of a dead-end street that has a turn-around area

6. _____ Located at the confluence or convergence of two streets

7. _____ Located so that access can be had only at the side of another lot

8. _____ The least desirable type of lot because of lack of privacy and visibility

9. _____ Refers to an incline or slant

10. _____   Access to the site or property

11. _____   Exit from the site or property

12. _____   Surplus land beyond that which is needed to support the property's highest and best use

13. _____   The nature of the surface of land

14. _____   Earth used to raise the existing ground level

15. _____   The slope of the surface of the ground expressed as a percentage

16. _____   Holds back earth

17. _____   Improvements not directly on the site that add to the site's utility

18. _____   Limitations that dictate certain uses that may or may not be made of the property

19. _____   A non-possessory right to enter or use someone else's land for a specified purpose

20. _____   A right of passage on, over, or under another person's land

MULTIPLE CHOICE QUESTIONS

Instructions: Circle your response and go to Appendix A to read the complete explanation for each question.

1. In which of the following cases would it be necessary to value the site separately from the improvements?
    a. Market approach
    b. For listing purposes
    c. For refinancing purposes
    d. When the existing improvements do not represent the highest and best use of the land

2. When appraising a property, an appraiser first has to determine its:
    a. location.
    b. highest and best use.
    c. utility.
    d. value.

3. Which of the following is generally the most important in determining the value of a parcel of land?

    a. Size

    b. Shape

    c. Location

    d. Slope

4. Appraisers can often find the size of the appraisal site in official legal documents. Legal documents do not report the _____ of the site, which is more important than gross area.

    a. usable area

    b. measurements

    c. zoning requirements

    d. shape

5. Buyers usually pay a premium for a(n) _____ location because these lots offer more seclusion and safety than other lots.

    a. cul-de-sac

    b. corner

    c. key lot

    d. T-intersection

6. Which of the following is generally the most common type of residential lot?

    a. Corner

    b. Interior

    c. Cul-de-sac

    d. Flag

7. A moderately sloping lot has a steepness of approximately:

    a. 0 - 3%.

    b. 3 - 10%.

    c. 10 - 15%.

    d. 30 - 45%.

8. When evaluating a site with excess land, an appraiser has to:

    a. assume a sizable adjustment.

    b. adjust only if the site has a view.

    c. determine the market's reaction.

    d. determine if the excess land is usable or not.

9. In which of the following areas should an appraiser feel least qualified to render an opinion?

   a. View
   b. Floor plan
   c. Drainage
   d. Lot size

10. Sometimes the level or elevation of the ground has to be changed or altered using bladed machines that literally scrape the earth. This process is known as:

    a. sloping.
    b. pitching.
    c. elevating.
    d. grading.

11. In considering exposure to the sun, an appraiser generally gives the most value to a backyard facing:

    a. north.
    b. south.
    c. east.
    d. west.

12. Which of the following is not classified as an off-site improvement?

    a. Utilities
    b. Roads
    c. Retaining walls
    d. Sewer system

13. The most widely available utility service for residential homes is:

    a. natural gas.
    b. electricity.
    c. sanitary sewers.
    d. cable television.

14. One primary difference between a sanitary sewer hookup and a septic tank system is:

    a. the necessity for a percolation test.
    b. a sufficient supply of fresh water at the site.
    c. the installation of a septic tank system that will not endanger other water sources or supplies in the area.
    d. all of the above.

15. The impact of close proximity to nuclear power plants or hazardous waste disposal sites is generally obvious by:

    a. lack of sales in the area.

    b. depressed sales of those properties that do sell.

    c. the long-term effects of land and people.

    d. both (a) and (b).

Property Inspection: Improvements

5
Chapter

INTRODUCTION

An appraiser's inspection of a property is significantly different from one completed by a home inspector. Although the roles of appraiser and home inspector are not the same, an appraiser must be familiar with much of the home inspection terminology. For example, while appraisers perform unbiased valuation services for their clients, home inspectors work in the interest of their buyers. A home inspector never assigns value. He or she merely examines the home for defects or signs of possible defects. Home inspectors perform a more thorough visual inspection and have different standards than appraisers.

In the last chapter, we covered key features and characteristics of the site itself. This chapter covers the key features and characteristics of the improvements located on the site. Most appraisers start their career appraising single-family homes. Therefore, inspecting and describing the characteristics and systems of a residence is the focus of this chapter.

LEARNING OBJECTIVES

After reading this chapter, you will be able to:

- describe functional utility.
- list the items included in an exterior inspection.
- list the items included in an interior inspection.

- identify equipment and mechanical systems.
- identify energy-saving features of a residence.
- describe automobile, storage, and yard utility.

IMPROVEMENT ANALYSIS

An appraiser's inspection of a residence usually has two main parts: the exterior inspection and interior inspection. In a typical appraisal, the appraiser sketches, measures, and photographs the exterior and interior of the home. Appraisers also look at the mechanical systems and equipment within the home, as well as the available car storage, and any other site improvements affecting the home's value.

When appraising a new home or appraising a home from the plans, an elevation sheet for the home can aid the appraiser. The **elevation sheet** is a labeled diagram or cutaway of the home detailing its features and building components, both interior and exterior.

Throughout the inspection, the appraiser judges the condition and quality of the building. Terms such as good or average are used to describe features that are adequate and equal in quality and utility to that same feature in similar homes. Fair or poor are used to describe features that are less than adequate and below average for the neighborhood. Each term has a meaning, and anything less than average may actually require some lenders to reject the loan. In order to judge effectively the condition and quality of the building and its features, an appraiser must have at least a general knowledge about the different aspects of house construction and the advantages and disadvantages.

In the inspection process, the appraiser determines the design, layout, and construction details of the subject property.

Common Building Feature Description

- The current building use
- Building size, model (for tract homes) and custom or tract construction
- Master plans, zoning, deed restrictions affecting this use
- Type of construction with descriptions of exterior and interior features including framing, roofs, facade, special features, storage, stairs, and ramps

- Substructures including basements, slabs, raised foundations, and foundation walls
- Painting and finishing
- Flooring and floor coverings
- Number of bedrooms and bathrooms
- Kitchen including types of appliances, countertops, and islands
- Special features including air conditioning, fireplace, security systems, entertainment centers, and built-ins
- Garages, carports, and other parking
- Energy efficiency features such as insulation, dual pane windows, low water use dishwashers, solar panels, and skylights
- Outside amenities such as pools and spas
- Outdoor courts (basketball, volleyball), gazebos, BBQ facilities, covered patios, landscaping and irrigation, and hardscape
- Other buildings such as detached garages, pool rooms, mother-in-law units, dog kennels, electronic gates and fencing

FUNCTIONAL UTILITY

The architectural needs of a residence are not met until a useful floor plan is designed to make the living unit as desirable as possible. Architects are often confronted with the choice of sacrificing style for functional utility or vice versa. Each component is important, and only with the proper blend of style and utility does the residence reach its maximum desirability. Two residences may be practically identical from the outside and have the same square footage inside. However, one may be much more desirable because its interior has been designed for functional utility.

ROOM LAYOUT

Most homeowners prefer a home organized to move people from the front to the back of the residence. The entryway is usually an alcove or hallway in the front used to greet guests and for guests' coats in an entryway closet. The living room generally connects directly with the entryway. There are various alternatives for the rest of the room layout. Sometimes, the kitchen and family room area are off to one side, with the bedrooms and

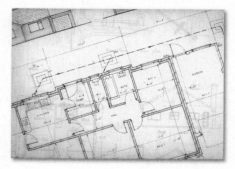

baths to the other. Or the living areas—living room, dining room, kitchen, family room, and an extra bathroom—may be separated from the rest of the residence.

Basic common sense in room and access layout provides maximum livability. It is generally undesirable, for example, to direct any foot traffic through one room to get to another. Some states' building codes prohibit bathrooms directly off a kitchen or dining room. If such an arrangement is allowed, no fewer than two doors should separate the two rooms. A bedroom directly off a dining room or kitchen is also undesirable.

An appraiser must be aware of popular room layouts and floor plans and know why they are popular. Common sense is helpful. A good floor plan embodies many of the factors discussed, such as an entryway designed for adequate traffic flow.

Undesirable Features Found in a Poor Floor Plan

- Entry directly into the living room makes it difficult for guests to avoid other household traffic.
- There is no inside (covered) access from the garage to the house for use in bad weather.
- The kitchen is too far from the garage, which makes carrying groceries into the kitchen inconvenient.
- The view from the living room is of either the driveway or the utility yard, neither of which is desirable.
- Corner bedrooms do not have two windows for cross ventilation.
- Family room is next to master bedroom.

ROOM SIZES

Most residential buyers want a medium-sized living room, a kitchen large enough to hold all equipment, a dining area with enough space to accommodate family and a few guests, a master bedroom larger than the secondary bedrooms, an adequate family room or den, and bathrooms large enough to provide comfort and utility. Buyers also want ample hallway width, and closet and cupboard space. The relative size of the rooms, of course, depends on the size and quality of the whole unit.

ROOM COUNTS

Room counts are provided in MLS listings and are included in many form appraisal reports. There are no national standards for defining a room. The FHA counts an alcove opening off the living room as one-half room, but does not count a dining space within a kitchen as a room. The generally accepted rule is to include those spaces that are effectively divided as separate rooms and to exclude bathrooms.

Whether a room qualifies as a bedroom is a function of whether the room has a closet and direct access to a hallway, living room, or other common area. A den could be considered a bedroom if there is closet space.

EXTERIOR INSPECTION

Two sections make up the exterior of a home: (1) the superstructure and (2) the substructure. The **superstructure** refers to all the above grade improvements. **Above grade** refers to anything above ground level. These include the wood framing, the materials used to finish both the interior and exterior walls, as well as the various coatings, doors, and windows. The **substructure** refers to all the below grade improvements. **Below grade** refers to improvements below ground level. The main underground component is the foundation. If there is a basement, it is part of the substructure.

When an appraiser arrives at a site, one of the first things he or she notices is the type of home and its architectural influence or style. The appraiser will take note of the exterior characteristics of the home and use a tape measure to get the accurate dimensions of the home. Then, the appraiser sketches the dimensions on graph paper, a laptop computer, or a handheld computer.

FOUNDATIONS

The **foundation** or substructure of a home has two purposes: (1) it supports the entire building and (2) it transfers the weight of the building to the ground. The foundation material used most often is **concrete**, a mixture of sand, gravel, and cement. It is strong, durable, relatively inexpensive, available, adaptable, and can usually be poured by machines or by hand, saving a great deal of time. The concrete foundation usually takes the form of the exterior load-bearing walls. Pre-cast concrete piers are sometimes used with supporting girders of lumber or lightweight steel for interior load-bearing walls.

Local climate and soil conditions often affect the choice of materials used, as do the size and weight of the structure and the location of the water table. Foundation problems can be the cause of a multitude of other problems including plumbing leaks, squeaky and uneven floors, sticking doors, and cracked walls.

SLAB-ON-GRADE

Depending on the climate, soil conditions, and architectural requirements, the builder may use a **slab-on-grade** foundation, in which the structure sits directly on the ground. In this case, the foundation and footings are one integral unit. Slab-on-grade foundations support the weight of the entire structure and are very sturdy when properly designed and constructed.

A **monolithic slab** is poured in one piece. It requires a wide base and steel reinforcement. The slab floor alone will not support interior load-bearing walls so an interior footing is trenched in before the slab is poured. A **floating slab** is composed of one section for the floor and another for the foundation wall, each poured separately. An expansion joint separates the two parts. A **screeded slab** is a wooden floor built on a concrete slab with no crawlspace underneath. The space under the wood flooring is usually used as a return for the heating and cooling system.

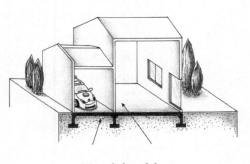

Monolithic slab

Steel bars or mesh reinforce poured concrete slabs. In some cases, a technique called post-tensioning is used. In a **post-tensioned slab**, cables laid in the wet concrete and put under tension after the concrete has cured give the foundation added strength. This technique increases the strength of the finished foundation.

CONCRETE OR CINDER BLOCK

Concrete masonry units (CMUs) are a very common material for foundation wall construction. This is especially true in remote and rugged areas where cement trucks do not have access because of terrain or distance from a cement plant. Both concrete and cinder blocks, also called building blocks, can be made water resistant. This material is strong and durable if proper techniques are employed during its construction. To increase the strength and resistance to cracking, reinforcing steel should always be used in conjunction with masonry or poured concrete.

WOOD FOUNDATIONS

In areas free from wood-destroying pests, such as termites, wood can be an excellent foundation material. In fact, wood is still the most popular, versatile material for residential framing. The frame consists of bottom horizontal boards, known as **sills**, to which are nailed vertical boards called **studs**. A variety of bracings, called joists, fire stops, and headers complete the frame. For the most part, the frame is not readily visible once the structure is complete, except in the

Using cinder blocks in foundation wall construction.

garage, where the skeletal framing and roof support members are often visible. The average appraiser makes no specific allowance for framing in comparing one residence with another.

BASEMENTS AND CRAWLSPACES

Buildings with raised foundations will have either a basement or a crawlspace. A **basement** is the lowest story of a building and is partially or entirely below ground. In colder parts of the country where the frost line may be 5 or 6 feet deep, many homes are built with basements, which can add value to a home. In many cases, the basement is a finished space with livable area. **Finished areas** are the enclosed areas in a home that are suitable for year-round use. These areas have flooring and insulation similar to the rest of the house. **Unfinished areas** are the areas of a home that do not meet these criteria.

Crawlspace with concrete footing

Sometimes, a finished basement can be what is known as a walkout basement. In this case, the basement is not entirely underground. At least one side is exposed and a door connects the livable space to the grade-level outside.

A **crawlspace** is an unfinished accessible space below the first floor of a building with no basement. Crawlspaces often provide access to wiring and plumbing. In moderate climates, homes built on a raised foundation will often have a crawlspace. The crawlspace is not large enough to be a finished space since it is often only 18-inches to 4 feet tall beneath the first floor. It serves the same purpose as the basement. It connects the foundation of the home to footings and piles that are pounded into the earth below the frost line.

Often a drainage system is located below basements or crawlspaces and begins with a drain and a sump. A **sump** is a pit or tank that catches liquid runoff for drainage or disposal. The water is pumped by a sump pump to the storm sewer or away from the structure to head off flooding. **Sump pumps** are essential in keeping a basement or crawlspace dry and preventing moisture and mildew problems. Sump pumps also help keep these areas from flooding altogether.

ROOFING

The material used to construct the roof is usually very visible in residential buildings, especially single-family residences. There is more variety of materials for roof construction than for any other component of a residence. The style and condition of a roof can affect the value of a home, and a roof in poor condition can significantly detract from the value of the home.

Common Roofing Materials

- Built-up roofing
- Slate
- Concrete tile
- Composition shingles
- Metal roofing and shingles
- Wood shingles and shakes

Other roofing materials exist, but those listed above are the ones most commonly used. Each material has a unique advantage, depending on the desires of the builder and the buyer as to appeal, cost, and durability.

Although the material most common in single-family residential construction is the composition shingle, the wood shingle and shake roofs often have more appeal and give better insulation. In general, the thicker the shake, the greater the advantage. A cedar shingle roof might last 30 years, while a heavy shake roof could last 40 years or more. The wood roof generally has one big disadvantage—its propensity to burn. Many homes burn because the wood roof is so susceptible to flying embers that land on it. Unless the roof is treated continually with a fire-retardant mixture, it becomes a fire hazard, especially in those areas with extremely hot and dry weather conditions, and where there is dense, dry vegetation including grass, undergrowth, and trees that might provide fuel for a devastating fire.

Wood shake roof

The metal roof is used widely in heavy snow areas. The slickness of metal when properly sloped prevents layers of heavy snow from accumulating on the roof. Roofs of conventional roofing material may collect 10 or more feet of snow, necessitating constant, laborious snow removal or exceptional beams and framing to support the added weight. Concrete tile, used mostly in warm areas, has a long life and excellent insulation qualities because of the layer of air inside the curved portion of the tile. Slate, anodized aluminum, and copper are practically indestructible by the elements. Roofs made of these materials will last almost indefinitely.

Roofing represents a main area of architectural style. There are many types of roofing available, but there are eight main styles of which to be aware.

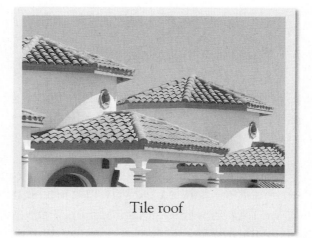

Tile roof

Common Roof Styles

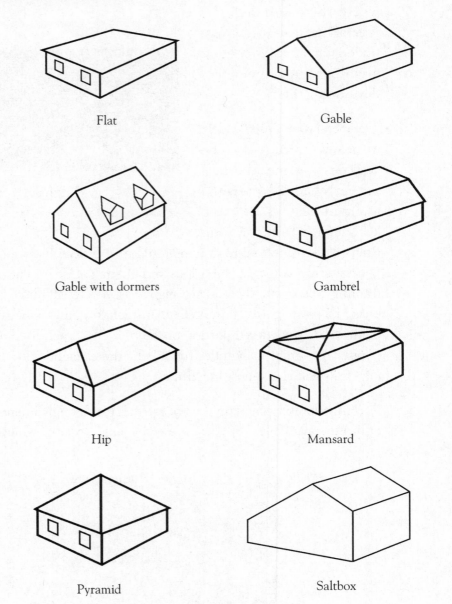

Flat

Gable

Gable with dormers

Gambrel

Hip

Mansard

Pyramid

Saltbox

Some roofs are constructed with gutters and downspouts to carry rainwater and melting snow into surface and underground drainage facilities. Gutters are usually made of galvanized iron, aluminum, copper, or other sheet metal and are generally painted. Vinyl is also common in modern residences. Some quality residences lack gutters and downspouts, as these items are often omitted to save money.

EXTERIOR WALLS

A common exterior wall material, **stucco** is a popular cement-like substance frequently used for wall cladding. It is the most versatile, and one of the least expensive. Stucco is applied after diagonal wood sheathing or plywood has been covered with building paper and chicken wire. The chicken wire supports the stucco, which is applied with a trowel in a wet, muddy consistency. Once dry, this material can be sealed with a waterproofing compound and painted.

Another popular exterior covering is wood. Often a rustic (wood) finish is applied to the front of a stucco residence to add to the appeal of the structure, or the entire exterior siding may be of quality wood. Wood surfaces require more maintenance than stucco surfaces, especially in areas where the chemical action of salty air deteriorates painted surfaces. Untreated redwood is impervious to termites and adverse weather conditions. Many untreated redwood-exterior homes are still in good condition after more than 80 years of exposure to the weather. The years seem to add charm to the surface of redwood siding. With dwindling redwood and other forest resources, it is likely that wood will not be used as often in the future.

With the increasing use of non-wood products, other exterior building materials—mineral laminated shingles, urethane plastics, fiberglass, vinyl, and other long-lasting materials—may become the preferred exterior residential siding materials. Most of these materials can be made to look surprisingly like wood, yet are immune to most of the things that harm wood siding, such as pest infestation, warping, peeling, cracking, and even burning.

Other Common Exterior Wall Materials

- Building board (composition board)
- Concrete building blocks
- Brick
- Adobe brick
- Stone
- Arizona flagstone
- Weatherproofed construction plywood
- Corrugated sheets
- Painted aluminum siding
- Tarpaper, wood shingles, and some materials more commonly used for roofing

INTERIOR INSPECTION

Once the basic examination of the outside is complete, the appraiser can then move to the inside of the home. At this point, the appraiser has already drawn a sketch of the exterior of the house. The appraiser now uses the perimeter sketch and fills in the room layout and other interior details.

Size for the interior of the home is reported in terms of **gross living area** (GLA), which is the total amount of finished, above ground habitable space. In most cases, attics, crawlspaces, and basements are unfinished and do not count in the GLA measurement. The **gross building area** (GBA) is the total amount of all enclosed floor areas and does include basements and attics. The American National Standards Institute (ANSI) has developed a standard method for calculating floor areas in single-family dwellings, *Square Footage - Method for Calculating, ANSI Z765-2003*. In some states, the state appraisal regulatory agency has adopted this standard method as a supplement standard that appraisers must follow. Copies may be purchased from the NAHB Research Center, a subsidiary of the National Association of Home Builders (NAHB).

The appraiser also takes note of the construction features present in the interior of the home. Most appraisal reports contain a checklist to remind the appraiser to check all the important features and provides a space for noting the condition of features present.

In many cases, the current owner can provide additional information about the condition or quality of improvements. If the homeowner is present during the appraiser's on-site inspection, he or she is usually happy to talk about the remodeling of the kitchen, when the interior of the home was last painted, and what major repairs have been completed recently.

FLOORS

Floors exist in homes to provide walking spaces and to support furniture. Most residential floors have diagonal sub-flooring—2-inches of tongue and groove or heavy plywood over supporting beams. Floors can be made of numerous materials including concrete, hardwood, carpet, resilient tile, and ceramic or quarry tile (stone and marble). Flooring in good condition and of certain materials, like finished wood or marble, can certainly add value to a home. Carpeting is most popular, particularly in high-traffic areas because it is quiet, warm, safe (non-skid), and easy to maintain.

For kitchens, bathrooms, and service rooms, vinyl, asphalt, and rubber tile are popular floorings. Some homes still have linoleum floors, but vinyl is more resilient and maintenance free. Even in these rooms, serviceable new blends of wall-to-wall carpeting are being used. Foam-backed indoor-outdoor carpet, laid wall-to-wall, are easy to maintain and surprisingly durable in utility rooms, laundry rooms, bathrooms, and even kitchens.

CEILINGS

The ceilings in most residences are covered with the same material as the walls. Materials used in ceilings include plaster, drywall, wood, and paneling. Other ceiling materials include acoustical tile, acoustical sprayed-on material with the appearance of rough stucco, heavy plywood, and even two-by-fours laid edgewise abutting one another for a special effect. Heavy beams can create a special architectural effect—the beamed ceiling. Exposed 4- by 8-inch wooden beams, 3 to 4 feet apart, support the roof with either a gable or a horizontal effect.

Some pre-1970 homes used acoustical materials consisting of asbestos, which has since been outlawed in residential construction. **Asbestos** is a mineral fiber, which has since been implicated in causing lung and stomach cancer. The appraiser should refer to experts in the asbestos removal field, if this material is evident, and should disclaim any expertise in the detection or treatment of this substance in the appraisal report.

INTERIOR WALLS

The interior wall material most often used in residential construction is **drywall**—also called sheetrock, plasterboard, or gypsum board. Drywall panels are used in place of wet plaster to finish the inside of buildings. Lath and plaster used to be the most common material, however drywall is more widely used because it costs less to install. It is nailed to the studs in sheets, the butted sides are taped, and a textured material is either sprayed or troweled on to give the effect of plaster. A 5/8-inch sheetrock layer has the same fire protection qualities as a plastered wall.

Other interior wall coverings are plywood, simulated wood paneling, hardwood paneling, and tile. Exterior support materials are sometimes carried through to the interior, in wall-bearing masonry, such as brick, adobe brick, or concrete block.

Drywall is a durable material, relatively inexpensive, and easy to paint, cover, or wallpaper. Additionally, it is easy to fix when damaged, resistant to rodents and insects, and good for blocking sound.

EQUIPMENT AND MECHANICAL SYSTEMS

The quality of the facilities provided in a residence has an influence on its attractiveness. Advanced knowledge of environmental control is increasingly reflected in the equipment offered in newer and remodeled residences. Today's buyers are making increasing demands for comfort and convenience.

Most equipment is installed during initial construction of the residence. However, older residences—both multiple as well as single family—are being modernized according to the desires of owners and renters. Each year, more homes are constructed with built-in features as standard equipment.

The main systems are electrical, plumbing, heating, and cooling. Homes vary in their type and quality of systems. Similarly, although almost every home has plumbing and electricity, there can be wide variations in the quality of plumbing fixtures and electrical capacity.

The appraiser must be aware of equipment and know how it adds to the utility and desirability of a residence. Since many items do not last the lifetime of the residence, the appraiser should know the items needing replacement during its economic life. He or she can then compute a realistic depreciation figure.

ELECTRICAL

The most important basic equipment of any residence is the power source—the electrical system. Most homes and apartments have many appliances and other electrical conveniences. Electrical power arrives at the home in two ways. In older communities, the power will come from an overhead transmission line or power pole. In newer communities, the power comes from subterranean lines run to the home. In some homes, solar panels on the roof capture solar energy to provide the majority of power for a home.

The main **electrical panel** (service panel) is the entrance and main distribution for electrical energy in the home. Most modern residences have 150-amp or 200-amp service panels to ensure the capacity to meet contemporary needs. The service panel also contains the main disconnect and the individual circuit breakers. The main disconnect allows for all the electricity in the home to be shut off with one switch. Circuit breakers provide a method to turn off different areas of the electrical system for servicing. A **circuit breaker** is an electrical device, which automatically interrupts an electric circuit when an overload occurs.

Circuit breaker and fuse box

Newer homes have a 220-volt system, controlled by an electrical service panel with circuit breakers. Older houses have a fuse box system. When an overload occurs, a fuse blows and it must be replaced. In the old days, a home was wired for 110-volt capacity. Today, that would be insufficient for all the modern appliances, entertainment systems, and computers. An appraiser should be able to identify a 220-volt or 240-volt wiring set-up (as noted by a three-wire service entrance) for newer homes. Additionally, an appraiser should be able to distinguish between 15 and 20 circuits for all appliances powered in a modern home.

PLUMBING

As residences increase in size and utility, they require more plumbing facilities. The average buyer or appraiser does not analyze the actual piping and the conduits in the walls and under the house, but does notice the quality of such plumbing fixtures as toilets, sinks, tubs, and showers. Are the toilets the silent flush type? Is there a wet bar or additional sink with water facility, in the family room? Is there a double sink (or even a triple sink) in the kitchen? Is there a double laundry tub in the laundry area? Are the faucets and spouts of good quality? Do the showerheads adjust for various water concentrations? In short, is the hardware of good quality? All these features add desirability, and therefore, value to the residence.

Pipes may have to be replaced if they are rusted, clogged, or corroded beyond use. It is often difficult for an appraiser to discover pipe deterioration unless there is outside evidence of leaks, such as water stains on walls or floors. Clogging by hardened mineral deposits will sometimes render a system inefficient in older homes. This is evidenced by lack of water flow when more than one faucet is turned on at the same time. If the pressure is found to be insufficient (this can be checked at the meter point by the local water department), then new pipes will have to be installed to restore the flow volume.

HEATING

One of the most common heating systems in homes is the gas furnace. In this system, natural gas is piped in as the fuel source and burned to heat air. A furnace or ducting system with return and supply registers distributes the air through the home. The heated air is forced through the home with the use of blowers or fans, so this system is often referred to as a forced air system. Most residences equipped with central heating have an automatic thermostatic control unit, which can be set to maintain a constant desired temperature. The heat registers are located on the floor in the baseboard, or in or near the ceiling.

If the valuation of a residence depends on great sophistication in analyzing the type of forced air heating system, the appraiser should consult a person experienced in this area. Generally, the appraiser's knowledge of the major types of heating systems, such as forced air, perimeter baseboard, solar, or radiant is sufficient for appraisal purposes.

AIR CONDITIONING

Air conditioning units can be simple, inexpensive window units used to cool one room of a home or expensive or elaborate central units capable of completely cooling a large residence. The cost and the resultant added value can range from $150 to many thousands of dollars.

In many parts of the country, because of relatively oppressive, muggy summer weather, a central air conditioning unit is essential in homes of good quality construction. The appraiser generally includes the depreciated cost of the air conditioning unit as a value increment to the residence.

Innovative modifications of existing forced air systems are meeting consumer acceptance because of a desire to combat general air pollution. In addition, many people are allergic to dust and pollen. Because of this, buyers desire greater control over the climate in their homes.

SPECIALTY EQUIPMENT

Specialty equipment, such as intercom systems, security alarms, and central vacuum systems can be found in high-quality residences. A central vacuum system is especially useful and efficient in two-story homes because it avoids the necessity of carrying heavy equipment up and down stairs or having separate vacuum cleaners in different parts of the house.

The value of specialty items depends heavily on the value of the whole residence. It is doubtful that a small, modest residence in an area of similar houses would realize a market value increase proportionate to the cost of installing a central vacuum system, or even an alarm system.

SMOKE DETECTOR UNITS

Studies have indicated that most deaths due to fire in homes are actually caused by smoke inhalation. Therefore, most states now require the installation of smoke detector units for all residential construction. Many states have implemented additional laws requiring that smoke detectors be installed or upgraded at the time of sale, regardless of the age of the home.

Self-contained smoke-sensitive detectors can be installed in a house to alert residents to a fire to satisfy these requirements. One popular type is the individual unit that can be affixed to the ceiling in the hallway near the bedrooms. These inexpensive battery-powered units, small enough to be held in a person's hand, buzz when smoke reaches a certain density. If the residents are cigarette smokers, or if excessive smoke results from cooking, the units can be adjusted to a less sensitive position. Periodic
adjustment is necessary because the battery can lose power over time. The units can be installed by the resident with nothing more than a screwdriver. Another type of smoke detector, powered by the residential electrical system,

is simply plugged into a socket. Unfortunately, if the electrical power is off in the house, the unit will not work.

The value increment to a residence equipped with one or several smoke detectors should offset their cost.

INTERIOR SPRINKLER SYSTEMS

For new residential construction, many communities in high fire danger areas now require ceiling sprinklers in every room. In today's market, this adds approximately $3 per square foot (SF) to the construction cost.

ENERGY EFFICIENCY

As energy becomes more expensive (and it appears it will), energy-efficient homes will realize maximum value. The appraiser should be aware of these basic energy-saving features of residences. The value increment of a particular residence equipped to be partially or fully energy efficient can only be determined on an individual basis.

Factors that Determine Energy Efficiency

- Local cost of gas, oil, or electricity
- Extremes in local weather
- Construction quality
- Size and shape of the structure
- Availability of other similar residences in the marketplace

INSULATION

Typically, the energy efficiency of homes is directly related to the type and quality of insulation methods used in construction. Title 24 of the federal building codes established minimum insulation requirements and established a rating system. Using this system, local building commissions set insulation standards for their areas based primarily on weather conditions and the type and purpose of the structure. Different types of insulating materials have varying degrees of resistance to heat flow. An R-value, or rating, is given to each type of material. **R-value** is the rating that measures how well insulation resists heat. For example, the minimum R-values in a warm valley area, located in an annually temperate climate zone, are different from an area with radical season temperature changes, such as a mountain resort.

OTHER ENERGY-EFFICIENT ITEMS

Some common energy-efficient items in a home are double, triple, or low-energy glazed windows, which decrease the amount of heat loss in cold months and prevent the cool air from escaping during warm months. Use of double-pane windows is another Title 24 requirement. Homes constructed since Title 24 regulations took effect will generally have higher energy-efficiency ratings than those built previously.

A home is also more energy efficient when it is properly caulked and weatherstripped, which prevents heating and cooling loss. The efficiency of water heaters rises when they are properly insulated or jacketed to prevent loss of heat. An appraiser should also note any built-in energy-efficient appliances in the home, such as a low water-use dishwasher.

USE OF SOLAR ENERGY

The use of solar energy can also make a home much more energy efficient. **Solar panels** gather the sun's heat for use in a solar water heater, solar heating system, and even as a source of electricity in the residence. A 3-kilowatt can supply about 75% of the electrical needs of a home.

Many homes now use solar energy to help defray the rising cost of heating the swimming pool or heating water for household use. In addition, rooms can be space heated with solar heating panels, plastic tubing, or a number of other ways to use this relatively pollution-free, inexpensive power source.

Solar panels

Although appraisers need not be experts in solar energy systems, an appraiser should stay abreast of trends and learn how different systems can add to, or detract from, value. This judgment is best supported by comparable sales information of homes with similar systems. If no such comparable sales are available, the appraiser must judge what value increment a particular solar energy system adds to, or subtracts from, a particular residence in a specific location. The advice of a solar engineering expert might be worthwhile in some cases. In general, an efficiently functioning unit should add value relative to the cost of its installation.

WIND ENERGY

Another form of natural, inexpensive, non-polluting energy being reconsidered in certain areas is wind energy. The windmill helped develop much of the farmland of the midwestern and western United States. Simple, efficient, modern windmills are now being manufactured and installed in some areas where sufficient winds prevail to supply a small portion of home energy needs. These units are usually functional only if the wind has an average velocity of 6 to 10 miles per hour. They are often no more visible or objectionable than a television aerial.

Wind energy is changed to electrical energy by means of a generator that powers electrical appliances. Excess electrical power is converted to chemical power by storage in batteries in the basement or below the house. It is then reconverted to electrical power during wind-less days and nights, when the electrical appliances are run by the power stored in the batteries. The cost of installing a wind energy system is reasonable, usually about 1% of the cost of the structure. If proper comparables are unavailable, an appraiser must make a value judgment of the value increment such a unit adds to a residence.

AUTOMOBILE AND STORAGE UTILITY

Once the appraiser has examined the exterior and interior of the home, he or she should also make note of any space designed for car storage. Many homes have facilities for parking at least two cars under a roof, sometimes three or more. The appraiser should note whether the garage is attached to or detached from the home, its size, and the number of cars it accommodates. An appraiser usually includes the garage in his or her sketch of the home. The architectural style of the garage generally follows the style of the house. Sometimes a carport substitutes for an enclosed garage. Unlike garages, carports are not enclosed. Carports have no walls or doors with which to control access.

An appraiser should be sure to consider the on-site parking facilities of a residence. Sometimes a full-sized car cannot fit into the existing garage of an older home. Most modern garages are large enough for two cars with room left for storage, a workbench, or even a laundry area.

GARAGE CONVERSIONS

In some single-family residences, the garage has been converted into a family room, another bedroom, or for some other use. An appraiser must judge whether the conversion is aesthetically pleasing and functionally sound, and whether it will increase the appeal of the residence. Sometimes the appraiser must balance the benefits of the added room against the disadvantage of not having a garage. This can be important to the potential buyer. In addition, lenders and loan insurers may not approve a loan if the garage has been converted to an extra room. This could adversely affect the marketability of the residence.

Many garage conversions result in additional living space lacking the heating and electrical facilities found in the main part of the house. This factor is important not only in the market approach, requiring a judgment by the appraiser, but also in the cost approach.

> Example: A 400 SF garage has been converted to a family room by finishing the interior walls and laying a vinyl floor covering over the concrete pad. No extensions of the forced-air heating system and the electrical system have been completed. In this case, the garage conversion would not be computed in the cost approach at the same cost per square foot as the other living areas of the house.

If building costs for average construction is $60 per square foot, then such a garage conversion would be computed at a cost between the square-foot cost of a simple garage and the square foot cost of building the house. If the square-foot cost of a garage is $20 per square foot, and the square-foot cost of a house is $60 per square foot—in such a case, $40 per square foot might represent a realistic cost to replace the converted garage.

In some cases, there is no garage, carport, or a driveway for parking cars. In which case, the owner of the home must resort to parking his or her car on a public street in front of the home. If encountered, an appraiser would note this on his or her report.

Before attempting a garage conversion, homeowners should always consult their deed restrictions (if any) to make sure the conversion is allowable. As well, appraisers should always verify with the homeowner or real estate agent (if an agent is involved) whether the conversion is permitted.

YARD UTILITY

The minimum size of most yards—front, side, and rear—is usually set by local zoning ordinance. To permit unrestricted access to the main structure during construction, yard improvements are usually installed after the residence has been completed. It is difficult to install a major yard improvement, such as a swimming pool, after the house, landscaping, and fencing are completed. Yet, many homeowners install pools years after construction of the residence. Major yard improvements for multiple residential units are usually installed during construction. The important consideration in valuing a yard is its present utility and desirability, not when the yard improvements were installed.

The functional utility of the yard should relate to the residence. In addition to aesthetic appeal, the yard should have room for outdoor living facilities. Depending on the size of the lot and the style of the house, patios, fences, planting, and a utility area should be considered. Yard utility is extremely important in southern and western states because of the moderate weather throughout most of the year.

These yards do not have curb appeal.

The landscaping gives these homes curb appeal.

PATIOS AND WALKS

Many residential yard areas have a patio and walkways for added outdoor enjoyment. **Patios** are surfaced exterior areas used for outdoor enjoyment of the home. Most of these improvements are made of concrete, either exposed aggregate or smooth finished. Patios and walks may be brick, Arizona flagstone, redwood, adobe brick, building block, or some other material. The cost generally determines the value increment to the residence. Concrete patios and walks are popular for the same reasons concrete foundations are popular—it can be installed quickly, it is adaptable to different contours, and it is serviceable and relatively inexpensive. Part of the cost of installing patios and walks is offset by an increase in value. Cost per square foot of the patio or walkway is the unit used in computing value by the cost approach.

An outdoor patio and an enclosed patio

LAWNS, SHRUBS, AND TREES

For every type, size, and quality of residence, there is a standard of adequate landscaping. Extensive landscaping does not always add value proportionate to its cost. A large lawn can be a drawback, since it requires extensive maintenance.

What is the value increment to a property of a large ornamental shade tree? Many people believe a 300-year-old, 6-foot thick, live oak in excellent condition, growing in a perfect spot, is worth what it would cost to replace the tree. Actually, the cost of installation of a tree of that age and size would be prohibitive. The cost of digging, wrapping the roots, transporting, and planting a giant tree weighing more than 40 tons would greatly exceed the expected value increment. In exclusive areas, the existence of such a tree might add 10% to the value of the lot—that is, a $400,000 lot with such a tree might sell for $440,000. Trees of all types—fruit, ornamental, and shade—contribute only to the value of the whole property and are seldom appraised separately.

LANDSCAPING

Landscaping is the use of vegetation around a house to prevent erosion and improve its aesthetic appearance. Different types of landscaping are

appropriate for different climate zones. For example, desert climates use a form of landscaping known as **zeroscaping**, in which little or no water is needed. Another type is called **xeriscaping**, in which water efficiency is achieved by using plants appropriate for the natural environment.

Xeriscaping

Appropriate landscaping has the ability to increase the value of the home. The actual valuation of the plantings can be judged only in comparison to residences with similar landscaping. Conversely, poorly landscaped properties can lose value because of the lack of curb appeal, the visual appeal of a property when viewed from the street. In more severe cases, poor landscaping can actually cause structural, roof, and cosmetic damage to homes. This happens when the grade slopes towards a home and water penetrates the home as a result.

OUTDOOR SPRINKLER SYSTEMS AND LIGHTING

As Americans seek more leisure time, they increasingly want to eliminate the drudgery of garden maintenance. Since hand watering is time-consuming for most people, built-in sprinkler systems are becoming more popular. Many are made of plastic pipe with fixed or pop-up heads. Some are of galvanized metal or other metal pipe. Some sprinkler systems have Rain Bird™ systems or revolving sprinkler heads.

Outdoor lighting is generally an extension of the home's interior lighting. Both sprinkler systems and outdoor lighting may add value to the overall value of the property. Both may require periodic maintenance and even replacement during the economic life of the residence.

FENCING

In the previous section, we discussed retaining walls as part of an appraiser's site analysis. In terms of improvements, appraisers must also look at fencing. **Fences** add to the security of a property and can add to its value. Residents in many parts of the country demand privacy in their outdoor living. In these cases, backyards are completely fenced. They are usually made of masonry (brick or block) or various types of wood. Vinyl fencing, which often emulates the look of wood without the maintenance, is becoming more popular as well.

The depreciation of such improvements is generally not separated from that of the whole property, although wood fencing might occasionally need periodic maintenance.

Fence types

ADDITIONAL SITE IMPROVEMENTS

In addition, the appraiser should note other improvements made to the exterior site. These improvements include things around the perimeter of a building like patios, pools, fences, lighting, ponds, out buildings, and even sports courts.

The appraiser also has to give **contributory value** to site improvements after identifying them. Sometimes the contributory value of site improvements does not equal the cost of building the improvement. For example, swimming pools contribute to the overall value of a home, but the contributory value is generally less than the expense of building the pool itself. As with all other property features, the appraiser determines the value of site improvements by considering market data.

SWIMMING POOL

One of the more popular major yard improvements in many parts of the country is the swimming pool. To estimate the value increment for a swimming pool, the appraiser must study the market to learn what value swimming pools have added in comparable sales. The addition of a $35,000 swimming pool will not necessarily add $35,000 to the value of the whole property. In the case of a $150,000 house, a $35,000 pool might add only $10,000 to $15,000 value to the whole property. Yet the same addition to a $400,000 home might add the full cost of $35,000 to the total value of the residence.

SPECIALTY OUTDOOR EQUIPMENT

Unusual outdoor improvements are occasionally included in a residential property—a tool shed, playhouse, thermostatically controlled greenhouse, or even a bomb shelter installed more than 35 years ago in the early 1960s.

The valuation of an expensive greenhouse or bomb shelter installation might be difficult even for an experienced appraiser, since comparable sales are not often available. Generally, such installations add some value to a residence, although the increment is not in proportion to their cost. A $15,000 bomb shelter in the backyard of a $200,000 single-family residence would probably not bring a commensurate increase in the sales price, because it is unlikely that many people would want such a structure.

A prospective buyer might want to convert such a structure into a workshop, photographic darkroom, or other hobby shop, and would be willing to pay $5,000 more for that residence than for one without a bomb shelter. The appraiser must be practical when valuing a property with such improvements. Similar sales should be considered. If they are not available, the appraiser should make a reasonable estimate of possible use and resultant value.

A greenhouse   A treehouse

ADDITIONS AND REMODELING OF EXISTING RESIDENCES

Room additions, whether vertical or horizontal, and remodeling can affect the value of a residence positively or negatively. When considering additions or remodeling, appraisers should ask the following questions.

- Does the addition or remodeling increase the utility of the residence to potential buyers?
- Does the addition or remodeling architecturally fit the existing structure and the neighborhood?
- Are the other residences of sufficient size and utility, whether originally constructed or added to, so that the house does not suffer by regression?
- Does the addition or remodeling conform to local building codes? Was a building permit obtained and were all other legal zoning requirements satisfied before construction?
- Does the addition or remodeling conform to all private legal deed restrictions? For example, does the addition or remodeling have to be approved by an architectural committee composed of adjoining property owners? Was such approval received?

ADDITIONAL MULTIPLE RESIDENTIAL UTILITY FACTORS

An appraiser should realize that many of the desires of buyers are the same for single- and multiple-family residential units. However, some basic considerations of functional utility are unique to multiple-family residences, since most of these are built for rental.

Functional Utility Considerations in Multiple-Family Residences

- Economic use of space in exterior and interior planning
- Easy exterior and interior maintenance, including landscaping
- Availability of off-street parking
- Inexpensive utility services

UNDESIRABLE STYLE AND FUNCTIONAL UTILITY FACTORS

When considering architectural style and utility, the appraiser should be aware of obvious undesirable features. Some of the following negative factors apply only to single-family residences, but most apply to multiple-family residences.

Common Undesirable Factors

- Unappealing mixture of exterior architectural styles
- Misplaced architectural style that does not fit the site or is incompatible with other styles in the neighborhood
- Improper situation of residence on the site
- No central hallway or entryway
- No hall closet or linen closet
- Minimum-sized bedroom closets
- Inadequate closet or cupboard space for bathroom and kitchen storage
- No separate pantry
- No separate laundry room
- Fewer than three entrances to the residence (an entrance to the kitchen through the garage counts as an entrance)
- Windows too few or too small to provide adequate cross ventilation and light to all rooms
- No dining area separate from the kitchen
- No den or family room
- Inadequate or excessive room size

PROBLEM AREAS

When conducting an inspection, it is not uncommon for the appraiser to have a homeowner make a special request—for example, that he or she not inspect a certain room. There might be a sick child at home or one who is taking a nap. Does this fact require the appraiser to make an extraordinary assumption about the condition of the unseen room? Yes, because residential appraisers are required to make a "complete interior and exterior inspection" of the property. If any normally accessible area were not inspected, the appraiser would have to make an extraordinary assumption as defined by USPAP. To be conservative, no one would criticize the appraiser for using an extraordinary assumption about the condition of the unseen room.

Sometimes appraisers encounter small problems, such as the example above, during a property inspection.

Problems Encountered During a Property Inspection

- Inaccessible parts of the house
- Requested to value only five acres of land when the site is actually larger
- Requested to ignore some buildings
- Non-permitted conversions and structures
- Possible contamination of the property
- Possible drug use and/or drugs being grown or processed

SUMMARY

In this chapter, we discussed several important items for the appraiser to consider in his or her property inspection. An appraiser should study functional utility to determine its effect on the salability of the residence. It is important to consider style and utility as objectively as possible.

An appraiser's inspection of a residence usually has two main parts: the **exterior inspection** and **interior inspection**. Throughout the inspection, the appraiser judges the condition and quality of the residence. He or she determines the design, layout, and construction details of the subject property. This includes the property's functional utility: **room layout, room size,** and **room counts.** The exterior inspection includes examination of the **foundations, roofing,** and **exterior walls.** An interior inspection includes making note of the **floors, ceilings,** and **interior walls.** The style, materials used, and overall condition of the items may significantly influence value and desirability.

An appraiser must also recognize the quality of the equipment and mechanical facilities provided in a residence. There are four main systems in a home: **electrical, plumbing, heating,** and **cooling.** The appraiser must determine how each adds to the utility and desirability of a residence. Appraisers should be aware of **energy efficiency items** and basic energy-saving features.

Once an appraiser has examined the exterior and interior of the home, he or she should also make note of **automobile, storage,** and **yard utility.** The appraiser should consider the on-site parking facilities of a residence, as well as any garage conversions. The appraiser should note the functional utility of the yard as it relates to the residence. Depending on the size of the lot and the style of the house, patios, fences, landscaping, and a utility area should be considered. Additional site improvements, room additions, and/or remodeling should also be noted in the appraiser's report. When considering architectural style and utility, the appraiser should be aware of obvious undesirable features and be able to recognize common undesirable factors and problem areas.

CHAPTER 5 REVIEW EXERCISES

MATCHING EXERCISE

Instructions: Write the letter of the matching term on the blank line before its definition. Answers are in Appendix A.

Terms

A. asbestos

B. basement

C. circuit breaker

D. concrete

E. concrete masonry units

F. contributory value

G. crawlspace

H. drywall

I. elevation sheet

J. fences

K. finished areas

L. foundation

M. gross building area (GBA)

N. gross living area (GLA)

O. landscaping

P. monolithic slab

Q. R-value

R. slab-on-grade

S. stucco

T. substructure

U. sump

V. superstructure

X. unfinished areas

Y. xeriscaping

Z. zeroscaping

Definitions

1. _____ A labeled diagram or cutaway of the home detailing its features and building components, both interior and exterior

2. _____ Above grade improvements

3. _____ Below grade improvements

4. _____ Supports the entire building and transfers the weight of the building to the ground

5. _____ Mixture of sand, gravel, and cement

6. _____ Foundation in which the structure sits directly on the ground

7. _____ Lowest story of a building and is partially or entirely below ground

8. _____ Unfinished accessible space below the first floor of a building with no basement

9. _____ Pit or tank that catches liquid runoff for drainage or disposal

10. _____ Cement-like substance frequently used for wall cladding

11. _____ The total amount of finished, above ground habitable space

12. _____ The total amount of all enclosed floor areas and does include basements and attics

13. _____ Mineral fiber which has since been implicated in causing lung and stomach cancer

14. _____ Interior wall material most often used in residential construction

15. _____ Electrical device which automatically interrupts an electric circuit when an overload occurs

16. _____ Rating that measures how well insulation resists heat

17. _____ Use of vegetation around a house to prevent erosion and improve its aesthetic appearance

18. _____ A form of landscaping in which little or no water is needed

19. _____ Adds to the security of a property

20. _____ Given by appraisers to site improvements after identifying them

MULTIPLE CHOICE QUESTIONS

Instructions: Circle your response and go to Appendix A to read the complete explanation for each question.

1. An appraiser's inspection usually has two main parts:
    a. drive-by and walk-through.
    b. exterior and interior.
    c. construction and amenities.
    d. subject property and neighborhood.

2. Which of the following best illustrates an undesirable floor plan feature?

    a. Living room is connected with the entryway
    b. Kitchen and family room are located to one side
    c. Bedroom is located directly off the kitchen
    d. Garage is adjacent to the kitchen

3. When an appraiser is performing a room count, he or she includes all of the following, except the:

    a. family room.
    b. bathrooms.
    c. living room.
    d. den.

4. Which part of a structure is the support for the entire building?

    a. Crawlspace
    b. Flooring
    c. Foundation
    d. Superstructure

5. A foundation composed of one section for the floor and another for the foundation wall, each poured separately, is known as a _____ slab.

    a. monolithic
    b. post-tension
    c. screeded
    d. floating

6. The most popular, versatile material for residential framing is:

    a. wood.
    b. concrete.
    c. steel.
    d. slate.

7. There is more variety of materials for _____ than for any other component of a residence.

    a. roof construction
    b. interior walls
    c. flooring
    d. ceilings

8. When measuring the gross living area (GLA), which of the following is most likely not included?

    a. Basement

    b. Attic

    c. Crawlspace

    d. All of the above

9. Of the following types of flooring, which is most likely to add value to a residence?

    a. Wall-to-wall carpet

    b. Finished wood

    c. Ceramic tile

    d. Linoleum

10. Drywall is also called:

    a. sheetrock.

    b. plasterboard.

    c. gypsum board.

    d. any of the above.

11. Today, most residences have a _____ controlled by an electrical service panel with circuit breakers.

    a. 110-volt system

    b. 210-volt system

    c. 220-volt system

    d. 420-volt system

12. Many states have implemented laws requiring _____ be installed or upgraded at the time of sale, regardless of the age of the home.

    a. air conditioning

    b. security alarms

    c. smoke detectors

    d. central heating

13. Which of the following are considered energy efficiency features?

    a. Dual pane windows

    b. Solar panels

    c. Low water-use dishwashers

    d. All of the above

14. Which of the following characteristics best distinguishes a garage from a carport?

    a. Carports are not enclosed.

    b. A full-sized car cannot fit into a carport.

    c. Garages are attached; carports are detached.

    d. The garage is included in the appraiser's sketch.

15. In determining contributory value, which of the following site improvements would contribute less than the building expense of the improvement?

    a. Wood fencing

    b. Swimming pool

    c. Landscaping

    d. Covered patio

Sales Comparison Approach

6 Chapter

INTRODUCTION

Using the sales comparison approach, the appraiser develops an opinion of value by analyzing similar properties that have sold and comparing these properties with the subject property. The techniques of analysis used in the sales comparison are fundamental to the valuation process. In fact, all valuation approaches are related to the sales comparison in one way or another. The sales comparison method should not be confused with the cost and income approaches, in which the basic data also come from the market.

LEARNING OBJECTIVES

After reading this chapter, you will be able to:

- describe applications of the sales comparison approach.
- describe the factors affecting the sales comparison approach.
- list the steps in the sales comparison approach.
- describe sources for collecting market data.
- describe the process for selecting comparables.
- describe how to verify comparable information.
- describe the types of adjustments made to the comparable properties and reconciliation.
- list the appraisal reporting options.

WHAT IS THE SALES COMPARISON APPROACH?

The **sales comparison approach** is one of the three classic approaches to value, involving comparison of the subject property to similar properties that have recently sold. The sales comparison approach is also known as the direct sales comparison approach or the market data approach.

APPLICATIONS OF THIS APPROACH

The sales comparison approach is applicable when appraising all kinds of real property interests. It is most reliable in situations in which there are a sufficient number of arm's-length sales transactions to indicate patterns within that market.

Although it is not usually the primary method employed, sales comparison analysis is often useful when appraising many kinds of commercial property. If sufficient sales data is available, appraisers use this approach as a check on the reasonableness of the value estimates obtained from the income and cost approaches to value.

Uses of the Sales Comparison Approach

- Property types that are bought and sold on a regular basis
- Single-family residences
- Condominiums
- Small multi-residential properties
- Vacant land

LIMITATIONS OF THIS APPROACH

In order for the sales comparison approach to be useful, there must be a sufficient number of recent, reliable transactions to analyze. This helps determine trends or value patterns in the market.

Analysis of sales provides the most straightforward and direct manner for the appraiser to use to develop a credible opinion of value. This would include, among other considerations, the ability to determine whether the comparable sales reflected the actions of knowledgeable buyers and sellers. Also, it would include the ability to analyze various financing arrangements. If market data is not present in adequate quantities, the approach can be unreliable and may not apply.

The sales approach is rarely used when appraising special-use properties. **Special-use property** also known as special-purpose property, has unique usage requirements—such as a church or a museum—making it difficult to convert to other uses. Special-use properties present some interesting appraisal challenges, as there are often few comparable sales to properly use the sales comparison approach. Likewise, there is often personal property, such as pews or artifacts, that needs to be valued. For these reasons, the sales comparison approach is generally not used when appraising special-use property. The cost approach to value is often the best value indicator for these types of appraisals.

A church is an example of a special-use property.

On the other hand, the sales comparison approach is often used for commercial and industrial buildings that have owner-users. These properties are usually not purchased for their income-producing capabilities—and as such, the appraiser finds the sales comparison approach to be very useful.

If a property is purchased for its income-producing capabilities, and it is sufficiently large, the sales comparison approach may not be as useful—for there are other factors that affect its use.

Limited Uses of the Sales Comparison Approach

- Property types that are bought and sold infrequently
- Properties in a market with few arm's-length transactions
- Property in a rapidly changing market
- Special-use properties
- Unique or custom-built properties

FACTORS AFFECTING THE SALES COMPARISON APPROACH

Many factors affect the sales comparison approach. As such, it is important to consider the guidelines presented in USPAP. In USPAP 2006, the new Scope of Work Rule was introduced.

SCOPE OF WORK RULE

The **Scope of Work Rule** has three basic parts: (1) the problem to be solved has to be identified, (2) the appraiser needs to determine and perform the scope of work necessary to develop credible assignment results, and (3) the appraiser needs to discuss the scope of work in his or her report.

What is Included in the Scope of Work

- Property identification
- Property inspection
- Type and extent of data researched
- Type and extent of analysis applied to solve the appraisal problem

When an appraiser performs a direct sales comparison, he or she must keep in mind the scope of work chosen to achieve a credible appraisal result. Before we get into the specific techniques used, let us review how the foundations of appraisal affect the use of the sales comparison approach.

In Chapter 2, we discussed anticipation and change. These two factors are the underlying principles of supply and demand, substitution, balance, and externalities as they affect the appraisal process.

SUPPLY AND DEMAND

Besides the interactions between buyers and sellers, interest rates and the activities of banks also influence property prices. Buyers provide the market demand and the properties offered for sale make up the supply. This assumes a market in which there are sufficient buyers and sellers for the market to operate in a manner, which fits the definition of value used by most lenders. It is assumed that buyers and sellers are fully informed, operating in their best interests, and under no duress.

Appraisers can estimate demand by considering the number of potential buyers for a particular property type. **Demand** is the desire to possess plus the ability to buy—an essential element of value. **Supply** is the total amount of a given type of property for sale or lease, at various prices, at any given point in time. Interest rates have a profound effect, because lower interest rates create more effective demand and higher rates can virtually stop real estate activity. This was seen in the early 1980s when mortgage rates reached 18% in some areas.

Buyers provide the market demand.

SUBSTITUTION

Substitution is particularly important, as a buyer should not pay more for a property than the cost of a substitute property of equal utility and desirability. If there are not sufficient properties offered for sale as part of supply, then the sales comparison approach is diminished and is not as reliable as it is when supply and demand are operating in an open market.

BALANCE

When supply and demand are in balance, the market is said to be in equilibrium. For this to occur, the relationship between a property and its environment must also be in balance. The relationship between land and improvements must be in equilibrium in order for a property to achieve its optimum market value. Equilibrium is almost never attained.

EXTERNAL FORCES

External forces, also known as **externalities**, are outside influences that may have a positive or negative effect on property value—as periods of economic development are positive and economic depression has the opposite effect.

An appraiser's job is to determine how these factors are operating in the local market area. The sales comparison approach is well suited to the appraisal of residential properties, especially single-family residences. The reliability of any method of valuation depends largely on the availability of data necessary for its application. Because people today are so mobile, data on home sales are usually readily available. The average ownership period for a single-family residence is approximately five to seven years. In any given neighborhood, there is a high probability that the appraiser will find similar properties that have sold within a reasonable period. In addition to properties sold, appraisers also compare properties under contract and those offered for sale.

Average ownership of a single-family home is five to seven years.

STEPS IN THE SALES COMPARISON APPROACH

USPAP requires appraisers to "collect, verify, and analyze all information applicable to the appraisal problem" when using the sales comparison approach.

The Sales Comparison Approach has a Systematic Procedure

1. **Collect market data.** The appraiser has to research the market for information on actual sales, listings, offers to purchase, and properties in contract. These properties should be homogeneous to the subject.

2. **Select market data.** After collecting information, appraisers must select the comparables that are the most appropriate. Buyers and sellers rely upon information gathered from the market in making their buying or selling decisions. In performing appraisals, appraisers should rely on the same information.

3. **Verification of data.** One of the most important aspects of this process is verification of sales data. Fannie Mae and many state offices indicate that appraisers are not doing an adequate job in this area. Most appraisers do some verification through public records and multiple listing services (MLS), but they often do not perform primary verification. This involves talking to someone who is or was involved in the transaction. Buyers, sellers, and/or real estate agents should be interviewed to make sure the conditions of sale match those used in the definition of value.

4. **Applying adjustments.** The major categories of adjustment for all comparable sales are time, location, and physical characteristics. The application of the sales comparison approach is essentially the same in

the valuation of all types of property—although the units of comparison between the sale properties and the subject may vary. The comparable sales, listings, and properties under contract that an appraiser uses need to be adjusted to the subject property. If the comparable is superior, the appraiser makes a downward adjustment, which is based on market data. If the comparison is inferior, then it has to be adjusted upwards as the subject is superior in this unit of comparison.

5. **Reconcile adjusted comparable property values.** The nature of the reconciliation depends on the appraisal problem, the approaches used, and the reliability of the value indications derived. The adjusted sale prices of the comparable sales should bracket the value of the subject property.

COLLECTING MARKET DATA

The first step in the process is for the appraiser to collect data from closed sales, contracts for sale, options, and listings of properties that are considered comparable to the subject property.

Questions to Ask Before Collecting Market Data

- What are the characteristics of the subject property?
- What area should be searched for sales?
- What period should be investigated for sales?
- What sources should be used to find sales?

CHARACTERISTICS OF THE SUBJECT PROPERTY

Before a search can be conducted, the characteristics and features of the subject must be defined. This information can be found in the MLS (if the property has been listed for sale), in county records, from previous appraisals done for tax or mortgage loan purposes, and from online and CD-ROM subscription services offering sales histories and property profiles. Companies such as DataQuick® provide data that is a composite of these resources, offering such pertinent information as lot size, square footage of improvements, number of bedrooms and bathrooms, and previous sales transaction data. Often, the name of the subdivision or development is included, along with the assessor's parcel and census tract numbers.

AREA OF SEARCH

The area to be searched for sales obviously depends on sales activity and the type of development surrounding the subject property. The immediate neighborhood or subdivision will usually yield adequate sales data for the appraisal of a tract home. In the case of an unusual residence or an apartment house, it may be necessary to extend the search area. If sales are not available in the immediate neighborhood, the appraiser attempts to find other

The best comp comes from the immediate neighborhood.

areas that may yield sales of properties similar to the subject. Generally, investigations are confined to the neighborhood of the subject property, the search area widening only if a preliminary analysis does not furnish adequate sales data.

TIME PERIOD FOR SALES

The time period for comparable sales depends on the sales activity in the area of the subject property. Sales close to the valuation date for the subject property are most desirable, especially when the market is rapidly changing.

Sales considered too old for direct comparison with the subject property are often useful for establishing a trend in sale prices of a particular type of property. Often an appraiser can find a sale-resale of the same property and use this data to determine appropriate time adjustments.

The valuation date for the subject property is usually the date of the current appraisal. If the property is being valued as of some prior date, sales both before and after the valuation date can be used.

SOURCES OF SALES DATA

The data sources appraisers use may vary from area to area and from property type to property type. **Data sources** are the variety of sources used by appraisers when collecting general, local, and specific information. Since no single data source is absolutely complete or accurate, appraisers need to rely upon multiple data sources. Local practices often dictate which data sources an appraiser will use for a particular assignment. Consulting multiple data sources will help the appraiser to minimize discrepancies, inaccurate details, and incomplete records. If discrepancies are found between differing data sources or if data is incomplete, the appraiser needs to do additional research to determine why the discrepancy exists or where to find the missing information.

Only if the data used is the most complete and accurate to be found will the appraiser be able to provide the best analysis of the assignment.

Important Sources of Information

- Real estate appraisers' workfiles

- Parties to the transaction

- Public record information

- Title insurance companies

- Multiple Listing Service (MLS)

- Subscription data services

- Computerized services

- Other sources such as newspaper and Internet

Assessment data is normally not used as it has reliability problems and assessments can be a function of law—not necessarily value.

Each appraiser develops sources for sales data. Most use more than one source. The intended use of the appraisal and the type of property being appraised often influence the selection of the sales data source.

REAL ESTATE APPRAISERS' WORKFILES

Most real estate appraisers maintain a workfile of the sales data collected from prior appraisals. While this may be a very good source of information, appraisers have to be careful to maintain confidentiality. Sometimes, the appraiser is precluded from using information obtained in an earlier assignment since using it would violate confidentiality laws. Appraisers need to be aware of the Confidentiality section of the Ethics Rule of USPAP in order to comply with this requirement.

PARTIES TO THE TRANSACTION

Parties to the transaction are the people directly involved—the buyer, seller, buyer's broker, and seller's broker. Particularly, real estate agents (salespersons and brokers) are a valuable asset for an appraiser. They often specialize in certain markets and are very helpful when the appraiser needs to become geographically competent to meet USPAP's Competency Rule. Sometimes, they can be hired to assist an appraiser in an important assignment to provide local knowledge and assist in comparable sales research. When going to another geographic area, using local REALTORS® can be worth any expenditure.

In many cases, buyers and sellers are often willing to talk to appraisers about the property they just purchased or sold. Although the information an appraiser learns from people in the field can be very helpful, particularly if the property was not listed on the MLS, it must be verified and corroborated. Principals in the transaction (buyers and sellers) have a stake in the property and may misrepresent facts.

PUBLIC RECORD INFORMATION

Information recorded at county recorder's offices, as well as some property tax assessor's information, is considered to be public. **Public records**, like those in the county recorder's office, are documents disclosing all

important facts about properties. Data obtained from these sources varies in accuracy, quality, and completeness from county to county and state to state. In areas of low population or rural locations, this information may not be computerized. The appraiser is required to manually search through cumbersome card catalogues and property lists. Sometimes, sales information does not appear on public record systems until months after the actual sale occurred.

While most states do provide public records, some states are non-report states. State law allows sales to be completed without reporting the sales price. This makes it very difficult for appraisers to get information about sales in these areas. Appraisers in these states have to develop networks of real estate agents and lenders who are willing to share sales information.

TITLE INSURANCE COMPANIES

Title insurance companies maintain files of all recorded county documents. Real estate transfer deeds are usually filed according to the physical location of the sale properties. This filing system facilitates the appraiser's job of obtaining sales within a specified area. Many title companies gather sales data as a service to customers. They usually charge an hourly fee.

Since competition is so high among title companies, many of them offer online services to companies and individuals who may be a source of business or may be in a good position to refer business. Having access to a title company website that allows the appraisers to gain information about properties, area demographics, sales data, plat maps, schools, churches, and other helpful information is a valuable asset. It is worth the effort to see if you can form a relationship with a title company that will allow you to access this information.

MULTIPLE LISTING SERVICE

The **multiple listing service** (MLS) is a cooperative listing service conducted by a group of brokers (usually members of a real estate association) to provide an inventory of all available properties in an area. While not specifically designed as a data source for appraisers, MLS systems are an invaluable source of information.

There are some exciting trends with multiple listing services. In the past, each area or small city had its own MLS, and appraisers had to join several of them if they worked in larger areas. Now, the smaller MLS systems are combining into larger geographic areas. In fact, some areas are now allowing appraisers who belong to one MLS to access all of them in their general area. This trend is likely to occur all over the country—as it greatly benefits appraisers who are working in several geographic regions.

The MLS is a good source of data.

It is important to keep in mind, that although MLS systems are an excellent source of data, listings found on MLS systems are designed to sell properties—not specifically to assist appraisers. Since listing records are generated by listing agents desiring to sell properties, there is a tendency toward overstating positive attributes and understating negative factors of a property.

SUBSCRIPTION DATA SERVICES

There are numerous companies engaged in the business of selling data to real estate appraisers, called **data services**. Almost all of these data services obtain their data from information disseminated by local county recorders and assessors. Some of the services provide information that has been submitted by real estate appraisers and lenders. A good number of these online data sources provide unlimited access to their database for a flat monthly fee. Others may charge per record, and, in some instances, the data is free. Some of these systems are geared toward providing data to residential real estate appraisers, while others specialize in providing data for commercial appraisers. Sometimes, private online data sources provide their data in conjunction with local MLS services. Additionally some data providers may also publish books containing sales data on a monthly or quarterly basis. Some of these services provide data that is updated monthly on CDs sent to appraisers and others provide data online over the Internet.

Data services available to an appraiser include the Internet, CDs, and books.

Computerized Services

All of the services discussed in the previous section are accessible using a computer and an Internet connection. Most form reports sent to lenders are now transmitted electronically. These companies provide appraisers with secure ways to transmit reports for a fee.

Changes occur so rapidly with computerized services that it is a challenge to keep up with new standards. In 1995, the Appraisal Standards Board (ASB) wrote Statement 8 to guide appraisers on how to properly deal with the electronic transmission of reports. In 2001, this statement was retired for it was impossible for the ASB to keep up with all the changes and have this part of USPAP apply to most appraisal situations. It is up to the appraiser to ensure that his or her appraisal reports meet USPAP—especially the guidelines found in SR 2-2.

OTHER SOURCES OF MARKET DATA

There are numerous other sources available to appraisers. Though these sources rarely provide all the information appraisers require to perform their services, they may provide a starting point for further investigation by an appraiser.

Newspapers

Real estate classified ads, as well as the real estate and public notices sections of a newspaper, often provide data regarding properties for sale and the parties involved in transactions. Information found in newspapers fills in gaps in the information obtained from other sources, such as the MLS and public records. The classified ads in newspapers are also a good source for current rental data information. The real estate sections of newspapers often provide local market trend information.

Internet Research

The Internet is a useful resource when researching real estate. As time goes on, more and more properties are listed on national Internet databases. In addition to sales and listing data, market area trends, and in some cases, local zoning and assessors' information is available.

SELECTING THE COMPARABLES

After an appraiser collects market data, he or she must select the appropriate comparables. The appraiser needs to identify which data is appropriate and applicable to the assignment at hand.

> Example: Sales from high-rise condominium developments are usually not good indicators of value for single-family detached homes. However, in some instances, sales of single-family detached condominiums are very strong indicators of value for detached, single-family homes in nearby planned unit developments.

The geographic area an appraiser would typically search for comparable sales data depends upon the nature of the real estate being appraised. If similar properties are commonly bought and sold within a neighborhood, such as single-family residences, an appraiser would typically limit the search for sales data to similar properties located within that area.

ELEMENTS OF COMPARISON

When appraising single-family residential properties, the appraiser considers numerous elements of comparison. An **element of comparison** is any aspect of a real estate transaction or any characteristic of the property that may affect the property's sales price. Appraisers will need to consider different elements of comparison for different assignments. Selecting truly comparable sales minimizes the amount and size of adjustments.

Elements of comparison are used to explain the differences of prices paid for real estate. Appraisers determine elements of appraisal by using research and then support these elements with market data. All adjustments made to properties should be the result of market data.

Elements of Comparison Considered by the Appraiser

1. Property rights conveyed

2. Financing terms

3. Terms and conditions of sale

4. Market and time conditions

5. Location

6. Physical characteristics

7. Other characteristics, including:
   - economic factors
   - costs and expenditures
   - permitted uses (zoning, master plans, redevelopment zones)
   - any personal property or other non-realty components of the sale

There are other factors that have to be considered for some properties such as restrictions caused by open space easements, historical preservation easements, CC&Rs that restrict uses, water and other riparian rights, and other kinds of easements. In Chapter 7, we will define the elements of comparison and discuss the derivation, identification, and measurement of adjustments as they affect the elements of comparison.

HIGHEST AND BEST USE

As discussed in Chapter 2, the highest and best use of a property is the main factor determining its value. For this reason, most appraisers will not use a comp if its highest and best use is different from that of the subject property. One of the simplest ways to check highest and best use is to see if there is a difference in zoning.

Differences in zoning may have a large influence on a property's value. An appraiser should attempt to use comparable sales that have the same zoning designation as the subject. When comparable sales have zoning different from the subject property, an adjustment may be necessary. Typically, properties that have zoning which allows a more intensive use are more valuable than ones that have zoning which allows less intensive development. This is because the owner of the more intensively zoned property has more options for how the property can be used.

UNITS OF COMPARISON

After selecting and processing the sales data, it must be arranged systematically to make analysis convenient for the appraiser. An appraiser must learn to discriminate in the selection of sales data, discarding information not relevant to the appraisal of the subject property.

Analysis involves separating comparable sales into parts that can be more readily examined. The appraiser can make meaningful comparisons between the desirability and utility of the comparable property and the subject property. The appraiser needs to make the arrangement in terms of the units of comparison that are appropriate for the particular assignment, the appraisal problem, and the nature and characteristics of the property that is appraised. Converting sale prices to size-related unit prices typically eliminates the need to make adjustments for differences in size. Differences in size and economy of scale are considered in reconciliation. If the subject property and one of the comparables are significantly different in size, then this may not be a good comparable as the price per unit examined will not be meaningful. The table on the following page indicates typical units of comparison for different property types.

Typical Units of Comparison Table	
Property Type	**Typical Units of Comparison Expressed as Price/Unit**
Single-Family Residence	
	Total property price Square foot of living area
Apartments	
	Living unit Bedroom Gross building area Gross rent multiplier
Office Properties	
	Gross building area Net rentable area
Industrial Properties	
	Gross building area Cubic foot of gross building area
Vacant Land	
	Square foot Acre Front foot

In the appraisal of single-family residences, total properties are compared after making adjustments for differences between the sale and subject properties. A common denominator is established.

Design, size, and utility of apartment houses usually differ too greatly to allow a direct comparison between total properties. However, several units of comparison have been developed for analysis of such sales. Appraisers often use three or four units of comparison when analyzing sales of apartment houses.

Common Units of Comparison

- Per square feet of living area
- Per living unit
- Per room
- Gross rent multiplier

VERIFYING COMPARABLE INFORMATION

After selecting the most appropriate comparable properties, the next step is to verify the information. The verification process is extremely important since it is used to identify which possible comparable properties are, or are not, reflective of activity in the open market. **Verification** is an inquiry into the circumstances surrounding and affecting a sale. This includes the reason for the sale of the property and any items affecting its price. The appraiser must be careful to ensure that data used to formulate the appraiser's opinions and conclusions reflect arm's-length transactions within the market.

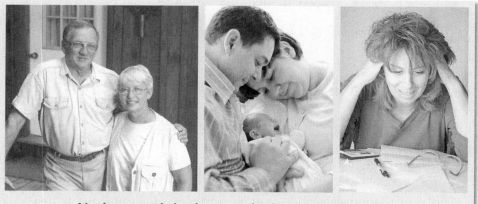

Verification includes the reason for the sale of the property
(downsizing, increase in family size, financial reasons).

PRIMARY VERIFICATION

Primary verification involves talking to someone who was involved in the transaction. Ideally, all comparable sales used in an appraisal should be confirmed with one of the principals in the transaction, the real estate broker or salesperson who handled the sale, or someone familiar with the terms and conditions of the sale. Sales may be confirmed either in person or by telephone. More information can usually be obtained by interviewing in person than by telephone, but personal interviews may be impractical.

Sales that are not arm's-length in terms of the definition of value should not be used or used with extreme caution. **Arm's-length** is normally defined as a transaction between unrelated parties under no duress to perform the transaction.

The data solicited in an interview with the buyer, seller, or real estate broker depend on the type of property and the information already available. In addition to the sales price, the appraiser should confirm other data pertinent at the time of the sale.

Pertinent Sales Data to Confirm

- Terms of sale
- Any extenuating circumstances in the sale (such as imminent foreclosure)
- Description of improvements (number of rooms, bathrooms, etc.)
- Occupancy status
- Rental, if not owner-occupied
- Condition of property at the date of sale
- Personal property included in the sale
- Assessments or encumbrances against the property at the date of sale

INSPECTION OF PROPERTIES

Many appraisers have questions about whether they can appraise a property without inspecting it. There are also questions concerning drive-by appraisals, and the appropriateness of appraising a property without seeing the inside. USPAP indicates that the appraiser has to indicate his or her level of inspection. The inspection can be no physical inspection, a drive-by exterior only inspection, or a full interior-exterior inspection. The appraiser must be able to achieve a credible result.

For most types of lender appraisals, the appraiser must inspect the subject property with at least a drive-by, as well as perform a drive-by inspection of the comparable properties. This inspection may be a brief observation of the property, or it may be as thorough as the inspection of the subject property itself. A thorough inspection of the sale properties allows the appraiser to make a more precise comparison between the comparable and subject properties. However, an appraiser seldom inspects the interior of comparable residences, as it is often difficult to gain entry to an occupied home, and a thorough inspection is time-consuming. If an appraiser works a certain area for much of his or her career, it is often possible to inspect comparable properties when they are offered for sale. The appraiser then has the opportunity to make notes about the comparable and take pictures.

The appraiser should inspect the subject property with at least a drive-by.

SECONDARY VERIFICATION

Most lenders require an appraiser to use at least two sources to confirm the sale. Most often, the appraiser uses the MLS and a title company or the county assessor's records. It is common practice to include the document number of the sale so that the reader of the appraisal report can verify the information. This confirmation is referred to as **secondary verification**. Information gained from interviews and physical inspections is primary verification.

APPLYING ADJUSTMENTS

Once the appraiser has collected, analyzed, and verified sales data, this information must be applied in the appraisal. At this point in the process, the appraiser has already narrowed down the number of sales, listings, and pending sales to those most similar to the subject. The next step is to apply adjustments to the comps. In the sales comparison approach, an **adjustment** is a dollar or percentage amount that is added to or subtracted from the sales price of a comparable property. The adjustment is to account for a feature that the property has or does not have which differentiates it from the subject property.

The most difficult and important aspect of the sales comparison approach is the adjustment for differences between comparable sales and the subject property. No property is identical to the subject property. The appraiser attempts to find properties as similar as possible to the subject property and adjusts for differences. To be considered comparable, the sale property must be similar to the subject property in location, utility, and date of sale, and the transaction must be voluntary and open.

The sale price of the comparable property is always adjusted upward or downward to reflect the differences between the comparable and the subject property. The major categories of adjustment for all comparable sales are time, location, and physical characteristics.

Adjustment Methods

- Percentage of sale price
- Dollar amount (the most common and practical method)
- Pluses or minuses

No property is identical to the subject property.

When measuring differences between comparable properties and the subject, the appraiser must avoid personal preferences and attempt to reflect only those differences that affect sellers and buyers. Adjustments are normally not made for elements less than 1% of the sales price of the comparable sale, as market data is not precise enough to permit the appraiser to discern minor differences in value amounts.

RECONCILIATION OF SALES COMPARISON APPROACH

Reconciliation is the adjustment process of weighing results of all three appraisal methods to arrive at a final value estimate of the subject property's market value. Reconciliation is also known as correlation. The **final value estimate** is an appraiser's opinion of the defined value of the subject property, arrived at by reconciling the estimates of value. The nature of the reconciliation depends upon the appraisal problem, the approaches used, and the reliability of the value indications derived.

When all three approaches are used—sales comparison, cost, and income— the appraiser examines the spread among the three indications. This will be discussed in more detail in Chapter 13. A wide spread may indicate that one or more of the approaches is not truly applicable to the appraisal problem. The appraiser must always consider the relative dependability and applicability of each approach in reconciling the value indications into a final value estimate of defined value. In reconciliation, the appraiser can explain variations among the indications and account for any inconsistencies among the value conclusions and methods with which they were derived.

The validity of the sales comparison approach is that it takes into account all of the valuation factors, including supply-demand, financing, and market conditions. As such, this approach has the most validity in appraising single-family homes, lots, and land. The sales comparison approach is thought of as the acid test of the valuation process. All of the other approaches to value are based, in one way or another, on the sales comparison approach.

ADJUSTMENT GUIDELINES

There comes a time when a comp ceases to be an appropriate comparable. This occurs when one has to make too many adjustments to the comparable. But, what is too many? The Federal National Mortgage Association (Fannie Mae or FNMA) has established **adjustment guidelines**.

Some lenders state that a single line item adjustment should not exceed 10% of the sales price of the comparable. For example, if a property sold for $200,000, no single adjustment should exceed $20,000. Keep in mind that this is not a steadfast rule—it is a guideline. The appraiser can still make the adjustment, even if it exceeds the 10% guideline for a single line item, as long as market data supports it.

Fannie Mae has also established guidelines for the total adjustment amounts. The two types of totals are net and gross.

The **net adjustment** amount is determined by combining all the adjustments and adding or subtracting them as indicated. The appraiser divides this amount by the sales price to determine the percentage of net adjustments. FNMA's guideline is that the percentage of net adjustments should not exceed 15%.

However, the net adjustment guideline is not enough, since the net adjustment amount allows for offsetting adjustments. In theory, an appraiser could apply 100 different adjustments that balance each other out and result in a net adjustment amount of $0. Fannie Mae has also established a guideline for the acceptable percentage of gross adjustments in a single comparable sale.

The amount of the **gross adjustment** is determined by adding all individual adjustments, without regard to whether they are positive or negative adjustments. Then, the appraiser divides that sum by the comparable property's sales price to determine the percentage of gross adjustment. Fannie Mae states that this percentage should not exceed 25% of the sales price of the comparable.

Adjustment Grid	
Sales Price	$100,000
Condition Adjustment	+$5,000
Bedroom Adjustment	− $3,000
Bathroom Adjustment	− $2,000
Pool Adjustment	− $7,500
Location Adjustment	+$5,000
Age Adjustment	+$3,000
Gross Living Area Adjustment	+$2,000
Net Adjustment	$2,500
Percentage of Net Adjustments	2.5%
Gross Adjustment	$27,500
Percentage of Gross Adjustments	27.5%

In this case, the percentage of net adjustments is well within the guideline at only 2.5%. However, the gross percentage of adjustments is too high. This is a clear red flag, as there appears to be too many significant quality differences between the two properties for them to be comparable. Again, this is only a guideline that can be exceeded within reason. In those occasional cases, an appraiser needs to include discussion about why such large adjustments were necessary.

FORM OF THE APPRAISAL REPORT

USPAP allows three reporting options: (1) Self-Contained Appraisal Report, (2) Summary Appraisal Report, and (3) Restricted Use Appraisal Reports.

These options are described in Advisory Opinion 11, as well as SR 2-2 of USPAP. If the appraisal is for a federally related transaction, then the appraiser has to use a self-contained or summary report. The restricted use report can only have one intended user, and as such, is not suitable for federally related transactions. Form reports approved by Fannie Mae and Freddie Mac are examples of summary reports.

SR 2-2 provides the appraiser a considerable amount of flexibility in how the appraisal report is organized. The 11 points that must be discussed are the basic components of the scope of work decision.

USPAP allows three
reporting options

Required Elements in an Appraisal Report.

1. State the identity of the client and any intended users, by name or type.

2. State the intended use of the appraisal.

3. State the real property interest appraised.

4. Indicate the type and definition of value and cite the source of the definition.

5. State the effective date of the appraisal and the date of the report.

6. Describe the scope of work.

7. Describe the information analyzed, the appraisal methods and techniques employed, and the reasoning that supports the opinion of value.

8. Summarize the information analyzed, the methods and techniques used, and the appraiser's reasoning.

9. State the use of the real estate as of the date of value.

10. State all extraordinary assumptions and hypotheticals used in the appraisal.

11. Include a signed certification in accordance with SR 2-3.

USPAP does not prescribe the order of these elements. Some appraisers prefer to put the signed certification in the front of the appraisal report right after the table of contents and others place the certification in the back of the report.

SUMMARY

The **sales comparison approach** is one of the three classic approaches to value, involving comparison of the subject property to recently sold, similar properties. When using the sales comparison approach, USPAP requires the appraiser to "collect, verify, and analyze all information applicable to the appraisal problem."

The sales comparison approach has a systematic procedure: (1) collect market data, (2) select market data, (3) verify data, (4) apply adjustments, and (5) reconcile adjusted comparable property values. The data sources appraisers use may vary from area to area and from property type to property type. **Data sources** are the variety of sources used by appraisers when collecting general, local, and specific information. These include Multiple Listing Services, public records, title insurance companies, and other real estate appraisers.

After an appraiser collects market data, he or she must select the appropriate comparables. When appraising single-family residential properties, the appraiser considers numerous elements of comparison. An **element of comparison** is any aspect of a real estate transaction or any characteristic of the property that may affect the property's sales price.

After selecting the best comparable properties, the next step is to verify the information. **Verification** is an inquiry into the circumstances surrounding and affecting a sale. Primary and secondary verification techniques should be used. Primary verification includes inspection of the property and first-hand interviews, while secondary verification is confirmation through the MLS or public records.

Once the appraiser has collected, analyzed, and verified market information, this information must be applied in the appraisal. An **adjustment** is a dollar or percentage amount that is added to or subtracted from the sale price of a comparable property. The adjustment is to account for a feature that the property has or does not have which differentiates it from the subject property.

Reconciliation is the adjustment process of weighing results of all three appraisal methods to arrive at a final estimate of the subject property's market value. In reconciliation, the appraiser can explain variations among the indications and account for any inconsistencies among the value conclusions and methods with which they were derived. Of course, there comes a time when a comp ceases to be an appropriate comparable. As such, the Federal

National Mortgage Association (Fannie Mae) has established **adjustment guidelines**. Fannie Mae states that a single line item adjustment should not exceed 10% of the sales price of the comparable.

Lastly, USPAP allows three reporting options: (1) self-contained, (2) summary, and (3) restricted use reports. These options are described in Advisory Opinion 11 as well as SR 2-2 of USPAP.

CHAPTER 6 REVIEW EXERCISES

MATCHING EXERCISE

Instructions: Write the letter of the matching term on the blank line before its definition. Answers are in Appendix A.

Terms

A. adjustment

B. adjustment grid

C. data services

D. data sources

E. demand

F. element of comparison

G. external forces

H. final value estimate

I. financing terms

J. gross adjustment

K. Multiple Listing Service (MLS)

L. net adjustment

M. parties to the transaction

N. physical inspection

O. public records

P. reconciliation

Q. special-use property

R. supply

S. title insurance company

T. verification

Definitions

1. _____ One that has unique usage requirements making it difficult to convert to other uses

2. _____ The desire to possess plus the ability to buy—an essential element of value

3. _____ The total amount of a given type of property for sale or lease, at various prices, at any given point in time

4. _____ Outside influences that may have a positive or negative effect on property value

5. _____ The variety of sources used by appraisers when collecting general, local, and specific information

6. _____ Documents disclosing all important facts about properties

7. _____ Cooperative listing service conducted by a group of brokers to provide an inventory of all available properties in an area

8. _____ Any aspect of a real estate transaction or any characteristic of the property that may affect the property's sales price

9. _____ An inquiry into the circumstances surrounding and affecting a sale

10. _____ A form of primary verification

11. _____ A dollar or percentage amount that is added to or subtracted from the sale price of a comparable property

12. _____ The adjustment process of weighing results of all three appraisal methods to arrive at a final estimate of the subject property's market value

13. _____ An appraiser's opinion of the defined value of the subject property, arrived at by reconciling the estimates of value

14. _____ Determined by combining all the adjustments and adding or subtracting them as indicated

15. _____ Determined by adding all individual adjustments, without regard to whether they are positive or negative adjustments

MULTIPLE CHOICE QUESTIONS

Instructions: Circle your response and go to Appendix A to read the complete explanation for each question.

1. The sales comparison approach is most applicable when:
   a. appraising vacant land.
   b. there is a sufficient number of comparable sales.
   c. appraising properties in an active market area.
   d. appraising all of the above.

2. The Scope of Work Rule has three basic parts. Which of the following is not one of the three parts?
   a. The problem to be solved has to be identified.
   b. The appraiser must use each of the three approaches in each appraisal.
   c. The appraiser needs to determine and perform the scope of work necessary to develop credible assignment results.
   d. The appraiser needs to discuss the scope of work in his or her report.

3. Many factors affect the sales comparison approach, but the most important single factor is:
   a. anticipation.
   b. change.
   c. substitution.
   d. balance.

4. The sales comparison approach has a systematic procedure. Which of the following is the first step?
   a. Verify data
   b Collect market data
   c. Select market data
   d. Apply adjustments

5. Which of the following lists the steps for the sales comparison approach in order?
   a. Collect, verify, select, reconcile, adjust
   b. Select, collect, adjust, vilify, reconcile
   c. Collect, select, verify, adjust, reconcile
   d. Verify, select, collect, adjust, reconcile

6. When researching market data, the appraiser is concerned with:
   a. characteristics of the subject property.
   b. area of search.
   c. time period for sales.
   d. all the above.

7. All of the following are important sources of information, except:
   a. real estate appraisers' workfiles.
   b. multiple listing services.
   c. assessment data.
   d. title insurance companies.

8. One of the simplest ways to check highest and best use is to see if there is a difference in:
   a. square footage.
   b. zoning.
   c. building materials.
   d. price per unit.

9. The appraiser needs to make the arrangement in terms of the units of comparison that are appropriate for the:

    a. particular assignment.
    b. appraisal problem.
    c. nature and characteristics of the property that is appraised.
    d. all of the above

10. Primary verification of comparable sales includes:

    a. talking to someone involved in the sale.
    b. checking with the county recorder's office.
    c. checking MLS data.
    d. all the above.

11. Many appraisers have questions about whether they can appraise a property without inspecting it. USPAP indicates that the appraiser has to:

    a. indicate his or her level of inspection.
    b. conduct a full interior-exterior inspection.
    c. inspect comparable properties.
    d. inspect at minimum the exterior of the subject property.

12. Adjustments are not normally made for elements less than _____ of the sales price of the comparable sale.

    a. 1%
    b. 3%
    c. 5%
    d. 10%

13. Fannie Mae states that gross adjustments should not exceed what percentage of the sales price of the comparable?

    a. 10%
    b. 15%
    c. 25%
    d. 30%

14. A comparable sold recently for $200,000 and requires a positive adjustment for physical differences of $22,000 and a negative adjustment for locational differences of $18,500. Under normal practice, should an appraiser use this comp?

    a. Yes, it meets the FNMA guidelines for single item adjustments.
    b. No, because it exceeds the FHA guideline for net adjustments.
    c. No, because it exceeds the GNMA guidelines for gross adjustments.
    d. No, because it exceeds the FNMA guideline for single line item adjustments.

15. Appraisal reports for federally related transactions frequently request just one approach to value. The report type for federally related transactions does not include the:

    a. Restricted Use Appraisal Report.

    b. Summary Appraisal Report.

    c. Self-Contained Appraisal Reports.

    d. URAR 1004 Form Report.

Measurement of Adjustments

7 Chapter

INTRODUCTION

The goal of the sales comparison approach is to select the market sales that are most homogeneous to the subject property. These sales are the most similar—the ones that buyers and sellers consider when using the principle of substitution. The comparable sales then need to be adjusted for the differences between them and the subject. These sales are always adjusted to the subject. If the comparable is superior to the subject in a particular feature or amenity, the adjustment made is downward. If the comparable is inferior to the subject in an area, an upward adjustment is made. This chapter covers the ways to determine what adjustments to make and to consider them in both quantitative and qualitative manners.

LEARNING OBJECTIVES

After reading this chapter, you will be able to:

- describe the appraisal step of selecting comparables.
- determine how to adjust comparable sales.
- describe how to apply adjustments.

SELECTING THE COMPARABLES

Comparative analysis is the general term used when considering elements of comparison. As introduced in the last chapter, an **element of comparison** is any aspect of a real estate transaction or any characteristic of the property that may affect the property's sales price. When an appraiser considers the data collected in order to choose the best comparables, the goal is to select properties that are most like the subject.

If comparables are found that require no adjustments, then the comparables are truly homogeneous. This happens occasionally, but most of the time, the appraiser has to adjust the comparables to the subject property.

In addition to similar physical, legal, and economic characteristics, for the typical residential appraisal, the comparables should have a:

- sales date as close to the subject as possible.
- similar chronological age or have a similar effective age.
- similar location.

After the sales information has been collected and confirmed, it can be organized in a variety of ways. Standards Rule (SR) 2 in USPAP offers the appraiser flexibility in how data should be organized and discussed. Many appraisers use one of the Fannie Mae or Freddie Mac forms for federally related transactions. These forms—such as the 1004 (URAR) and the 2055 (Desktop Underwriter Quantitative Analysis Appraisal Report)—list the elements of comparison in a grid format.

Exterior-Only Inspection Residential Appraisal Report

File #

| There are | comparable properties currently offered for sale in the subject neighborhood ranging in price from $ | | to $ | |
| There are | comparable sales in the subject neighborhood within the past twelve months ranging in sale price from $ | | to $ | |

FEATURE	SUBJECT	COMPARABLE SALE # 1		COMPARABLE SALE # 2		COMPARABLE SALE # 3	
Address							
Proximity to Subject							
Sale Price	$		$		$		$
Sale Price/Gross Liv. Area	$ sq. ft.	$ sq. ft.		$ sq. ft.		$ sq. ft.	
Data Source(s)							
Verification Source(s)							
VALUE ADJUSTMENTS	DESCRIPTION	DESCRIPTION	+(-) $ Adjustment	DESCRIPTION	+(-) $ Adjustment	DESCRIPTION	+(-) $ Adjustment
Sale or Financing Concessions							
Date of Sale/Time							
Location							
Leasehold/Fee Simple							
Site							
View							
Design (Style)							
Quality of Construction							
Actual Age							
Condition							
Above Grade Room Count	Total Bdrms. Baths	Total Bdrms. Baths		Total Bdrms. Baths		Total Bdrms. Baths	
Gross Living Area	sq. ft.	sq. ft.		sq. ft.		sq. ft.	
Basement & Finished Rooms Below Grade							
Functional Utility							
Heating/Cooling							
Energy Efficient Items							
Garage/Carport							
Porch/Patio/Deck							
Net Adjustment (Total)		☐ + ☐ -	$	☐ + ☐ -	$	☐ + ☐ -	$
Adjusted Sale Price of Comparables		Net Adj. % Gross Adj. %	$	Net Adj. % Gross Adj. %	$	Net Adj. % Gross Adj. %	$

I ☐ did ☐ did not research the sale or transfer history of the subject property and comparable sales. If not, explain

My research ☐ did ☐ did not reveal any prior sales or transfers of the subject property for the three years prior to the effective date of this appraisal.
Data source(s)
My research ☐ did ☐ did not reveal any prior sales or transfers of the comparable sales for the year prior to the date of sale of the comparable sale.
Data source(s)
Report the results of the research and analysis of the prior sale or transfer history of the subject property and comparable sales (report additional prior sales on page 3).

ITEM	SUBJECT	COMPARABLE SALE # 1	COMPARABLE SALE # 2	COMPARABLE SALE # 3
Date of Prior Sale/Transfer				
Price of Prior Sale/Transfer				
Data Source(s)				
Effective Date of Data Source(s)				

Analysis of prior sale or transfer history of the subject property and comparable sales

Summary of Sales Comparison Approach

Indicated Value by Sales Comparison Approach $

Indicated Value by: Sales Comparison Approach $ Cost Approach (if developed) $ Income Approach (if developed) $

This appraisal is made ☐ "as is", ☐ subject to completion per plans and specifications on the basis of a hypothetical condition that the improvements have been completed, ☐ subject to the following repairs or alterations on the basis of a hypothetical condition that the repairs or alterations have been completed, or ☐ subject to the following required inspection based on the extraordinary assumption that the condition or deficiency does not require alteration or repair:

Based on a visual inspection of the exterior areas of the subject property from at least the street, defined scope of work, statement of assumptions and limiting conditions, and appraiser's certification, my (our) opinion of the market value, as defined, of the real property that is the subject of this report is
$, as of   , which is the date of the inspection and the effective date of this appraisal.

The Fannie Mae forms do not include all items that may need to be adjusted. Elements such as zoning, landscaping, auxiliary units, and detached buildings are not included. Later in this chapter, a typical grid will be presented and discussed.

In the sections below, we consider each of the elements of comparison used to select the comparables.

PROPERTY RIGHTS CONVEYED

In a majority of appraisal assignments, appraisers are asked to appraise the fee simple interest in a property. In other instances, appraisers are requested to estimate partial interests in a property. As a reminder, a **partial interest** is an interest in real estate that represents less than the fee simple estate (i.e., a leased fee or leasehold estate). The owner of a leasehold interest in a property does not own the complete bundle of rights in that property. A **leasehold estate** is the tenant's interest in the leased property during the term of the lease. This type of estate only has value if the agreed-upon rent is less than the market rent. It is also known as a less-than-freehold estate.

There are also examples of single-family homes and condominiums in which the owner does not own the land. Housing near some universities is often built on leased land. In this case, the appraiser determines the value of the leased fee estate—not the fee simple estate. It is important to find other properties on leased land to use for comparables.

Sometimes appraisers are asked to value life estates. A **life estate** is an estate that is limited in duration to the life of its owner or the life of another designated person. These are just a few types of leasehold interests that are less than fee estate.

Though it is not always possible, appraisers should try to use comparable properties that include the same property rights as the subject property in their analyses—since property rights tend to have a large influence on value. Once the property rights for the subject and the comparable sales are established, the appraiser can relate and, if necessary, adjust the market data for the comparable properties to the subject property.

FINANCING TERMS

The financing terms used to purchase a property can affect the price a seller is willing to accept. In fact, differences in financing can cause the sales price of one property to be significantly higher than another almost identical property that sold in the same period.

Financing can vary in many ways. Sometimes, in order to facilitate a sales transaction, a seller will pay fees that a buyer would traditionally pay, such as discount points and closing costs. In those situations, the seller will usually add those additional fees to the sales price. Wraparound loans, installment sales contracts, seller financing, or a loan assumption can have a significant impact on sales prices.

Adjustments for financing are different from other adjustments in one very significant way. Other adjustments are based upon differences between the comparable sale and the subject. However, adjustments for financing are based upon the difference in financing for the comparable sale and financing typically found in the market. If typical financing was used, the sale is referred to as a **cash equivalent sale**—a sale in which the financing does not affect the price.

When adjusting for financing, appraisers typically adjust for cash equivalency. The **cash equivalency technique** is a procedure in which the sales prices of comparable properties selling with atypical financing are adjusted to reflect financing that is typical in a market. The calculations used to derive cash equivalency adjustments will vary depending on the type of financing used to purchase the comparable property and the terms associated with that financing.

> Example: Situations often arise in which the seller of a property will pay discount points to a lender so that a buyer may get financing at a below-market rate. (Points refers to prepaid interest lenders accept in order to finance a loan at below-market interest rates.) In these situations, the seller usually incorporates the additional points into the sales price he or she is willing to accept. If using this sale as a comp, an appraiser would typically deduct from the sales price a dollar amount equal to the amount paid by the seller.

In some cases when atypical financing is used, the appraiser may not be able to adjust for its effect on the sales price, and he or she will have to use a different comp.

Financing and cash equivalency will be discussed in greater detail in the next chapter.

TERMS AND CONDITIONS OF SALE

One of the reasons appraisers are encouraged to use primary verification of comparable sales is that it allows the appraiser to discover a buyer and seller's motivation. Primary verification is accomplished by talking to someone who was involved in the transaction—not just relying on printed data. If the buyer's motivation is atypical for the market, the sales price may be atypical as well. The appraiser looks for arm's-length transactions in which all parties involved are knowledgeable, acting in their own self-interest, and under no undue influence or pressure from other parties.

Oftentimes, the conditions of sale affect the market price. When properties are assembled, the whole is often worth more than the sum of the parts. The parts assembled are worth more to the new property than they would be to a buyer at large.

> Example: The owner of a movie theatre purchases a vacant lot adjacent to the theatre. This lot then becomes part of the theatre complex and is more valuable as part of the complex than it would have been if it were sold for another use.

The conditions of a sale can sometimes lead to a lower price. A seller who wants to sell quickly may discount the property's price, or family members may sell at a discount to other family members.

Obviously, it is best to use comparable sales that have no unusual conditions of sale. If the appraiser finds it necessary and unavoidable to use a sale of this type, an appraiser must exercise great care. The appraiser must make appropriate, market-based adjustments to compensate for these conditions and their effect on the sales price of the comparable property.

MARKET CONDITIONS AND TIME CONSIDERATIONS

An appraisal is an opinion of value as of a specific date. Adjustment for time reflects the change in value between the date of the comparable sale and the valuation date of the subject property. Changing market conditions are also reflected over time. It is difficult to accurately measure differences in value over time. If enough sales of similar properties are available, a value trend can sometimes be established and measured. Published studies summarize surveys measuring changes in various types of property values. In a rapidly changing market, the most recent sales and listings of property for sale should be given considerable weight in the sales comparison approach. The question of how long a comparable is worthy of consideration is one that appraisers wrestle with in many assignments. Because of this, Fannie Mae has a general guideline that comparable sales over six months old should not be used.

There are some theoretical problems with this guideline as some properties have the contracts for sale negotiated much sooner than the property sales close. This often occurs in land deals, in which the buyer is securing entitlements during escrow or settlement. This time consideration can greatly skew the units of comparison.

In some regions—desert and resort areas—sales occur infrequently and appraisers have to use comparables that are more than a year old. As such, time of sale is a function of market conditions, the number of comparable sales available, and the quality of these sales. Appraisers must exercise judgment in determining how to treat the important time factor.

Example: Appraiser Dan identifies a comparable within the same planned development (PUD) as the subject. The comparable sold ten months ago for $450,000. Because each property has the same floor plan and is in the same PUD, only the time of sale must be adjusted. From his research, Dan concludes that the property values in the local market have increased an average of 4% per year. To convert this to a monthly percentage, he will divide the yearly percentage by twelve (the total number of months in a year) and then multiply this by the number of months for which he must account.

$$0.04 \div 12 = 0.00333$$
$$0.00333 \times 10 = 0.0333 \text{ or } 3 \text{ } 1/3 \text{ } \% \text{ } (3.33\%)$$

The final step is to adjust the comparable's sales price up by the percentage.

$$\$450,000 \times 3.33\% = \$14,985$$

$$\$450,000 + \$14,985 = \$464,985, \text{ or } \$465,000 \text{ (rounded)}$$

LOCATION

Adjustment for location includes differences in desirability between neighborhoods or between specific locations within a neighborhood. When appraising single-family residences, comparable sales are normally limited to the neighborhood of the subject property. Dissimilarity exists between neighborhoods in public transportation, shopping facilities, schools, parks, natural amenities, socioeconomic status of residents, and care and condition of properties.

Ideally, the location of comparable properties should resemble that of the subject property within the market area. Unless there is a shortage of comparable sales in the market area, comparable properties adjacent to stores or highways should not be used. Sales affected by natural amenities, such as trees, views, creeks, or mountains can provide problems, as the value of these amenities are often difficult to measure. In general, these should not be used unless the subject property also includes natural amenities. Likewise, if the subject property has any undesirable amenities or characteristics associated with its location, only similar sales should be used for comparison.

PHYSICAL CHARACTERISTICS

One of the more challenging aspects of appraisal is determining how to treat physical differences between the subject and the comparable properties. Some physical aspects correlate much higher with value than others. An appraiser must be aware of quality, quantity, and design differences between the sale and subject properties and must be able to express them in terms of market data.

Physical characteristics are generally classified as site (or land) improvements and building improvements. As discussed in the property inspection chapters, site and land improvements include lot size, street improvements, utilities, and natural amenities—all of which are considered in relation to their effect on the total property.

When adjusting for differences in building improvements, an appraiser must consider age, condition, size, type, and quality of construction. A comparable property must have major similarities to the subject property. Adjustments should be necessary only for minor differences. A two-story house should not be compared to a one-story house, a brick building to a wood-frame building, or a two-bedroom, one-bathroom home to a three-bedroom, two-bathroom home. The goal, as mentioned before, is to use homogeneous comparable sales.

The following pictures show two houses that are model matches. The first house has a two-car garage and the second a three-car garage. However, the first home has an additional bedroom downstairs in lieu of a three-car garage. Both homes are on the same side of the street and have the same view.

Model with two-car garage has extra square footage and an additional downstairs bedroom.

Model with a three-car garage and less square footage. It has four bedrooms vs. five for the model with the two-car garage.

The appraiser has to decide how the typical buyer would treat the three-car garage option as compared to having a two-car garage with an additional bedroom. Property owners in this particular subdivision indicated that they considered the difference a trade-off. There was not a significant difference in sales prices of the two models as compared over a five-year period. Even though three-car garages are popular in the area, many homeowners with children consider the additional bedroom a desirable amenity.

An appraiser must adjust for differences by analyzing market response. How much more will buyers pay for an inside utility room, additional bathroom, remodeled kitchen, pool and spa, or extra garage space? Each significant difference between the comparable property and the subject property must be translated into dollars.

OTHER CHARACTERISTICS

Other physical, legal, and economic characteristics of the subject and comparable properties should be considered. Properties with similar zoning (legal) or similar income-producing capacity (economic) are better indicators of value than properties that differ in these characteristics.

ECONOMIC CHARACTERISTICS

Most beginning appraisers start with residential property appraisals. However, the sales comparison approach can also be used with income-producing properties. Ideally, if the subject property is producing income, the comps should produce similar amounts. If not, an adjustment may be necessary.

> Example: Appraiser Kate is using the sales comparison approach to value a convenience store that has annual revenue of $900,000. Two similar convenience stores sold recently. One with annual revenue of $820,000 sold for $700,000. The other with annual revenue of $600,000 sold for $490,000. In this situation, the first comp is more similar to the subject in its capacity to produce income.

As discussed in Chapter 1, economic considerations are considered in terms of the financial capacity of a market or neighborhood's occupants and their ability to rent or own property, to maintain it in an attractive and desirable condition, and then to perform renovations when applicable.

With the trend toward urban and suburban sprawl, communities tend to overlap one another. This results in many people living in one market area and working in another. An appraiser often analyzes job opportunities available in a given area, and must analyze where homeowners in a given market area are traveling for work.

COSTS AND EXPENDITURES

A knowledgeable buyer often analyzes a potential purchase in terms of improvements needed to make it suitable to his or her needs. This is often seen in very expensive properties, in highly desirable areas. The discriminating buyer in a high-end market is going to consider what needs to be done to the property immediately after the purchase.

> Example: Consider an appraiser valuing a property worth more than $5,000,000. The search for comparable sales resulted in discovering that nearly every sale involved an extensive remodel immediately after purchase. In many of these comparables, it appears that the majority of the sales price was attributable to the location of the property and its land value.

Other Reasons for Expenditures Immediately After Purchase
- Curing deferred maintenance
- Removing and remodeling parts of the structures
- Change in use with special use permits and sometimes zoning changes
- Costs for remediation of any contamination

Often, the buyer does not know exactly what the costs will be—though the buyer and seller are likely to negotiate some kind of price adjustment to reflect the potential expenditures. This is another example of why primary verification is so important and should not be overlooked by the appraiser.

NON-REALTY COMPONENTS OF VALUE

On occasion, **non-realty components** (personal property) may be sold along with real property. If the sales price of the comparable includes such items, the appraiser may need to make an adjustment. For a residential appraiser, most of the non-realty components involve furniture, fixtures, and appliances. Vacation homes, for example, are often sold furnished. It is important in these cases for the appraiser to perform enough market research to determine how much of a premium was paid for furniture and decorating. In comparison, using a comparable that does not include furniture can be problematic.

For the most part, appraisers have to determine if the refrigerator, washer and dryer, and other appliances add value to the property as personal property. Generally, they have little resale value and are not included in the final estimate of value.

ADJUSTING THE COMPARABLES

Upon identifying the elements that are applicable to the subject appraisal, each has to be compared to the subject to see if an adjustment is warranted. If sufficient information is available, a quantitative adjustment can be made. If not, the element can be addressed using a qualitative analysis.

In the sales comparison approach, the appraiser uses quantitative and/or qualitative analysis to derive an opinion of value. The two techniques can be used separately or in combination.

The goal of the adjustment process is to make each comparable sale equivalent to the subject as of the date of value. Adjustments to comparable properties may be made to the total property price, to a common unit price or a mixture of both. The appraiser has to ensure that all comparables are treated the same. The magnitude of the adjustment should reflect the degree of difference between the comparable and the subject. Appraisers are cautioned to consider all appropriate elements of difference—but not to adjust for the same difference twice.

QUANTITATIVE ANALYSIS

When quantitative adjustments are applied, the appraiser constructs a range of value. **Quantitative analysis** compares data on properties to obtain results that are then applied to other properties in the same market. Using reconciliation, the appraiser determines where the subject property fits along the continuum of the range of value and what the point estimate of value should be. In this approach, the appraiser ensures that the subject properties most similar to the subject are given the most weight.

TYPES OF QUANTITATIVE ADJUSTMENTS

The ways to determine quantitative adjustments as they apply to comparable properties include data analysis, statistical analysis, and graphic and trend analysis.

DATA ANALYSIS

When there is sufficient data, the paired sales or sale-resale techniques can be very useful—but when the appraiser substitutes his or her judgment for market-derived adjustments, the results can be misleading. It is very important for an appraiser to explain how his or her adjustments were derived so that the reader of the report understands the rationale and methods used to obtain specific adjustments.

Many appraisers are not doing an adequate job of justifying adjustments in this area. The appraiser should estimate the amount of adjustment indicated by market data and use other analytical techniques and/or secondary data to test the reasonableness of the adjustment used.

Paired Sales Analysis

The **paired sales analysis** is a method of estimating the amount of adjustment for the presence or absence of any feature by pairing the sales prices of otherwise identical properties with and without that feature. A sufficient number of sales must be found to allow the appraiser to isolate the effect on value of the pertinent factor.

Although paired sales analysis is a theoretically sound method, it is sometimes impractical. There is often a limited supply of model matches with only one major difference. An adjustment determined from a single matched pair does not necessarily indicate a true difference—just as one comparable sale is insufficient to determine the market value of a subject property.

> Example: Assume two properties sold in a tract of homes all developed by the same builder. Both of the homes have the exact same floor plan and both are in a similar location. The two homes are virtually identical in all aspects except one has an upgraded kitchen and the other is in original condition. The home with the upgraded kitchen sold for $425,000 and the one without sold the same month for $410,000. Both homes sold with conventional financing in a market with stable values.

In the above scenario, the difference in price is $15,000. The only significant difference between the two properties is the kitchen. Therefore, it would be reasonable to assume that the upgraded kitchen in this tract of homes has a contributory value of $15,000. Appraisers would then be able to state, with a high degree of certainty, that a similar kitchen in the same neighborhood would warrant a $15,000 adjustment upwards or downwards. The direction of the adjustment would be dependent upon whether the subject or the comparable sale was the property with the upgrade.

Upgraded kitchen   Original kitchen

Suppose an appraiser needs to know the value of a pool in a particular marketplace. He or she searches for two sales that are similar in all characteristics, except for the pool. The grid on the following page illustrates this concept.

Adjustment Grid					
Sale 1	3 Bedroom	2 bath	1600 SF	pool	$200,000
Sale 2	3 Bedroom	2 bath	1625 SF	no pool	$192,000

This paired sales analysis reveals that a pool in this marketplace is worth about $8,000. The two properties have the same number of bedrooms and bathrooms. They are close enough in size that no adjustment needs to be made (a 25 square foot difference is not perceptible in the marketplace). Assuming that all other characteristics are similar, the only recognized difference is the pool. This marketplace appears to support the value for a pool at $8,000.

Following the verification principle—as well as strengthening the position that a pool in this marketplace is worth $8,000—more evidence is needed. The diligent appraiser continues to search and finds another pair to analyze.

Adjustment Grid					
Sale 1	4 Bedroom	2.5 bath	2000 SF	pool	$232,000
Sale 2	4 Bedroom	2.5 bath	2000 SF	no pool	$223,500

This time, the two properties have the exact same square footage, room count, and floor plan. The only recognized difference is Sale 1 has a pool while Sale 2 does not. The difference in the selling prices is $8,500. Since the properties are a bit more expensive, the slightly higher pool value can be justified. However, the difference is not significant and further supports the opinion that a swimming pool in this marketplace is worth approximately $8,000.

> **The more evidence an appraiser can extract from the marketplace, the stronger his or her opinion of value.**

This method is accurate. But, it is often impractical. Typically, very few sales are available that have only one significant difference between them. When sales like this do exist, the difference between the two is not the item the appraiser is trying to identify.

When this method is used, frequently a series of adjustments is required in order to isolate the effect of a single characteristic. In this scenario, the problem arises in knowing how much to adjust for the other items when attempting to isolate the effect of that single characteristic.

Even though the data available to perform the paired sale analysis may be limited, appraisers should not discard this method of extracting adjustments. In many cases, the paired sales method will provide meaningful results, in spite of limited available data. In these cases, the appraiser should check the reasonableness of the data by using some of the other available analytical methods.

Sale-Resale Analysis

The sale-resale analysis is a method for determining adjustment or depreciation amounts that is useful when a property is sold and resold in a relatively short period. Assuming both sales are arm's-length, open-market transactions, and assuming that there have been no significant changes to the property during the time between the two sales, the difference in price could be a basis for a time adjustment.

> Example: Assume a property was purchased for $375,000 on June 1st and resold on the following year on April 1st for $395,000. The increase in value over that period was $20,000. This $20,000 increase was spaced over a 10-month period and was a 5.33% increase over the original sales price. The 5.33% increase equals a .53% increase in value per month. Rounding this figure, it would be safe to say that property values in this property's market are increasing at approximately 1/2% per month or approximately 6% per year.

In some instances, a property may be in a stable market in which values are not changing to any significant degree. If the properties have been remodeled during the time between the two sales, the sale-resale analysis method could identify the contributory value of the remodeling.

Like the paired sale analysis, this method is not always practical. Rarely do properties sell and resell with no other changes taking place. In many instances, properties are purchased, remodeled, and resold in markets that are also increasing in value. To identify how much of the increase in value between the two sales was attributable to the remodeling and how much was attributable to the increasing market may be difficult to determine. The sale-resale analysis can prove to be a powerful analytical tool in the appraiser's overall set of analytical techniques.

Flipping is another possible threat to the quality of an appraiser's sale-resale analysis. **Flipping** occurs when a person buys a property at one price and quickly sells it to another at an inflated price, usually within a short period. The sale may appear to be an arm's-length transaction. However, the inflated sales price is often designed to defraud the lender. That is, if the second sale occurs on the same day or within a few days of the initial closing. There is nothing fraudulent about buying a property, and flipping it at a higher price, so long as all information is known. With proper verification, the appraiser should be able to avoid flipped properties.

STATISTICAL ANALYSIS

Statistical analysis techniques can be useful to determine adjustments if there is a sufficient number of sales to justify statistical analyses. Most of these are correlational in technique. The appraiser has to understand basic statistics and how those statistics apply to a given assignment. The appraiser wants results that are mathematically sound, but must be sure the results are meaningful and appropriate for the particular appraisal assignment.

In statistical analysis, a **correlation** is a relationship among variables that is demonstrated when an observed change in the value of one variable is related to a corresponding change in the value of another variable. The correlation is positive if an increase in one variable is associated with an increase in another variable. A negative correlation occurs when the presence of one variable

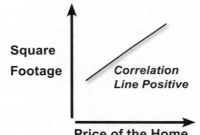

is associated with a decrease in a second variable. Correlational relationships can be either linear or non-linear.

This first example shows a positive correlation in which the price of the home increases as the square footage increases.

This second example indicates a negative correlation. The effect of street noise is compared to the sales price.

The price of the home goes down as street noise increases.

Linear regression is a specific type of correlation that is often used by appraisers to determine how one or more independent variables affect a dependent variable. **Regression** is a statistical analysis assessing the association between two variables.

Uses of Linear Regression to Predict the Value of a House

Dependent Variable	Independent Variables
Value of Property	Square footage
	Lot size
	Bedrooms
	Bathrooms
	Garage space
	View

Multiple Regression Analysis

Multiple regression analysis is a statistical technique for estimating a particular variable, such as a probable sales price, using more than one other known variable. The theory of multiple regression analysis has been around for a long time. However, it was of little value to most appraisers because even the simplest analysis required a large number of calculations.

With the advent of personal computers and the development of software capable of quickly performing the numerous computations required, appraisers now use this technique much more easily. Appraisers use multiple regression analysis not only to identify the amount of an adjustment, but also to help estimate property values. The problem with using multiple regression is that all sales in an area are usually factored into the analysis, not just the sales that are comparable to the subject. Less than arm's-length transactions and fraudulent sales often get included in these analytical models. Obviously, these non-market based transactions can distort the results obtained from a multiple regression analysis.

Like the other methods, multiple regression analysis has benefits and limitations. Since it is a statistical method, multiple regression analysis works best when distinct, quantifiable data can be identified. Items such as age, building size, sales price, room count, and site area are easily quantifiable. Other items having an effect on value such as quality, condition, view, design, and location are subjective and not easily quantifiable. These items are not as readily applicable in a program that is based upon mathematical calculations.

In areas where properties have a high degree of homogeneity and are approximately the same age, size, quality, condition, design, and appeal, multiple regression analysis may produce credible results. In areas where the properties are custom built or no two properties are similar, multiple regression analysis usually does not produce meaningful results.

GRAPHIC AND TREND ANALYSIS

Two other quantitative procedures that are used are graphic analysis and trend analysis. **Graphic analysis** is a technique used to identify and measure adjustments to the sale prices of comparable properties. It is a variant of statistical analysis in which the appraiser uses graphically displayed data visually or through using a curve fit analysis. A simple graphic display of grouped data is used to illustrate market reaction to variations in the units of comparison.

Trend analysis uses an arrangement of statistical data in accordance with its time of occurrence, usually over a period of years. A series of related changes may be identified and projected into a probable future pattern. It is especially useful when there are many sales, but not necessarily similar to the subject property. The problem with trend analysis is that some appraisers apply the trend to a large market area. Normally, real estate markets are a series of sub-markets. One sub-market may indicate that values have increased and another that values have declined. For example, to say that the value of homes in Boston has gone down 7% in the last year can be misleading—as parts of Boston may have increased in value and other parts may be down.

Depending on how the appraiser calculated the adjustments, adjustments using quantitative techniques can be applied as a percentage or a dollar amount. For example, data may indicate that property values in the subject market area have increased 12% in the past year. This corresponds to a 1% per month adjustment if one assumes a straight-line increase. Further analysis indicates that properties in the subject's location sold for 7% more than properties in an area a mile away. Percentages are normally converted to a dollar amount that may be used for upward or downward adjustments as appropriate.

QUALITATIVE ANALYSIS

When the appraiser uses qualitative techniques, the comparable sales are normally divided into two groups: (1) those superior to the subject property and (2) those that are inferior.

Qualitative analysis compares data on properties to obtain relative comparisons between properties in the same market. The adjusted prices of these two groups will bracket the value of the subject by indicating a probable range of value. This technique is useful when the comparables are not as homogeneous as one would like them to be.

TYPES OF QUALITATIVE ADJUSTMENTS

After the appraiser has applied quantitative adjustments—or in cases in which this is not possible because of lack of homogeneity in sales comparables—the appraiser can apply qualitative adjustments. There are three basic categories of qualitative adjustments: (1) relative comparison analysis, (2) ranking analysis, and (3) contingent valuation methodology (CVM).

RELATIVE COMPARISON ANALYSIS

If an appraiser uses relative analysis, he or she considers the comparable sale in terms of whether it is superior, equal, or inferior to the subject. This technique is helpful when conditions in the real estate market are not uniform and there are insufficient properties that are similar enough to the subject to allow for quantitative analysis. It is similar to the paired sales analysis mentioned earlier, but there are too many differences to use paired analysis.

BRACKETING

When performing a qualitative adjustment using relative comparison, the appraiser uses a bracketing technique. **Bracketing** is the selection of market data so that the subject is contained within a range of data. It is based on the idea that the sales prices of the comparables chosen for the appraisal are not higher than the value of the subject property, nor will they all be lower. When considering the marketplace, bracketing produces a much more solid conclusion.

> Example: A property appraised for $300,000, and all of the comparable sales sold for a price in the low $290,000s. How can the appraiser justify his opinion of value when all of the comparable properties are lower? If the appraiser cannot find an appropriate comp that sold for $300,000 or more, then the value derived may be questionable.

Similarly, if all of the comparables are higher in price than the value of the subject property, a question should arise as to whether or not appropriate comparables were used.

In the appraisal of a relatively new residence within a subdivision of similar houses, the bracket range will not normally exceed 5% between the high and low adjusted sale prices. The spread may exceed 5% for older or unusual residences. The appraiser should not average the adjusted sale prices to find a final estimate value. If a large number of comparable sales are used, an appraiser may narrow the indicated price range by eliminating some of the less comparable sale properties and give the greatest weight to the sales that are most comparable to the subject property.

RANKING ANALYSIS

Ranking analysis is used when the appraiser takes the next step and ranks the qualitative comparables in terms of their similarity to the subject. There are two ways to use this approach. One is to rank the comparables in ascending or descending order. Then the appraiser analyzes each sale to determine the relative position of the subject in the array.

A second way to use a ranking analysis is to rank the comparables and then assign a weight to each comparable in terms of its similarity to the subject.

The table below illustrates this technique. The unit of comparison used is price per square foot and we are using a vacant lot as an example. The subject lot is 0.6 acres and residentially zoned. The site is nearly all usable. The comparables are also residential lots, but are different in sizes. Assume the sales prices have been adjusted prior to building the table.

	Comparable Sales				
	Lot Size	Sales Price	Price Sq. Ft	Weight Assigned	Weight Contribution
1	.75 acres	100,000	$3.07	25%	$.77
2	.78 acres	125,000	$3.68	20%	$.78
3	.85 acres	110,000	$2.97	20%	$.59
4	.65 acres	130,000	$4.59	20%	$.92
5	.9 acres	145,000	$3.33	15% 100%	$.50 $3.56

The price per square foot of the subject is the sum of all of the weighted contributions. The weights assigned must equal 100%. The various ranked weighted contributions are added giving a total weight to be applied to the subject lot.

Using this technique, the value of the vacant lot would be $93,000.

Calculation:

>   Step 1: Convert 0.6 acres to square feet (unit of comparison)
>   0.6 acres x 43,560 SF / acre = 26,136 SF
>
>   Step 2: Multiply lot size by cost per square foot
>   26,136 SF x $3.56 / SF = $93,000 (rounded)

CONTINGENT VALUATION METHODOLOGY

The contingent valuation methodology, if performed properly, can yield very good results. The **contingent valuation methodology** is a method used to identify how a particular feature affects the value of a property by asking those who are knowledgeable about that market (i.e. other appraisers and agents). It is also called the survey method.

Contingent valuation methodology is generally used when there is no sales data available. There are participants in any given market that are knowledgeable about and active in that market. To identify how much a particular feature affects the value of a property, asking those who are knowledgeable about that market is often all the appraiser needs to do. If an appraiser surveys enough knowledgeable participants within a market in a systematic manner, the appraiser can generate data that is not found elsewhere.

Since this method does not rely on sales data to determine the adjustment value, the major benefit to this method is that it can be used when there is no sales data available. This method also has its limitations. Like any type of survey, a significant number of interviews need to be performed in order to obtain accurate and quantifiable results. The appraiser needs to exercise care in creating questions that are not leading. Also, the appraiser should ask all interviewees exactly the same questions in order to obtain meaningful results.

APPLYING ADJUSTMENTS

Once the appraiser has collected sufficient data, analyzed it, and verified the sales information, he or she is ready to apply adjustments in order to make the comparable properties equal to the subject property. An **adjustment** is a dollar or percentage amount that is added to or subtracted from the sale price of a comparable property.

This process applies to confirmed sales, pending sales, as well as any active listings considered as part of the comparison. The accuracy of the sales comparison approach is determined by the appropriateness of the comparables used and how the appraiser makes adjustments. The adjustments need to come from market data. In general, it is hard to determine a market adjustment that is less than 1% of the sales price of the comparables. Many appraisers make a whole series of adjustments that have no basis from market data.

Three Adjustment Methods

1. Dollar amount (the most common and practical method)

2. Percentage of the sales price

3. Using pluses or minuses

The sale price of the comparable property is always adjusted upward or downward to reflect the differences between the sale property and the subject property. The major categories of adjustment for all comparable sales are time, location, and physical characteristics.

MAKE ADJUSTMENTS IN ORDER

Since appraisers use both dollar amount and percentage adjustments, the adjustments must be made in a specific sequence. This is true if percentage adjustments are made alone, or if they are made in combination with dollar adjustments. If the adjustments are made strictly on a dollar basis, the sequence in which adjustments are made is unimportant.

Adjustments that affect overall property value are made first, followed by adjustments that only affect individual property features. Typically, appraisers make adjustments in a certain sequence. The appraiser then adjusts for those differences that only affect specific property features.

Elements of Comparison - Typical Order of Adjustments

1. Property rights conveyed

2. Financing terms

3. Conditions of sale

4. Market conditions and time adjustments

5. Location adjustments

6. Physical characteristics

7. Other characteristics, including economics, expenditures, use and zoning, and personal property

The following table illustrates how these adjustments may be made using a grid.

Sequence of Adjustments		
Element of Comparison	**Market Data Adjustment**	**Applied Adjustment**
1. Sales Price		$300,000
2. Property Rights Conveyed	0	
3. Financing (favorable)	-5%	$285,000
4. Conditions of Sale	0	
5. Expenditures after purchase	-$27,500	$257,500
6. Market Conditions (market slowing)	+3%	$265,225
7. Location (superior)	-5%	$244,625
8. Physical Characteristics (inferior)	-7%	$261,749
9. Use and zoning	0	
10. Non-realty components	0	
Reconciled value of comparable (rounded)		**$262,000**

WORKING WITH DOLLAR ADJUSTMENTS

Comparables with dollar adjustments only are relatively uncomplicated. This is because the sequence in which adjustments are made is unimportant when using a dollar adjustment only.

Example: A comp sold for $335,000 but required several adjustments

Since this example only involves dollar adjustments, the appraiser can add up the adjustments in any order, and the adjusted price will always be $326,000. The appraiser can even total the adjustments, and then combine the net adjustment amount with the sales price to get the adjusted price.

Comparable	
Sales Price	$335,000
Condition	- $5,000
1/2 Bath	+ $8,000
Garage	- $12,000
Adjusted Price	$326,000

WORKING WITH PERCENTAGES ADJUSTMENTS

Since a percentage adjustment affects the overall property value, applying several percentage adjustments can cause the outcome to vary considerably. Unlike dollar adjustments, one cannot simply add the percentages together and then apply the ultimate percentage to the comparable's price. When applying percentage adjustments, intermediate adjusted prices are calculated. Subsequent adjustments are applied to the previous intermediate price thereby calculating a new intermediate price. This results in a cumulative value estimate that could be significantly affected by the sequence in which adjustments are applied.

Example: A suitable comparable has been found and it sold for $310,000. However, three percentage adjustments are required to account for its differences to the subject. The location of the comparable is superior to the subject, which requires a 10% negative adjustment to make up for its superiority. The appraiser has also discovered that the financing used to purchase the property was atypical for that market. Therefore, the sales price of the comp needs to be adjusted up by 2%. Finally, it sold 14 months ago, and due to changing market conditions, it will need to be adjusted up 5%.

The examples below examine two different ways to determine the adjusted sales price.

1) First, following the logic of dollar adjustments, one could simply add the three percentages together to get a net percentage of -3% (2% + 5% - 10% = -3%). If you subtract 3% from the sales price of the comparable, its adjusted value is $300,700.

Combined	
Sales Price	$310,000
Net %	x .97
Adjusted Price	**$300,700**

2) We get a different result if we apply the adjustments in the correct sequence.

As you can see, there is a difference of almost $2,000 when using systematic percentage adjustments, and with larger numbers, the discrepancy becomes more glaring.

Sequence	
Sales Price	$310,000
Financing Terms	x 1.02
	$316,200
Market Conditions	x 1.05
	$332,010
Location	x .90
Adjusted Price	**$298,000 (rounded)**

WORKING WITH PERCENTAGE AND DOLLAR ADJUSTMENTS

When this scenario arises, it is crucial to follow the sequence of adjustments, for any improperly applied adjustment will affect the following adjustment(s).

Example: Jane is appraising a large, multi-million dollar home. She found a comparable property that recently sold for $5,500,000 that required several adjustments: a $20,000 adjustment for a pool, a 7% adjustment for market conditions, and a -10% adjustment for external obsolescence associated with proximity to a highway. In addition, Jane discovered during her research that the seller bought down the buyer's loan, which accounted for $111,000 of the sales price.

Sequence 1	
Sales Price	$5,500,000
Financing	- $111,000
	$5,389,000
Market Conditions	x 1.07
	$5,766,230
Location	x .90
	$5,189,607
Physical Characteristics	+ $20,000
Adjusted Price	**$5,209,600 (rounded)**

When applied properly, the sequence of adjustment reveals that the proper adjusted value of this particular comparable is $5,209,600 (rounded).

If the adjustments are applied in any other order, the appraiser's result will be off from as little as $4,000 to as much as $12,500.

Sequence 2	
Sales Price	$5,500,000
Physical Characteristics	+ $20,000
	$5,520,000
Location	x .90
	$4,968,000
Financing Terms	- $111,000
	$4,857,000
Market Conditions	x 1.07
	$5,196,990

Questions to Consider When Applying Adjustments
- What are the major differences between the comparable and the subject?
- Do the differences make the comparable more or less valuable?
- What is the value of the difference?

IDENTIFY DIFFERENCES

When looking at the various elements of comparison, appraisers have to identify if there is a difference for which adjustment is necessary. We discussed earlier the different elements of comparison that appraisers look at when selecting the most appropriate comparables. Now that comps have been chosen, the appraiser looks at the same elements of comparison and checks for any special sales and financing considerations and any differences between the comps and the subject property in time-related, location, and physical characteristics.

In performing the sales comparison analysis, the subject and the comparable sales are usually entered onto an **adjustment grid**, or matrix. The **adjustment grid** lists important items affecting value such as site area, location, design and appeal, quality, condition, gross building area, basement area, room count, view, age, and amenities. Using this grid helps to ensure that the comparable sales are adjusted consistently. It also shows, in an easy-to-read format, how the subject compares to the comparable properties in various characteristics and the adjustments the appraiser makes.

DECIDE IF THE COMP IS MORE OR LESS VALUABLE

Once differences are identified, the appraiser's next step is to analyze each of the differences one by one and determine if a particular difference makes the comparable sale superior or inferior.

Example: The comparable property shown in the grid below is not in as good condition as the subject property and does not have as many bathrooms. However, it does have a larger garage and a pool, while the subject property does not.

	Subject Property	Comparable Sale	
Sales Price	???	$205,000	
Condition	Good	Fair	Inferior
Bedrooms	4	4	Same
Bathrooms	3	2	Inferior
Garage	2-car	3-car	Superior
Pool	No	Yes	Superior

We already know the sales price of the comparable property, and we are trying to determine the probable sales price of the subject property. Since the comp's condition and number of bathrooms are inferior to the subject, we know that the subject property would be worth more than the comp in these areas. However, the comp has a larger garage and a pool, so the subject would be worth less than the comp in those areas.

By comparing the two properties in this way, the appraiser knows if he or she has to make a positive or a negative adjustment to the comparable sales price, even before determining the actual dollar value of the adjustment.

Direction of Adjustments

1. If the comparable property has a feature that is superior to the subject property or if the comparable property has a feature that is missing from the subject property, the comparable property is considered to be worth more than the subject in regard to that item. In that case, the sales price of the comparable would need to be adjusted down to account for the contributory value of that superior feature and its effect upon the sales price of that property.

2. If the comparable property has a feature that is inferior to the subject property or if the comparable property is lacking a feature that the subject property has, the comp is worth less than the subject in regard to that item. In that case, the sales price of the comparable property would be adjusted up to account for that difference.

Adjustments are always made to the comps. The appraiser cannot adjust the value of the subject property because the value of the subject is unknown.

DETERMINE THE ADJUSTMENT VALUE

When the appraiser identifies a characteristic in which the subject property and the comparable property differ, he or she must identify the amount the market would pay for that difference. By tabulating the pluses and minuses of all of the adjustments made to the comparable sale, we arrive at the adjusted selling price. The grid on the following page illustrates the concept.

Adjustment Grid			
	Subject Property	**Comparable Sale**	
Sales Price	???	$205,000	
Condition	Good	Fair	+ $5,000
Bedrooms	4	4	
Bathrooms	3	2	+ $5,000
Garage	2-car	3-car	- $5,000
Pool	No	Yes	- $10,000
Adjusted Sales Price		**$200,000**	

In this example, some features are superior to those of the subject property. These require a negative adjustment. Other features are inferior. These require a positive adjustment. This enables the appraiser to zero in on an indicated value for the subject property.

Adjustments made to the prices of the comparable sales may be applied either in dollars or as a percentage. For example, an enclosed patio may add $15,000 in value (dollar adjustment) or a home located adjacent to a noisy freeway may be found to be worth 15% less (percentage adjustment) than other homes not similarly affected.

The manner in which the adjustment is extracted from the market determines which way the adjustment is applied. Some adjustments are applied to reflect specific property features or physical characteristics. Views, swimming pools, and additional garage spaces fit this category. Dollar values are used for these types of adjustments. Other adjustments are made to the sales prices of comparable properties to reflect items affecting the overall value of that property. Sales and financing concessions as well as property rights conveyed would be items fitting this description. Since these items affect the overall value, the sales price of the comp is adjusted by a percentage.

In some appraisal assignments, the appraiser makes the adjustments to a particular unit of comparison rather than the property as a whole. For example, when appraising an apartment complex, or a large hotel, the appraiser may analyze comparable sales on the basis of price per unit. Theaters, sports facilities, and auditoriums may be analyzed in terms of price per seat.

RV parks, mobile home parks, and parking lots may be analyzed in terms of price per space. Some properties are analyzed on the basis of price per square foot, price per acre, or even price per cubic foot.

> Example: Alex is appraising a warehouse. He found a comparable that recently sold for $21 per cubic foot. Alex's market investigation reveals that a negative 4% adjustment for age should be made and a positive 7% adjustment for physical differences. Alex would first subtract 4% from the price per unit ($21 − 4% = $20.16), and then add 7% ($20.16 + 7% = $21.57) to find the adjusted value per unit, $21.57 per cubic foot.

Identifying how much to adjust for a particular item is the most difficult aspect of the sales comparison approach. Adjustments must be market derived, and in some situations, readily available market data is inconclusive. There are numerous methods for identifying how large an adjustment should be, and some methods work better than others. Appraisers need to be aware of all the methods and exercise sound judgment in determining the applicability of any particular method to the appraisal problem at hand.

SUMMARY

Comparative analysis is the general term used when considering elements of comparison. An **element of comparison** is any aspect of a real estate transaction or any characteristic of the property that may affect the property's sales price. When an appraiser considers the data collected in order to choose the best comparables, the goal is to select properties that are most like the subject.

Elements of Comparison Considered by the Appraiser
1. Property rights conveyed
2. Financing terms
3. Terms and conditions of sale
4. Market and time conditions
5. Location
6. Physical characteristics
7. Other characteristics, including economic factors, costs and expenditures, permitted uses (zoning, master plans, redevelopment zones), any personal property or other non-realty components of the sale

In the sales comparison approach, the appraiser uses quantitative and/or qualitative analysis to derive an opinion of value. The two techniques can be used separately or in combination. **Quantitative analysis** compares data on properties to obtain results that are then applied to other properties in the same market. There are several means to use to determine quantitative adjustments as they apply to comparable properties: (1) data analysis, (2) statistical analysis, and (3) graphic and trend analysis. **Qualitative analysis** compares data on properties to obtain relative comparisons between properties in the same market. There are three basic categories of qualitative adjustments: (1) relative comparison analysis, (2) ranking analysis, and (3) contingent valuation methodology (CVM).

Once the appraiser has collected sufficient data, analyzed it, and verified the sales information, he or she is ready to apply adjustments in order to make the comparable properties equal to the subject property. An **adjustment** is a dollar or percentage amount that is added to or subtracted from the sale price of a comparable property. In performing the sales comparison analysis, the subject and the comparable sales are usually entered onto an **adjustment grid**, or matrix. The adjustment grid lists important items affecting value such as site area, location, design and appeal, quality, condition, gross building area, basement area, room count, view, age, and amenities. Adjustments are always made to the comparables. The appraiser cannot adjust the value of the subject property because the value of the subject is unknown.

CHAPTER 7 REVIEW EXERCISES

MATCHING EXERCISE

Instructions: Write the letter of the matching term on the blank line before its definition. Answers are in Appendix A.

Terms

A. adjustment

B. adjustment grid

C. bracketing

D. cash equivalency technique

E. cash equivalent sale

F. contingent valuation methodology

G. correlation

H. data analysis

I. flipping

J. graphic analysis

K. leasehold estate

L. life estate

M. multiple regression analysis

N. paired sale analysis

O. qualitative analysis

P. quantitative analysis

Q. ranking analysis

R. regression

S. relative comparison analysis

T. sale-resale analysis

U. trend analysis

Definitions

1. _____ The tenant's interest in the leased property during the term of the lease

2. _____ An estate that is limited in duration to the life of its owner or the life of another designated person

3. _____ A sale in which the financing does not affect the price

4. _____ A procedure in which the sales prices of comparable properties selling with atypical financing are adjusted to reflect financing that is typical in a market

5. _____ Compares data on properties to obtain results that are then applied to other properties in the same market

6. _____ Compares data on properties to obtain relative comparisons between properties in the same market

7. _____ A dollar or percentage amount that is added to or subtracted from the sale price of a comparable property

8. _____ In performing the sales comparison analysis, the subject and the comparable sales are usually entered onto this

9. _____ A method of estimating the amount of adjustment for the presence or absence of any feature by pairing the sales prices of otherwise identical properties with and without that feature

10. _____ A method for determining adjustment or depreciation amounts that is useful when a property is sold and resold in a relatively short period

11. _____ Occurs when a person buys a property at one price and quickly sells it to another at an inflated price, usually within a short period

12. _____ A relationship among variables that is demonstrated when an observed change in the value of one variable is related to a corresponding change in the value of another variable

13. _____ A statistical technique for estimating a particular variable, such as probable sales price, using more than one other known variable

14. _____ The selection of market data so that the subject is contained within a range of data

15. _____ A method used to identify how a particular feature affects the value of a property by asking those who are knowledgeable about that market

MULTIPLE CHOICE QUESTIONS

Instructions: Circle your response and go to Appendix A to read the complete explanation for each question.

1. A homogeneous property is one that is _____ to the subject property.
    a. inferior
    b. superior
    c. similar
    d. all of the above

2. While researching comparable properties, Gary finds an identical comp in the same tract of homes. He notes that as part of the sales agreement, the seller partially financed the sale. Gary should:

    a. use the comparable with no further action.

    b. apply a cash equivalency technique to the comparable to adjust for the atypical financing.

    c. not use the comparable because it has atypical financing.

    d. apply a cash equivalency formula to the subject to adjust for the atypical financing.

3. Location adjustments may be based on:

    a. changes in highest and best use.

    b. proximity to negative factors such as highways.

    c. dissimilarity in natural amenities.

    d. all the above.

4. A comparable house sold nine months ago for $375,000. The appraiser concludes that property values have increased by 5% per year. The adjustment is:

    a. $13,750.

    b. $14,100.

    c. $18,675.

    d. $19,736.

5. In the sales comparison approach, the appraiser uses quantitative and/or qualitative analysis to derive an opinion of value. The two techniques:

    a. must always be used separately.

    b. can be used separately or in combination.

    c. should be combined for the best results.

    d. should only be combined if sufficient information is not available.

6. Adjustments are made:

    a. as a dollar amount only.

    b. as a percentage of the sales price.

    c. using pluses or minuses.

    d. in all of the above ways.

7. The sequence in which adjustments are made is unimportant if the adjustments are made:

    a. strictly on a dollar basis.

    b. in combination with dollar adjustments.

    c. on a percentage basis alone.

    d. on a case-by-case basis.

8. Kate located a comparable that recently sold for $450,000 that needed several adjustments: a $10,000 adjustment for a remodeled kitchen, a 5% adjustment for market conditions, and 3% for seller assisted financing. What is the adjusted value of the comparable?

    a. $449,000

    b. $463,175

    c. $468,300

    d. $475,000

9. Dawn locates a comparable sale that has three-car garage and a bonus room. The subject property has a two-car garage and no bonus room. On her adjustment grid, Dawn should apply a:

    a. positive adjustment to the comparable sale.

    b. negative adjustment to the comparable sale.

    c. positive adjustment to the subject property.

    d. negative adjustment to the subject property.

Use the following grid to answer 10 – 12:

Characteristic	Subject	Sale 1	Sale 2	Sale 3
Price		$400,00	$435,000	$390,000
Square Feet	1,600	1,600	1,600	1,600
Bedrooms	Four	Four	Four	Four
Bathrooms	Two	Two	Two	Two
Pool	Yes	No	Yes	No
Garage	2-car	3-car	3-car	2-car

10. What is the adjustment value for a pool in this neighborhood?
    a. $10,000
    b. $20,000
    c. $25,000
    d. $35,000

11. What is the adjustment value for an extra garage space in this neighborhood?
    a. $5,000
    b. $10,000
    c. $15,000
    d. $25,000

12. According to the adjustment grid on the previous page, what is the indicated value of the subject property?
    a. $400,000
    b. $415,000
    c. $425,000
    d. $432,000

13. Gayle purchased her home in the spring of 2006 for $225,000. She sold it 12 months later for $245,000. Using the sale-resale analysis, what is the annual rate of at which this market is increasing?
    a. 3%
    b. 9%
    c. 15%
    d. 20%

14. Linear regression is often used by appraisers to determine how one or more independent variables affect a dependent variable. Regression is a statistical analysis:
    a. assessing the association between two variables.
    b. measuring the decline in value of the subject property.
    c. determining the correlation of the estimates of value.
    d. used only for the valuation of non-realty components.

15. What is the primary limitation associated with using multiple regression analysis?
    a. It cannot be performed quickly
    b. It can only be used in areas where no two properties are alike
    c. Items having an effect on value such as condition or view cannot be estimated
    d. All sales in an area are usually factored into the analysis, not just the sales that are comparable to the subject

Finance and Cash Equivalency

Chapter

INTRODUCTION

The financing terms used to purchase a property can affect the purchase price. This is why primary verification is so important. Financing terms can vary in many ways. Sometimes a seller will pay buyer points in order to secure a lower rate or to secure a government-sponsored loan. When sellers are paying part of the buyer's costs, they often try to recoup this amount with a higher sales price. Wraparound loans, installment sales contracts, loan assumptions, and seller-carried financing can all affect the sales price of a property.

In this chapter, we will discuss the financing process and ways to take alternative financing and convert these terms into cash equivalency.

LEARNING OBJECTIVES

After reading this chapter, you will be able to:

- identify a cash equivalent sale.
- distinguish between the primary and secondary mortgage markets.
- identify the different types of financing techniques.
- identify special clauses found in real estate financing agreements.
- name common loan programs.

REAL ESTATE FINANCING PROCESS

Almost all real estate transactions involve some kind of financing. Few people have the cash to purchase a home, and even if they do, they often use financing since the federal government subsidizes homeowners who pay interest by making these payments tax deductible. As economic conditions change, the forces of supply and demand reshape the real estate market. Both of these factors affect the real estate market and help to create an evolving mortgage market. One of the biggest challenges facing residential appraisers is to keep up with the latest financing techniques and to determine how these affect sales prices.

With so many financing options available, homeownership has become easier in recent years. However, it has become more difficult for the appraiser to keep up—because of the various financing options.

As we indicated in the previous chapter, adjustments for financing are different from other adjustments in a significant manner. Other adjustments consider the differences between the subject and the comparable. However, financing adjustments consider the difference between the financing used for the comparable sale and that which is normally found in the market. A cash equivalent sale involves typical financing. A **cash equivalent sale** is a sale in which the financing does not affect the sales price. When appraisers adjust for financing, they are adjusting for the comparable's lack of cash equivalency that results from alternative or creative financing.

Some sellers agree to pay part of the buyer's closing costs including loan points that will result in a lower interest rate for the buyer. This is seen often in VA and FHA guaranteed loans, discussed later in the chapter. Some sellers attempt to recoup these fees by charging the buyer a slightly higher purchase price. Therefore, if the appraiser is considering a VA sale, it is good to use comparables that were also sold with the VA guarantee. If these comparables are not available, then a financing adjustment may be necessary.

CASH EQUIVALENCY

As mentioned earlier, **cash equivalence** in appraising is the price expressed in terms of cash. This is in contrast to a price expressed totally or partly in terms of the face amounts of notes or other securities that cannot sell at their face amounts. Calculating the cash equivalent price requires an appraiser to compare transactions involving atypical financing to transactions involving comparable properties financed at typical market terms. These sales are analyzed to determine if an adjustment for non-cash equivalency is warranted. This is referred to as the cash equivalency technique.

Mathematical models are sometimes used to analyze cash equivalency. It is important to ascertain if these models are truly reflecting market behavior. If the cash discounts indicated by the calculations are not recognized by buyers and sellers, then the adjustment is not recognized.

Remember that securities that are short-term and highly liquid may qualify for cash equivalency status. Generally, only those investments with original maturities of three months or less qualify as cash equivalents. Cash equivalency is thus determined only once—at the acquisition date. The total of cash and cash equivalents is treated as one single amount. When preparing the cash flow statement, any cash equivalent items are added to cash and the total is the target amount of cash flow to be reconciled on the cash flow statement.

In the typical real estate transaction, the down payment plus the loan are considered as cash equivalent as the seller is receiving all cash when the transaction settles. The problems for appraisers appear with sales that are made with the alternative financing techniques mentioned above.

THE FEDERAL RESERVE SYSTEM

The **Federal Reserve Bank System (the Fed)** is the nation's central bank, whose job it is to regulate the flow of money and credit to promote economic growth with stability. The Fed is divided into 12 districts across the country.

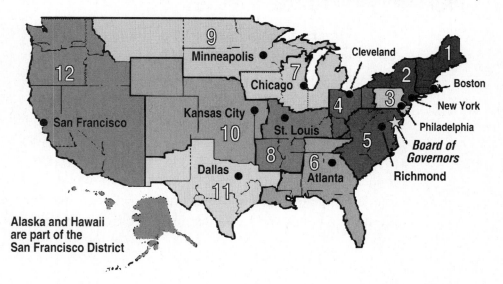

The goal of the Federal Reserve System is to maintain sound economic conditions. Part of this involves sound credit policies. The Fed works hard to control inflation and to make sure there is no deflation as well. The Fed regulates the flow of money in the marketplace indirectly through its member banks by controlling their reserve requirements and discount rates. The **discount rate** is the interest rate that is charged by the Federal Reserve Bank to its member banks for loans. The Fed requires member banks to keep a certain amount of their assets on hand as reserve funds. These reserves are not available for loans or any other use. By increasing the reserve requirements, the Fed in effect limits the amount of money that member banks can use to make loans. When the amount of money available for loans decreases, then interest rates increase.

Increasing interest rates are often the catalyst that leads buyers and sellers to use alternative financing. Interest rate increases also have a tendency to slow down an over-heated economy. Lowering interest rates can cause the economy to heat up and the prices of homes have a tendency to increase, as there is more effective demand as more people can qualify for loans. Home prices tend to be inversely proportional to interest rates. Lower rates yield higher home prices and the opposite is true as well.

Federal Reserve member banks are permitted to borrow money from the district reserve banks to enhance their lending capabilities. The interest rate the banks pay for the federal funds is called the discount rate. The **prime rate**, which is the rate the bank charges its strongest customers (those with the highest credit ratings), is heavily influenced by the discount rate.

PRIMARY MORTGAGE MARKET

The **primary mortgage market** is the market in which lenders make mortgage loans by lending directly to borrowers. The primary mortgage market is the source of much of the appraiser's business as it concerns federally-related transactions. If the federal government regulates the agency, and it provides loans, then the transaction is defined as a federally-related transaction. However, the argument is made that the federal legislation does not control government programs so loans going to them are not federally related. Federal law governs the banks that are processing the loans. Is a lender's appraisal a federally-related transaction? Since the loans begin with banks or savings and loans that are federally controlled, it is reasonable to answer, "Yes."

Appraisal regulations apply to real estate-related financial transactions entered into by the agencies or by federally regulated financial institutions. This includes commercial banks, savings and loan associations, credit unions, bank holding companies, and the non-bank subsidiaries of bank holding companies. If a real estate-related transaction exceeds $250,000, the appraiser may presume that it is a federally-related transaction, unless specifically notified by the institution that it is not a federally-related transaction.

For a federally-related transaction, the appraiser must be licensed or certified by his or her respective state office of real estate appraisal. Federal Law (Title XI, FIRREA) mandated this.

The primary mortgage market is made up of the lenders who originate real estate loans. These institutions make money available to borrowers. The borrower is seeking financing in order to make a purchase or to refinance an existing loan. The lender is looking for a loan that is an investment. The lender requires enough income to be attractive as an investment.

Basic Sources of Income for Lenders

1. Finance charges such as loan origination fees and discount points. **Discount points** are fees equal to a percentage of the loan amount and are used to buy down the interest rate.

2. Recurring income such as interest payment for loans that are kept as part of the bank's portfolio.

3. Service fees for collecting payments from the borrower on behalf of whoever purchased the loan from the originator.

Since lenders derive much of their income from loan fees, they sell their loans as soon as possible to the secondary mortgage market to obtain more money. This allows the bank to make more loans and collect more loan fees. Part of the role of the appraiser is to determine if the seller of a property paid any of these fees and what impact it had on the purchase price.

Servicing loans can be very profitable as well and some companies buy the servicing contracts from other mortgage lenders or the investors who have purchased the loans. **Servicing loans** is the act of supervising and administering a loan after it has been made.

Loan Servicing Activities

- Collecting payments and impounds
- Accounting
- Bookkeeping
- Preparing insurance and tax records
- Following up on loan payments and delinquencies

The latter has become very important as many homeowners have variable rate loans that they are not able to pay as interest rates rise. Some of the major lenders in the primary market can serve as potential clients for the appraiser.

Potential Appraiser Clients

- Savings and Loans
- Commercial banks
- Credit Unions
- Mortgage banking companies
- Mortgage brokers
- Insurance companies
- Pension funds
- Endowment funds

The savings and loan institutions and commercial banks are known as fiduciary lenders. A **fiduciary lender** is a lender with an obligation to protect and preserve their depositors' funds. These fiduciary lenders are supervised by the FDIC and governed by FIRREA and the Office of Thrift Supervision (OTS).

Credit unions are cooperative organizations whose members send money into savings accounts. Credit unions have moved from short-term loans, such as home improvement loans and short-term consumer loans, to long-term mortgage lending. Credit unions often offer desirable loans to their own members.

Insurance companies generate large sums of money from the premium charges. A certain amount of money is kept to service policies, but a great deal of money is available for real estate loans. Insurance companies generally provide funds for large commercial enterprises, apartment buildings, and industrial sites.

Mortgage banking companies originate mortgage loans with money belonging to insurance companies, pension funds, and their own funds. This makes them direct lenders. **Direct lenders** lend their own funds and handle the entire loan process from origination to funding. Like the other banks, they derive income from loan fees and servicing fees. Mortgage banking companies are often organized as stock companies.

Mortgage brokers are not direct lenders but they bring the borrower to the lender. A mortgage broker originates a loan by taking the application from a borrower and selling that unclosed loan to another mortgage lender. Appraisers have to be very careful when working with mortgage brokers as they often put pressure on the appraiser to "hit the number" so that a loan will be made. Appraiser independence is extremely important. Part of the appraiser's job when working with mortgage brokers is to educate them on what can and cannot be part of the appraisal process. Fannie Mae now has a policy of making lenders buy back loans in which values were substantiated by faulty appraisals. Fannie Mae also reports appraisers who perform these faulty appraisals to the appropriate state office for possible disciplinary action.

SECONDARY MORTGAGE MARKET

In contrast to the primary mortgage market, in which lending institutions make mortgage loans directly to borrowers, the **secondary mortgage market** refers to the market that involves the buying and selling of existing

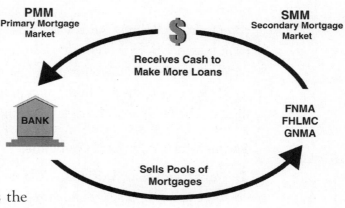

mortgage loans from the primary mortgage market or from each other. The secondary market serves as a source of funds for the primary lenders so they can continue to make loans and generate income. The activity of the secondary market is vital when the supply of money is low. The secondary market stimulates both the housing construction industry and the mortgage market by buying existing loans and expanding the types of loans that are available.

As we indicated above, when a loan is sold, the originator often retains the loan servicing. When payments are collected, they are passed along to the investor who purchased the loan. The investor is charged a fee for this service. It is interesting to note that the original lender often acts as if it still owns the loan and makes demands upon the borrower for late fees and prepayment penalties even though the lender has loaned this money out again many times.

The process of assembling a number of mortgage loans into one package prior to selling them to an investor is called **warehousing**. Securities that represent shares in these pooled mortgages are then sold to investors. There are specific underwriting requirements for the pooled loans designed to protect the investors. It is important to ensure that there is adequate collateral to provide a degree of safety.

Major Purchasers of Pooled Mortgages

- FNMA or Fannie Mae

- GNMA or Ginnie Mae

- FHLMC or Freddie Mac

The **Federal National Mortgage Association (FNMA)**—also known as Fannie Mae—is a privately-owned corporation that issues its own stock (NYSE: FNM). FNMA buys conventional, FHA, and VA loans in the secondary mortgage market to make sure mortgage money is available for people in communities all across America. Fannie Mae buys a block or pool of mortgages from a lender in exchange for mortgage-backed securities. Fannie Mae also develops appraisal guidelines that help to standardize the appraisal process in the lending industry. Every appraiser who performs appraisals for lenders needs to be familiar with these guidelines.

Fannie Mae's Appraisal Guidelines

1. **Appraiser Qualifications.** Chapter 1 discusses the lender's responsibility for selecting appraisers and for reviewing their appraisals both initially and through an on-going basis. It also covers the use of supervisory or review appraisers and Fannie Mae's right to refuse to accept appraisals prepared by specific appraisers.

2. **Appraisal Documentation and Certifications.** Chapter 2 describes the various appraisal report forms that are to be used to document an appraisal

and any required exhibits to them. It also discusses requirements related to the age of an appraisal report, explains the types of appraisals needed for proposed and existing construction, and references the various certifications that an appraiser must make.

3. **Special Appraisal Considerations.** Chapter 3 discusses considerations that should be given to properties with unusual features. It points out the need for properties to meet specific eligibility criteria in order for the mortgage to be delivered to FNMA, and explains the detrimental effect that certain environmental conditions can have on a property's value.

4. **Reviewing the Appraisal Report.** Chapter 4 discusses the requirements for analyzing a property and its appraisal.

Unlike Fannie Mae, the **Government National Mortgage Association (GNMA)**—also known as Ginnie Mae—is a governmental agency created as a wholly-owned corporation within the Department of Housing and Urban Development (HUD) that serves low-to-moderate-income homebuyers. It is part of HUD and organized as a corporation without capital stock. Using their tandem plan, FNMA and GNMA can join forces in times of tight money. The tandem plans allow FNMA to purchase high-risk, low-yield loans at full market rates.

The **Federal Home Loan Mortgage Corporation (FHLMC)**—commonly known as Freddie Mac—is also a government-sponsored, shareholder-owned (NYSE: FRE) company whose mission is to provide liquidity, stability, and affordability to the housing market. FHLMC links Main Street to Wall Street by purchasing, securitizing, and investing in home mortgages. This provides homeowners and renters with lower housing costs with better access to home financing. Freddie Mac can sell bonds on the open market and use the pools of mortgages as security. However, Freddie Mac does not guarantee the payment of the loans it purchases.

FINANCING TECHNIQUES

There are many different ways to finance a purchase and these can affect the appraisal process. The borrower provides the lender with a promissory note that contains the terms of the loan, interest rates, payment dates, late payment fees, pre-payment penalties, and balloon payments (if any). These notes are secured by a mortgage or a trust deed—depending in which state the property is located. The equity in the property is offered for security for the loan.

When the note is offered for a refinance, all of the borrower's assets are available to secure the loan. The two basic kinds of loans are those secured with a straight note and those that are amortized. A **straight note** is a promissory note in which payments of interest only are made periodically during the term of the note, with the principal payment due in one lump sum upon maturity. Many home equity lines of credit are like this—the borrower only pays the interest amounts due on the loan. The principal is paid through a separate payment when the borrower wants to pay off the loan amount. This is called a balloon payment. Under an installment loan, a **balloon payment** is a final payment that is substantially larger than any other payment and repays the debt in full.

> Example: What is the monthly payment on a straight note if the principal is $100,000, the interest rate is 8.25%, and the term is 10 years?
>
> Solution: Since this is a straight note, there is no amortization. $100,000 x 8.25% = $8,250.00 annual interest. Divide this by 12 months to get a monthly payment of $687.50. At the end of the 10 year, the entire $100,000 is due.

A **fully-amortized note** is the most common type of loan with institutional lenders. Interest is charged on the outstanding principal balance at the rate and term agreed upon by the lender and borrower in a loan. Most of the early payments are interest with little going toward the principal balance. Each payment is first applied to the interest owed and the balance is applied toward paying down the principal.

FIXED-RATE MORTGAGE

A common type of fully-amortized note is a **fixed-rate mortgage (FRM)**. This type of loan consists of regular, periodic payments of both interest and principal, which pay off the debt completely by the end of the term. These types of loans are available for 40 years, 30 years, 20 years, 15 years, and even 10 years. This is why it is important for appraisers to ensure the property being appraised has an economic life equal to at least the term of the loan. The following table illustrates the relationship of interest and principal payments over time in a 15-year loan.

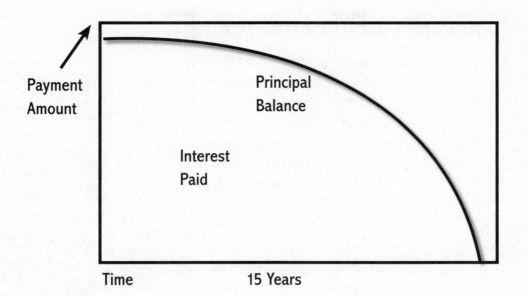

ADJUSTABLE-RATE MORTGAGE

As home prices rise, adjustable-rate mortgages are more popular. An adjustable note, or **adjustable-rate mortgage (ARM)**, is one with an interest rate that adjusts to a movable economic index. The interest rate in the note varies upward or downward over the term of the loan, depending on the agreed-upon index. A variable rate must be based on a publicly available index such as the prime rate published in some major daily newspapers, LIBOR, or a U.S. Treasury bill rate.

ARMs are used to qualify buyers for larger loans because they normally start with a low rate and then fluctuate depending upon the index used. The buyer is qualified at the low rate with the smaller payment. Details about how the note rates will change is contained in the promissory notes.

Many of these notes allow for negative amortization with the unpaid interest being added to the loan balance. **Negative amortization** occurs when monthly installment payments are insufficient to pay the interest, so any unpaid interest is added to the principal due. As interest rates rise, the payments also rise, and the borrower can end up losing his house and other assets if the loan was a refinance. As this is written, interest rates have slowly been increasing as have the number of foreclosures. Some appraisers are spending the bulk of their time appraising houses that are in the foreclosure process. In order to minimize further risk, lenders are currently implementing guidelines that qualify borrowers on their ability to make payments at the adjusted rate in addition to the initial rate.

REVERSE ANNUITY MORTGAGE

Older homeowners with equity in their property, but not much of a monthly income, can use a reverse annuity mortgage. A **reverse annuity mortgage** is

a loan for homeowners 62 years of age and older who have paid off their mortgages or have only small remaining mortgage balances. With this type of mortgage, the lender makes payments to the homeowner. The payments are based upon the equity the homeowner has remaining in the property that is given as security for the loan.

Reverse annuity mortgages are becoming more popular as baby boomers reach retirement age. Reverse annuity mortgages allow seniors to supplement fixed income and enjoy life more with the extra income. The loan is paid off when the borrower dies and the estate pays off the loan or the property is sold and the lender is paid from the proceeds.

HOME EQUITY LINE OF CREDIT

A **home equity line of credit (HELOC)** is an example of an open-ended loan in which a borrower's home serves as collateral. A HELOC is a type of second lien that taps into a property owner's equity and creates a revolving credit line.

The lender commits to the full amount of the line of credit, but the borrower has the choice to use it as needed. If there is no balance, there are no fees on the line of credit. The interest rate on the initial amount borrowed can be fixed, but it is popular to tie these loans to the bank's prime lending rates. Open-ended loans are preferable to most home improvement loans as well as credit card lines of credit. These loans give the borrower a great deal of flexibility and financial power.

Different Uses for Home Equity Lines of Credit

- Purchase additional real estate
- Finance the purchase of expensive items

- Consolidate existing installment loans on credit card debt

- Medical, dental, home improvement, or other expenses

ALTERNATIVE FINANCING

A special challenge is presented when the appraiser is considering a comparable sale that was sold with alternative or creative financing. Alternative financing occurs most often when the borrower is unable to obtain financing through conventional methods.

Common Types of Alternative Financing

- Seller carry-back

- Installment sale

- Assuming existing financing

- Wraparound loan

- Equity sharing

SELLER CARRY-BACK

The simplest form of alternative financing is a purchase money mortgage when the seller carries a note to help the buyer who does not have an adequate down payment for conventional financing. The note normally is for at least five years. This is a junior loan—as the primary mortgage is placed ahead of the seller loan. Sellers need protection in case the buyer defaults on the first mortgage, for the seller's note can be erased. Most sellers record a **request for notice** with the county recorder and the recorder notifies the seller if the buyer's first loan goes into default. The seller then has the right to bring the first mortgage current and file a notice of default on the second.

Appraisers should remember that their opinion of value is determined in terms of cash equivalency. As discussed in the previous chapter, adjustments for financing are significantly different from other adjustments. Other adjustments consider the differences between the subject and the comparable. However, financing adjustments consider the difference between the financing used for the comparable sale and that which is normally found in the market.

Typical financing presupposes that the sale is a cash equivalent sale. When appraisers adjust for financing, they are adjusting for the comparables lack of cash equivalency resulting from the alternative or creative financing.

INSTALLMENT SALES CONTRACT

The installment sales contract is a financing instrument with many different names. It may be called an installment sales contract, a contract of sale, an agreement of sale, a conditional sales contract, a contract for deed, or a land sales contract.

An **installment sales contract** provides a real estate financing instrument in which the buyer agrees to purchase the property, but the seller keeps the title until certain conditions are met. The buyer is given possession and use of the property. For this use, the buyer agrees to make regular payments to the seller. In essence, the seller becomes the lender in this type of sale. Once the buyer is in a position to secure his or her own financing, then the title passes to the buyer in a manner similar to a normal sale.

The lack of immediate ownership poses some risks for the buyer. Should the seller have financial problems, declare bankruptcy, become incompetent, or encumber the title during the contract period, the buyer could encounter legal problems trying to obtain ownership per contract.

The seller has some risks, as well. If the buyer defaults on his or her payments to the seller, it can be very difficult to remove the buyer from the property. This could lead to a protracted legal battle, which defeats the purpose of the agreement. With these risks to both buyer and seller, installment sales are not very common.

ASSUMING THE SELLER'S LOAN

Using existing financing can provide an alternative means to purchase a property. If the buyer is well qualified and has enough cash for the down payment, it is normally less expensive to take over an existing loan than to secure a new loan. An **assumption clause** allows a buyer to assume responsibility for the full payment of the loan with the lender's knowledge and consent. With the approval of the lender, the buyer takes over primary liability for the loan, with the original borrower secondarily liable if there is a default. Many of the loan costs are avoided, and in some cases, the interest rate on the seller's loan is less than the prevailing interest rates on new real estate loans.

A buyer may also purchase a property subject to the existing loan. A **subject to clause** allows a buyer to take over a loan, making the payments without the knowledge or approval of the lender. The original borrower remains responsible for the loan, even though the buyer takes title and makes the payments. The seller retains liability for the loan and can have his or her credit impacted in a negative manner if the buyer is late making payments.

WRAPAROUND LOAN

A **wraparound loan**, also known as an all-inclusive trust deed (AITD), is another type of seller financing. This type of loan wraps an existing loan with a new loan, and the borrower makes one payment for both. The wraparound loan provides additional financing for the buyer without paying off the senior loan(s). The second lender (seller) gives the buyer a new increased loan that wraps around the existing financing. The buyer then makes payment to the seller on the larger loan. This device has benefits to the seller because the new loan normally has a higher interest rate than the original loan.

There are some important negotiation aspects of a wraparound. For example, who gets the amortization on the first mortgage? A wraparound can be used to refinance a property as well as to finance a purchase. The lender who has the senior loan does not normally permit a wraparound. Therefore, the borrower has to have a plan if the lender calls the loan. Almost all loans from banks and savings and loan institutions have an acceleration clause.

EQUITY SHARING

Equity shares present another alternative financing technique to help buyers who do not have an adequate down payment to purchase a property. Equity shares are normally done when the buyer has the ability to increase the value in the house by providing remodeling tasks. The equity partner normally supplies the cash for the purchase or qualifies for a loan using his or her credit. A partnership agreement is drafted that sets the time limits for the partnership and explains how the partner living in the property can buy out the equity partner. If this is not possible, then the property is sold and the proceeds are divided in accordance with the provisions of the equity share contract.

FINANCING CLAUSES

In addition to repayment terms, most real estate financing agreements contain special clauses or conditions that give the lender the power to call the loan.

When a borrower signs loan documents, he or she is agreeing to the following clauses that are currently used in most loan agreements.

Special Clauses in Real Estate Finance Agreements

1. Acceleration clause

2. Alienation clause

3. Prepayment clause

An **acceleration clause** gives the lender the right to call the loan due and demand repayment immediately on occurrence of a specific event. If the borrower fails to pay real property taxes, loan payments or willfully damages the property.

The **alienation** or **due-on-sale clause** is a type of acceleration clause. A lender may call the entire note due if the original borrower transfers (alienates) ownership of the property to someone else. Federal law allows banks to enforce due on sale clauses except for transfers between spouses and transfers to family trusts.

A **prepayment clause** is a real moneymaker for banks and other financial institutions. This clause allows a lender to collect a certain percentage of a loan as a penalty for an early payoff. A typical prepayment penalty is six months' interest on the amount prepaid that exceeds 20% of the original principal amount of the loan.

> Example: Assume that the original loan amount is $200,000. Two years later the balance of the loan principal is $197,000. The interest rate is 6%. If the buyer pays the loan off, the penalty is as follows:
>
> $200,000 is the original loan amount. 20% of this is $40,000.
>
> $197,000 is the existing loan balance.
>
> $40,000 can be paid with no penalty.
>
> There is a penalty on $157,000. (197,000 − 40,000)
>
> $157,000 subject to prepayment penalty. The interest rate is 6% per annum or 3% for six months.
>
> $157,000 x 3% = $4,710 which is the prepayment penalty

Not all loans carry a prepayment penalty, but those that do can be expensive if the property owner needs to sell the property.

LOAN PROGRAMS

All loans can be classified according to their loan terms, loan-to-value ratio, and whether they have government backing. First, as we have already learned, all of the various loans are classified by their terms—fixed-rate loans, adjustable-rate loans, and their combinations.

In addition, mortgage loans are classified by the loan-to-value ratio or LTV. The **loan-to-value ratio (LTV)** is the ratio of debt to the value of the property. Lenders, especially mortgage brokers, use the LTV to pressure appraisers to hit the number so the loan package can be put together.

> Example: For a conforming loan of $417,000, the lender may be looking at a LTV of 75%. The value they "need" is determined by calculating the appraised value.
>
> $417,000 is 75% of what amount?
>
> $417,000 ÷ .75 = $556,000

The order is placed for the appraisal and the appraiser is told by the lender, "We need a value of $556,000." Some appraisers choose to risk their license and hit the number regardless of whether there is data to support this position. This is often done in order to secure repeat business from a particular lender. However, there are buyers who are extremely thankful when an honest appraiser refuses to hit the number—thereby keeping the buyer from overpaying for the property. Appraiser independence is an important factor toward achieving the goal of USPAP, which is to create public trust.

Finally, loans are classified by whether they have government backing— conventional or government loans. Some lenders specialize in only conventional conforming loans, whereas full service lenders offer a wide selection of loan programs including conventional, government-sponsored FHA and VA loans, and non-conforming loans, which include jumbo and subprime loans.

CONVENTIONAL LOANS

A **conventional loan** is any loan made by lenders without governmental guarantees (FHA-insured or VA-guaranteed). Conventional loans provide the least amount of risk for the lender as the LTV is lower than many other programs. A low LTV results from a large down payment and a corresponding low risk loan. If the loan is issued as part of a purchase money transaction, then the property is security for the loan. If the loan is issued for a refinance, the borrower loses his or her purchase money status and all of his or her assets are available as security for the loan. Some lenders loan amounts that exceed the value of the property if the borrower has many assets and a good credit score. Many lenders prefer a drive-by inspection of the building as the property is only part of the security for the loan. Conventional loans may be conforming or non-conforming.

CONFORMING LOANS

Even though lenders can set the criteria for evaluating a borrower's credit-worthiness, **conforming loans** have terms and conditions that follow the Fannie Mae and Freddie Mac guidelines, which sets loan limits to a certain amount. These loans are called "A" paper loans, or prime loans, and can be made to purchase or refinance homes (one-to-four residential units). Fannie Mae and Freddie Mac guidelines establish the maximum loan amount, borrower credit and income requirements, down payment, and suitable properties. As mentioned previously, FNMA is forcing lenders to buy back loans that were made with faulty appraisals.

When borrowers need a higher LTV than is available with conventional loans, they can often get a loan with private mortgage insurance (PMI). **Private mortgage insurance (PMI)** is a type of mortgage guarantee insurance required by conventional lenders on the first part of a high-risk loan. PMI is required for most homebuyers who obtain loans that are more than 80% of their new home's value. With the higher LTV, the lender wants more security and PMI provides this additional security. The problem with PMI is it is expensive and sometimes it is hard for the borrower to get enough home equity to be able to drop the additional insurance. Some lenders will provide loans up to 95% of the appraised value if the borrower gets PMI.

NON-CONFORMING LOANS

Sometimes either the borrower's creditworthiness or the size of the loan does not meet conventional lending standards. In that case, a non-conforming loan is used. **Non-conforming loans** do not meet the standards of Fannie Mae and Freddie Mac—these include jumbo loans and subprime loans.

JUMBO LOANS

Loans that exceed the maximum loan limit set by Fannie Mae and Freddie Mac are called **jumbo loans**. Because jumbo loans are not funded by these government-sponsored entities, they usually carry a higher interest rate and some additional underwriting requirements.

SUBPRIME LOANS

Loans that do not meet the borrower credit requirements of Fannie Mae and Freddie Mac are called **subprime loans**—also known as "B" and "C" paper loans as opposed to "A" paper conforming loans. Subprime loans are offered to borrowers who may have recently filed for bankruptcy or foreclosure, or have had late payments on their credit reports. Their purpose is to offer temporary financing to these applicants until they can qualify for conforming "A" financing. Due to the higher risk associated with lending to borrowers that have a poor credit history, subprime loans typically require a larger down payment and a higher interest rate.

Prior to 1990, it was very difficult for anyone to obtain a mortgage if he or she did not qualify for a conventional FHA or VA loan. Many borrowers with bad credit are good people who honestly intended to pay their bills on time. Catastrophic events such as the loss of a job or a family illness can lead to missed or late payments or even foreclosure and bankruptcy. Subprime loans were developed to help higher risk borrowers obtain a mortgage.

GOVERNMENT PARTICIPATION IN REAL ESTATE FINANCE

Two federal agencies help make it possible for people to buy homes they would never be able to purchase without government involvement. These two federal agencies that participate in real estate financing are the Federal Housing Administration (FHA) and the Veterans Administration (VA).

FEDERAL HOUSING ADMINISTRATION (FHA)

The **Federal Housing Administration (FHA)** is a federal government agency that insures private mortgage loans for financing of homes and home repairs. The FHA operates as part of HUD and it does not build homes or lend money. The agency insures loans against borrower default. These loans are made through FHA approved lenders who use FHA approved appraisers. Appraisers on the FHA panel are required to perform some home inspection duties as part of the appraisal inspection.

The most popular FHA program is Title II, Section 203(b), which deals with fixed-rate loans with terms of 10 to 30 years for one to four units. In recent years, there has been a great deal of real estate fraud perpetrated on loans that had FHA guarantees. Because of this type of fraud, the FHA hired a Certified General Appraiser as part of a federal task force to investigate and stop this kind of fraud. A budget of $50,000,000 was set aside for this task.

Requirements for FHA Loan Guarantees

- The borrower is charged a percentage of the loan as a premium for the FHA insurance. The borrower or some other party at the closing of the loan pays this premium. If the other party is the seller, this could affect the appraiser and require a financing concession. This fee may be financed as part of the loan. FHA sometimes also charges a monthly premium. The insurance premiums vary depending upon the type of loan and whether or not the property is a single-family residence.

- FHA has standards that cover the type and construction of the buildings, quality of the neighborhood and the creditworthiness of the borrower. Once again, this requirement can have repercussions for the appraiser and affect his or her scope of work.

- The real estate has to be appraised by an appraiser who is approved by FHA. If the purchase price exceeds the FHA-appraised value, the buyer may pay the difference in cash as part of the down payment. FHA varies the amount of loans that will be approved—depending upon what part of the country the property is located.

A key feature of FHA insured loans is that they may be prepaid at any time with no penalty. If the loan was initiated after August 2, 1985, no prior notification of the exercise of the pre-payment option is required.

An important aspect of FHA insured loans that affects appraisers is whether or not the loans can be assumed. This depends upon when the loans were issued since FHA has changed its rules over time. If the loans were originated before December 1986, there is normally no problem with assuming the loan. If the loan was originated after December 1989, the loan can only be assumed if the buyer is completely qualified. This requires the buyer to go through the complete qualification process.

With FHA appraisals, the discount points have to be considered as part of the financing analysis. For a loan guaranteed by FHA, the lender has the option to charge discount points in addition to loan origination fees. These fees include the mortgage insurance premium, buy-down fees, prepaid items, and impound or escrow amounts in addition to the loan origination fees. In some transactions, the seller pays all of these fees and this can affect the purchase price. Loan points are deductible to the buyer regardless of who pays them.

VA GUARANTEED LOANS

The **Department of Veteran Affairs (VA)** functions to guarantee loans to purchase and construct homes for eligible veterans and their spouses. This includes spouses of veterans who died in a service related incident. The VA also guarantees loans for mobile homes including a lot to place a mobile home. The VA has criteria that are spelled out on their website that discuss eligibility and how to obtain VA benefits including loan guarantees.

The VA assists veterans in purchasing a home with little or no down payment. The interest rates are competitive with conventional loans. Like FHA, VA does not loan money—but it does guarantee loans made by lending institutions approved by the VA. There is no limit on the amount of a loan a veteran can obtain placed by the VA. The lender is responsible for making this determination. The VA guarantees for the typical loan of $144,000 to $203,000 is the lesser of $36,000 or 40% of the loan amount. For larger loans, the VA will guarantee the lesser of $50,750 or 25% of the loan amount.

The VA issues a **certificate of reasonable value (CRV)** for the property being purchased. The CRV states the value of the property as determined by a VA-approved appraiser. The CRV sets the upper limit on what VA will insure and the veteran can pay purchase prices higher than the appraisal amount as indicated on the CRV. The buyer using his or her VA benefits pays a loan origination fee to the lender, as well as a funding fee of 1.25 - 2% depending upon how much the veteran provides as a down payment. Reasonable discount points may be charged on a VA loan and either the buyer or the seller may pay them. This is another area the appraiser has to investigate before he or she decides if a financing adjustment is needed.

As with FHA, there is no prepayment penalty for a VA loan, and the veteran may repay the loan at any given time. Once the loan is repaid, the veteran may become eligible to obtain another VA guaranteed loan. VA loans are assumable under certain conditions—the VA has to approve the new buyer and the assumption agreement.

SUMMARY

This chapter covered real estate financing, which is important data relevant to the appraisal process. Almost all real estate transactions involve some kind of financing. Few people have the cash to purchase a home, and even if they do, they often use financing since the federal government subsidizes homeowners who pay interest by making these payments tax deductible. One of the big challenges facing residential appraisers is to keep up with the latest financing techniques and to determine how these affect sales prices.

The mortgage market is composed of the primary and secondary mortgage markets. The **primary mortgage market** is the market in which lenders make mortgage loans by lending directly to borrowers. The **secondary mortgage market** refers to the market that involves the buying and selling of existing mortgage loans from the primary mortgage market or from each other. The secondary market serves as a source of funds for the primary lenders so that they can continue to make loans and generate income.

There are many different ways to finance a purchase and these can affect the appraisal process. Some of the conventional ways include a **fixed-rate mortgage (FRM)**, **adjustable-rate mortgage (ARM)**, and a **reverse annuity mortgage**. When conventional methods of financing do not suffice, alternative financing is available in the form of seller carry-back loans, **equity shares**, **installment sales contracts**, **wraparound loans**, and **home equity lines of credit (HELOC)**.

In addition to repayment terms, most real estate financing agreements contain special clauses or conditions like an **acceleration clause**, **alienation clause**, and **prepayment clause**.

The **loan-to-value ratio (LTV)** is the ratio of debt to the value of the property. A **conventional loan** is a type of loan that does not contain any government guarantees or insurance. Loans that carry these guarantees are insured by the **Federal Housing Administration (FHA)** and the **Department of Veteran Affairs (VA)**.

Appraisers have to be careful in their valuation analysis by reviewing the purchase documents as mandated in USPAP SR 1-5. They need to analyze the financing to see if it is resulting in higher purchase prices than the market data will support.

CHAPTER 8 REVIEW EXERCISES

MATCHING EXERCISE

Instructions: Write the letter of the matching term on the blank line before its definition. Answers are in Appendix A.

Terms

A. acceleration clause

B. adjustable-rate mortgage (ARM)

C. amortized loan

D. cash equivalent sale

E. conventional loan

F. direct lender

G. discount point

H. discount rate

I. Federal Housing Administration (FHA)

J. Federal Home Loan Mortgage Corporation (FHLMC)

K. Federal National Mortgage Association (FNMA)

L. fiduciary lender

M. fixed-rate amortized mortgage

N. Government National Mortgage Association (GNMA)

O. home equity line of credit (HELOC)

P. installment sales contract

Q. prepayment clause

R. private mortgage insurance (PMI)

S. primary mortgage market

T. reverse annuity mortgage

U. secondary mortgage market

V. servicing loans

W. straight note

X. The Federal Reserve Bank System (the Fed)

Y. warehousing

Z. wraparound loan

Definitions

1. _____ A sale in which the financing does not affect the sales price

2. _____ The nation's central bank, whose job it is to regulate the flow of money and credit to promote economic growth with stability

3. _____ The interest rate that is charged by the Federal Reserve Bank to its member banks for loans

4. _____ The market in which lenders make mortgage loans by lending directly to borrowers

5. _____ The act of supervising and administering a loan after it has been made

6. _____ A lender with an obligation to protect and preserve its depositors' funds

7. _____ A lender that lends its own funds and handles the entire loan process from origination to funding

8. _____ The market that involves the buying and selling of existing mortgage loans from the primary mortgage market or from each other

9. _____ The process of assembling into one package a number of mortgage loans, prior to selling them to an investor

10. _____ A government-sponsored, shareholder-owned company that works in the secondary mortgage market to make sure mortgage money is available for people in communities all across America

11. _____ A governmental agency created as a wholly-owned corporation within the Department of Housing and Urban Development (HUD) that serves low to moderate-income homebuyers

12. _____ A government-sponsored, shareholder-owned (NYSE: FRE) company whose mission is to provide liquidity, stability and affordability to the housing market

13. _____ A promissory note in which payments of interest only are made periodically during the term of the note, with the principal payment due in one lump sum upon maturity

14. _____ A type of loan consisting of regular, periodic payments of both interest and principal, which pay off the debt completely by the end of the term

15. _____ A type of loan with an interest rate that adjusts to a movable economic index

16. _____ A type of loan that uses its built-up equity to pay the borrower a fixed annuity, based on a percentage of the property value

17. _____ A real estate financing instrument in which the buyer agrees to purchase the property, but the seller keeps the title until certain conditions are met

18. _____ A type of loan that wraps an existing loan with a new loan, and the borrower makes one payment for both

19. _____ A type of second lien that taps into a property owner's equity and creates a revolving credit line

20. _____ Mortgage guarantee insurance required by conventional lenders on the first part of a high risk loan

MULTIPLE CHOICE QUESTIONS

Instructions: Circle your response and go to Appendix A to read the complete explanation for each question.

1. The Federal Reserve Bank System (the Fed) indirectly manipulates the flow of money by:
   a. controlling the reserve requirements and discount rates.
   b. offering loans directly to consumers.
   c. allowing banks to set their own reserve requirements.
   d. selling mortgage-backed securities to the public.

2. Lenders make their income from:
   a. origination fees.
   b. interest payments from loans.
   c. service fees.
   d. all of the above.

3. Pat recently received his appraiser's license. After deciding on a marketing budget, Pat makes a list of potential clients. Who are Pat's potential clients?
   a. Savings and loan institutions
   b. Mortgage brokers
   c. Commercial banks
   d. All of the above

4. Mortgage banking companies originate mortgage loans that can come from their own funds. This is an example of a:
   a. direct lender.
   b. mortgage broker.
   c. mortgage servicer.
   d. credit union.

5. One of the functions of the Federal National Mortgage Association (FNMA), otherwise known as Fannie Mae, includes:

    a. developing appraisal guidelines.

    b. determining reserve requirements for banks.

    c. determining interest rates for the primary mortgage market.

    d. manipulating the flow of money in the economy.

6. Tom, a mortgage broker, asks Sally if she could appraise a property for a client. Sally willingly accepts the assignment and travels to the property. Upon arrival, she notices the home has unusual features. In order to comply with Fannie Mae's appraisal guidelines for this property's unique features, she should refer to:

    a. Chapter 1.

    b. Chapter 2.

    c. Chapter 3.

    d. Chapter 4.

7. Which of the following is not a function of Freddie Mac?

    a. Guaranteeing the payments of purchased loans

    b. Helping homeowners and renters with low housing costs

    c. Investing in home mortgages

    d. Providing increased access to home financing

8. A(n) _____ is the most common type of loan with institutional lenders.

    a. fixed-rate mortgage

    b. adjustable-rate mortgage

    c. interest-only loan

    d. fully-amortized note

9. Fred is currently exploring different financing options. After doing some initial research, he prefers a fully-amortized loan that will provide regular payments that cover interest as well as principal for the life of the loan. He wants the lowest payment possible so a 40-year term is not out of the question. What type of loan should Fred seek?

    a. Adjustable-rate mortgage (ARM)

    b. Fixed-rate mortgage (FRM)

    c Interest-only mortgage

    d. Reverse annuity mortgage

10. Which of the following is used to help figure out the adjusted rate in an ARM?

    a. Any economic index
    b. LIBOR
    c. LABOR
    d. Both (a) and (b)

11. Ted is quickly reaching retirement age and needs a way to supplement his social security income to fund his hobbies. He has owned his property for 25 years so he has a lot of equity in his home. What type of mortgage would be ideal for Ted?

    a. Adjustable-rate mortgage (ARM)
    b. Interest-only mortgage
    c. Reverse annuity mortgage
    d. Seller carry-back financing

12. Pam is planning to remodel her kitchen. She receives bids ranging from $40,000 – $50,000 for the project. Which of the following is often used for home improvements?

    a. Seller carry-back financing
    b. Home equity line of credit (HELOC)
    c. Reverse annuity mortgage
    d. Credit card

13. A(n) _____ clause gives the lender the right to call the loan due and demand repayment immediately on occurrence of a specific event.

    a. acceleration
    b. alienation
    c. due-on-sale
    d. prepayment

14. John's loan has an LTV of 80%. The loan amount is $330,000. What is the purchase price of John's property?

    a. $366,000
    b. $408,600
    c. $412,500
    d. $660,000

15. A jumbo loan is a type of _____ loan.

    a. conforming
    b. non-conforming
    c. subprime
    d. government-sponsored

Income Approach: Analysis of Income and Expenses

9

Chapter

INTRODUCTION

An investor typically purchases income-producing property and the earning power is the critical element affecting the property value. In general, the higher the earning power of the property, the higher the value. These two are directly proportional. The analysis of cost and sales data is often an integral part of the income capitalization approach. Capitalization techniques are also used in the cost and sales comparison approaches. In the sales comparison approach, income capitalization can be used to analyze and adjust sales data. In the cost approach, obsolescence is often measured by capitalizing an estimated income loss.

This chapter explains the process that an appraiser uses to determine effective gross income (EGI) and net operating income (NOI). It also provides a broad overview of the steps involved in developing a reconstructed operating statement.

The basic theory of the income approach applies to the valuation of all income-producing properties. However, the techniques vary slightly, depending on the type of property appraised.

LEARNING OBJECTIVES

After reading this chapter, you will be able to:

- describe the principles, application, and limitations of the income approach.
- identify commonly used measures to analyze income.
- classify expenses as fixed, variable, or replacement reserves.
- describe a reconstructed operating statement.

THE INCOME APPROACH

The **income approach** is an appraisal method that estimates the present worth of future benefits from ownership of a property to determine that property's value. It is also known as the income capitalization approach.

The income approach is applicable to property in which future benefits are measured by the expected net income to the owner. This includes most investment property—apartments, stores, offices, and in some cases, vacant land or air rights. The income approach measures the present worth of the net income a property will produce during its remaining economic life. **Economic life** is the estimated period over which a building may be profitably used. It is also known as useful life.

APPLICATION OF INCOME APPROACH

Application of the income approach is straightforward. The income approach is most useful when appraising properties in which a property's ability to produce income is considered by potential buyers.

The income approach to value is solely dependant on a property's income—real or potential. If a property's ability to produce income is an important factor to potential buyers, then this approach is the best indicator of value. Even if the property is not currently producing income, this approach can convert its potential income into a current value. If an income property is encumbered by a below-market long-term lease, potential income may not be relevant.

An Appraiser Uses Seven Basic Steps with the Income Approach

1. Estimate the potential gross income.

2. Estimate an allowance for vacancy and collection loss.

3. Subtract the allowance for vacancy and collection loss from the potential gross income estimate to determine the effective gross income.

4. Estimate fixed expenses, variable expenses, and reserves for replacement of short-lived items.

5. Deduct estimated expenses and reserves from effective gross income to determine net operating income.

6. Select a capitalization rate applicable to the subject property.

7. Capitalize, or discount, the estimated net income to indicate the present value of the property.

Any property that generates income can be valued using an income approach to value. If the property is very expensive in terms of the present market, the income approach may understate the value.

> Example: John purchased a home 20 years ago for $75,000. He moved but kept the property. His mortgage payment is $480 per month. However, he rents the house for market rent, which is $1,200 per month. Property values have greatly increased in the area and the current market value for the property is $395,000. If a new buyer purchased the home for $375,000 with 25% down, the mortgage payment would be approximately $1,780.

Is it likely that a knowledgeable buyer would purchase this property for its income-producing capability and the present value of its future income stream? The answer, of course, is no. Reason being, the property would not rent for anywhere close to $1,780 per month. Therefore, purchasing this home for its income-producing capabilities would not make any sense.

If an appraiser valued the property based upon its current income-producing capability, he or she would arrive at a value of approximately $250,000. This would grossly understate the market value, and the income approach would not apply to this appraisal even though the property is being used as a rental. The appraiser would consider the income approach to value as mandated in USPAP Standards Rule (SR) 1-4, but would not use it—as it does not apply and would not be part of the scope of work.

When the income approach does apply and more than one approach to value is being used, the income approach is often given the most weight in the final reconciliation.

LIMITATIONS OF THE INCOME APPROACH

The income approach has limited usefulness when current rental data and operating statements are not available.

The income approach will require current market data for rentals of like properties as well as careful analysis of the operating statements. Sometimes these pieces of information are difficult to obtain and analyze. When quality data is not available, determining the appropriate capitalization rate is very difficult, and at times, can become very complex. This approach is not applicable if the income-producing capability of the subject and comparable properties is not a factor to potential buyers.

Considerations When Using the Income Approach

1. The income approach is generally not applicable to single-family residences. When used on single-family or smaller multiple-family residential income properties, the gross rent multiplier (GRM) is most often employed in the real estate industry. This approach is discussed thoroughly in the next chapter. The sales comparison approach—or market data approach—considers only gross income and may not properly account for differences in operating expenses, management, maintenance, and reserve accounts, which might have a dramatic effect on net income.

2. The income approach requires a proper determination of capitalization rates with knowledge of how these rates relate to borrowed capital (first and secondary financing), safe investment (bank savings accounts), risk factor of property management, non-liquidity, and tax benefits (depreciation and capital gains). The income approach also requires knowledge of hypothecation (lending ability) possibilities of property along with general national, state, regional, and local economic conditions that may affect the appreciation or depreciation of the property.

3. It may be difficult to find enough properties that are homogeneous to the subject property to develop meaningful capitalization rates using market data. An example of this is seen with properties that have rental units that are purchased for the possible conversion to condominium units. The resulting capitalization rates tend to be low (which indicates high

values), and these units have cap rates which are not applicable to rental units purchased for their rental incomes.

4. When using direct capitalization, an appraiser assumes that the property's income and expenses are stabilized. Direct capitalization is performed using data for one year. If there is deferred maintenance and repairs needed after the first year, direct capitalization could misstate the value unless the appraiser has adequately allowed for future expenditures.

5. In determining the rate of return by the comparative sales method, it is sometimes difficult to obtain proper income and expense information of comparable properties. This is especially true for smaller income properties that are managed by the owner.

6. There are also problems using the yield capitalization such as predicting future appreciation, determining proper discount rates, predicting future land values for reversion purposes and the challenges of using discounted cash flow models. These subjects are not thoroughly discussed in this chapter, but they are problems with the income approach to value. You will encounter these subjects in advanced courses.

INTERESTS TO BE VALUED

Income properties are usually leased, which creates legal estates of the lessor's interest (leased fee) and the lessee's interest (leasehold). A lease is a contract—or rental agreement—between landlord (owner/lessor) and tenant (renter/lessee) which gives the tenant an interest in the property.

A lease creates two types of estates. The owner's fee estate becomes a leased fee estate when the property is leased. A **leased fee estate** is the property owner's interest in the leased property. The tenant now owns a **less-than-freehold estate**, which is also known as a **leasehold estate**. A leasehold estate only has value if the agreed-on rent is less than the market rent. There are times when the government (state and federal) may require an appraiser to value the property with its fee simple absolute value as part of eminent domain proceedings. If the property is transferred or sold with no conditions or limitations on its use, it is known as an estate in fee simple absolute. **Fee simple absolute** is the largest, most complete degree of ownership recognized by law.

When it is mandated that the fee simple be valued, it is also necessary to value the leasehold estate under certain circumstances. Depending upon the requirements of the lease and the relationship of the contract rent to the economic rent, the leasehold could have a positive, negative, or zero value. It is not proper appraisal technique to determine the fee simple value and leasehold value—and then determine the leased fee estate as the difference between the two. Both the leased fee estate (owner) and the leasehold estate (tenant) have to be determined on their own merit. The important thing that an appraiser has to remember is that the fee value of a leased property is probably not equal to the leased fee value. Most appraisals of leased properties are actually appraisals of the leased fee estate.

LEASE PROVISIONS

A lease may be set up as a gross lease or a net lease. A **gross lease** means that the tenant pays a fixed amount of rent, and the owner pays all the expenses of ownership, such as maintenance, insurance, taxes, and assessments. This type of lease is typically used with residential property. If a tenant and landlord share expenses in accordance to the provisions of the lease, it becomes a **modified gross lease**.

Net leases vary from single net leases, to double net leases, and triple net leases. A **single net lease (N)** is a lease in which the tenant pays an agreed-upon sum as rent, plus certain agreed upon expenses per month (e.g., taxes and insurance). This type of arrangement is more common with commercial property—with the tenant paying rent plus at least some of the ownership expenses. With a **double net lease (NN)**—also known as a net-net lease—the tenant pays rent, utilities, taxes, and insurance. The owner pays for structural repairs and property maintenance. This generally only occurs with commercial property. A **triple net lease (NNN)** indicates the tenant is paying rent and virtually all of the expenses. In this situation, the owner does not have to put any of the rental income back into the property. This is also known as a net-net-net lease or absolute net lease.

Keep in mind, not every part of the country interprets these the same way. For example, in some areas, there can be a triple net lease with the landlord paying for the common area maintenance (CAM). **Common area maintenance** is a charge directly to the tenants for the upkeep of common areas, such as sidewalks, landscaping, parking lot lighting, and snow removal.

> ### Review – Lease Types and Payments
>
> - **Gross lease** – The tenant pays a fixed amount of rent, and the owner pays all the expenses of ownership, such as maintenance, insurance, taxes, and assessments.
>
> - **Modified gross lease** – The tenant and landlord share expenses in accordance to the provisions of the lease.
>
> - **Single net lease** – A lease in which the tenant pays an agreed-upon sum as rent, plus certain agreed upon expenses per month (e.g., taxes and insurance).
>
> - **Double net lease** – The tenant pays rent, utilities, taxes, and insurance. The owner pays for structural repairs and property maintenance.
>
> - **Triple net lease** – The tenant is paying rent and virtually all of the expenses.

PRINCIPLES USED IN THE INCOME APPROACH

In its simplest form, the income approach is based upon the premise that there is an identifiable relationship between the income a property can generate and the value of that property. All of the income approach techniques rely upon the expectation that a property will produce income.

ANTICIPATION AND CHANGE

The basic goal of every income analysis is to use capitalization techniques, to attempt to estimate future benefits and determine their present value. The main principle behind the income approach is the principle of anticipation. As discussed in Chapter 2, the **principle of anticipation** states that value is created by the benefits to be derived in the future. The amount a buyer will typically pay for a property is directly proportional to the future income benefits the buyer expects to derive from that property. The appraisal of income-producing property estimates a present value for the future benefits of real property. The income approach directly measures the present value of property based on its expected future benefits, expressed in dollars.

Like anticipation, the **principle of change** holds that it is the future, not the past, which is of prime importance in estimating value. This may involve forecasting the anticipated future income or estimating a capitalization rate that reflects the anticipated pattern of change in income over time. The residential appraiser is normally limited to one-to-four units, but the procedures described in this chapter and the next apply to larger units as well.

Benefits vary with the type of property. The expected future benefits from ownership of a single-family residence include not only the basic utility of housing but also pride of ownership, stability, prestige, and freedom of use. Typically, single-family residences are not sold based on revenue potential. Therefore, the income approach is seldom used in the valuation of single-family residences. In single-family residence appraisal, we substitute the income approach for a method called the gross income multiplier (GIM). This method is more fully described in Chapter 10.

SUPPLY AND DEMAND

The analyses of supply and demand—along with the expected competition a property will encounter—are useful in forecasting future benefits that a property owner will receive. This analysis also provides valuable information the appraiser can use in determining capitalization rates. As previously discussed, the **principle of supply and demand** states that market value is affected by the intersection of supply and demand forces in the market as of the appraisal date. Prices and rent levels tend to increase when demand is greater than supply, and tend to decrease when supply exceeds demand. The market determines rental rates, income, and rates of return.

If the demand for rental space exceeds the supply, this leads to an increase in rental and lease rates. This often occurs when interest rates begin to climb and people find it less expensive to rent than to buy property. To estimate the rates of return and to predict future benefits, appraisers must consider present demand along with forecasted demand for a particular type of property. A second part of this analysis is to forecast how this demand relates to present as well as future supply.

The economic theory of supply and demand states that for real estate, price varies directly but not necessarily proportionally with the demand, and inversely, not proportionally with existing supply. Usually property values vary directly with changes in supply. This results in what are known as buyer's markets (large supply) and seller's markets (limited supply).

Real property has value so long as there is a desire for its use. Its value increases as the supply of land decreases—as more and more people compete for the available land. The highest land values are found in the most populated cities, where small parcels of available land often bring very high prices.

ANALYZE INCOME

An appraiser examines an income property's income statement and analyzes the information to measure the income properly. Commonly used measures include potential gross income (PGI), effective gross income (EGI), and net operating income (NOI).

POTENTIAL GROSS INCOME

The simplest income to calculate is the potential gross income, which is the maximum income a property could generate. **Potential gross income (PGI)** is a property's total potential income at full occupancy from all sources before operating expenses are deducted.

The most obvious income a property produces is the rent paid by tenants. However, potential gross income includes all receipts generated by the property. This is usually classified as either rental income or service income. **Rental income** for an apartment building is the total of the economic, or fair, rent for each of the apartment units. **Service income** includes receipts from laundry facilities, vending machines, and selling of utility services to tenants.

Rental Income

Service Income

Contract rent is the amount of rent being paid under contractual terms binding owners and tenants. **Economic rent**—or market rent—is what a leased property would be expected to rent for under current market conditions if the property were vacant and available for rent. Market rent should be estimated for all living units, including manager and janitor's units, even if the rent is not actually being collected. If parking or storage space is rented separately from the living unit, such income should also be included. The gross rental estimate assumes that the property is in good, rentable condition and has competent management. The estimated cost of repairing any deferred maintenance is deducted from the value of the property indicated by the income approach.

When contract rent exceeds economic rent, this condition is called excess rent. **Excess rent** can be the result of leases being negotiated in a stronger market, locational considerations, or conditions of the property. What is typically done is the economic rent (market) is capitalized at normal rates and the amount of the excess rent that exceeds economic rent is capitalized at a higher rate because of the risk that it may not continue throughout the economic life of the property.

Rental data comes from two sources: (1) the present rent schedule and (2) a survey of rents from similar properties. A **rental survey** is an analysis of competitive rents. The purpose of this task is to identify the amount of income the subject property might generate. Although the rent schedule and rental history are an important source of data, they should never be used for a gross income estimate without first being compared with other apartment rentals in the area.

If it is practical, the rental survey should cover only those apartments in the general area that are of similar age and construction. Usually, apartment units with the same number of bedrooms are compared. There are additional, more detailed, bases for comparison—such as rent per room or rent per square foot of living area. Since most tenants choose apartments to fit their bedroom requirements, bedroom count is usually the most practical unit of comparison.

In collecting rental data, it is important to obtain enough information for meaningful comparison with the subject units. The appraiser must determine basic facts such as rent, furnishings, utilities, number of rooms, acceptance of children or pets, vacancies, date or rent schedule, and type of tenants. Property managers usually will provide this type of information. An inspection of the comparable apartment building will provide additional data on the age and condition of the building, recreation, laundry, storage, and parking facilities.

SINGLE FAMILY COMPARABLE RENT SCHEDULE

This form is intended to provide the appraiser with a familiar format to estimate the market rent of the subject property. Adjustments should be made only for items of significant difference between the comparables and the subject property.

ITEM	SUBJECT	COMPARABLE NO. 1		COMPARABLE NO. 2		COMPARABLE NO. 3	
Address							
Proximity to Subject							
Date Lease Begins Date Lease Expires							
Monthly Rental	If Currently Rented: $	$		$		$	
Less: Utilities Furniture	$	$		$		$	
Adjusted Monthly Rent	$	$		$		$	
Data Source							
RENT ADJUSTMENTS	DESCRIPTION	DESCRIPTION	+(−) $ Adjustment	DESCRIPTION	+(−) $ Adjustment	DESCRIPTION	+(−) $ Adjustment
Rent Concessions							
Location/View							
Design and Appeal							
Age/Condition							
Above Grade Room Count Gross Living Area	Total ¦ Bdrms ¦ Baths Sq. Ft.	Total ¦ Bdrms ¦ Baths Sq. Ft.		Total ¦ Bdrms ¦ Baths Sq. Ft.		Total ¦ Bdrms ¦ Baths Sq. Ft.	
Other (e.g., basement, etc.)							
Other:							
Net Adj. (total)		☐ + ☐ − $		☐ + ☐ − $		☐ + ☐ − $	
Indicated Monthly Market Rent		$		$		$	

Comments on market data, including the range of rents for single family properties, an estimate of vacancy for single family rental properties, the general trend of rents and vacancy, and support for the above adjustments. (Rent concessions should be adjusted to the market, not to the subject property.)

Final Reconciliation of Market Rent:

I (WE) ESTIMATE THE MONTHLY MARKET RENT OF THE SUBJECT AS OF _____   TO BE $_____

Appraiser(s) SIGNATURE _____   Review Appraiser SIGNATURE _____
(If applicable)

NAME _____   NAME _____

This form must be reproduced by the Seller.

It may be necessary to adjust the comparable rental units with the subject units. After analyzing the comparable rental data, the appraiser estimates a rental schedule for the subject property. The economic rent schedule may be less than, greater than, or the same as the actual rent schedule. If the economic schedule differs substantially from the existing schedule, that should be well documented and supported. Rent schedules are usually established on a monthly basis. They are converted to annual income for use in the income approach. It is important to consider long-term leases, as these give the tenant a leasehold interest in the property.

If the actual rent schedule is substantially below the estimated economic rent schedule, the appraiser must consider the probability of raising existing rents to current economic levels. In areas governed by rent control, it may be necessary to use the existing rent schedule. In such cases, it is important to use rent-controlled comparables. The appraiser must be familiar with any municipal regulations that may affect rental property and develop an estimated rent schedule accordingly.

Some personal property, such as refrigerators and window coverings, is usually included in the rental of an apartment unit. In addition, it is often included in the sale of the real property and treated in the appraisal as real property. Any personal property included in an appraisal of real property should be clearly identified. In the appraisal of an apartment building that includes all furnishings, estimated value should be categorized as real property or personal property. In this case, the estimated economic rent must be allocated between real and personal property.

In a small apartment building, the service income usually comes only from laundry facilities. The appraiser should determine whether the machines are to be included in the appraisal or if they are in the building on a rental basis. In a large apartment complex, utilities may be purchased wholesale by the apartment building and sold to the individual units. In either case, the service income estimate can usually be based on past income to the property.

Review – Steps to Determine Potential Gross Income
- Identify the subject property's current gross income.
- Identify properties that are comparable to the subject property and perform a rental survey of those properties.

EFFECTIVE GROSS INCOME

The concept of effective gross income accounts for the discrepancy between potential and actual income. An allowance must be made for vacancy and collection loss. This allowance is deducted from the potential gross

income (PGI) to determine the effective gross income (EGI). The **effective gross income (EGI)** is the amount of income that remains after vacancy and collection losses are deducted from potential gross income. **Vacancy loss** is the loss of potential income because of a vacant unit. A **collection loss** is incurred if tenants do not pay their agreed-upon rents. Sometimes, it takes months to evict a tenant legally. In these situations, it may cost an owner hundreds or thousands in collection losses.

The vacancy and collection loss allowance is not estimated solely on conditions existing at the date of appraisal, but reflects the expected vacancy and collection loss over an extended time. The appraiser estimates an average loss, knowing that vacancy and collection loss may sometimes exceed this estimate while at other times there may be no loss.

The vacancy and collection loss allowance in apartment properties is typically estimated at 2 - 7% of the gross income. The allowance set by the appraiser is based on his or her judgment of the subject property and the surrounding neighborhood. Remember, the estimated allowance is for future vacancy and rent loss.

If a property has a history of no vacancies, the rent schedule has probably been too low. Any apartment building should experience some vacancy and

rent loss. It is often desirable to have a vacancy period between tenants to facilitate interior painting and maintenance. Remember that the allowance is considered in relation to the prevailing economic rent, not the existing contract rent.

NET OPERATING INCOME

Net operating income (NOI) is the income remaining after the operating expenses are deducted from the effective gross income, but before mortgage debt service and tax depreciation. Net operating income is probably the best value indicator for income property since it most accurately reflects the income for any given property.

To calculate NOI, an appraiser deducts operating expenses from effective gross income (EGI).

$$EGI = PGI - \text{Vacancy and Collection Losses}$$
$$NOI = EGI - \text{Operating Expenses}$$

ANALYZE OPERATING EXPENSES

In appraisal, expenses are estimated on an annual basis regardless of the period in which they are incurred or paid. These are known as operating expenses. **Operating expenses** are necessary to maintain the property and to help ensure the continued production of income. They include, but are not limited to, items such as property management, insurance, property taxes, utilities, and maintenance. Operating expenses will vary from property to property.

Expenses must be considered in relation to the future productive life of the property, and expressed as a yearly figure at costs prevailing as of the date of appraisal.

The operating expenses deducted from effective gross income are usually classified as fixed expenses, variable expenses, or reserves for replacement.

FIXED EXPENSES

Property taxes, license fees, and insurance are the only items normally classified as fixed expenses. **Fixed expenses** are operating costs that are more or less permanent and that vary little from year to year regardless of occupancy. Property taxes, for example, are a fixed expense. These

taxes may vary slightly from year to year and they must be paid on a fixed annual basis. Generally, property taxes are assessed on a calendar year or fiscal year and are usually paid in two installments. The assessed value usually increases over the previous assessment, and the taxes increase. A fiscal year is often used for tax purposes as compared to a calendar year (January through December). A **fiscal year** is a 12-month accounting period not related to the actual calendar year.

The definition of market value assumes the sale of the subject property. In estimating taxes, the appraiser must use the anticipated taxes to the potential buyer, not the past taxes to the present owner. The tax rates are set by each state and the local assessor, and are generally based on property value plus any outstanding bonds or assessments.

Most communities require property owners to have an operating license for each residential property. Typically, the fee is based on the number of dwelling units per building. Commercial building owners are not exempt. Many cities require building owners (even owner-operators) to obtain a business tax permit for the building, which is separate from a business license for the operation of a business.

Insurance on a property usually includes fire, liability, and extended coverage. The insurance coverage typical for the type of property being appraised should be used as a cost basis. The appraiser must be careful when extracting insurance charges from the owner's operating statement. Many policies are

written and paid for on a 3-year basis and must be prorated for one year. Separate policies may have been written for fire and liability coverage, while the payment indicated may include only one of the policies. If the accuracy of the insurance charges is doubtful, it is important to obtain current rates from a local insurance agent.

VARIABLE EXPENSES

The level of occupancy, amount of income a property generates, and the amount of services provided by the owner to the tenants are some of the variables associated with income-producing property. **Variable expenses** are operating expenses that vary with occupancy level or intensity of use of a property.

Common Variable Expenses

- Advertising
- Building maintenance
- Cleaning
- Decorating
- HVAC
- Landscape maintenance
- Marketing
- Parking area maintenance

- Payroll
- Pest control
- Property management
- Repairs
- Security
- Snow removal
- Trash removal
- Utilities

Utilities furnished by an owner vary with the type of property and the terms of the rental agreement. In an apartment building, the owner usually provides water, garbage service, electricity for common area lighting and utility rooms, and gas for central water heaters. In some cases, the owner provides all utilities, except telephone and cable. Utilities may also be charged to tenants at a flat monthly rate and included in the rent. Owner and tenant can both save by purchasing each utility service through one meter—rather than through separate meters for each apartment. The appraiser should determine what utilities the owner provides to the tenants before estimating the economic rent schedule and utility expenses.

If it is practical, the appraiser should itemize separately the estimated cost of the various utilities—water, electricity, gas, garbage service, and any others present. The cost of utilities also varies with type and age of the apartment building, size of the units, and type of occupancy. Obviously, expenses for electricity and water are greater in a garden-style apartment with extensive landscaping and outside lighting than in a high-rise apartment. A two-bedroom apartment occupied by a family may use four times the amount of utilities used by a single-occupancy, one-bedroom unit. Utility expenses can be obtained from the operating statement of the subject property. Appraisers should analyze the expenses for at least one full year to compensate for seasonal differences in utility costs.

The cost of direct management and services related to the management of property is the **administration expense**. In a small apartment building, the only administrative expense is usually the wages of a resident manager—or property manager—who shows and leases apartment units, collects rent, maintains grounds, and may perform minor maintenance and repairs. Payment to the resident manager is usually in the form of reduced rent for the living unit, amounting to approximately 6 - 10% of rent collected. Additional payments are often made for maintenance and repair work. If the property has no resident manager and the owner performs the management functions, an estimated cost for management must still be included as an expense.

In a large apartment complex, administrative expenses may also include supervisory management, leasing fees, office expenses, and legal and accounting fees. Many real estate and property management companies will completely operate an apartment complex—hiring resident managers and other personnel, arranging for repairs and maintenance, leasing units, and keeping the books. The owners receive a monthly statement accounting for rent collection and disbursements of funds. Real estate and property management companies generally charge approximately 6 - 10% of collected gross income for their supervisory management, in addition to the normal costs of the resident manager, repairs, and maintenance.

Maintenance expenses include the buildings and grounds. Building maintenance and repairs are closely allied and usually grouped. The annual cost of maintenance and minor repairs should be estimated. When estimating maintenance and repair expenses, an appraiser should not rely on the owner's operating statement. Many major maintenance items, such as painting, may

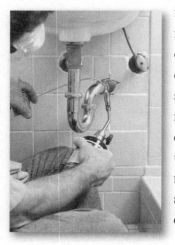

incur only once every five years—and may not be included in the owner's operating statement as an expense item in any given year. If the operating expenses of the property for the past five years are available, an appraiser can estimate average maintenance and repair expenses from the history of the property. The actual operating expenses are useful for establishing monthly or yearly maintenance costs for items under service contract—such as a swimming pool, gardening, elevator, and air conditioning.

Estimates for maintenance and repairs are often based on a percentage of gross income or on dollars per square foot of building area. Although guidelines have been established for various types of property, expenditures vary widely with facilities. In a small apartment building, the major maintenance expense is usually painting. A large apartment complex may have five to ten major maintenance items. An appraiser will make the most accurate expense estimate by considering major maintenance items separately from the allowance included for miscellaneous repairs.

REPLACEMENT RESERVES

Replacement reserves are funds set aside by the property owner to pay for the replacement of certain building components and fixtures that periodically wear out in a property. These are items that wear out more rapidly than the building itself.

Replacement items may be grouped as (1) components that are an integral part of the building, (2) personal property normally included in the sale and lease of the real property, and (3) furniture.

Items Typically Paid for with Replacement Reserves
- Appliances
- Exterior painting
- Floor coverings
- Kitchen, bath, and laundry equipment
- Re-roofing
- Resurfacing driveway or parking areas
- Window coverings

Building components having a shorter economic life than that of the total structure include roofing, floor coverings, water heaters, furnace, elevators, and air conditioners. These items may be replaced two or three times during the economic life of the building. Many appraisers agree that replacement of major building items increases the economic life of the building and improves the structure, and as such, these expenses should be treated as a capital improvement rather than as an annual expense. A **capital improvement** is any permanent improvement made to real estate for the purpose of increasing the useful life of the property or increasing the property's value. While these items are generally treated as capital improvements, some allowance must be made for replacement of these items during the life of the building—and the period in which the anticipated income was estimated.

The annual allowance for replacement of building components is usually determined by estimating the replacement cost new of each item and dividing it by the anticipated useful life of that item (assuming the item was new).

> Example: If the replacement cost of a furnace is $2,400 and its estimated useful life is 20 years, an annual reserve of $120 would be made for each furnace. An allowance is made in this manner for each applicable building component.

In practice, one lump sum is usually included as a reserve for all short-lived building components. In estimating the useful life of building components, the appraiser should consider the estimated expense for maintenance and repairs, which is also deducted from gross income. Maintenance and repair extend the useful life of building components.

Personal property that is typically included and considered real property (refrigerators, lighting fixtures, and window coverings) have shorter economic lives than the building itself. Reserve allowances similar to those for short-lived building components must be estimated for replacement of these items. The amount of reserve for replacement is estimated in the same manner as the reserve for the building components.

If furniture is included with an apartment, a reserve for replacement of these items is established only if the gross income estimate includes the income attributable to the furniture. The annual reserve for furniture replacement is estimated in the same manner as the reserve for replacement of building components.

EXCLUDED EXPENSES

Accountants record property expenses in a different manner from that of appraisers. Expense and operating statements prepared by accountants for property owners and supplied to appraisers typically include all the expenditures an owner makes for a property, even those that are not operating expenses. Items such as financing expenses, income taxes, book depreciation charges, and capital improvements are all expenses that property owners incur. An appraiser rectifies the operating statement by omitting these expenses since they are not operating expenses and vary from owner to owner.

FINANCING EXPENSES

If a property is owned free and clear, there are no financing expenses. If there are financing expenses, they will vary from owner to owner. One owner may take out a mortgage with a fixed interest rate while another owner may have a variable rate. In almost all cases, a property's value is independent of financing.

INCOME TAXES

Federal and state income taxes vary in each situation. Property may be owned by a corporation or by an individual. Each form of ownership has different tax implications, but the property itself is not worth more or less because of an owner's tax situation. A buyer would not pay more for a property simply because the seller is in a low tax-bracket. Property values are independent of an owner's tax obligations. As such, income taxes are not included in operating expenses.

BOOK DEPRECIATION

Book depreciation is an accounting concept, which refers to an allowance taken to provide for recovery of invested capital. A formula strictly for income tax purposes, book depreciation is not typically reflective of actual market conditions. This expense will also vary from owner to owner, so it is not included in an appraiser's estimate of operating expenses.

INSURANCE EXPENSES

Sometimes, operating expense charges are not segregated from other expenses. For example, an insurance bill may include coverage not just for the building, but also for business inventory, furniture, machinery, equipment, or other personal property. In this case, portions of the insurance bill that do not cover the real estate need to be deducted from the overall insurance charge.

Review – Types of Income and Expenses

- **Potential gross income** – A property's total potential income from all sources during a specified period.

- **Effective gross income** – Amount of income that remains after vacancy and collection losses are deducted from gross income.

- **Operating expenses** – Expenses necessary to maintain the property and to help ensure the continued production of income.

- **Net operating income** – Amount of income remaining after the operating expenses are deducted from the effective gross income.

RECONSTRUCT THE OPERATING STATEMENT

When an appraiser determines expenses for comparable properties, he or she often starts with an operating statement provided by a real estate broker or an owner. An **operating statement** is a written record of a property's gross income, expenses, and resultant net income for a given period. Some items normally included in an owner's operating statement, such as interest and principal payments on loans, and depreciation (accounting depreciation) are not included in the operating statement prepared by the appraiser. This information must be modified because the income and expense may be presented in a way that may not meet appraisal standards.

The summary of income and expenses prepared by the appraiser is called a reconstructed operating statement. A **reconstructed operating statement** is one that eliminates the inapplicable expense items for appraisal purposes and adjusts the remaining valid expenses, if necessary. An appraiser's reconstructed operating statement is intended to reflect a stabilized estimate of income and expenses. Allowances for vacancy and collection loss, reserves for replacements, and management expense (in which the owner performs management) may be incorporated in the appraiser's operating statement but not in the owner's accounting statement. Although appraisers should not incorporate the actual income and expenditures of the subject property into their reconstructed operating statements, they must be prepared to support their estimates, which may differ from the actual history of the property.

Differences Between Owner and Reconstructed Operating Statements

- The appraiser estimates an economic rent schedule for the property. The owner's statement is based on the actual income schedule.

- Owner's statement may not allow for vacancy and rent loss.

- Only the actual recurring expenses are deducted in computing the owner's statement. Existing taxes are used rather than increased taxes caused by a change in ownership.

- Owner's statement provides only a minimal allowance, if any, for repairs and maintenance and no allowance for replacement of short-lived building components and personal property.

Many publications outline typical expenses in apartment operations. Expenses are usually expressed as a percentage of gross income. Since expenses in apartment buildings vary so greatly, published averages should only be used as a guide in analyzing the expenses reported for the appraised property.

FORECASTING NET OPERATING INCOME

Assessing the earning power of a property means the appraiser has to forecast its expected cash flow and net operating income. To make this determination, an appraiser must evaluate the income and expense history for the subject and for competing properties. Normally this is a minimum of a three-year period. The history should include actual vacancy levels and management expenses for the subject and comparables. The appraiser must analyze the leases of the subject and comparable properties to the extent possible. Additionally, the appraiser must forecast expected changes in taxes, energy costs, and other operating expenses.

The following table shows a reconstructed operating statement for a 4-unit garden apartment. The total expenses for a modern garden apartment are normally between 30 - 40% of the gross income from the apartment. As the building ages, expenses usually increase in relation to income.

Reconstructed Operating Statement—4 Units

Category		Amount
Potential Gross Income		
4 Units @ $800 per month	$38,400	
Laundry @ $50 per month	$600	
Total Potential Gross Income		$ 39,000
Less: Vacancy and collection loss (5%)		– $1,950
Effective Gross Income		$37,050
Expenses		
Fixed expenses		
Taxes	$6,000	
Insurance	$2,000	
License	$100	
Total Fixed Expenses	$8,100	
Operating Expenses		
Property Manager	$2,400	
Water	$1,200	
Trash	$1,200	
Landscaping	$1,200	
Maintenance	$750	
Total Operating Expenses	$6,750	
Less: Total Expenses		– $14,850
Less: Reserves for Replacement		– 5,000
Net Operating Income (NOI)		$17,200

SUMMARY

The **income approach** is an appraisal method that estimates the present worth of future benefits from ownership of a property to determine that property's value. In this chapter, we discussed how income-producing property typically affects an investor and examined how earning power is the critical element affecting the property value. In general, the higher the earning power of the property, the higher the value.

We discussed the applications and limitations of the income approach and considered definitions of key terms such as **leased fee estate** and **leasehold estates**. Various lease types include **gross, modified gross, single net, double net**, and **triple net leases**.

When estimating income, an appraiser examines **gross income** and **net operating income (NOI)**. The simplest income to calculate is the **potential gross income (PGI)**, which is a property's total potential income from all sources during a specified period. The concept of effective gross income accounts for the discrepancy between potential and actual income. **Effective gross income** is the property's income after vacancy and collection losses are deducted from the estimate of projected potential gross income. **Net operating income (NOI)** is the income remaining after the operating expenses are deducted from the effective gross income. Net operating income is probably the best value indicator for any income property since it most accurately reflects the income for given property. To calculate net operating income, an appraiser deducts operating expenses from effective gross income. **Operating expenses** are those expenses necessary to maintain the property and to help ensure the continued production of income. When analyzing operating expenses, an appraiser must consider **fixed expenses, variable expenses**, and **replacement reserves**.

The operating statement and reconstructed operating statements were also discussed. An **operating statement** is a written record of a property's gross income, expenses, and resultant net income for a given period. The summary of income and expenses prepared by the appraiser is called a reconstructed operating statement. A **reconstructed operating statement** is one that eliminates the inapplicable expense items for appraisal purposes and adjusts the remaining valid expenses, if necessary.

CHAPTER 9 REVIEW EXERCISES

MATCHING EXERCISE

Instructions: Write the letter of the matching term on the blank line before its definition. Answers are in Appendix A.

Terms

A. administration expense

B. book depreciation

C. capital

D. capital improvements

E. collection loss

F. contract rent

G. economic life

H. economic rent

I. effective gross income (EGI)

J. fee simple absolute

K. fiscal year

L. fixed expenses

M. gross lease

N. income approach

O. leased fee estate

P. leasehold estate

Q. modified gross lease

R. net operating income (NOI)

S. operating expenses

T. operating statement

U. potential gross income (PGI)

V. reconstructed operating statement

W. rental survey

X. replacement reserves

Y. vacancy loss

Z. variable expenses

Definitions

1. _____ Appraisal method that estimates the present worth of future benefits from ownership of a property to determine that property's value

2. _____ Estimated period over which a building may be profitably used

3. _____ Property owner's interest in the leased property

4. _____ Tenant's interest in the leased property during the term of the lease

5. _____ Tenant pays a fixed amount of rent, and the owner pays all the expenses of ownership

6. _____ A property's total potential income from all sources during a specified period

7. _____ Amount of rent being paid under contractual terms binding owners and tenants

8. _____ What a leased property would be expected to rent for under current market conditions if the property were vacant and available for rent

9. _____ Amount of income that remains after vacancy and collection losses are deducted from gross income

10. _____ Loss of potential income because of a vacant unit

11. _____ Loss incurred if tenants do not pay their agreed-upon rents

12. _____ Income remaining after the operating expenses are deducted from the effective gross income

13. _____ Expenses necessary to maintain the property and to help ensure the continued production of income

14. _____ Operating costs that vary little from year to year regardless of occupancy

15. _____ Operating expenses that vary with occupancy level or intensity of use of a property

16. _____ Funds set aside by the property owner to pay for the replacement of certain building components and fixtures that periodically wear out in a property

17. _____ Any permanent improvement made to real estate for the purpose of increasing the useful life of the property or increasing the property's value

18. _____ An accounting concept, which refers to an allowance taken to provide for recovery of invested capital

19. _____ Eliminates the inapplicable expense items for appraisal purposes and adjusts the remaining valid expenses, if necessary

20. _____ A written record of a property's gross income, expenses, and resultant net income for a given period

MULTIPLE CHOICE QUESTIONS

Instructions: Circle your response and go to Appendix A to read the complete explanation or calculation for each question.

1. The income approach is applicable to property in which:
    a. future benefits are measured by the expected gross income to the owner.
    b. current benefits are measured by the expected potential income to the owner.
    c. future benefits are measured by the expected net income to the owner.
    d. past benefits are measured by the expected gross income to the owner.

2. An appraiser uses seven basic steps with the income approach. Which of the following is the first step?
    a. Estimating an allowance for vacancy and collection loss
    b. Estimating the potential gross income (PGI)
    c. Estimating operating expenses
    d. Estimating effective gross income (EGI)

3. Most appraisals of leased properties are of which type of estate?
    a. Leasehold
    b. Less-than-freehold
    c. Leased fee
    d. Fee simple

4. If a tenant and landlord share expenses in accordance to the provisions of the lease, it becomes a(n) _____ lease.
    a. absolute net
    b. double net
    c. gross
    d. modified gross

5. In a triple net lease (NNN), the tenant pays for:
    a. utilities.
    b. taxes.
    c. insurance.
    d. all the above.

6. In considering potential gross income for appraisal purposes, which of the following is used?
   a. Effective rent
   b. Economic rent
   c. Contract rent
   d. Service rent

7. Income derived from laundry facilities, vending machines, and selling of utility services is known as _____ income.
   a. gross
   b. rental
   c. service
   d. administrative

8. For appraisal purposes, when contract rent exceeds economic rent, the appraiser should capitalize:
   a. the economic rent at normal rates.
   b. excess rent at a higher rate.
   c. the contract rent at a higher rate.
   d. both (a) and (b).

9. A rental survey is an analysis of which of the following?
   a. Competitive rents
   b. Rent schedule
   c. Rental history
   d. Operating expenses

10. Effective gross income (EGI) is determined by:
    a. deducting vacancy and collection loss from the gross income.
    b. adding a vacancy rate to the gross income.
    c. deducting contract rent from economic rent.
    d. adding operating expenses to the gross income.

11. The vacancy and collection loss allowance is based on:
    a. the existing contract rent.
    b. an extended time.
    c. the date of appraisal.
    d. all of the above.

12. Net operating income (NOI) is determined by:

    a. adding operating expenses to gross income.

    b. deducting operating expenses from potential gross income (PGI).

    c. deducting operating expenses from effective gross income (EGI).

    d. adding vacancy and/or collection losses to potential gross income (PGI)

13. Property taxes fall into which of the following expense categories?

    a. Variable expenses

    b. Fixed expenses

    c. Reserves for replacement

    d. Administrative expenses

14. Replacement reserves, as an expense item, affect which of the following?

    a. Components that are an integral part of the building

    b. Personal property normally included in the sale and lease of the real property

    c. Furniture and appliances

    d. All of the above

15. An owner's operating statement usually differs from the appraiser's net income estimate in which of the following ways?

    a. The owner's statement does not consider actual recurring expenses

    b. The owner's statement does not allow for vacancy and collection loss

    c. The owner's statement does not allow for reserves for replacement

    d. Both (b) and (c)

Income Approach: Multipliers

10
Chapter

INTRODUCTION

The income approach measures the present worth of the income a property will produce during its remaining economic life. The process of estimating the present worth of a property based on its anticipated income is called **capitalization**. While there are several methods of capitalizing income, this chapter will discuss the multiplier approach to value. Direct and yield capitalization will be discussed in Chapter 11.

Income multipliers are used by many investors and appraisers when evaluating smaller income-producing properties. The multipliers include the gross rent multiplier (GRM) and the gross income multiplier (GIM). Though the two are similar, there is a difference between GRM and GIM.

The gross rent multiplier (GRM) is often applied when appraising single-family residences used as rental property, as well as smaller income-producing properties such as duplex and fourplex units. The gross income multiplier (GIM), on the other hand, is generally reserved for larger income-producing and commercial properties.

LEARNING OBJECTIVES

After reading this chapter, you will be able to:

- describe the use of multipliers in the income approach.
- describe how a gross rent multiplier is calculated.
- determine a gross income multiplier and use it to calculate the value of a property.

USING INCOME MULTIPLIERS

The key benefit of using a multiplier is its relative ease of use. A **multiplier** is a number that, when multiplied by the income, gives an indicator of value. The advantage of this approach is that it is widely used and understood by both the investing public and the appraisal community.

In order to use multipliers as means of deriving income to value, an appraiser needs to research comparable properties' sale prices, income, expenses, financing arrangements, and market conditions at the time of sale. Inexperienced appraisers may make a mistake by using multipliers derived from properties that are not truly similar to the subject property. Care must be used to ensure the income or rent of the properties used to derive the multiplier is comparable to that of the subject. The specific multiplier has to be applied to the same income base.

GROSS RENT MULTIPLIER

In earlier chapters, the difficulty of relating home ownership amenities to dollar income was discussed. The appraisal of a single-family residence is generally not adapted to the theory of the income approach. Because many single-family homes are rented, the income potential may be considered if the subject property is tenant-occupied.

In single-family residence appraisal, the gross rent multiplier is applied through the income method of valuation. The **gross rent multiplier (GRM)** is a figure which, when multiplied by the monthly rental income, will give an indication of the property's market value. The **gross rent (GR)** is income (calculated annually or monthly) received from rental units before any expenses are deducted. The GRM is also used in appraising multiple-family residential and commercial properties, but is included as part of the sales comparison approach.

> **Formula – Gross Rent Multiplier**
>
> GRM = Value ÷ GR
>
> Value = GRM × GR

The gross rent multiplier is a factor of the ratio between gross rent and sales price. The gross rent multiplier for the subject property is estimated based on an analysis of the ratio between the sale price and gross rent for a number of comparable properties. The sale price of a property is divided by its gross monthly rent to determine a gross rent multiplier factor. The rent multipliers of several comparable sales should be determined and analyzed to estimate the proper gross rent multiplier for the subject property.

Gross rent multipliers for single-family residences, duplexes, and small apartment buildings are usually expressed as a monthly multiplier factor. Multipliers applicable to large apartment buildings and commercial properties are expressed on a yearly income basis. The appraiser converts a monthly multiplier to an annual factor by dividing by 12. For example, a monthly multiplier of 130 would be the same as a yearly multiplier of 10.8.

The GRM is a reliable method of valuation only when sufficient sales data are available. As with the income approach, the gross rent for the subject property must be estimated from or substantiated by comparable rents in the area. Many investors in small residential income properties, such as duplexes and fourplexes, rely strongly on the GRM when purchasing investment property.

There are three main steps to apply when using the GRM: (1) select the comparable properties and calculate GRM, (2) reconcile the comparables, and (3) apply the GRM to the subject property.

First select comparable properties and calculate the GRM for each. Once the comparables are selected, determine which comps are most like the subject property.

Guidelines for Selecting Comparable Properties

- The sales should be recent. Rent multipliers may change with economic conditions.

- The sale properties should be located in the same or equal neighborhoods as the subject property.

- The sale properties should be reasonably similar to the subject in all essential physical elements.

- The rent for the sale properties must be their fair market rent at the time of sale.

- The ratio of expenses to rent should be similar for sale property and subject.

Analyze the sale properties and select the multiplier to be applied to the subject property. After the GRM is derived from comparable sales, it must be applied to the subject in the same manner as it was derived. The GRM is a ratio between price and income at the time of sale, and no adjustments are necessary.

Example: The subject property is a fourplex located in a suburban neighborhood. There are two 1-bedroom/1-bathroom units and two 2-bedroom/1-bathroom units. The appraiser performed a rental survey for the subject property and determined that the 1-bedroom units rent for $750 per month and the 2-bedroom units for $850 per month. The actual rents were reasonably close to the economic rents, but the appraiser used economic rents—as this is proper appraisal practice.

Subject Property

Two Units × $750 rent/month	=	$1,500
Two Units × $850 rent/month	=	$1,700
Total Forecasted Monthly Income	=	$3,200

Step 1: Find Comps and Calculate GRM

GRM is found by dividing the sales price by the gross monthly rent.

Comparable Sale #1

This property is a 5-unit apartment house with three units that are 1-bedroom/1-bathroom and two units that have 2-bedrooms/1.5-bathrooms. The 1-bedroom units rent for $725 per month and the 2-bedroom units for $875 per month. This property recently sold for $608,350.

Three Units × $725 rent/month = $2,175
Two Units   × $850 rent/month = $1,700
Total Forecasted Monthly Income = $3,875
GRM = $608,350 ÷ $3,875 = 156.99 (rounded to 157)

Comparable Sale #2

This property is a triplex with one unit that has 1-bedroom/1-bathroom and two units that have 2-bedrooms/1-bathroom. The 1-bedroom unit rents for $735 per month and the 2-bedroom units for $850 per month. This property recently sold for $433,400.

One Unit × $735 rent/month = $ 735
Two Units × $850 rent/month = $1,700
Total Forecasted Monthly Income = $2,435
GRM = $433,400 ÷ $2,435 = 177.98 (rounded to 178)

Comparable Sale #3

This property is a fourplex with three units that have 1-bedroom/1-bathroom and one unit that has 2-bedrooms/1-bathroom. The 1-bedroom units rent for $750 per month and the 2-bedroom units for $875 per month. This property recently sold for $525,000.

Three Units × $750 rent/month = $2,250
One Unit   × $850 rent/month = $ 850
Total Forecasted Monthly Income = $3,100
GRM = $525,000 ÷ $3,100 = 169.35 (rounded to 169)

Step 2: Reconciliation of the Comparables

The three sales used produced gross income multipliers that range from 157 to 178 (summarized on grid below). Commonly known as the average, the mean is calculated by adding the average prices or numeric values of a statistical sample and dividing that by the number of values in the sample.

Comparable	Monthly Income	Sales Price	GRM
Comp 1	$3,875	$608,350	157
Comp 2	$2,435	$433,400	178
Comp 3	$3,100	$525,000	169
Averages/Mean	$3,137	$522,250	168

The appraiser thought that the comparables were usable—as they were all within six blocks of the subject. He considered all three comps, but gave Comp 3 the most weight as it had the same number of units as the subject. Comp 2 had more curb appeal and two extra parking spaces, which put this sale at the upper limit of the value range. The subject had some deferred maintenance—which none of the comparables had—so the appraiser reconciled the GRM between Comps 1 and 3. The reconciled GRM was 163.

Step 3: Derivation and Application

After the GRM is derived from comparable sales, it must be applied to the subject in the same manner that it was derived.

Value of the Subject $=$ GRM $\times$ Gross Rent

Value of the Subject $=$ 163 $\times$ $3,200

Value of the Subject $=$ $521,600

GROSS INCOME MULTIPLIER

One of the simplest ways to form an opinion of a property's value based on its income is to use a gross income multiplier (GIM). A **gross income multiplier (GIM)** is a figure which, when multiplied by the annual gross income, will equal the property's market value.

The gross income multiplier (GIM) is similar to the GRM method. The distinction between the two is that GIM accounts for all possible potential income, whereas GRM accounts only for the property's rental income. It is faster to calculate the GRM, but consequently, it is not as accurate or detailed as the GIM. Like GRM, the amount of the GIM must be obtained from recent comparable sales since it varies with specific properties and areas. The **potential gross income multiplier (PGIM)** is the ratio between the value or sales price of a property and its potential gross income. **Potential gross income (PGI)** is the amount of income a property could potentially generate assuming 100% occupancy at market rental rates.

DERIVATION AND APPLICATION

To derive a GIM, the appraiser must have market data of comparables that were rented at the time of sale, or were anticipated to be rented within a short time period. The GIM used to value the subject property is estimated based on an analysis of the ratios between the sales prices and gross incomes for a number of comparable properties. The sale price of a property is divided by its gross monthly rent to determine a gross income multiplier (GIM).

Gross income multipliers can be used with either monthly or yearly income. Monthly income is used primarily when appraising small multi-family residential properties or in cases where there are no seasonal variations in a property's projected income. In most situations, an appraiser uses the annualized income multiplier.

Formulas

Value $=$ PGI $\times$ GIM

PGIM $=$ Value $\div$ PGI

Effective Gross Income Multiplier (EGIM)

The second ratio the appraiser will use is the effective gross income multiplier (EGIM). The **effective gross income multiplier (EGIM)** is the ratio between the effective gross income and the value of the property. **Effective gross income (EGI)** is the amount of income remaining after vacancy and credit losses are deducted from gross income. It is especially important for the appraiser to be sure the potential income and vacancy factor for each of the comparable sales used is calculated in the exact same manner as it is for the subject.

Although GIMs can be based upon monthly data, annualized data is used here to determine a capitalization rate.

Formulas

Value $=$ EGI $\times$ EGIM

EGIM $=$ Value $\div$ EGI

Example: Assume a property has a value (sales price) of $380,000. Its EGI is $80,000. What is the EGIM?

EGIM $=$ Value $\div$ EGI

EGIM $=$ $380,000 $\div$ $80,000

EGIM $=$ 4.75

An income multiplier derived from potential income can only be applied to the potential income of the subject. The same is true for income derived from effective gross income. This process can be used for all of the comparable sales.

> **Review – GRM vs. GIM**
> - Gross rent multiplier (GRM) is used only with rental income.
> - Gross income multiplier (GIM) suggests that some of the income used comes from sources other than rent.

Differences between the Gross Income Multipliers

Value of the subject property		$400,000
PGI	$ 90,000	
Less: 5% Vacancy/Collection Loss	($ 4,500)	
EGI	$ 85,500	

Deriving PGIM	Deriving EGIM
PGIM = Sale Price ÷ PGI	EGIM = Sale Price ÷ EGI
PGIM = $400,000 ÷ $90,000	EGIM = $400,000 ÷ $85,500
PGIM = 4.44	EGIM = 4.68

LIMITATIONS OF INCOME MULTIPLIER TECHNIQUES

The main drawback in using multiplier techniques is that they are based on gross income and rent—ignoring the net income that a property may generate. In many cases, buyers and sellers are more interested in net than gross income.

The appraisal process should be reflective of the attitudes of buyers and sellers in the market. It may be inappropriate to use a gross rent or income multiplier analysis—since it is not always reflective of the actions of buyers and sellers in the market. Two properties may generate very similar levels of gross income. However, one may have significantly higher net income since it has lower operating expenses. All other things being equal, the property with the higher net income would tend to be in greater demand and more valuable. Using a multiplier technique, this difference is ignored.

Factors to Consider When Using Income Multipliers

- Use comparables similar to the subject and each other in terms of physical, locational, and investment characteristics.

- Be sure the rental data used with the comparables is fair market rent. At times, properties sell with low rents because the property owner did not want to disturb the tenants, even though their cooperation was needed to show the property. This is potentially the biggest source of error in use of income multipliers.

- Gross income multipliers (GIMs) suggest some of the income used in this approach comes from sources other than rent. A gross rent multiplier (GRM) is used only with rental income.

- The types of leases in the comparable rentals have to be similar to those analyzed in the subject. For example, GIMs derived from gross leases cannot be compared to net leases.

- The appraiser can use either the potential gross income (PGI) or the effective gross income (EGI), but the data and measure must be used consistently throughout the analysis to produce credible results. The income measure selected is a function of market data and the purpose of the analysis.

SUMMARY

The income approach measures the present worth of the income a property will produce during its remaining economic life. The process used to develop an opinion of property value from its income stream is called **capitalization**. Income multipliers are used when evaluating smaller income-producing properties. The advantage of this approach is that it is widely used and understood by both the investing public and the appraisal community. The multiplier approach includes the gross rent multiplier (GRM) and the gross income multiplier (GIM). A **multiplier** is a number that, when multiplied by the income, gives an opinion of value.

The **gross rent multiplier (GRM)** is a figure which, when multiplied by the monthly rental income, will equal the property's market value. The **gross rent (GR)** is income (calculated annually or monthly) received from rental units before any expenses are deducted.

The gross income multiplier (GIM) is similar to the GRM method. The distinction between the two is that GIM accounts for all possible potential income, whereas GRM accounts only for the property's rental income. Like GRM, the amount of the GIM must be obtained from recent comparable sales since it varies with specific properties and areas. The **potential gross income multiplier (PGIM)** is the ratio between the value or sales price of a property and its potential gross income. **Potential gross income (PGI)** is the amount of income a property could potentially generate assuming 100% occupancy at market rental rates.

CHAPTER 10 REVIEW EXERCISES

MATCHING EXERCISE

Instructions: Write the letter of the matching term on the blank line before its definition. Answers are in Appendix A.

Terms

A. annualized data

B. capitalization

C. derivation

D. effective gross income (EGI)

E. effective gross income multiplier (EGIM)

F. gross income multiplier (GIM)

G. gross rent

H. gross rent multiplier (GRM)

I. multiplier

J. potential gross income (PGI)

K. potential gross income multiplier (PGIM)

L. ratios

M. reconciliation

N. rental income

Definitions

1. _____ The process of estimating the present worth of a property based on its anticipated income

2. _____ A number that, when multiplied by the income, gives an indicator of value

3. _____ A figure which, when multiplied by the monthly rental income, will equal the property's market value

4. _____ Income (calculated annually or monthly) received from rental units before any expenses are deducted

5. _____ A figure which, when multiplied by the annual gross income, will equal the property's market value

6. _____ The ratio between the value or sales price of a property and its potential gross income

7. _____ The amount of income a property could potentially generate assuming 100% occupancy at market rental rates

8. _____ The ratio between the effective gross income and the value of the property

9. _____ The amount of income remaining after vacancy and credit losses are deducted from gross income

MULTIPLE CHOICE QUESTIONS

Instructions: Circle the correct response and go to Appendix A to read the complete explanation for each question.

1. The process of estimating the present worth of a property based on its anticipated income is called:
   a. amortization.
   b. appreciation.
   c. capitalization.
   d. depreciation.

2. Which statement is incorrect regarding GRM and GIM?
   a. The GRM is based on income derived from rent.
   b. The GRM and the GIM are identical.
   c. Both use a number that, when multiplied by the income, gives an estimate of value.
   d. GIM is used on small income-producing properties.

3. How is the GRM calculated?
   a. Divide PGI by the value
   b. Multiply the value by gross rent
   c. Divide the value by gross rent
   d. Multiply PGIM by the value

For questions 4 – 8, consider the following data:

Value of the subject property	$400,000
PGI	$ 80,000
Vacancy and collection loss	(5%)?
Potential Gross Income Multiplier (PGIM) =	Value ÷ PGI
Effective Gross Income Multiplier (EGIM) =	Value ÷ EGI

4. From the information above, what is the vacancy and collection loss?

    a. $3,000

    b. $4,000

    c. $4,300

    d. $3,750

5. What is the EGI?

    a. $40,000

    b. $56,000

    c. $76,000

    d. $84,000

6. How is the PGIM calculated?

    a. Divide the PGI by the value

    b. Divide the PGI by the EGI

    c. Divide the value by the PGI

    d. Add the value to the vacancy factor

7. What is the PGIM in the previous example?

    a. 4.5

    b. 5.0

    c. 5.3

    d. 4.75

8. What is the EGIM in the previous example?

    a. 5.26

    b. 5.56

    c. 4.76

    d. 6.0

For questions 9 – 15, use the data presented below:

Comparable	Annual EGI	Sales Price	EGIM
Comp 1	$50,000	$600,000	?
Comp 2	$?	$575,000	10.00
Comp 3	$56,410	$?	9.75
Comp 4	$45,000	$495,000	11.00
Comp 5	$60,526	$575,000	?

9. What is the EGIM for Comp 1?

    a. 8
    b. 9
    c. 12
    d. 13

10. What is the effective annual income for Comp 2?

    a. $57,500
    b. $60,000
    c. $55,000
    d. $47,500

11. What is the sale price for Comp 3?

    a. $499,000
    b. $500,000
    c. $600,000
    d. $550,000

12. What is the monthly income for Comp 4?

    a. $2,000
    b. $3,750
    c. $4,275
    d. $5,250

13. What is the monthly EGIM for comparable 4?

    a. .92
    b. 120
    c. 1.92
    d. 132

14. What is the monthly EGIM for Comp 5?

    a. 9.5
    b. 11.25
    c. 114
    d. 144

15. What is the mean (average) EGIM for all the comps above?

    a. 11
    b. 12
    c. 9.55
    d. 10.45

Income Approach: Capitalization

INTRODUCTION

There are several methods used to convert income into an estimate of value. The two techniques using gross income—gross rent multiplier (GRM) and gross income multiplier (GIM)—were discussed in Chapter 10. This chapter will focus on methods using net income—direct capitalization and yield capitalization. In capitalization, the estimate of value results from dividing the net operating income estimate by an appropriate capitalization rate.

While several methods of capitalizing net income are discussed in this chapter, the method emphasized is direct capitalization, which uses the technique of deriving capitalization rates from comparable sales. **Direct capitalization** is an income capitalization technique in which value is estimated by dividing net operating income by the overall capitalization rate. This estimate of value is accomplished in one basic step, which is illustrated in this chapter. We will also discuss yield capitalization, which is another more complex method for valuation of income-producing property.

LEARNING OBJECTIVES

After reading this chapter, you will be able to:

- define income capitalization.
- identify the rates used in the capitalization process.
- describe the relationship between risk and capitalization rates.
- describe how to select capitalization rates.
- apply the formulas used with direct capitalization.

INCOME CAPITALIZATION

Real estate investors most often purchase or develop properties with the expectation of deriving a cash flow. The more income a property generates for its owner, the more valuable the property. The income capitalization approach is based on the premise that there is an identifiable relationship between the net income a property generates and the value of the property. The process of estimating the present worth of a property based on its anticipated income is capitalization. Capitalization converts income to capital value.

The income approach generally involves a three-step process: (1) estimate net operating income, (2) select an appropriate capitalization rate, and (3) capitalize the income.

Capitalization Formulas				
Determine a property's value:	V	= NOI	÷	OAR
Determine the cap rate:	OAR	= NOI	÷	V
Calculate a property's NOI:	NOI	= V	×	OAR

An appraiser examines an income property's operating statement, analyzes the information, and reconstructs the operating statement. Income and expense analysis and the preparation of a reconstructed operating statement were discussed in Chapter 9.

CAPITALIZATION RATES

When an investor considers buying a property for its income-producing capabilities, he or she obviously wants the investment to be profitable. For an investor, the **return on investment** is the profit produced by the investment.

It answers the question, "How much will I earn from making this investment?" The return or profit from an investment is also known as the **yield**.

A second factor each investor considers is "Will I be able to recoup my investment when I decide it is time to sell?" Another aspect of this analysis is whether the property will sell for more than the original purchase price. The recapture or conversion of the investment to cash or other valuable assets is known as the **return of investment**.

TYPES OF CAPITALIZATION RATES

There are four basic types of rates used in the capitalization process. Interest rate is the return on an investment necessary to attract capital funds. The **interest rate** is the RETURN ON INVESTMENT and is the rate of interest considered to be a reasonable return on an investment. It is applicable only to the net income from the land. It is also described as the yield rate necessary to attract the money of the average investor to a particular type of investment.

The **recapture rate** is the RETURN OF INVESTMENT and is the rate that an investor recovers invested money. It is applicable only to the net income from improvements. When buildings or other improvements contribute to the production of income, an allowance must be made for recapture of the value of the improvements. Structural improvements have a limited economic life, while land may generally be used indefinitely.

The **overall capitalization rate** (OAR), or simply the cap rate, is a market-derived ratio reflecting the relationship between the net operating income a property generates and its value. It is used to convert expected net operating income (NOI) generated by a property into a value estimate (V) for that property. It provides for both the return on investment and return of invested capital, but the proportions are unknown. Generally, an appraiser uses a capitalization rate provided by the client/investor for appraisals in which investment value, rather than market value, is desired.

> **Example:** Find the overall capitalization rate if a property sold for $800,000 and has a NOI of $72,000.
>
> Cap Rate = NOI ÷ Sales Price
>
> Cap Rate = $72,000 ÷ $800,000
>
> Cap Rate = .09 or 9%

The type of capitalization rate selected depends on the capitalization technique used.

Example: An income-producing property has a NOI of $80,000. The overall cap rate (OAR) is estimated to be 6%. What is the value of the property?

$$Value = NOI \div OAR$$
$$Value = \$80,000 \div 0.06$$
$$Value = \$1,333,333$$

A **composite capitalization rate** provides both a return on the investment and a return of the investment value. It differs from an overall capitalization rate because it is derived from known proportion of both interest rate and recapture rate.

CAPITALIZATION RATES AND RISK

Because real estate competes with all other types of investment for available investment funds, when estimating the rate of return demanded by investors, an appraiser must consider many characteristics of the particular investment.

Characteristics to Consider when Evaluating an Investment

1. **Reliability of net income.** The appraiser must evaluate certainty of future income and expenses. Most real estate involves greater risk as to the reliability of net income than most bonds and mortgages. A property on a long-term net lease to a responsible lessee is more desirable—and would probably attract capital funds at a lower rate—than a similar property on a month-to-month tenancy.

2. **Liquidity.** An investment that can be readily sold, such as stocks and bonds, is usually preferable to an asset like real estate or machinery that may require weeks or months to sell. Real estate does not have the liquidity of stocks and bonds. Similarly, an investment that can be acquired in relatively small denominations has a much wider market of prospective purchasers than a larger investment.

3. **Burden of management.** The burden of management is usually greater for real estate than for other investments. In this case, we mean general supervision and care of the investment, not management of the type that would be deducted from the income as an operating expense. Investment assets require different degrees of management. Bonds and

mortgages require virtually none. A real property under a long-term net lease requires less management than a property under a month-to-month tenancy.

4. **Probability of increase or decrease in value.** The probability of a change in value varies with the type of investment and individual asset. Bonds and mortgages are likely to remain stable in capital value. One of the most important characteristics of real estate and of corporate common stocks is the potential appreciation in value as a hedge against inflation. If buyers and sellers anticipate an increase in the capital value of an asset, the present yield rate will be less than the rate for an asset of stable or decreasing value.

5. **Taxation.** The income tax treatment of anticipated future benefits from an investment can influence the capitalization rate. Tax-free municipal bonds are purchased at a lower yield rate than similar taxable bonds. Real estate investors benefit more from preferential income tax treatment than do other investors.

6. **Hypothecation.** Being able to use a capital asset as collateral for borrowing money is an advantage. Because real estate is fixed, it is considered secure, as collateral. Real estate is one of the best assets as collateral for loans. Assets that fluctuate rapidly in value do not normally serve as good collateral.

7. **Leverage.** Investment in real estate typically requires a small percentage of capital as a down payment, minimizing the investor's cash output. Leveraging may require as little as 10 - 30 % of the total property value, allowing the investor to control the property with the least amount of down payment. Less capital is necessary for a real property purchase down payment than for many other forms of investment.

Just as real estate competes with other investments for capital funds, each parcel of real estate competes with every other parcel. Capitalization rates for real property vary with the type, age, and condition of the property, location, and surrounding developments, and existing economic conditions.

Capitalization rates and value are inversely proportional. If there is a high-risk property, there will be a high capitalization rate and a low value. Low risk investments are those with a lower possibility of losing money, along with the possibility of less income. If the risk factor is low, the capitalization rate will be low and the value will be high.

Review – Cap Rates and Risk

Low risk = Low OAR = High value

High risk = High OAR = Low value

The more secure the future net income, the lower the capitalization rate. A lower rate would be used in capitalizing the income from an apartment house in a well-maintained and stable neighborhood than in an area of declining economic conditions.

The difference in capitalization rates would reflect people's judgment of the quality of the properties in relation to the characteristics of a good investment. In an undesirable neighborhood, the capitalization rate might be higher because the reliability of income is poorer, the probability of appreciation in value is less, and the burden of management is greater. It is similar to investors who purchase second and third mortgages. These are not as safe as a first mortgage but can have a higher return. If these mortgages are sold, they require a higher discount than the first mortgage.

The age, condition, and construction of the buildings on improved properties have a direct effect on the capitalization rate. The resulting discounting rate is a combination of interest rate and recapture rate. The value of improvements must be recaptured during the remaining economic life. The shorter the future economic life of the improvements, the greater the annual allowance for recapture. The value of a building with an estimated future economic life of 50 years must be recaptured at a rate of 2% per year. The value of a building with an estimated future economic life of 20 years must be recaptured at a rate of 5% per year. Usually, the older the building, the cheaper the construction, or the poorer the condition, the shorter will be the estimated future economic life and the greater will be the annual recapture rate.

SELECTING CAPITALIZATION RATES

The appraiser attempts to select a capitalization rate that reflects the actions of buyers and sellers for the particular type and class of property. Selecting the capitalization rate is one of the most important parts of the capitalization process. A minor change in the rate will cause a substantial difference in property value. A rate increase from 8-9% will result in an 11% decrease in value.

Example: Find the percentage decrease in value of a property if $60,000 NOI is capitalized at 8% and 9%.

Step 1: Value = NOI ÷ Cap Rate

Value = $60,000 ÷ 0.08

Value = $750,000

Step 2: Value = $60,000 ÷ 0.09

Value = $666,670

Step 3: Calculate the decrease in value

$750,000 − $666,670 = $83,330

Step 4: Calculate the percentage decrease in value

Percentage decrease = $83,300 ÷ $750,000

Percentage decrease = 11%

METHODS TO DERIVE CAPITALIZATION RATES

Three methods have been developed to aid the appraiser in selecting a capitalization rate: (1) comparative sales method, (2) band of investment method, and (3) summation method.

COMPARATIVE SALES METHOD

If there is sufficient data, it is preferable to derive the capitalization rate from comparable sales. The appraiser needs to determine if the income, expenses, financing terms, and market conditions at the time of the sale of the comparable are appropriate to use with the subject property. This is especially true for the net operating income (NOI) as the expenses for the comparables may represent the year that just ended and may have to be adjusted to the date of value used for the subject. Besides income and expense data, the appraiser also needs to consider allowances for replacement and needs to ensure these are adjusted to the current conditions as of the date of value. As we discussed earlier, it is also important for the appraiser to ensure that there are no special financing concessions that may affect the sales price of the comparable properties.

When the appraiser derives the capitalization rate using comparable sales, the overall rate is applied to the subject property in a manner consistent with its derivation. If the capitalization rate of the comparables is based upon the NOI and expenses for the next year, then this capitalization rate should be applied to the subject property and its projected NOI for the next year as well.

Once comparable sales have been identified and verified, and appropriate adjustments made, the appraiser can determine the capitalization rate of the comparable sale by dividing its NOI by the sales price. The capitalization rate chosen by the appraiser from those indicated by the comparable sales would be the one indicated by the sale that is most similar to the subject property.

At times, actual operating expense information for the comparable sales is unavailable; but, the gross income and sales price information is available. As a reminder, **operating expenses** are expenses required to run a property (i.e., to maintain its income). In those situations, an appraiser must analyze the market to determine typical market operating expenses. From this market estimate, an appraiser can estimate operating expenses for the chosen comparable property. Then, the appraiser subtracts the estimated operating expenses from each comp's effective gross income to determine the property's NOI.

Example: The operating statement for the subject property shows that its NOI is $575,000. After researching the market area, the appraiser came up with the following comparable information.

Comparables	NOI	Sales Price	Cap Rate
Comp 1	$450,000	$5,000,000	9.%
Comp 2	$357,750	$3,578,000	10.%
Comp 3	$1,506,800	$25,113,000	6.%
Comp 4	$600,000	$6,316,000	9.5%

After further analysis, the appraiser concludes that Comp 3 is not especially indicative of the market, even though on the surface it appeared to be wholly comparable to the subject. Looking at the remaining comps, the appraiser concludes that the cap rate most likely should be in between 9-9.5%. The appraiser ultimately selects 9.5% because Comp 4 was the most comparable to the subject. $575,000 ÷ 9.5% = $6,052,631. The subject has a value of $6,053,000 (rounded).

Selection of a capitalization rate from comparative sales involves a direct analysis of transactions between buyers and sellers in the market. The capitalization rate indicated by a sale is determined by dividing the sale price into the net income from the property. A sales price of $600,000 for a property with an annual net operating income of $57,000 would indicate a cap rate of 9.5%. ($57,000 ÷ $600,000 = .095 or 9.5%)

Sales of several similar properties must be analyzed in the same manner and the indicated rates correlated into one. This method does not take into account possible fluctuations in future cash flows, but uses data from a fixed period in time—the time of sale. It assumes that expected changes in income performance will be the same for the subject and comparable properties.

Selection of a capitalization rate by the comparative sales method is considered the most appropriate method, since it directly reflects the capitalization rates at which properties are bought and sold. Even though the calculations used in this method are simple, its application has many hazards. The appraiser must use good judgment in selecting a capitalization rate.

Before accepting a rate estimated by the comparative sales method, several factors must be considered.

1. The comparative sales should be recent. Capitalization rates change with general economic conditions.

2. The net income imputed to the sale properties must be derived in the same way as that of the subject property. If applicable, the same type of expenses must be deducted from the gross income of the sale parcel as from the gross income of the subject property. Often, the same ratio of gross income to net income as was estimated for the subject property is used for the sale property.

3. The sale property should be located in the same neighborhood as the subject property or in a neighborhood considered equally desirable.

4. The improvements of the sale property should be similar to those of the subject property in type or class, age and condition, size, construction, and ratio of building to land.

In appraisal practice, it is often difficult to obtain sufficient sales data to derive a capitalization rate directly applicable to the subject property. It may be necessary to adjust the capitalization rates indicated by the sales to the rate proper for the subject property. Adjustment of rates indicated by other comparable sales and correlation of these rates to select a capitalization rate for the subject property involves the appraiser's judgment.

As we said before, differences in capitalization rates reflect the quality of the properties in relation to the features of a good investment. If a comparable sale property indicates a rate of 11%, any features of the comparable sale property superior to the subject property indicate a rate higher than 11% for the subject. Conversely, features of the subject property superior to the sale property indicate a rate lower than 11% for the subject. A capitalization rate from a comparative sale may be adjusted up or down for any number of differences. The more adjustments necessary, the less reliable the indicated capitalization rate.

Capitalization rates derived from properties with structural improvements include both an interest rate and a recapture allowance. Since the recapture portion of the capitalization rate applies only to the income attributable to the improvements, you must segregate land and building values for the sale property.

Estimate the remaining economic life of the building. Multiply the annual recapture rate by the building value to determine the annual recapture in dollars. Deduct this figure from the net income to determine net income after recapture. Dividing the sale price into the net income after recapture yields the interest rate.

Example: Compute the interest rate by the comparative sales method using the following information.

Sales price	$800,000
Building value (75%)	$600,000
Remaining life of building	50 years
Annual net income	$72,000

Step 1: Calculate the Recapture Rate

Recapture rate = 100% ÷ 50 years

Recapture rate = .02 or 2%

Step 2: Calculate the Recapture

Recapture = Building Value × Recapture Rate

Recapture = $600,000 × .02

Recapture = $12,000

Step 3: Calculate the Net Income After Recapture

Net income = NOI − Recapture

Net income = $72,000 − $12,000

Net income = $60,000

Step 4: Calculate the Interest Rate (ROI)

ROI = Net Income ÷ Sales price of the property

ROI = $60,000 ÷ $800,000

ROI = 7.5%

Estimating a capitalization rate by the comparative sales method is the most practical method. In practice, an appraiser keeps abreast of current capitalization rates by a continual analysis of property sales and listings and by discussions with informed buyers and sellers.

DERIVING CAPITALIZATION RATES FROM OPERATING DATA

If the appraiser cannot derive a capitalization rate because stringent data requirements cannot be met, he or she has the option to derive a cap rate by using operating statement ratios. If there is not sufficient expense data for the comparable sales, the appraiser can determine typical expense ratios from other parts of the marketplace and published data. To do this, he or she needs reliable data about the gross incomes and sales prices for each comparable. The appraiser can determine what the typical expenses are for the comparables in question. Then using market data, the appraiser determines the net operating income (NOI) for each comparable by subtraction. To determine the NOI, subtract the operating expenses from the effective gross income (EGI).

OPERATING STATEMENT RATIOS

The market estimate of operating expenses can be expressed as a ratio—the operating expense ratio and the net income ratio. The **operating expense ratio (OER)** is the relationship of a property's expenses to income, found by dividing total operating expenses by effective gross income (EGI).

The **net income ratio (NIR)** is the ratio between the net operating income of a property and its effective gross income. It is calculated by dividing the net operating income (NOI) by the effective gross income (EGI).

Example: Calculate the net income ratio (NIR) for a property with an effective gross income (EGI) of $80,000 and operating expenses (from market data) of $45,000.

Step 1: Calculate the Net Operating Income (NOI)

$$NOI = EGI - Operating\ Expenses$$
$$NOI = \$80,000 - \$45,000$$
$$NOI = \$35,000$$

Step 2: Calculate the Net Income Ratio (NIR)

$$NIR = NOI \div EGI$$
$$NIR = \$35,000 \div \$80,000$$
$$NIR = 0.4375\ or\ 44\%$$

Because the operating expense and net income ratios are complementary, adding them together will result in 1.0 or 100%. This relationship is useful when an appraiser is able to calculate one but needs the other. To do this, subtract the known ratio from 1.0 or 100%

Example: A property has an effective gross income of $78,000 and operating expenses totaling $31,200. The NOI is $46,800 ($78,000 − $31,200). The following chart shows how the operating expense ratio and net operating income ratio are inverses of one another.

Net income ratio	$46,800 ÷ $78,000 =	60% (0.6)
Operating expense ratio	$31,200 ÷ $78,000 =	40% (0.4)
		100% (1.0)

BAND OF INVESTMENT

Band of investment is a method of estimating interest and capitalization rates, based on a weighted average of the mortgage interest rate (or other cost of borrowed funds) and the rate of return on equity required.

When a property is purchased, it is normally financed with a combination of equity from the purchaser and a loan from some bank or investor. Lenders anticipate receiving a competitive interest rate associated with the credit worthiness of the borrower and the perceived risk of the investment. The lender normally wants both returns on the investment as well as a return of investment, so the typical loan is amortized.

In a similar manner, equity investors (buyers) want a competitive equity cash return at an appropriate rate or they will seek investments elsewhere. The band of investment is a technique in which the capitalization rates demanded by the lender as well as the investor are weighted and presented as a percentage, which represents a capitalization rate. This procedure uses a weighted-average rate attributable to the total investment. Using this technique, the appraiser determines a capitalization rate for both the equity and the debt position for a property and then combines these two rates into an overall rate.

> **Example**: Assume a property was purchased for $900,000. The loan to value ratio is 70%, which is typical for this kind of investment. The following ratio between equity and loan apply:
>
> Equity Value (30%)   = $270,000
>
> Mortgage Value (70%) = $630,000
>
> Property Value (100%) = $900,000

The band of investment derives a capitalization rate by combining the mortgage constant (capitalization rate) with the investor capitalization rate. The **mortgage constant** or **mortgage capitalization rate (R_M)** is the ratio of annual debt service to the principal amount of the mortgage loan. The mortgage constant is affected by the loan interest rate, the term of the loan, and the frequency of the payments of interest and principal. Mortgage constants can be calculated on a financial calculator or by referring to financial tables. We will illustrate how to calculate this in Chapter 12, which deals with the financial calculator.

Formula – Mortgage Constant

R_M = Debt Service ÷ Mortgage Principal

The capitalization rate for the equity is referred to as the equity capitalization rate (R_E). The **equity capitalization rate** is the factor used to estimate the value of the equity in the band of investment method of capitalization and other mortgage and equity techniques. There are different ways to calculate this depending upon the nature and size of the investment. R_E is used to convert an equity dividend into an equity value indication.

Formula – Equity Capitalization Rate

R_E = Equity Dividend ÷ Equity Invested

The formula reflects one way to calculate the equity capitalization rate, which is to divide the pretax cash flow by the equity investment into the property. This amount is often difficult to confirm, as many buyers do not want to share this information. If it can be obtained, it is a very strong indication of the capitalization rate assigned to the equity.

Appraisers often determine R_E by comparing the interest rates being paid on other investments to the return expected for the subject property. For a safe conservative investment, the appraiser may use rates from treasury bills or other similar investments. For riskier investments, the appraiser may use the rates being paid on subprime loans or the interest rates for second and third mortgages.

As previously indicated, the cap rate from the band of investment must satisfy both the mortgage component and the equity dividend requirement of the investor. For mortgage-equity analysis, the cap rate can be thought of as a composite rate. Thus, the cap rate is a weighted average of the mortgage capitalization rate and the equity capitalization rate. This relationship is shown below.

Percent of Property Value	x Cap rate	= Weighted Component
Mortgage (%)	$\times R_M$ =	From Mortgage
Equity (%)	$\times R_E$ =	From Equity

Example: The subject property is a 10-unit apartment building. The buyer is putting 30% down and securing a loan for the remaining 70%. The interest rate for the mortgage is 6.5%. The loan term is 25 years. This is an average risk purchase so the investor wants to see a return of at least 8% as this is more than the current rate for T-Bills and other secure investments. Using the formula presented above, compute the cap rate.

Percent of Property Value	$\times$ Cap Rate		=	Weighted Component
Mortgage:	70 %	$\times$ 0.0806*	=	0.0564
Equity:	30 %	$\times$ 0.08	=	0.0240
Overall Cap Rate			=	0.0804 or 8% rounded

*This represents the mortgage constant for an amortized loan at 6.5% with a 25-year term. We will illustrate how to calculate this on the financial calculator in Chapter 12.

SUMMATION METHOD

Estimating a capitalization rate by the summation method requires considerable subjective judgment on the part of the appraiser. For this reason, it is best to use this method only as a check against one of the other available methods.

The **summation method** establishes a safe rate for an investment and adds or subtracts from this basic rate according to the proper interest rate for the subject property. The summation method is another name for the cost approach to estimating value. The safe rate chosen is usually that of a risk-free investment, such as savings deposits or government bonds. Additions or subtractions are made by percentages for investment characteristics considered more or less desirable than the safe-rate investment.

> ### Review – Seven Considerations When Evaluating an Investment
> 1. Reliability of net income
> 2. Liquidity
> 3. Burden of management
> 4. Probability of increase or decrease in value
> 5. Taxation
> 6. Hypothecation
> 7. Leverage

Those are the major characteristics of any investment. The relative importance of any particular characteristic depends on the type of investment being evaluated. Although other investment characteristics might be added to the list, enlarging it would result in overlapping of elements or including items of minor importance. For instance, risk is a major consideration in an investment. However, risk is considered with both the reliability of net income and the probability of increase or decrease in value. The appraiser prepares a chart showing how the subject property differs in investment characteristics from the safe rate investment.

Safe rate		8.0%
Adjustments		
Reliability of net income	+	2.0%
Liquidity	+	1.5%
Burden of management	+	1.0%
Probability of appreciation	−	4.0%
Indicated interest rate		8.5%

The rate derived by the summation method is an interest rate. Any allowance necessary for the recapture of improvement cost must be added to this rate.

CAPITALIZATION TECHNIQUES

The two most widely used methods for converting income into an estimate of value are direct capitalization and yield capitalization. **Direct capitalization** converts an estimate of a single year's income into an indication of value. **Yield capitalization** mathematically discounts future benefits at appropriate yield rates, producing a value that explicitly reflects the income pattern, value change, and yield-rate characteristics of the investment.

DIRECT CAPITALIZATION

Direct capitalization is most often used when properties are already operating with a stabilized income and expense basis and there are sufficient comparable sales. Comparables should have similar risk levels, incomes, expenses, physical and locational characteristics and the expectation that future income levels will be similar to the subject property. This method is less useful for properties during initial lease-up or for properties with varying income and expense levels in the future. The advantage of direct capitalization is that it is simple to use, easy to explain, provides strong market evidence of value and expresses what the participants in the market are thinking.

Using the direct capitalization method, a buyer who will pay $1 million for a property yielding an annual net operating income (NOI) of $90,000 is indicating a willingness to purchase the property at a 9% capitalization rate. If a number of sellers and buyers are willing to transfer similar property on the same terms, the capitalization rate indicated for this particular type of property is 9%.

Applying this data to the capitalization process, an annual net operating income (NOI) of $90,000 divided by the capitalization rate of 9% indicates a property value of $1 million.

Property Value = NOI   ÷   Cap Rate

Property Value = $90,000 ÷   0.09

Property Value = $1,000,000

In practice, it is very difficult to obtain true NOI from buyers or sellers of comparable properties.

In the **property residual technique**, net income from a property is segregated between land and improvements. The method is the same one used for capitalizing the income from vacant land. Instead of capitalizing with an interest rate only, a composite rate of interest and recapture is used. Income to the land is capitalized at the interest rate and income to the improvements is capitalized at a rate, which combines the interest rate and an annual recapture rate. The recapture rate is computed by dividing the remaining economic life of the improvements into 100%. For example, the annual recapture rate for a building with an estimated remaining life of 50 years would be 2%; for 40 years, it would be 2.5%.

> **Example**: If net income to the property is $90,000 per year and the overall capitalization rate is estimated to be 12%, the property value indicated by the income approach would be computed by dividing the NOI by the overall capitalization rate.
>
> Property Value   = $90,000 ÷ 0.12
>
> Property Value   = $750,000

The most important element in the property residual technique is selection of the capitalization rate. The rate should be developed by the comparative sales method. The comparative sales must be similar to the subject property in location and improvements and in the manner in which net income is estimated.

RESIDUAL TECHNIQUES

Residual techniques are procedures used to capitalize the income allocated to an investment component of unknown value after all investment components of known values have been satisfied.

Ways to Use Residual Techniques
- Physical components (land and buildings)
- Financial interests (mortgage and equity)
- Legal estates (leased fee and leasehold)

It is important to remember that residual techniques should only be used when the assumptions upon which they are developed are reasonable. If an appraiser uses residual techniques, he or she is using some known variables to determine unknown variables.

The following table illustrates the different known and unknown variables for residual techniques:

Use of Residual Techniques with Known and Unknown Variables		
Technique Used	**Known**	**Variable Sought**
Land Residual	NOI	Land or site value
	Value of Building	
	Building Cap Rate	
	Land Cap Rate	
Building Residual	NOI	Building Value
	Building Cap Rate	Land or site value
		Land Cap Rate
Mortgage Residual	NOI	Amount of Mortgage
	Amount of Equity	
	Equity Cap Rate	
	Mortgage Constant	
Equity Residual	NOI	Amount of Equity
	Mortgage Amount	
	Mortgage Constant	
	Equity Cap Rate	

Using comparable sales or one of the residual techniques (if comparables are not available), an appraiser can calculate an overall cap rate using the band of investment. In some yield capitalization techniques, net income from a property is segregated between land and improvements. The appraiser uses comparable sales to determine the capitalization rates of the land and the improvements. Just as a cap rate is developed for the weighted mortgage rate and the rate of return for the equity component using the band of investment, a similar process can be used using the land and building components to the value of a property. This is also a weighted formula and the appraiser has to determine the relative contributions of the land and the improvements to the total estimate of value.

Example: A commercial strip mall has an annual NOI of $200,000. It is determined that the land is contributing 45% to the NOI and the improvements are contributing 55%. Using a similar methodology to the band of investment, in this case, the land and improvement capitalization rates are used, not investor equity. If comparable sales indicate that the cap rate for the land is 7.5%, and the rate for the improvements is 8%, what is the overall cap rate?

% of Property Value	×	Cap Rate	=	Weighted Component
Land (45 %)	×	0.075	=	.03375
Improvements (55%)	×	0.08	=	.044
				.07775
Overall Cap Rate			=	.07775 or 8% rounded

The value is then determined by dividing the NOI by the overall cap rate as we have done previously.

Value	=	NOI	÷	Cap Rate
Value	=	$200,000	÷	0.08
Value	=	$2,500,000		

BUILDING RESIDUAL TECHNIQUE

The total value of a property can be estimated using direct capitalization, if the land value is known, the NOI is known, and the capitalization rates for both land and improvements have been determined. The **building residual technique** is an income capitalization technique in which the net income to the building (after deducting the income required for the land) is capitalized into an estimated value for the building.

Example: Assume that the appraiser has determined the cap rate for the land to be 8% and the rate for the improvements is 9%. The NOI is $225,000. The land value was determined to be $2,000,000 using comparable land sales.

a. Land Value = $2,000,000

b. NOI = $225,000

c. Income Attributable to Land

NOI_{Land} = Land value x Land cap rate

NOI_{Land} = $2,000,000 x .08

NOI_{Land} = $160,000

d. Income Attributable to Improvements = (b − c)

Income Attributable to Improvements = $65,000

e. Building Value = $NOI_{Building}$ ÷ Cap Rate$_{Building}$

Building Value = $ 65,000 ÷ .09

Building Value = $722,000

f. Value of Property = Land + Improvements

Value of Property = $2,000,000 + $722,000

Value of Property = $2,722,000

For this approach to work, the appraiser needs to have information about the current land value, NOI, and the cap rates for the land and improvements. This information is often a challenge to extract from the marketplace.

This method is used in situations when the improvements have suffered significant accrued depreciation. In some instances, the appraiser can use this approach to calculate accrued depreciation. The depreciation would be the value determined using the building residual technique and subtracting this amount from the cost of replacement new.

LAND RESIDUAL TECHNIQUE

In a similar manner, the value of the land can be determined using the NOI attributable to the land with a land cap rate determined from other sources. The **land residual technique** is an income capitalization technique in which the net income remaining to the land (after income attributable to the building has been deducted) is capitalized into an estimate of value for the land.

Example: Using the same data in the previous example, the land value is calculated when the improvement value is known.

a. Improvement Value $= \$722,000$

b. NOI $= \$225,000$

c. Income Attributable to Improvements

$\text{NOI}_{\text{Building}} = \text{Building value } \times \text{ Cap Rate}_{\text{Building}}$

$\text{NOI}_{\text{Building}} = \$722,000 \times .09$

$\text{NOI}_{\text{Building}} = \$65,000$

d. Income Attributable to Land (b − c)

$\text{NOI}_{\text{Land}} = \$225,000 - \$65,000$

$\text{NOI}_{\text{Land}} = \$160,000$

e. Land Value $= \text{NOI}_{\text{Land}} \div \text{Cap Rate}_{\text{Land}}$

Land Value $= \$160,000 \div .08$

Land Value $= \$2,000,000$

f. Value of Property $=$ Land $+$ Improvements

Value of Property $= \$2,000,000 + \$722,000$

Value of Property $= \$2,722,000$

The land residual technique is often used in cases when there are no comparable land sales. It is often used in the cost approach to value. Like the building residual technique, the appraiser has to know the appropriate cap rates for land and improvements, the NOI, and the value of the building.

EQUITY AND MORTGAGE RESIDUAL TECHNIQUES

The equity residual technique and the mortgage residual technique are determined in a similar manner. For a discussion of these techniques, see The Appraisal Institutes' publication, *The Appraisal of Real Estate, 12 ed.*

YIELD CAPITALIZATION

Yield capitalization, or discounted cash flow analysis, is another more complex method for valuation of income generating property. **Yield capitalization** is a method in which the value of future benefits is discounted to a present value. Future benefits include the periodic flow of income generated by a property for its owner (return on investment) as well as a reversion. **Reversion** is the lump sum amount the investor expects to receive upon sale of a property at some future point in time (return of investment).

The process in which the periodic future income flows and the reversion are converted into a present value estimate is called discounting. **Discounting** is a form of capitalization, which is specifically concerned with calculating present worth based upon future income. The **discount rate** is the yield rate to the investor and assumes a satisfactory return on and return of investment to the investor.

Conceptually, it is helpful to look at the property being appraised as an investment over time and note the direction of cash flow. When the initial purchase of a property is made, funds flow from the buyer to the seller. While not always the case, there is usually an expectation that the property will generate funds, which will flow to the investor who just bought the property. There is also an expectation that at some point in the future, the property will be sold with the investor receiving a lump sum amount of capital. Yield capitalization converts these various cash flows into a value estimate.

Steps when Performing Yield Capitalization

1. Project the holding period of the investment. The **holding period** is the length of time the property will be used as an investment.

2. Estimate and forecast all the future cash flows associated with the investment. At times, monies will flow from the investor toward the investment. This is called **negative cash flow**. At other times, income generated by the property flows toward the owner resulting in **positive cash flow**.

3. Identify an appropriate discount rate. The rate chosen needs to be reflective of investor's expectations and provide for an acceptable return on investment and return of investment.

4. Convert the future benefits into a present value estimate.

SIX FUNCTIONS OF ONE DOLLAR

To understand yield capitalization, it is necessary to have an understanding of the time element of money. The classic illustration of the change in values over time is the **Six Functions of One Dollar** chart, which expresses the results of six types of calculations meaningful to investors.

The chart on the next page identifies six individual functions. Columns 1 and 2 are for compounding, columns 3 and 6 are for asset accumulation or debt retirement, and columns 4 and 5 are for discounting.

7.00% Annual Interest Rate

Years	1 Future Value of $1	2 Future Value of $1 Per Period	3 Sinking Fund Factor	4 Present Value of $1 (Reversion)	5 Present Value of $1 Per Period	6 Installment to Amortize $1
1	1.070000	1.000000	1.000000	0.934579	0.934579	1.070000
2	1.144900	2.070000	0.483092	0.873439	1.808018	0.553092
3	1.225043	3.214900	0.311052	0.816298	2.624316	0.381052
4	1.310796	4.439943	0.225228	0.762895	3.387211	0.295228
5	1.402552	5.750739	0.173891	0.712986	4.100197	0.243891
6	1.500730	7.153291	0.139796	0.666342	4.766540	0.209796
7	1.605781	8.654021	0.115553	0.622750	5.389289	0.185553
8	1.718186	10.259803	0.097468	0.582009	5.971299	0.167468
9	1.838459	11.977989	0.083486	0.543934	6.515232	0.153486
10	1.967151	13.816448	0.072378	0.508349	7.023582	0.142378
11	2.104852	15.783599	0.063357	0.475093	7.498674	0.133357
12	2.252192	17.888451	0.055902	0.444012	7.942686	0.125902
13	2.409845	20.140643	0.049651	0.414964	8.357651	0.119651
14	2.578534	22.550488	0.044345	0.387817	8.745468	0.114345
15	2.759032	25.129022	0.039795	0.362446	9.107914	0.109795
16	2.952164	27.888054	0.035858	0.338735	9.446649	0.105858
17	3.158815	30.840217	0.032425	0.316574	9.763223	0.102425
18	3.379932	33.999033	0.029413	0.295864	10.059087	0.099413
19	3.616528	37.378965	0.026753	0.276508	10.335595	0.096753
20	3.869684	40.995492	0.024393	0.258419	10.594014	0.094393
21	4.140562	44.865177	0.022289	0.241513	10.835527	0.092289
22	4.430402	49.005739	0.020406	0.225713	11.061240	0.090406
23	4.740530	53.436141	0.018714	0.210947	11.272187	0.088714
24	5.072367	58.176671	0.017189	0.197147	11.469334	0.087189
25	5.427433	63.249038	0.015811	0.184249	11.653583	0.085811
26	5.807353	68.676470	0.014561	0.172195	11.825779	0.084561
27	6.213868	74.483823	0.013426	0.160930	11.986709	0.083426
28	6.648838	80.697691	0.012392	0.150402	12.137111	0.082392
29	7.114257	87.346529	0.011449	0.140563	12.277674	0.081449
30	7.612255	94.460786	0.010586	0.131367	12.409041	0.080586
31	8.145113	102.073041	0.009797	0.122773	12.531814	0.079797
32	8.715271	110.218154	0.009073	0.114741	12.646555	0.079073
33	9.325340	118.933425	0.008408	0.107235	12.753790	0.078408
34	9.978114	128.258765	0.007797	0.100219	12.854009	0.077797
35	10.676581	138.236878	0.007234	0.093663	12.947672	0.077234
36	11.423942	148.913460	0.006715	0.087535	13.035208	0.076715
37	12.223618	160.337402	0.006237	0.081809	13.117017	0.076237
38	13.079271	172.561020	0.005795	0.076457	13.193473	0.075795
39	13.994820	185.640292	0.005387	0.071455	13.264928	0.075387
40	14.974458	199.635112	0.005009	0.066780	13.331709	0.075009

Typically, people place funds in investments with the expectation those funds will earn interest. The investor is a "lender" and the investment is the "borrower." The individual invests (loans) capital in an investment, which is expected to compensate the investor with some kind of return. If an individual puts $100 into a savings account at a bank and it pays 7% per year, at the end of one year, the initial $100 investment has grown to $107. In a different light, to accumulate $107 in one year, it would be necessary to deposit $100 into an account bearing 7% interest.

Three Overall Ways to View Money

1. The future worth (amount) can be calculated based upon compounding.

2. The present worth (amount) of money may be calculated through discounting.

3. The amount of equal payments to retire a debt or to accumulate a specific amount of money may also be analyzed.

Overall, the six functions of a dollar are tied to the time element of money. With computer technology and modern financial calculators, charts like the one following this discussion have essentially become obsolete. These charts are helpful in illustrating the various functions of a dollar, which is why this chart is included.

The following includes the six functions of a dollar calculated at a 7% interest rate and projected out for 40 years. In order to use this chart, simply multiply the appropriate factor by the appropriate amount of money. The result includes the original investment plus any interest or discount.

> **Example**: To find out how much $250 would be worth if it were placed in a savings account untouched for 15 years, look at column 1 (Future Value of $1.00) for 15 years. Multiply that factor (2.759032) by $250. At the end of 15 years, the original investment of $250 will have grown to $689.76.

COLUMN 1, FUTURE VALUE OF $1

This column is used to calculate the future worth of a present amount assuming the amount invested draws interest at the rate stated at the top of the chart.

> **Example**: The future value factor of $1.00 invested for 17 years is 3.158815. If $100 were invested for 17 years with a rate of 7% per year, the interest plus the initial investment of $100 would total $315.88.

COLUMN 2, FUTURE VALUE OF $1 PER PERIOD

This column is used to calculate the future value if regular additions of $1.00 are made every year and the interest stays constant during the investment period. In this instance, not only is interest added to the original investment amount, but additional capital is added to the investment at regular intervals as well.

> **Example:** If $100 is invested at the end of every year for five years and that amount earns 7% per year, the investment will build up to $575.07 at the end of the fifth year.

COLUMN 3, SINKING FUND FACTOR

This column will tell the investor how much must be invested each year to accumulate to a specific amount at the end of the stated period.

> **Example:** If a person wants to accumulate $1,500,000 in savings over a 20-year period, an annual deposit of $36,589.50 ($1,500,000 × 0.024393) must be placed into an account bearing 7% interest every year for those 20 years.

COLUMN 4, PRESENT VALUE OF $1

This column is used to calculate the present value of a future amount.

> **Example:** A person who will inherit $750,000 in 5 years could sell his or her rights to the inheritance. If the investor buying the rights to the inheritance required a 7% return on his or her investment, he or she would pay $534,739.50 ($750,000 × 0.712986).

COLUMN 5, PRESENT VALUE OF AN ANNUITY OF $1 PER PERIOD

This column is much like Column 4, but instead of one future lump payment, it is used to discount future cash flows into a present worth.

> **Example:** Assume a woman won a $20,000,000 state lottery payable at $1,000,000 per year for 20 years. If the state required a 7% discount, the woman would receive $10,594,014 ($1,000,000 × 10.594014) as a lump sum (prior to taxes).

Column 5 is used most frequently by real estate appraisers because it estimates the present value of an annuity.

COLUMN 6, INSTALLMENT TO AMORTIZE $1

This column is often used to identify the size of regular payments (annually in this case) required to pay off a debt over a specified period.

> **Example:** If homeowner Pat obtained a 30-year, $300,000 loan at 7% to buy his house, he would have to make annual payments to the lender of $24,175.80 ($300,000 × 0.080586).

ANNUITY METHOD OF CAPITALIZATION

Since real estate income flows in a similar pattern, it is reasonable to analyze real estate income from the point of view of an annuity. An **annuity** is a sum of money received at fixed intervals, such as a series of assured equal or nearly equal payments, to be made over a period of time. Though the term annuity technically refers to an annual amount, it applies to any kind of regular payment of a specific amount. For any income-producing property, tenants pay rent at regular intervals (usually monthly) to the property owner. Because of this, proprietors come to expect a regular amount of income generated at a predictable schedule. Estimating the present value of an annuity is the same process used to value real estate that produces a predictable steady stream of income at regular intervals.

When discounting, the present value of an annuity is always assumed to be less than the sum total of all the cash flows during the period of the annuity. This procedure is tied to the premise that benefits received today are worth more than benefits received in the future.

The formula for calculating the present value of an annuity is rather complex and beyond the scope of this discussion. However, the factors found in the previous table can be used to calculate the value of an income-producing property.

> **Example:** An income-producing property has been leased to a very reliable tenant for 18 years. The property produces a net annual operating income of $250,000 to the owners. The yield on the property has been estimated to be 7%. Though it would not work out this way in the real world, for purposes of simplicity, the net operating income is forecast to be level for the next 18 years. This would be making the assumption that taxes, maintenance, and management costs would not go up for the next 18 years. At the end of the 18-year lease period, the subject property's building is estimated to be at the end of its remaining economic life and have no value. Consequently, at the end of the lease period, all the value of the subject property will be solely in its land.

Current comparable land sales indicate the current value of the land at $450,000. On average, land value has historically appreciated 1% per year for the last 20 years and is forecast to increase at this rate into the near future. The future value of a property is obviously very difficult to predict. This assumption is made for illustration purposes. The assignment is to estimate the current value of this property.

SOLUTION

To solve this valuation problem, the present value (PV) of the income stream needs to be estimated as well as the present value of the reversion.

Step 1

PV of NOI = NOI × Annuity Factor at 7% for 18 years

PV of NOI = $250,000.00 × 10.059087

PV of NOI = $2,514,772.00

Step 2. To estimate the value of the land, the subject's land is currently estimated to be worth $450,000. Assuming it increases in value by 1% per year, 18 years in the future it is estimated to be worth $538,300 (rounded).

FV Land = Current Land Value × FV of $1/18 years @ 1%

FV Land = $450,000 × 1.196147

FV Land = $538,266 rounded to $538,300

Step 3. The future value (FV) of the land needs to be discounted to its present value by multiplying it by the reversion factor (Column 4) for 7% at 18 years.

PV Land = FV Land × PV of the Reversion Factor

PV Land = $538,300 × 0.295864

PV Land = $159,264 rounded to $159,300

Step 4. The final step is to add the present values of the net operating income and of the reversion.

PV of the Reversion = PV NOI + PV Land

PV of the Reversion = $2,514,772 + $159,300

PV of the Reversion = $2,674,072 rounded to $2,675,000

SUMMARY

The process of estimating the present worth of a property based on its anticipated income is **capitalization**, which is used to convert income to value. The two most widely used methods for converting income into an estimate of value are **direct capitalization** and **yield capitalization**. The estimate of value results from dividing the income estimate by an appropriate capitalization rate.

The **capitalization rate** is the rate of interest—which is considered a reasonable return on the investment. It is also described as the yield rate necessary to attract the money of the average investor to a particular type of investment. Selecting the capitalization rate is one of the most important parts of the capitalization process. Three methods have been developed to aid the appraiser in selecting a capitalization rate: (1) **comparative sales method**, (2) **band of investment method**, and (3) **summation method**.

Residual techniques are procedures used to capitalize the income allocated to an investment component of unknown value after all investment components of known values have been satisfied. This chapter discussed **property residual technique**, **building residual technique**, and **land residual technique**.

CHAPTER 11 REVIEW EXERCISES

MATCHING EXERCISE

Instructions: Write the letter of the matching term on the blank line before its definition. Answers are in Appendix A.

Terms

A. annuity

B. band of investment

C. building residual technique

D. comparative sales method

E. direct capitalization

F. discount rate

G. discounting

H. equity capitalization rate

I. equity dividend

J. holding period

K. hypothecation

L. land residual technique

M. liquidity

N. mortgage capitalization rate

O. negative cash flow

P. net income ratio (NIR)

Q. operating expense ratio (OER)

R. overall capitalization rate (OAR)

S. positive cash flow

T. residual techniques

U. return of investment

V. return on investment

W. reversion

X. six functions of one dollar

Y. summation method

Z. yield capitalization

Definitions

1. _____ An income capitalization technique in which value is estimated by dividing net operating income by the overall capitalization rate

2. _____ Profit produced by the investment

3. _____ Recapture or conversion of the investment in real estate to cash or other valuable assets

4. _____ Market-derived ratio reflecting the relationship between the net operating income a property generates and its value

5. _____ The relationship of a property's expenses to income, found by dividing total operating expenses by effective gross income (EGI)

6. _____ The ratio between the net operating income of a property and its effective gross income

7. _____ Method of estimating interest and capitalization rates, based on a weighted average of the mortgage interest rate (or other cost of borrowed funds) and the rate of return on equity required

8. _____ Capitalization rate of the debt

9. _____ Factor used to estimate the value of the equity in the band of investment method of capitalization and other mortgage and equity techniques

10. _____ Establishes a safe rate for an investment and adds or subtracts from this basic rate according to the proper interest rate for the subject property

11. _____ Procedures used to capitalize the income allocated to an investment component of unknown value after all investment components of known values have been satisfied

12. _____ Income capitalization technique in which the net income remaining to the land (after income attributable to the building has been deducted) is capitalized into an estimate of value for the land

13. _____ Method in which the value of future benefits is discounted to a present value

14. _____ The lump sum amount the investor expects to receive upon sale of a property at some future point in time (return of investment)

15. _____ Form of capitalization specifically concerned with calculating present worth based upon future income

16. _____ Yield rate to the investor and assumes a satisfactory return on and return of investment to the investor

17. _____ Length of time the property will be used as an investment

18. _____ Income generated by the property flows toward the owner

19. _____ Expresses the results of six types of calculations meaningful to investors

20. _____ Sum of money received at fixed intervals

MULTIPLE CHOICE QUESTIONS

Instructions: Circle the correct response and go to Appendix A to read the complete explanation for each question.

1. The appraisal process of estimating the present worth of a property based on its anticipated income is:
    a. band of investment method.
    b. capitalization.
    c. summation method.
    d. sales comparison.

2. Return on investment is also known as _____ whereas return of investment is also known as _____.
    a. yield, recapture
    b. profit, yield
    c. yield, income
    d. conversion, profit

3. Which of the following is not one of the seven characteristics to consider when evaluating an investment?
    a. Conversion
    b. Reliability of income
    c. Liquidity
    d. Taxation

4. Being able to use a capital asset, such as real estate, as collateral for borrowing money is known as:
    a. liquidity.
    b. capitalization.
    c. leverage.
    d. hypothecation.

5. Kelly owns a duplex, which has a NOI of $60,000. The cap rate is 4%. What is the value of the property?
    a. $800,000
    b. $1,150,000
    c. $1,500,000
    d. $2,250,000

6. Buyer Terry pays $800,000 for a property yielding an annual net operating income (NOI) of $75,000. What is the capitalization rate?

   a. 8.5%

   b. 9.375%

   c. 10.6%

   d. 12%

7. The lower the capitalization rate used, the:

   a. less secure the future income.

   b. higher the value result.

   c. lower the value result.

   d. higher the risk.

8. The method of capitalization rate determination that combines the mortgage interest rate with the equity rate necessary to attract investors is:

   a. band of investment method.

   b. comparative sales method.

   c. summation method.

   d. none of the above

For questions 9 – 12 use the following situation and data:

An apartment complex has an annual NOI of $200,000. It is determined that the land is contributing 55% to the NOI and the improvements are contributing 5%. We use a very similar methodology with the band of investment, but in this case, we use the land and the improvement capitalization rates and not investor equity. If comparable sales indicate that the capitalization rate for the land is 6.5% and the rate for the improvements is 7.5%, then the overall capitalization rate is calculated as follows:

> Weighted component = % of Property Value × Cap rate
> Weighted component = Land (55 %) × 0.065
> Improvements (45%) × 0.075
> Value equals the NOI divided by the overall cap rate.
> Value = NOI ÷ Cap Rate

9. In the table above, what is the weighted component for the land?

   a. 0.030

   b. 0.0358

   c. 0.065

   d. 0.0638

10. What is the weighted component for the buildings?

  a. 0.013
  b. 0.045
  c. 0.0338
  d. 0.0351

11. What is the capitalization rate using the property residual approach?

  a. 4%
  b. 6.3%
  c. 7%
  d. 9.5%

12. What is the value of the apartment units?

  a. $2,500,000
  b. $2,650,000
  c. $2,700,000
  d. $2,860,000

For questions 13 – 15 use the following situation and data:

This data represents a residual technique in which the appraiser is trying to determine the land value and the property value. The appraiser knows the value of the improvements ($750,000), the NOI ($250,000), the cap rates of the land (8%) and improvements (9%).

  a. Improvement Value = $750,000

  b. NOI = $250,000

  c. Income Attributable to Improvements

  $NOI_{Building}$ = Building value × Cap Rate$_{Building}$

  $750,000 × 0.09 = $65,000 = $67,500

  d. Income Attributable to Land (b – c)

  e. Land Value = NOI_{Land} ÷ Cap Rate$_{Land}$

  Land Value = _____ ÷ 0.08

  f. Value of Property = Improvements + Land

13. In the land residual technique analysis above, what is the NOI attributable to the land?

    a. $102,800

    b. $182,500

    c. $212,000

    d. $317,500

14. What is the value of the land (rounded)?

    a. $2,100,000

    b. $2,280,000

    c. $3,100,000

    d. $3,280,000

15. What is the value of the whole property?

    a. $2,280,000

    b. $2,565,000

    c. $3,030,000

    d. $3,335,000

12

Chapter

INTRODUCTION

In the old days, we made financial calculations using a slide rule. In the early 1980s, this changed as the financial calculator made its debut. For the past 25 years, the Hewlett Packard HP 12c financial calculator has been the financial calculator of choice among appraisers.

The HP 12c was the world's first horizontal financial calculator. Its innovative design and breakthrough Reverse Polish Notation (RPN) entry forever changed the way students and professionals reach their goals. After 25 years, this iconic calculator retains its world-famous horizontal design and sells under its original name and model number.

In this chapter, students will learn how to use this financial calculator to solve appraisal problems. If the reader currently uses an HP 12c, there should be enough new applications and problems to solve to make this chapter worthwhile. If you do not currently use a financial calculator, you will need to have one to use as you go through this chapter. We recommend either buying or borrowing an HP 12c as this is the calculator most often used by appraisers.

LEARNING OBJECTIVES

After reading this chapter, the student will be able to:

- describe the keyboard layout and the keys and functions that are used most often by appraisers.
- use the Reverse Polish Notation [f] and [g] functions, and other special keys.
- calculate typical problems encountered by appraisers.

THE CALCULATOR

A time-tested performer, the HP 12c has an easy-to-use Reverse Polish Notation (RPN) layout, one-line LCD display, and efficient data entry. There are over 120 built-in functions. There are four stack **registers** used to store numbers during calculations and the calculator is programmable.

Note gold keys on the face of the calculator to be used with [f] function.

Note blue keys on the down side of the button to be used with [g] function

THE KEYS

The HP 12c has 39 keys and we will discuss those of most use to the appraiser. Numerical keys are located where there are numbers on the right side.

 This is the key used to turn the calculator on and off. It is located in the lower left-hand corner.

 As the name implies, this key is used to enter data. You will note it is larger than all the other keys and is used for many operations.

 This function key is used with other keys with gold written above them to complete various operations.

 This function key is used with other keys with blue written in subscript to complete various operations.

 The STO key is used to store or place things into memory. One of the features of the HP 12c is that the user can create many memory spaces and the calculator is not limited to one memory, as are many adding machines.

 The RCL key is used to recall a number stored in one of the memory areas.

 The change sign key converts positive numbers into negative. All numbers are assumed to be positive unless the change key is used, so there is no need to indicate a positive number by using a plus (+) sign.

 This key computes problems using exponents.

The exchange key is used to change the numerator with the denominator.

Operators

 On the right-hand side of the calculators are the operators. After the numbers are properly entered, they are used to perform the function.

FUNCTION KEYS

Many keys on the HP 12c perform two or even three functions. The primary and alternate functions are indicated on the calculator by different colors. The primary function of a key is indicated by the characters printed in white on the upper face of the key.

The alternate function(s) of a key are indicated by the characters printed in gold above the key and the characters printed in blue on the lower face of the key.

The gold [f] is the function key to be used with characters printed in gold above the key. The blue [g] is the function key to be used with the characters printed in blue on the lower face of the key. Nearly all of the keys and numbers have a blue symbol on the base of the key.

These alternate functions are specified by pressing the appropriate prefix key after the function key. For example, consider the [i] key in the top row of the calculator on the left side. The directions to use the gold function, [INT/i]; the white function, [i] and the blue function, [i] are given in the dialog box below.

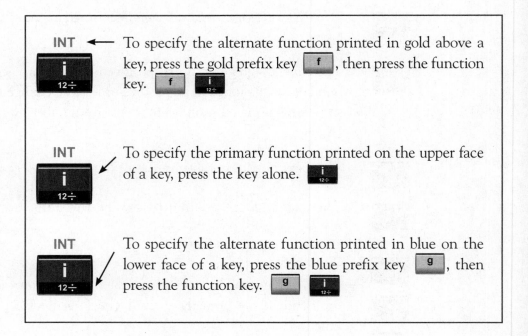

GOLD [f] FUNCTION KEY

It is important to remember that the gold [f] function key interacts with the gold superscripts that are above the keys on the left side of the calculator. We will use several of these keys in our financial calculations. So if a key box is displayed with a superscript, it means that this is a gold key. For example, amortization is used to calculate the principal and interest paid over a certain period of time. We solved a problem using this key above. Amortization is shown for this discussion as:

 This is used to clear the calculator.

BLUE [g] FUNCTION KEY

The blue keys are controlled by the blue [g] function key and they are designated as a subscript to the key pad. So the interest key has the subscript, which indicates that we are converting annual interest to monthly as we have done in several problems.

[g] + [CHS DATE] This is used to compute a future date.

[g] + [7 BEG] This is used to set the calculator so that it assumes that all payments in a compound interest problem are received at the beginning of each period. Using this key will result in the word BEGIN showing in the display.

[g] + [8 END] This resets the HP 12c to assume that all payments in a compound interest problem are received at the end of each period. The word END does **not** appear in the display.

LOAN AMORTIZATION KEYS

The time value keys are located at the top of the calculator. These are the five financial keys used for mortgages, discounting, the functions of a dollar, forecasting, discounted cash flows, compound interest calculations, and the like.

is used for the number of payments. If a loan is based upon a 30-year amortization, the number of monthly payments to be made is 30 years times 12 payments a year or 360 payments. The blue number at the base of the ![n] key indicates (12x).

To input a 30-year amortization, you use 30 ![g] ![n] and the display will show 360.

is used to indicate the interest rate. If we are solving for monthly payments, the annual interest rate has to be converted into monthly portions. Once again, the ![g] key is used but this time, with the ![i] key. To show an interest rate of 8% on a monthly basis, enter 8 ![g] ![i] and the display will show .67 (rounded from .666).

is the present amount of the loan balance and this is normally inputted without using either function key.

indicates the payment amount. Sometimes this is what we are solving for, other times we know the payment and are solving for something else.

represents the future value of the loan balance, or it can be used in forecasting to project the value of a property in the future.

GETTING STARTED

To begin using your HP 12c, press the ![ON] key. Pressing ![ON] again turns the calculator off. If not manually turned off, the calculator will turn off automatically 8 minutes after it was last used. Note that the ![ON] key is lower than the other keys to help prevent it being pressed inadvertently. If a {*} symbol shows up in the lower-left corner of the display, it means the battery power is nearly exhausted and you should replace the battery.

The display's readability depends on lighting, your viewing angle, and the display contrast setting. You can adjust the display contrast by holding down the [f] key and pressing [+] or [−].

USING REVERSE POLISH NOTATION (RPN)

There is no equal sign (=) on the calculator. This calculator is designed to solve problems without using the equal sign, brackets, and parentheses. This mathematic logic is known as **Polish Notation** and can be used in a reverse mode. It is more commonly referred to as RPN.

This works differently than a typical mathematical formula. When using an adding machine to solve for the quotient of "22 x 23", first input 22, hit the multiplication sign and then input 23 followed by the equal sign. Using RPN, the process is different.

Start by pressing the two key twice to come up with 22 and then hitting the [ENTER] key. Then indicate that 22 will interact with 23 by punching in the 2 and the 3 keys to make 23. Then specify the operation that will be accomplished—multiplication [×].

Problem: How much is 22 times 23?

Steps	Keystrokes	HP 12c Display on
Clear calculator	[f] [CLx]	0.00
1. First number	22	22.
2. Enter this number	[ENTER]	22.00
3. Second number	23	23.
4. Multiply	[×]	506.00

Problem: How much is 34,567 plus 54,698?

Steps	Keystrokes	HP 12c Display on
Clear calculator	f CLX	0.00
1. First number	34,567	34,567.
2. Enter this number	ENTER	34,567.00
3. Second number	54,698	54,698.
4. Add	+	89,265.00

The RPN or reverse notation becomes advantageous when the appraiser is performing several calculations in one sequence.

Problem: How much is 20 times 320 times 4 divided by 6? Try to solve this on your own. Here are the steps.

Steps	Keystrokes	HP 12c Display on
1. First number	20	20.
2. Enter this number	ENTER	20.00
3. Second number	320	320.
4. Multiply	×	6,400.00
5. Third number	4	4.
6. Multiply	×	25,600.00
7. Fourth number	6	6.
8. Divide	÷	4,266.67

Now suppose that you want to divide this remainder into another number, say 12,350. The display indicates 4,266.67 and if you keyed in 12,350 and divided, you would be dividing 4,266.67 by 12,350 and not the other way around. The solution for this dilemma is to change places of the two numbers. We want 4,266.67 to be the denominator and not the numerator. Using the exchange key, which is a very useful key, does this. So continuing the previous problem with the new twist, we perform the following:

Steps	Keystrokes	HP 12c Display on
9. Fifth number	12,350	12,350.
10. Exchange positions	x≷y x≤y	4,266.67
11. Divide	÷	2.8945

Once you finish an operation, it is a good idea to clear the registers. This is accomplished by using the ⬛ f key and the CLx REG (*gold letters*) above the CLx x=o (*white letters*) key. This is accomplished as the gold ⬛ f actually communicates with the gold function CLx REG. It clears all the memory in the registers.

SETTING THE DECIMAL POINT

The decimal point needs to be changed in some operations from the normal two places to more or less, depending upon the nature of the calculation. It is easy to change the decimal point so that you can see the data beyond two places. In the following example, we will show a number at 2 and 5 decimal points.

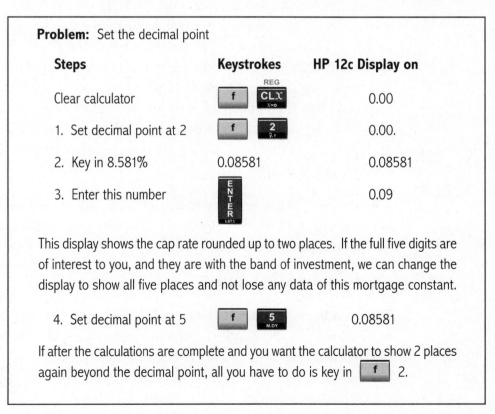

Problem: Set the decimal point

Steps	Keystrokes	HP 12c Display on
Clear calculator	f CLx (REG)	0.00
1. Set decimal point at 2	f 2	0.00.
2. Key in 8.581%	0.08581	0.08581
3. Enter this number	ENTER	0.09

This display shows the cap rate rounded up to two places. If the full five digits are of interest to you, and they are with the band of investment, we can change the display to show all five places and not lose any data of this mortgage constant.

| 4. Set decimal point at 5 | f 5 | 0.08581 |

If after the calculations are complete and you want the calculator to show 2 places again beyond the decimal point, all you have to do is key in f 2.

SETTING PAYMENT MODE

Calculations involving payments in advance yield different results than calculations involving payments in arrears. Usually lease payments are made in advance and mortgage payments are made in arrears. With mortgages, borrowers make the payment after they have had the use of the money. The calculator is set up to determine the payment amount in arrears as one has with the typical mortgage.

 This key is used to set the calculator so that it assumes that all payments in a compound interest problem are received at the beginning of each period. Using this key will result in the word BEGIN showing in the display.

 This resets the HP 12c to assume that all payments in a compound interest problem are received at the end of each period. The word END does **not** appear in the display.

STORING AND RECALLING NUMBERS

There are 20 addressable memories in the HP 12c, called **registers**. What this means is there are 20 places you can store information to be recalled at a later time. The problem is remembering what you have stored in which register. The first ten sites are the ten numbers on the keyboard from 0 to 9. The next ten are in different registers that are accessed by the same keys. For the second set of storage places, you access them by using the period sign and then the number. For example, we can store a number in 1 and also in .1. It is seldom that we need to use more than a few storage spaces at once, so the other ten registers are not used that often by appraisers, but they are available if needed.

For example, assume you need to convert acres into square footages. An acre is equivalent to 43,560 SF. Since we will be using the 43,560 more than once, we decide to store it in register 6.

Keystroke: 43,560 STO 6

That number is stored and can be recalled whenever we need it. To recall a number, you use the RCL key which is just to the left of the enter key. You tell the calculator what you are trying to recall by using the number that has the data stored. So to recall our acreage, we simply key in RCL 6 and the 43,560 will be displayed.

Problem: Assume that you are performing a land appraisal and you want to express the land sizes in acres. There are three parcels of 180,000 SF, 520,000 SF, and 230,000 SF. We can solve this problem and store the results if we like. We can also add up the total acreage by recalling what we have stored.

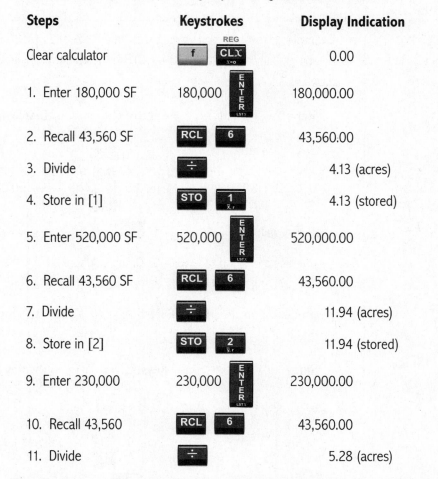

Steps	Keystrokes	Display Indication
Clear calculator	f CLX	0.00
1. Enter 180,000 SF	180,000 ENTER	180,000.00
2. Recall 43,560 SF	RCL 6	43,560.00
3. Divide	÷	4.13 (acres)
4. Store in [1]	STO 1	4.13 (stored)
5. Enter 520,000 SF	520,000 ENTER	520,000.00
6. Recall 43,560 SF	RCL 6	43,560.00
7. Divide	÷	11.94 (acres)
8. Store in [2]	STO 2	11.94 (stored)
9. Enter 230,000	230,000 ENTER	230,000.00
10. Recall 43,560	RCL 6	43,560.00
11. Divide	÷	5.28 (acres)

Thus far, we have converted all of the land square footages into acres and have stored the results except for the last calculation. To determine the total acreage, simply add the stored data. Use the recall key for each register and then add the results. Since the 5.28 acres is already on the display, we do not need to store and recall this data; we add the other stored data to it.

12. Recall 4.13 acres	RCL 1	4.13
13. Add	+	9.41
14. Recall 11.94 acres	RCL 2	11.94
15. Add	+	21.35

The display will show 21.35, which is the total acreage.

USING PERCENTAGE AND PERCENTAGE CHANGE KEYS

Two keys that are used frequently in appraisal problems are the percentage %INTG and the percentage change Δ%FRAC keys. Both of these functions are easy to use.

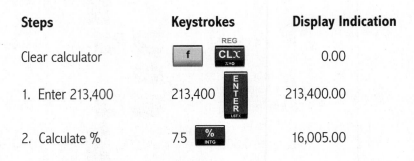

Example 1: Assume you want to calculate 7.5% of 213,400. You could solve this by multiplying the 213,400 by .075 or solve the problem directly with two easy steps.

Steps	Keystrokes	Display Indication
Clear calculator	f CLX	0.00
1. Enter 213,400	213,400 ENTER	213,400.00
2. Calculate %	7.5 %	16,005.00

The display will indicate 16,005.00, the solution.

Example 2: To determine 3.5% of 555,444, you would perform a similar operation.

Steps	Keystrokes	Display Indication
Clear calculator	f CLX	0.00
1. Enter 555,444	555,444 ENTER	555,444.00
2. Calculate %	3.5 %	19,440.54

The percentage change key Δ%FRAC is very useful in calculating market appreciation. One of the best ways to calculate appreciation is to use the sale-resale of the same property.

Example: A property sold two years ago for $375,000 and it recently sold for $425,000. How much market appreciation does this sale-resale indicate?

Steps	Keystrokes	Display Indication
Clear calculator	f CLX	0.00

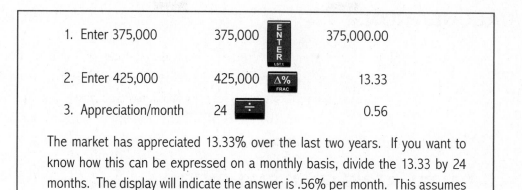

The market has appreciated 13.33% over the last two years. If you want to know how this can be expressed on a monthly basis, divide the 13.33 by 24 months. The display will indicate the answer is .56% per month. This assumes the appreciation is a straight-line function.

KEYING IN LARGE NUMBERS

Since the display cannot show more than 10 digits of a number, numbers greater than 9,999,999,999 cannot be entered into the display by keying in all the digits in the number. To enter numbers that have more than 10 digits, the numbers are converted to mathematical shorthand called **scientific notation**. Numbers entered in scientific notation can be used in calculations just like any other number.

To convert a number into scientific notation, move the decimal point until there is only one digit (a nonzero digit) to its left. The resulting number is called the **mantissa** of the original number. The number of decimal places you moved the decimal point is the **exponent** of the original number. If you moved the decimal point to the left, the exponent is positive; if you moved the decimal point to the right (this would occur for numbers less than one), the exponent is negative.

To express the number in the calculator, first key in the mantissa, press the **EEX** key, and then enter the number of decimal places.

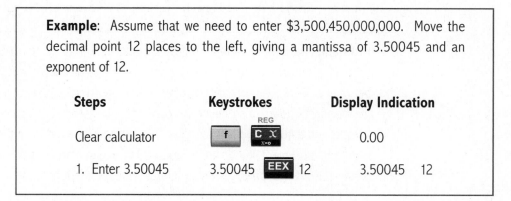

CALCULATIONS

Now that we have covered the basic keystrokes, we will practice with some typical calculations performed by appraisers. Starting with fairly simple operations, we will examine several problems that can affect appraisal practice. One of the major uses of the HP 12c for the appraiser is to perform time value of money calculations.

CALCULATING LOAN PAYMENTS

There are several ways to calculate loan payments such as using financial tables, computer amortization programs and other published data. However, this is often time consuming, and it is relatively easy to make these calculations using the HP 12c.

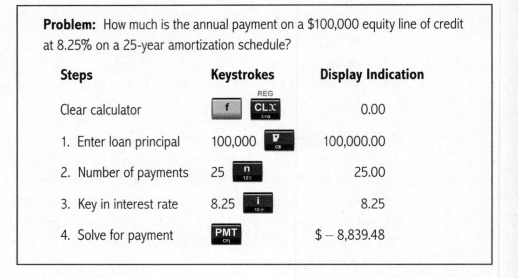

Problem: How much is the annual payment on a $100,000 equity line of credit at 8.25% on a 25-year amortization schedule?

Steps	Keystrokes	Display Indication
Clear calculator	f CLx	0.00
1. Enter loan principal	100,000 PV	100,000.00
2. Number of payments	25 n	25.00
3. Key in interest rate	8.25 i	8.25
4. Solve for payment	PMT	$ – 8,839.48

When we are calculating a payment of some kind, it will naturally show up on the display as a negative number. For example a payment of $8,839.48 will be indicated as –$8,839.48. This is the return of and return on capital.

Problem: As this is written, conforming loan amounts go up to $417,000. Assume a borrower wanted to know how much the payments would change between a 30-year amortization and a 40-year one. The buyer is trying to keep the payments down. The buyer discovers he can get a 30-year loan for 6% interest and a 40-year loan for 6.25%. Does it make sense to take the 40-year loan from a payment standpoint? The $400,000 loan amount is conforming so the borrower is not paying a higher interest rate required for jumbo loans.

Solution

First, solve for the 30-year loan.

Steps	Keystrokes	Display Indication
Clear calculator	f CLX	0.00
1. Enter loan principal	400,000 PV	400,000.00
2. Number of payments and convert to monthly	30 g n	360.00
3. Key in interest rate and convert to monthly	6 g i	0.50
4. Solve for payment	PMT	-$2,386.27

Next solve for the 40-year loan.

Steps	Keystrokes	Display Indication
Clear calculator	f CLX	0.00
1. Enter loan principal and change sign	400,000 PV	400,000.00
2. Number of payments and convert to monthly	40 g n	480.00
3. Key in interest rate and convert to monthly	6.25 g i	0.52
4. Solve for payment	PMT	-$2,259.19

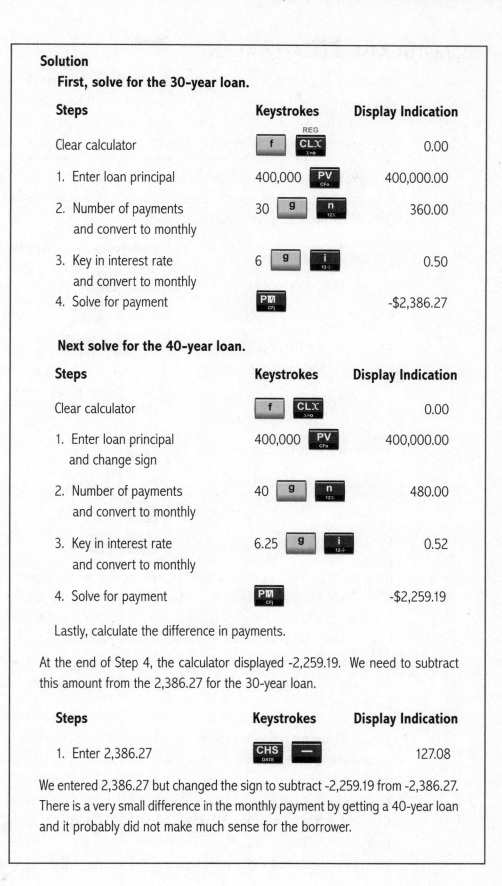

Lastly, calculate the difference in payments.

At the end of Step 4, the calculator displayed -2,259.19. We need to subtract this amount from the 2,386.27 for the 30-year loan.

Steps	Keystrokes	Display Indication
1. Enter 2,386.27	CHS —	127.08

We entered 2,386.27 but changed the sign to subtract -2,259.19 from -2,386.27. There is a very small difference in the monthly payment by getting a 40-year loan and it probably did not make much sense for the borrower.

CALCULATING LOAN BALANCE

You have been hired as an appraisal consultant to help the property owner decide whether or not it is feasible to perform a rehabilitation project on a property he owns. One of your concerns is the cost of the rehab and it is important to know the loan balance of the current property indebtedness.

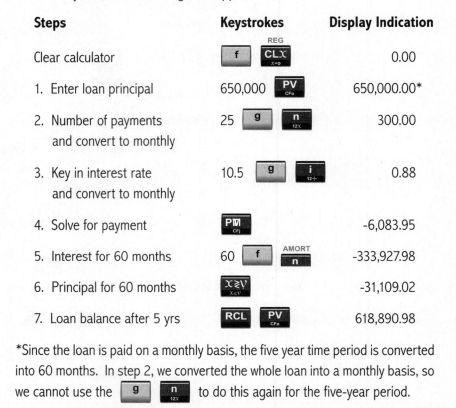

Problem: The original loan amount is $650,000 at 10.5% for 25 years. The loan has been in force for 5 years (60 months). What is the loan balance at the end of five years? The following data applies:

Steps	Keystrokes	Display Indication
Clear calculator	f CLX	0.00
1. Enter loan principal	650,000 PV	650,000.00*
2. Number of payments and convert to monthly	25 g n	300.00
3. Key in interest rate and convert to monthly	10.5 g i	0.88
4. Solve for payment	PM	-6,083.95
5. Interest for 60 months	60 f n (AMORT)	-333,927.98
6. Principal for 60 months	x≷y	-31,109.02
7. Loan balance after 5 yrs	RCL PV	618,890.98

*Since the loan is paid on a monthly basis, the five year time period is converted into 60 months. In step 2, we converted the whole loan into a monthly basis, so we cannot use the g n to do this again for the five-year period.

The loan amount was still high, and the interest rate is not favorable. Hopefully, with the rehabilitation, the property owner can negotiate a more favorable interest rate.

After the amortization for five years, we were able to calculate both the interest paid and the principal reduction. The total amount paid ($365,037) for the 60 pay periods is stored in the calculator as interest paid and the principal reduction. Step number 5 calls the calculator to perform the amortization. Note the gold f interacts with the amortization sign in gold n (AMORT) above the n key. The principal and interest are both calculated at the same time and they are sent to different registers. This is why the exchange positions key 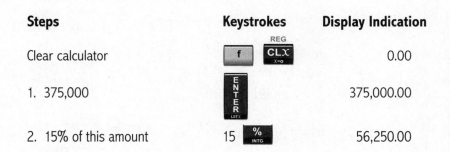 is used so that we can see the amount of principal reduction. If we hit the 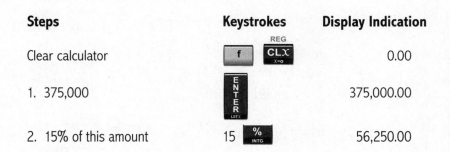 key again it would go back to interest.

CALCULATING BALLOON PAYMENTS

Appraisers need to determine if adjustments need to be made for financing concessions. In the following example, there is a seller carry-back involved in the sale and since most lenders require seller financing to be at least for five years, this example has a term of five years with a balloon payment at the end of that time. A **balloon payment** is the final installment payment on a promissory note that is significantly larger than the other installment payments provided under the terms of the promissory note.

Problem: Assume you are appraising a house that sold for $375,000 with a seller carryback of 15%. The interest rate is 7.75% amortized over 20 years and there is a balloon payment at the end of five years. The monthly payment is $458.82. What is the balloon payment due at the end of five years? The first thing we have to determine is the amount of the carry-back.

Steps	Keystrokes	Display Indication
Clear calculator	f CLx (REG)	0.00
1. 375,000	ENTER	375,000.00
2. 15% of this amount	15 % (INTG)	56,250.00

We are ready to use the financial keys to calculate the balloon payment. First, we enter the $56,250 into the PV register.

3. 56,250.00 (displayed)	PV	56,250.00
4. Enter monthly interest rate	7.75 g i (12÷)	0.65
5. Enter monthly payment	458.82 CHS PMT	-458.82
6. Enter number of periods to the balloon	5 g n (12x)	60.00
7. Solve for future value (amount of the balloon)	FV CHS	49,059.35

Now the appraiser has to decide if this carry-back requires some kind of adjustment when compared to the comparable sales that have no similar carry-back.

In most cases, you will find it necessary first to compute the monthly payment as it normally is not given to you. Then after you have this information, you can solve for the balloon payment in a manner similar to above.

Problem: Compute the balloon payment for a loan of $245,000, at 7.5% interest based upon a 30-year amortization. The balloon payment is due after 5 years.

The first part of the solution is to solve for the payment. Note that we are leaving this amount a negative number, as it will go into the financial register as a negative and the amount of the balloon payment will be a positive.

Steps	Keystrokes	Display Indication
Clear calculator	f CLX	0.00
1. Key in loan principal	245,000 PV	245,000.00
2. Key in number of payments (convert to monthly)	30 g n	360.00
3. Key in interest rate (convert to monthly)	7.5 g i	0.63
4. Solve for payment	PMT	-1,702.44
5. Number of periods to balloon	5 g n	60.00
6. Solve for balloon payment	FV CHS	231,812.72

CALCULATING NEGATIVE AMORTIZATION

Many loans today are written with teaser rates that result in negative amortization. **Negative amortization** is a loan repayment plan that results in the loan balance increasing instead of decreasing. The procedure we use for negative amortization is the same as the one for normal amortization.

Problem: Compute the balloon payment for a loan of $245,000, at 7.5% interest based upon a 30-year amortization. Assume that the monthly payment is $1,500 instead of $1,702.44 and is level for five years. Solve for the balloon payment or the new loan balance after 5 years.

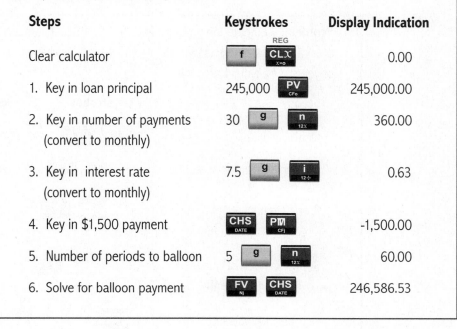

Steps	Keystrokes	Display Indication
Clear calculator	f CLX	0.00
1. Key in loan principal	245,000 PV	245,000.00
2. Key in number of payments (convert to monthly)	30 g n	360.00
3. Key in interest rate (convert to monthly)	7.5 g i	0.63
4. Key in $1,500 payment	CHS PMT	-1,500.00
5. Number of periods to balloon	5 g n	60.00
6. Solve for balloon payment	FV CHS	246,586.53

By reducing the amount of the monthly payment by $202.44 to help the borrower afford to make the loan payments, the lender shifted the loan to a negative amortization (-1,586.53) for the 5-year period. After 5 years, the principal balance and any balloon payment is greater than the original loan amount.

HANDLING VARIATIONS

Sometimes the user needs to look at variations and change part of the analysis when considering the financial functions. We do not clear the financial registers as we make changes.

Problem: Compute the payment for a $400,000 loan, at 6.25% interest based upon a 40-year amortization. Then compute various changes to interest, number of years, or payment amount.

Steps	Keystrokes	Display Indication
Clear calculator	f CLX	0.00
1. Key in loan principal	400,000 PV	400,000.00
2. Key in number of payments (convert to monthly)	40 g n	480.00
3. Key in interest rate (convert to monthly	6.25 g i	0.52
4. Solve for payment	PMT	-2,259.19

Change One. What would happen to the payment if there were a 30-year loan?

5. Key in number of payments	30 g n	360.00
6. Solve for payment	PMT	-2,450.11

Change Two. Suppose the borrower negotiated a 5.85 % interest rate for the loan to go with the 30-year amortization.

7. Key in new rate	5.85 g i	0.49
8. Solve for payment	PMT	-2,348.32

Change Three. The borrower received a salary increase and asked the banker about a 15-year loan at 5.65%. How does this affect the payment?

9. Key in number of payments	15 g n	180.00
10. Key in new rate	5.65 g i	0.47
11. Solve for payment	PMT	-3,284.79

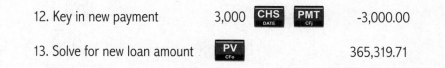

Change Four. The borrower decides that he wants the 15-year loan with the lower interest rate, but he can only afford payments of $3,000 per month. He is willing to borrow a lesser amount. What amount can he borrow with the payments limited to $3,000/month?

| 12. Key in new payment | 3,000 CHS PMT | -3,000.00 |
| 13. Solve for new loan amount | PV | 365,319.71 |

CALCULATING IRR

Other keys that are important for advanced and other functions such as the Internal Rate of Return $\overset{R}{\text{FV}}$ are not covered in detail. The keys used to calculate IRR are blue g function + PV, PM, FV and gold f function + $\overset{IRR}{\text{FV}}$

PRACTICE PROBLEMS

Work on solving the problems below on your own using the HP 12c. Do not look at the answers, which are shown at the end of this chapter, until you have completed all of the problems.

1. You are considering refinancing your house at an interest rate of 6.5% for a loan term of 30 years. The amount of the loan is $200,000. What is the monthly payment?

2. A colleague of yours sold a piece of property and decided to carryback a loan for $75,000. This is a **straight note** (interest only) with a term of 10 years. The note interest rate is 11%. What are the monthly payments? What will be the balloon payment in 10 years?

3. You have a loan on your home, which you have had for seven years. The original loan balance was $175,000. It is an adjustable-rate mortgage that has an interest rate of 5% for the first 7 years and then it adjusts upward. You need to decide whether to keep this loan or to refinance the property. To do this you need to know the loan balance. The loan is amortized over a 30-year period, but the interest rate will probably increase in the future. What is the loan balance? How much interest have you paid to date?

ANSWERS TO PRACTICE PROBLEMS

1. This problem is solved using the following sequence:

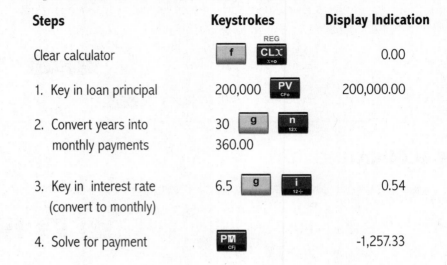

Steps	Keystrokes	Display Indication
Clear calculator	**f** **CLX**	0.00
1. Key in loan principal	200,000 **PV**	200,000.00
2. Convert years into monthly payments	30 **g** **n** 360.00	
3. Key in interest rate (convert to monthly)	6.5 **g** **i**	0.54
4. Solve for payment	**PM**	-1,257.33

2. There is no amortization for this problem as it deals with a straight note. So the monthly payment is interest only. The solution here is straightforward. Since there is no amortization, the loan amount does not change and the whole principal balance of $75,000 is due at the end of the ten years.

Steps	Keystrokes	Display Indication
Clear calculator	**f** **CLX**	0.00
1. Key in loan principal	75,000 **ENTER**	75,000.00
2. Calculate 11% of this amt.	11 **%** **CHS**	-8,250.00
3. Solve for payment	12 **÷**	-687.50

3. This problem requires the use of the financial functions. Here is the solution:

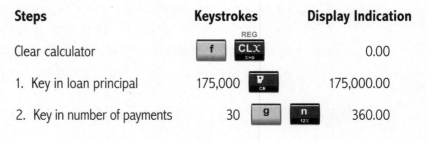

Steps	Keystrokes	Display Indication
Clear calculator	**f** **CLX**	0.00
1. Key in loan principal	175,000 **PV**	175,000.00
2. Key in number of payments	30 **g** **n**	360.00

(convert to monthly)

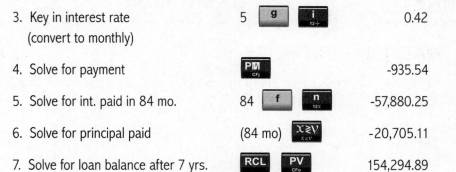

3. Key in interest rate (convert to monthly)	5 **g** **i**	0.42
4. Solve for payment	**PMT**	-935.54
5. Solve for int. paid in 84 mo.	84 **f** **n**	-57,880.25
6. Solve for principal paid	(84 mo) **x≷y**	-20,705.11
7. Solve for loan balance after 7 yrs.	**RCL** **PV**	154,294.89

SUMMARY

The financial calculator is a valuable tool and once you use it, it will be as important to you as your laptop and cell phone. We examined many of the features of the HP 12c and have indicated several appraisal functions associated with these features. We considered Reverse Polish Notation (RPN) and gave several examples of how this works. We discussed many of the keys and functions and indicated the step-by-step procedures to solve different kinds of problems.

There are many uses that we did not demonstrate such as those which are used in yield capitalization. The reader is encouraged to go to the next step and learn how to calculate discounted cash flows, internal rates of return, and reversion values. Future study will lead you to use the statistical functions, which are located on the blue subscripts of the first two rows of the numbers registers, and learn how to write programs for your own use.

CHAPTER 12 REVIEW EXERCISES

MATCHING EXERCISE

Instructions: Write the letter of the matching term on the blank line before its definition. Answers are in Appendix A.

Terms

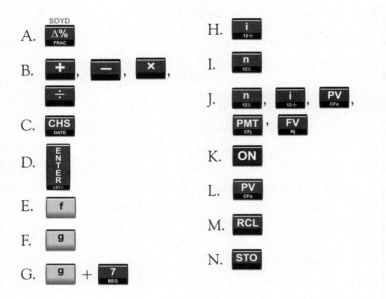

A.

B. , , ,

C.

D.

E.

F.

G.

H.

I.

J. , , , ,

K.

L.

M.

N.

O.

P. balloon payment

Q. display

R. mantissa

S. negative amortization

T. registers

U. Reverse Polish Notation

V. straight note

Definitions

1. _____ Used to view data or results

2. _____ Used to store numbers during calculations

3. _____ Key used to turn calculator on and off

4. _____ Key used to input numbers

5. _____ Key used to convert positive numbers into negative numbers

6. _____ Key used to change the numerator with the denominator

7. _____ Keys known as the operators

8. _____ Function key used with the "gold functions"

9. _____ Function key used with the "blue functions"

10. _____ Loan amortization keys

11. _____ Keys used to show the word BEGIN in the display

12. _____ Key used to input term of loan or length of note

13. _____ Key used for monthly and annual interest rates

14. _____ Key used for the present amount of the loan balance

15. _____ Mathematic logic without use of = sign and brackets

16. _____ Key used to calculate percentage change

17. _____ Numerical part of scientific notation

18. _____ The final installment payment on a promissory note that is significantly larger than the other installment payments provided under the terms of the promissory note

19. _____ Principal increases over time

20. _____ An interest-only note

MULTIPLE CHOICE QUESTIONS

Instructions: Circle the correct response and go to Appendix A to read the complete explanation for each question. For the math problems use the HP 12c even if you can solve some of them without the calculator.

1. What is 35 times 37?
   a. 1,225
   b. 1,295
   c. 1,325
   d. 1,395

2. What is 20 times 320 times 5 divided by 7?
   a. 4,570 (rounded)
   b. 457
   c. 45,700
   d. None of the above

3. If you are performing various operations on the HP 12c, how do you exchange numbers from one register to another?

    a. It cannot be done as the registers are secure.

    b. You need to use the [EEX] key.

    c. You need to use the [x≷y] key.

    d. Either (b) or (c)

4. How do you set or change the decimal point on the HP 12c?

    a. Use the g function key and then enter the number of decimal places that you need

    b. Use the [x≷y] key and indicate which number you are changing to

    c. Use the [CLx] key to clear the old decimal point then key in the new one

    d. Use the f function key and set the number of places you need

5. Since the display will only take 10 places, how do you key in 12,900,000,000?

    a. 1.29 [EEX] 10

    b. 12.9 [EEX] 10

    c. 1.29 [EEX] 11

    d. 12.9 [EEX] 9

6. To give yourself more financial flexibility, you negotiated an equity line of credit with the bank for $100,000. Assume that you use all of it and have an interest rate of 8.75% with a 25-year term. You were able to talk the bank into your making only one payment per year. What is your annual payment for year 1?

    a. $8,975

    b. $9,000

    c. $9,173

    d. $9,423

For questions 7 – 12 use the following situation:

The loan described below has been in force for 5 years (60 months). What is the loan balance at the end of five years? The following data applies:

Original loan amount	$550,000
Term	20 years
Interest rate	9.5%

Here is a partially filled in solution table. You will be asked questions that concern the areas that are designated with a question mark.

Steps	Keystrokes	Display indication
1. Clear calculator	f CLx x=o	0.00
2. Key in loan principal	550,000 PV CFo	550,000.00
3. Key in number of payments (convert to monthly)	?	?
4. Key in interest rate (convert to monthly)	?	?
5. Solve for payment	PM CFj	?
6. Solve: 60 mo. interest paid	60 f n 12x	-249,224.25
7. Solve: 60 mo. principal paid	x≷y x<v	-55,962.75
8. Solve: loan balance after 5 yr.	RCL PV CFo	?

7. What are the keystrokes to enter the number of monthly payments?

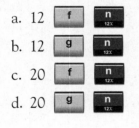

a. 12 f n 12x

b. 12 g n 12x

c. 20 f n 12x

d. 20 g n 12x

8. What is the display indication for the number of payments?

a. 144.00

b. 144.

c. 240.00

d. 240.

9. What are the keystrokes to enter the interest rate in the table above?

   a. 9.5 `f` `i 12÷`

   b. 9.5 `g` `i 12÷`

   c. 20 `f` `i 12÷`

   d. 20 `g` `i 12÷`

10. What is the display indication for the interest rate?

   a. 79.00

   b. 0.79

   c. 7.9%

   d. .79%

11. What is the payment amount?

   a. -4,076

   b. -5,086

   c. -4,086

   d. -5,076

12. What is the loan balance after five years?

   a. 494,037

   b. 550,000

   c. 490,000

   d. 513,038

For questions 13 – 15. Assume that you are performing a land appraisal and you want to express the land sizes in acres. There are three parcels of 280,000, 620,000, and 430,000 SF. Store 43,560 in one of the registers, and when you answer the following, save the results in another register.

13. How many acres are there in the 280,000 SF parcel?

   a. 28

   b. 7.12

   c. 6.43

   d. 4.55

14. How many acres in the 620,000 SF parcel?

   a. 13.5
   b. 14.23
   c. 11.3
   d. 13.3

15. What is the total acreage of the three parcels?

   a. 20.66
   b. 29.66
   c. 32.66
   d. 30.53

Reconciliation

13
Chapter

INTRODUCTION

As you have learned, there are three approaches to valuing real estate: the sales comparison approach, the income approach, and the cost approach. These are the three standard approaches for real estate appraisal. Each of the three approaches indicates a value for the subject property. **Reconciliation** is the adjustment process of weighing results from the three appraisal methods to arrive at a final estimate of the subject property's market value.

In reconciliation, the appraiser considers the appropriateness of each of the three approaches to the subject, the quantity and quality of available data, and the amount of judgmental adjustment required to reach each estimate. The final analytical step in the valuation process is the reconciliation of the value indications into a single value or a reasonable value range. The nature of the reconciliation depends upon the appraisal problem.

In this chapter, we will discuss the reconciliation process, approaches used, and the reliability of the value indications derived.

LEARNING OBJECTIVES

After reading this chapter, you will be able to:

- describe the factors involved in determining the final value estimate.
- describe the purpose of the re-evaluation and appraisal review process.
- solve problems regarding the measures of central tendency.
- list the appraisal reporting options and discuss when to use each type of report.

FINAL VALUE ESTIMATE

All data used in real estate appraising comes from the market; therefore, there should be some reciprocal relationship among the three approaches. The values indicated by each approach form a range of value for the subject property. The **range of value** is simply the difference between the highest and lowest variant. The final estimate of value should be within this range. The **final value estimate** is the appraiser's estimate of the defined value of the subject property, arrived at by reconciling the estimates of value derived from the sales comparison, income, and cost approaches. The values indicated by the three approaches should generally not differ more than 10%. If the spread in values exceeds 10%, the approaches should be re-examined and possibly adjusted to narrow the difference.

When all three approaches are used, the appraiser examines the spread among the three indications. A wide spread may indicate that one or more of the approaches is not truly applicable to the appraisal problem. The appraiser must always consider the relative dependability and applicability of each approach in reconciling the value indications into a final value estimate of defined value. In reconciliation, the appraiser can explain variations among the indications and account for any inconsistencies among the value conclusions and methods with which they were derived.

To reconcile the values indicated by the three approaches, an appraiser must judge and weigh the data that led to each value conclusion. The term weight is often used by appraisers. **Weight** implies judging the importance, influence, or authority of the specific data being considered. Throughout the appraisal process, an appraiser must correlate and weigh data to form conclusions.

FACTORS USED

The appraiser reviews the data and the approaches to value in relation to the type of property being appraised, the data available, and the intended use of appraisal.

These three factors form the guidelines for judging each of the approaches in reconciling a final value estimate. Of course, there is usually more than one approach to value used. If an appraiser has been objective and thorough, these factors result in different indications of value. With two or more indications of value, the differing values must be reconciled into a final opinion.

TYPE OF PROPERTY APPRAISED

The type of property being appraised often dictates a heavier weight on one or two of the three approaches to value. Single-family residences are generally purchased for the benefits of homeownership, not necessarily for producing income. Homebuyers predicate the price they are willing to pay on the sale prices of comparable homes or on the cost of constructing a similar house. As such, the sales comparison and cost approach are the most appropriate methods of valuing a single-family home. As the age of the house increases, the validity of the cost approach decreases because of the difficulty of estimating depreciation.

The Dakota building, New York

Properties purchased primarily for their income-producing capabilities, such as apartment buildings, are normally valued with the greatest emphasis on the income approach. However, the sales comparison and cost approaches should also be given full consideration. Usually, with an older apartment house, the sales comparison and cost approaches become less significant. This is due to the lessening of similarity between properties with age and the difficulty of accurately estimating depreciation.

DATA AVAILABLE

The data available to the appraiser is probably the most important aspect of reconciliation. Regardless of which approach is most applicable to a particular type of property, if adequate data is not available, a reliable value estimate cannot be developed using that approach.

All data used in appraisal comes directly or indirectly from the market. Sales of property similar to the subject are directly compared by the sales comparison approach. The same sales may also be used in estimating gross rent multiplier, capitalization rate, land value, or accrued depreciation. A direct market investigation may be used in estimating an economic rent schedule or the construction cost of a building.

Availability of data means both quantity and quality. Quantity is the amount of data. Quality refers to the reliability of the data and their relevance to the particular appraisal problem. Information that cannot be verified and substantiated is not dependable for use in making an appraisal. The relevance of the appraisal data to the subject property is of the utmost importance. It is better to have a limited amount of pertinent data than an abundance of information of questionable applicability.

INTENDED USE OF APPRAISAL

The intended use of the appraisal may have bearing on the weight given to any of the three approaches. If the appraisal is to be used in an eminent domain trial, sales of similar properties are usually considered the best demonstrable evidence of value. Likewise, evidence of value to be presented to persons unfamiliar with appraisal practices for purchase, sale, and taxation is often more understandable presented in the form of comparable sales.

When appraising investment properties for loan purposes, the lending institution wants to be sure that the income from the property will cover all expenses and repay the loan debt. When making loans on properties where improvements are to be constructed, the lending institution is concerned that the total value of the improved property be in relation to the cost of the improvements.

Appraising for insurance purposes requires primary consideration of the cost approach. Replacement cost less accrued depreciation is usually the basis for settlement of claims for destroyed or damaged real property.

Questions to Ask When Using the Sales Comparison Approach

- Are the sales comparables homogeneous to the subject?

- Are there an adequate number of sales?

- Are there sufficient units of comparison?

- Is the market relatively stable or is it moving up or down?

- Was it necessary to time adjust the comparable sales? Were the adjustments based upon market data?

- Were any of the adjustments qualitative? Are these well supported?

- How does the adjusted range of value compare to actual market sales?

- If the appraisal is for a loan, have the Fannie Mae Supplemental Standards been met? If not, have you explained why?

- Have you reconciled the direct sales comparison into one value indicator for this approach? Have you explained which units of comparison you have given the most weight?

- How does the sales comparison approach compare to the other approaches to value?

Questions to Ask When Using the Income Approach to Value

- Do you have owner records of income and expenses for the past three years?

- Do these records include all sources of income?

- Do these records include all expenses? This can be a problem when the owner is also managing the property. How reliable are these records?

- Is there adequate expense data for similar properties?

- Are the expense projections for the subject property in line with expenses for comparable properties?

- Has the owner set aside funds for replacement reserves?

- Does the typical buyer use capitalization techniques or does he or she use income multipliers?

- If a multiplier technique is used, have you made sure the rentals of the comparable sales are at market rents?

- Is there an adequate number of rental comparables?

- Are the unit mixes comparable?

- Is there market data to support any adjustments made?
- Are the adjustments made quantitative, qualitative, or a combination?
- Is there market support for using a capitalization technique?
- Is there market support for the overall rate?
- Does the capitalization approach reflect market thinking?
- Is the income approach to value the most important with this kind of property?
- Are the conclusions and reconciliation of the income approach consistent with the conclusions in the other approaches to value?

RE-EVALUATION

Once an appraiser has reconciled the individual approaches to value, he or she then prepares for final reconciliation by re-evaluating the entire appraisal. **Re-evaluation** is the review of the entire appraisal in which the appraiser makes sure the available data, analytical techniques, and logic applied have led to consistent judgments.

The appraiser considers the approaches by revisiting:

1. Scope of work

2. Quantity and quality of the data collected and verified in each approach

3. Inherent strengths and weaknesses of each approach as it applies to the subject property

4. Relevance of each approach to the subject property and market behavior

Reviewing the previous list of questions is helpful when re-evaluating. This final review also enables the appraiser to ensure the data is authentic, sufficient, and applicable to the assignment. At this time, the appraiser examines any differences in the value conclusions derived from the different approaches and resolves any inconsistencies and conclusions that do not seem reasonable.

When an appraiser considers the various approaches to value employed in the assignment, he or she determines if one approach to value is more significant than the others—or whether two out of the three approaches are more indicative than the third approach.

> Example: If an appraiser is valuing a custom home in an upscale neighborhood, he or she would probably discover the income approach to value is not indicative of the value of the property, even if the subject property was being used as a rental. Reconciliation would give the most weight to the sales comparison approach. If there are suitable land comparable sales, the cost approach could lend support to this and is sometimes useful to set the upper limit of the range of value.

It is probable that several indications of value may be derived from a single approach. An example of this is seen in the valuation of units. In which case, an appraiser may determine a value per unit, a value per square foot, value per room, and a value per bedroom. These normally are not the same—the sales comparison approach needs to be reconciled for the different results into a final value estimate when using this approach.

> **It is important to remember that all approaches to value use the sales comparison approach in one form or another. The principle of substitution underlies all of the approaches to value.**

Appraisal is both an art and a science. Much of the work completed within the three approaches to value represents the science of appraisal. Here, an appraiser applies his or her knowledge and experience. When the appraiser shifts to the final reconciliation, he or she shifts to the art of appraisal and uses judgment based upon experience. The final opinion of value is not the average of the approaches used. There is no magical formula—it is the result of proper appraisal techniques and appraiser judgment. This is why the appraisal process results in an OPINION of value and not a FACT of value. Different appraisers can be similarly professional in their approach and yet have different opinions.

APPRAISAL REVIEW

Although there are many reviews possible for any given appraisal report, the most important review begins in the appraiser's office. Someone should check all mathematical calculations other than the original appraiser. Math errors of any kind can diminish the client's confidence in the appraisal. The appraisal should be read for correct grammar and spelling. These errors, like math errors, do not project an image of professionalism. It is a good idea to ask the reviewer if the appraisal makes sense. This is another way to look at the logic used throughout the process and to determine if the reader is going to be able to follow the process. Standard 2 of USPAP stresses the importance of not misleading the reader.

In-House Review

- Does the appraisal solve the client's problem? The client may be purchasing the property as an investment and may need an allocation of purchase price to establish his or her basis for depreciation.

- Is the scope of work appropriate?

- Does the appraisal consider all meaningful data? There are many instances when an appraiser intended to include something in the appraisal and then left it out unintentionally.

JUDGMENT

All of the data analysis in the world is useless if the appraiser does not use proper judgment. Judgment is the product of experience and competency. It is used in reconciliation more than any other part of the appraisal process. An appraiser considers the relative significance and applicability of each value indication and decides where to place the most weight in the final reconciliation. Standards Rule 1-6 indicates the appraiser must reconcile the quality and quantity of the data available and analyze within the approaches to value used and reconcile the applicability or suitability of the approaches used to arrive at the valuation conclusions. This is the result of proper appraisal logic and judgment.

Completing an assignment competently requires proper judgment and proper execution. Proper judgment is alluded to in the Competency Rule when it says to "properly identify the problem to be addressed." Proper execution is referenced in the requirement to have "the knowledge and experience to complete the assignment competently." It is important to recognize the link between the Competency Rule and the Standards Rules—all Standards Rules are essentially extensions of the Competency Rule.

APPROPRIATENESS

The appropriateness of an approach to value in terms of the intended use is usually related to property type. For example, an appraiser might consider the income approach to value when considering an expensive custom home. Realistically, most buyers generally do not purchase a custom home to secure an income stream. A house that is 50-years old is probably not a good candidate for a detailed cost approach to value, but the cost approach can be helpful to determine the highest and best use for the property.

The final opinion of value is normally based upon the approach or the approaches that are most applicable, but the final opinion of value need not be the same as the value indicated by the most applicable approach. This is often seen with income properties in which the sales comparison is higher than the income approach to value and they both apply. If the buyer is more interested in the income stream than the resale value, the appraiser may decide to give more weight to the income approach—even if it results in a lower indication of value. As discussed in Chapter 6, the intended use of the appraisal and the type of property being appraised influences the approach an appraiser uses.

ACCURACY

The perceived accuracy of an appraisal is an indication of the appraiser's confidence in the data used and the adjustments made.

> Example: An appraiser is considering a house with a three-car garage and a similar house that has a four-car garage. Using the sales comparison approach, the appraiser makes an adjustment based on his experience on how much value the extra garage space provides—as there is not much data to support these conclusions since this is the only house with a four-car garage in the area. Local REALTORS® have their opinions, which are considered—but once again, there is no market data to support the opinions.

It is relatively easy to determine how much the extra garage space is worth using the cost approach to value—and the appraiser has a lot of confidence in approaching this amenity using the cost approach. The area does not have any garage rental, so there is nothing the income approach to value can contribute. The cost approach is also important in this example, as the appraiser needs to decide if the garage improvements represent an over-improvement (or superadequacy).

The number of comparable properties, whether or not they are homogeneous, the number of adjustments, and the gross and net dollar amounts of the adjustments also provide an indication of how accurate an approach is. If there are a larger number of properties supporting one approach to value over another, this will tend to give the appraiser more confidence in that approach.

QUANTITY OF EVIDENCE

The quantity of evidence is used to determine the appropriateness and accuracy of the value indication. Quantity of verifiable data also affects the quality and relevance. Any value indicator can be negatively affected by a lack of relevant data.

> Example: Consider an appraisal in which the appraiser is attempting to extract a gross income multiplier (GIM) from four comparable sales. All of the properties are appropriate when the appraiser considers their physical and locational characteristics. The first comparable is at market rents and there is a detailed statement which shows all additional income from laundry equipment and garage rentals. There is information that indicates the condition of the property, when the carpets were replaced, when the roof was replaced, and when the units were last painted. Since the subject was also in excellent condition, this was considered a good comparable.
>
> The other three comparables had data that was less detailed and they were all managed by the owner, so the financial data and condition of the units was not as readily discernable. Since there was so much more verified data about the first comparable, the appraiser has a lot more confidence in the GIM derived from this sale.

In this example, the confidence interval that the true GIM is closer to the first comparable than the others is governed by the homogeneity of the first comparable to the subject property. It will have a smaller standard deviation, and will receive the most weight. Although statistical analyses are important, it is an appraiser's job to derive a credible opinion of value, which is supported by data.

> **Review – Basis of Final Reconciliation**
> - Judgment as the product of experience and competency
> - Appropriateness of the value indication
> - Accuracy of the appraisal as a measure of the appraiser's confidence
> - Quantity and quality of the evidence used

STATISTICAL CONCEPTS

Most computerized-form programs for appraisers have automatic mathematical calculation capability for comparable property adjustments, and often for computing the average of the adjusted sales prices of the comparables. Appraisers must be careful to not simply average the adjusted values.

MEASURES OF CENTRAL TENDENCY

There are three common statistical measures—the mean, the median, and the mode. All three are used to measure central tendency and to identify the typical variate in a sample or population. In statistics, a **variate** is a single random variable with a numerical value within a particular sample. When averaging, the **deviation** is the measure of how far the average variate differs from the mean of all variates. The deviation is also referred to as the average absolute deviation.

MEAN

Commonly known as the average, the **mean** is calculated by adding the average prices or numeric values of a statistical sample and dividing that by the number of values in the sample. The result will provide a single figure that accounts for all variates, even ones that are significantly lower or higher than the majority.

> Example: The variates are 4, 5, 6, and 7. Add the variates together and divide by four (the number of variates): $22 \div 4 = 5.5$. If the variates are changed and are now 4, 5, 6, and 13, the mean for this sample changes from 5.5 to 7. Here, the majority of the variates are clustered around 5, but since one variate is significantly higher, it influences the conclusion significantly.

MEDIAN

The **median** equals the middle value in a statistical sample. The median home price in an area is the price, which is midway between the least expensive and most expensive homes sold in the area during a given period of time. Unlike the mean, the median is not significantly affected by one unusually high or low number.

> Example: Divide a sampling into two equal groups. The number in the middle is the median. It will provide a figure that is the midpoint. With a sampling of 12, 3, 6, 15, and 9, first place the numbers into an array: 3, 6, 9, 12, 15, and then divide them into equal groups: (3, 6) 9 (12, 15). Since 9 is in the middle of the list, it is the median.

If the number of variates is an even number, there will not be a single variate directly in the middle. In situations including an even number of variates, find the mean of the two numbers on either side of the midpoint.

MODE

The final measure of central tendency is called the mode. The **mode** equals the most frequently occurring price or value in a statistical sample. When analyzing comparable sales, the most frequently occurring sales price definitely warrants consideration.

Example:

Once	$299,500
Once	$300,000
Once	$301,000
Twice	$305,000
Once	$305,500
Once	$308,500
Once	$310,000
Once	$312,000
Once	$320,000

From the array above, the most frequently occurring variate is $305,000. In this sample of comparable sales, the sales range from $299,500 to $320,000 with a mean of $306,650, a median of $305,250, and a mode of $305,000. An appraiser could make an argument for any value within the range. However, after further analysis, there is a better argument for a value that fits the central tendencies.

When calculating market value using the sales comparison approach, an appraiser may use the median or the mode price—if the comparable properties are very similar. If there are greater variations, the appraiser may choose the mean price, as this would tend to smooth the differences. If a particular comparable sale is most like the subject, the appraiser will use this to weigh his or her evaluation of the estimated value.

FINAL RECONCILIATION AND REPORTING

USPAP indicates that the final opinion of value can be stated as a point estimate of value, a range of value, or a value in relation to some benchmark amount. **Point estimate of value** is the final value indication reported as a single dollar amount. It is the figure that best represents the value of the subject as indicated by the range of value. The point estimate of value is reconciled from the adjusted range of value. The point estimate of value is used for lender appraisals, estate purposes, real estate taxation, depreciation, rental values, and property transfer decisions. Most clients require a point estimate of value.

ROUNDING

Rounding of numbers is also an important consideration. **Rounding** is expressing an amount as an approximate number. The basic rule is that numbers should be rounded to reflect the degree of precision that the appraiser can associate with his or her opinion of value. Often the way the numbers are rounded is a matter of convention. It is important to keep in mind that an appraisal result is an opinion of value. An appraiser may come up with an opinion of value of $231,576 using a particular approach. Because this number appears to be very specific and scientific, an appraiser should round the final value estimate to emphasize the fact that it is indeed an estimate. In this example, an appraiser should recognize that reconciliation is not that precise, and would likely round the result to $231,000 or $231,600.

Sometimes rounding will take the opinion of value beyond the range of value suggested by the preliminary indications. For example, $239,600 and $239,450 may be expressed as $240,000. If a range of value is appropriate, the appraiser may indicate this value as between $239,000 and $240,000.

Using a range of value implies the true value is no lower than the bottom of the range and no higher than the top part of the range. The appraiser has to remember what the intended use of the appraisal is and must remember not to present the results in a manner that will mislead the client and other intended users.

SIGNIFICANT DIGITS

Throughout the appraisal process, one of the characteristics of a number is how many significant digits it contains. **Significant digits** are those that go from the first numeral on the left over to the last numeral on the right that is not a zero. All non-zero digits (1, 2, 3, 4, 5, 6, 7, 8, 9) are always significant. For example, 34 has two significant digits, and 34.2 has three significant digits. When zeros are added to the final value, it becomes more complicated.

Guidelines for Significant Digits

- Zeros placed before other numerals are not significant. The number 0.037 has only two significant digits.

- Zeros placed between other numerals are always significant. There are four significant digits in 2001.

- Zeros placed after other numerals, but behind a decimal point are significant. There are three significant digits in 4.50.

- Zeros at the end of a number are significant only if they are behind a decimal point (see c. above). In an amount such as $4,500, it is impossible to determine if the zeros are significant or not. Without a decimal point, there are at least two significant digits. With a decimal point followed by two zeros ($4,500.00), there are four significant digits.

- When adding or subtracting quantities, the number of decimal places (not significant digits) in the answer should be the same as the least number of decimal places in any of the numbers being added or subtracted.

Example: A number calculated in an appraisal may contain all significant digits, for example, $344,637.17. A final value estimate made using one technique and the available data may result in a value conclusion of two significant digits—$340,000, and another technique may result in a value of $344,637 or six significant digits. This difference implies the second value is more accurate, but both may be of equal accuracy.

There are two instances regarding significant digits that always should be avoided.

1. Do not write more digits in an answer (either intermediate or final) that is justified by the number of digits in the data.

2. Do not round off to two digits in an intermediate answer, and then write three digits in the final answer.

The reconciliation process can be very simple when all approaches used arrive at similar results. The difficulty comes when the three approaches do not arrive at similar results. The appraiser must consider the reliability of the data and the relative applicability of each approach. The appraiser must go back to the beginning—define the problem—and insure the final opinion of value is the solution to the defined problem. Once the final opinion of value is developed, all that remains is to prepare the report.

REPORTING THE APPRAISAL RESULTS

The data supporting an estimate of value is placed on an appraisal report. An **appraisal report** is a written statement in which an appraiser gives his or her opinion of value. Reports must be written in such as way as to provide the reader sufficient information without being misleading in any manner. Omitting relevant facts or choosing comparables for their sales price rather than their similarity are examples of being misleading. It is never acceptable to write a report that misleads the reader.

The completion of these reports is a synopsis of the appraiser's work product. The supporting data, analysis, and development of approaches are fully supported and documented in the appraiser's workfile. A **workfile** is the appraiser's record, which contains all the documentation necessary to support the appraiser's analyses, opinions, and conclusions conveyed in the appraisal report. Completing these reports in a competent and thorough manner helps maintain the appraiser's credibility, and supports the efficient working of the real estate market.

In fact, SR 2 in USPAP fully describes the essential elements of each report and the required certifications of that appraiser. All reports must meet all requirements of USPAP, including the certifications and assumptions and limiting conditions associated with the appraisal. USPAP sets forth all of the reporting requirements for real estate appraisal reports. A complete  workfile must be developed and maintained in accordance with the provisions of USPAP. As a matter of standard practice, an appraiser should always keep his or her workfiles in case he or she must revisit the appraisal or defend his or her appraisal.

TYPES OF APPRAISAL REPORTS

According to USPAP, reporting standards for appraisals require that the report must clearly and accurately set forth the appraisal in a manner that is not misleading. The report must contain sufficient information enabling the intended users of the appraisal to understand the report properly.

Three Types of Appraisal Reports

1. Summary Appraisal Report

2. Self-Contained Appraisal Report

3. Restricted Use Appraisal Report

The choice of report type goes back to the beginning, when the problem was defined. The client's needs were identified and the type of report was selected to meet those needs. The choice of report type does not affect the amount of work done to complete the appraisal. The client's needs determine the report type, but the entire appraisal process must be completed prior to preparing the report.

SUMMARY APPRAISAL REPORT

A **Summary Appraisal Report** is the most common as it fulfills the minimum requirements for lenders to process their loans. If the client does not specifically state the desired report format, the report should at least meet the requirements of a Summary Appraisal Report.

Uniform Residential Appraisal Report   File #

The purpose of this summary appraisal report is to provide the lender/client with an accurate, and adequately supported, opinion of the market value of the subject property.

| Property Address | City | State | Zip Code |

Borrower — Owner of Public Record — County

Legal Description

Assessor's Parcel # — Tax Year — R.E. Taxes $

Neighborhood Name — Map Reference — Census Tract

Occupant ☐ Owner ☐ Tenant ☐ Vacant — Special Assessments $ — ☐ PUD — HOA $ ☐ per year ☐ per month

Property Rights Appraised ☐ Fee Simple ☐ Leasehold ☐ Other (describe)

Assignment Type ☐ Purchase Transaction ☐ Refinance Transaction ☐ Other (describe)

Lender/Client — Address

Is the subject property currently offered for sale or has it been offered for sale in the twelve months prior to the effective date of this appraisal? ☐ Yes ☐ No

Report data source(s) used, offering price(s), and date(s).

I ☐ did ☐ did not analyze the contract for sale for the subject purchase transaction. Explain the results of the analysis of the contract for sale or why the analysis was not performed.

Contract Price $ — Date of Contract — Is the property seller the owner of public record? ☐ Yes ☐ No — Data Source(s)

Is there any financial assistance (loan charges, sale concessions, gift or downpayment assistance, etc.) to be paid by any party on behalf of the borrower? ☐ Yes ☐ No — If Yes, report the total dollar amount and describe the items to be paid.

Note: Race and the racial composition of the neighborhood are not appraisal factors.

Neighborhood Characteristics		One-Unit Housing Trends			One-Unit Housing		Present Land Use %	
Location ☐ Urban ☐ Suburban ☐ Rural	Property Values ☐ Increasing ☐ Stable ☐ Declining			PRICE	AGE	One-Unit	%
Built-Up ☐ Over 75% ☐ 25-75% ☐ Under 25%	Demand/Supply ☐ Shortage ☐ In Balance ☐ Over Supply			$ (000)	(yrs)	2-4 Unit	%
Growth ☐ Rapid ☐ Stable ☐ Slow	Marketing Time ☐ Under 3 mths ☐ 3-6 mths ☐ Over 6 mths			Low		Multi-Family	%
Neighborhood Boundaries				High		Commercial	%
				Pred.		Other	%

Neighborhood Description

Market Conditions (including support for the above conclusions)

| Dimensions | Area | Shape | View |

Specific Zoning Classification — Zoning Description

Zoning Compliance ☐ Legal ☐ Legal Nonconforming (Grandfathered Use) ☐ No Zoning ☐ Illegal (describe)

Is the highest and best use of the subject property as improved (or as proposed per plans and specifications) the present use? ☐ Yes ☐ No If No, describe

Utilities	Public	Other (describe)		Public	Other (describe)	Off-site Improvements—Type	Public	Private
Electricity	☐	☐	Water	☐	☐	Street	☐	☐
Gas	☐	☐	Sanitary Sewer	☐	☐	Alley	☐	☐

FEMA Special Flood Hazard Area ☐ Yes ☐ No — FEMA Flood Zone — FEMA Map # — FEMA Map Date

Are the utilities and off-site improvements typical for the market area? ☐ Yes ☐ No If No, describe

Are there any adverse site conditions or external factors (easements, encroachments, environmental conditions, land uses, etc.)? ☐ Yes ☐ No If Yes, describe

General Description		Foundation		Exterior Description	materials/condition	Interior	materials/condition
Units ☐ One ☐ One with Accessory Unit		☐ Concrete Slab ☐ Crawl Space		Foundation Walls		Floors	
# of Stories		☐ Full Basement ☐ Partial Basement		Exterior Walls		Walls	
Type ☐ Det. ☐ Att. ☐ S-Det/End Unit		Basement Area sq. ft.		Roof Surface		Trim/Finish	
☐ Existing ☐ Proposed ☐ Under Const.		Basement Finish %		Gutters & Downspouts		Bath Floor	
Design (Style)		☐ Outside Entry/Exit ☐ Sump Pump		Window Type		Bath Wainscot	
Year Built		Evidence of ☐ Infestation		Storm Sash/Insulated		Car Storage ☐ None	
Effective Age (Yrs)		☐ Dampness ☐ Settlement		Screens		☐ Driveway # of Cars	
Attic ☐ None		Heating ☐ FWA ☐ HWBB ☐ Radiant		Amenities ☐ Woodstove(s) #		Driveway Surface	
☐ Drop Stair ☐ Stairs		☐ Other Fuel		☐ Fireplace(s) # ☐ Fence		☐ Garage # of Cars	
☐ Floor ☐ Scuttle		Cooling ☐ Central Air Conditioning		☐ Patio/Deck ☐ Porch		☐ Carport # of Cars	
☐ Finished ☐ Heated		☐ Individual ☐ Other		☐ Pool ☐ Other		☐ Att. ☐ Det. ☐ Built-in	

Appliances ☐ Refrigerator ☐ Range/Oven ☐ Dishwasher ☐ Disposal ☐ Microwave ☐ Washer/Dryer ☐ Other (describe)

Finished area above grade contains: Rooms — Bedrooms — Bath(s) — Square Feet of Gross Living Area Above Grade

Additional features (special energy efficient items, etc.).

Describe the condition of the property (including needed repairs, deterioration, renovations, remodeling, etc.).

Are there any physical deficiencies or adverse conditions that affect the livability, soundness, or structural integrity of the property? ☐ Yes ☐ No If Yes, describe

Does the property generally conform to the neighborhood (functional utility, style, condition, use, construction, etc.)? ☐ Yes ☐ No If No, describe

Freddie Mac Form 70 March 2005   Page 1 of 6   Fannie Mae Form 1004 March 2005

The **Uniform Residential Appraisal Report (URAR)** is probably the most widely used summary report. The URAR is used to report the results of single-family residential appraisals. It allows for all three approaches, but emphasizes the sales comparison approach. The cost approach is located on the third page, below an area designed for the appraiser's comments regarding the appraisal. The results of all three approaches are reported on page two, which has room for reconciliation.

SELF-CONTAINED APPRAISAL REPORT

The **Self-Contained Appraisal Report** option is the most detailed of the three types of reports. The report is exactly what the name implies, a complete rendering of the entire appraisal process. The appraiser provides all of the data analyzed, his or her reasoning, the complete review of the techniques applied, and finally the results of his or her work product.

RESTRICTED USE APPRAISAL REPORT

A **Restricted Use Appraisal Report** is the briefest presentation of an appraisal and contains the least detail. It is called restricted use because the client is the only intended user of the report. It can be oral or written, one or multiple pages, a range, or just a single number. The amount of detail in the report depends upon the client's needs and the problem being addressed by the appraisal. Here, as in the summary report, the amount of work completed before preparing the report has nothing to do with the report type, but the scope of work defined earlier in the process.

SUMMARY

Reconciliation is the adjustment process of weighing results of all three appraisal methods to arrive at a final estimate of the subject property's market value. In reconciliation, the appraiser considers the appropriateness of each of the three approaches to the subject, the quality of available data, and the amount of judgmental adjustment required to reach each estimate. The **final value estimate** is the appraiser's estimate of the defined value of the subject property, arrived at by reconciling the estimates of value, derived from the sales comparison, income, and cost approaches.

The appraiser reviews the data and approaches to value in relation to the following factors: (1) type of property being appraised, (2) data available,

364 Residential Sales Comparison & Income Approaches

and (3) intended use of the appraisal. Once an appraiser has reconciled the individual approaches to value, he or she then prepares for final reconciliation by re-evaluating the entire appraisal. **Re-evaluation** is the review of the entire appraisal, in which the appraiser makes sure that the data available and the analytical techniques and logic applied have led to consistent judgments.

There are three common statistical measures—the mean, the median, and the mode. Commonly known as the average, the **mean** is calculated by adding the average prices or numeric values of a statistical sample and dividing that by the number of values in the sample. The **median** equals the middle value in a statistical sample. The **mode** equals the most frequently occurring price or value in a statistical sample.

The data supporting an estimate of value is placed on an appraisal report. An **appraisal report** is a written statement in which an appraiser gives his or her opinion of value. There are three types of appraisal reports: (1) Summary Appraisal Report, (2) Self-Contained Appraisal Report, and (3) Restricted Use Appraisal Report.

CHAPTER 13 REVIEW EXERCISES

MATCHING EXERCISE

Instructions: Write the letter of the matching term on the blank line before its definition. Answers are in Appendix A.

Terms

A. appraisal report
B. final value estimate
C. in-house review
D. mean
E. median
F. mode
G. point estimate of value
H. range of value
I. reconciliation

J. re-evaluation
K. Restricted Use Appraisal Report
L. rounding
M. Self-Contained Appraisal Report
N. significant digits
O. Summary Appraisal Report

P. Uniform Residential Appraisal Report (URAR)
Q. variate
R. weight
S. workfile

Definitions

1. _____ The adjustment process of weighing results of all three appraisal methods to arrive at a final estimate of the subject property's market value

2. _____ The difference between the highest and lowest variant

3. _____ Appraiser's estimate of the defined value of the subject property, arrived at by reconciling the estimates of value, derived from the sales comparison, income, and cost approaches

4. _____ Implies judging the importance, influence, or authority of the specific data being considered

5. _____ Review of the entire appraisal in which the appraiser makes sure that the data available and the analytical techniques and logic applied have led to consistent judgments

6. _____ Calculated by adding the average prices or numeric values of a statistical sample and dividing that by the number of values in the sample

7. _____ Equals the middle value in a statistical sample

8. _____ Equals the most frequently occurring price or value in a statistical sample

9. _____ The final value indication reported as a single dollar amount point

10. _____ Expressing an amount as an approximate number

11. _____ The first numeral on the left over to the last numeral on the right that is not a zero

12. _____ A written statement in which an appraiser gives his or her opinion of value

13. _____ The appraiser's record, which contains all the documentation necessary to support the appraiser's analyses, opinions, and conclusions conveyed in the appraisal report

14. _____ The most commonly used appraisal report, which fulfills the minimum requirements for lenders to process loans

15. _____ The most widely used summary report

MULTIPLE CHOICE QUESTIONS

Instructions: Circle the correct response and go to Appendix A to read the complete explanation for each question.

1. Which of the following is not a criterion for reconciliation?
   a. Final opinion of value
   b. Appropriateness
   c. Quality
   d. Judgment

2. There are three factors used to form the guidelines for judging each of the approaches in reconciling a final value estimate. Which of the following is not one of those factors?
   a. Type of property being appraised
   b. Location of subject property
   c. Data available
   d. Intended use of appraisal

3. The _____ is probably the most important aspect of reconciliation.

    a. intended use of the appraisal
    b. type of property being appraised
    c. relevance of each approach
    d. data available to the appraiser

4. Once an appraiser has reconciled the individual approaches to value, he or she then prepares for final reconciliation by _____ the entire appraisal.

    a. re-evaluating
    b. re-calculating
    c. re-estimating
    d. re-constructing

5. Kate was hired to appraise a single-family home built in 2001. Which of the following is the most appropriate approach to value?

    a. Cost approach
    b. Income approach
    c. Sales comparison approach
    d. Both (a) and (c)

6. In USPAP, which of the following stresses the importance of not misleading the reader?

    a. Standards Rule 1-6
    b. Standard 2
    c. Standards Rule 2-2
    d. Standard 3

7. Which of the following is used in reconciliation more than any other part of the appraisal process?

    a. Judgment
    b. Weight
    c. Experience
    d. Accuracy

For questions 8 – 11, use the following chart for a 3-bedroom, 2-bathroom house in Any City, FL 33000

183 Hill St.	$159,000
1245 N. Front St.	$162,500
210 Baker Ln.	$167,400
370 Mountain Ave.	$159,000
4312 Ocean Way	$175,700

8. What is the mean price for a 3-bedroom, 2-bathroom house in Any City, FL 33000?
    a. $162,400
    b. $164,700
    c. $166,000
    d. $173,200

9. What is the median price for a 3-bedroom, 2-bathroom house in Any City, FL 33000?
    a. $159,000
    b. $160,100
    c. $162,500
    d. $175,700

10. What is the mode for this sample of 3-bedroom, 2-bathroom homes in Any City, FL 33000?
    a. $159,000
    b. $162,500
    c. $167,400
    d. $170,000

11. Why should an appraiser round the final value estimate?
    a. To make the report easier to read
    b. To emphasize the fact that it is indeed an estimate
    c. Because exact figures are too confusing
    d. To allow room for error

12. When is a workfile required?
    a. When using a Self-Contained Appraisal Report
    b. Only when using the URAR
    c. Only when facts are omitted
    d. Anytime an appraisal is performed

13. Regarding appraisal reporting, all of the following are true, except the:
    a. type of report cannot be selected until the appraisal is complete.
    b. client's needs determine the report type.
    c. choice of report type does not affect the amount of work done to complete the appraisal.
    d. entire appraisal process must be completed prior to preparing the report.

14. Which is the most elaborate of the appraisal report options?
    a. Uniform Residential Appraisal Report
    b. Self-Contained Appraisal Report
    c. Summary Appraisal Report
    d. Restricted Use Appraisal Report

15. In which type of report does the amount of detail depend upon the client's needs and the problem being addressed by the appraisal?
    a. Summary Appraisal Report
    b. Self-Contained Appraisal Report
    c. Uniform Residential Appraisal Report (URAR)
    d. Restricted Use Appraisal Report

14

Chapter

INTRODUCTION

In this last chapter, we are going to consider some case studies based on appraisal experiences. A **case study** is the analysis of a real-life problem and is designed usually for training purposes. By reading and recognizing what caused the problems in the appraisal process, you will have additional means to spot possible problem areas and be able to avoid them in your appraisal practice.

A professional appraiser should be a critical thinker and a good listener. **Critical thinking** is the careful, precise analysis or examination of the facts. Problem solving requires not only the ability to listen, but also the need to ask the right questions, prior to accepting the assignment. Many appraisers make the mistake of accepting every appraisal assignment that comes their way. It is better to decline an assignment then to find yourself in trouble with the regulatory agencies for improper actions and unsupported conclusions.

Although some of the scenarios used in these case studies are exaggerated situations that you may not encounter, they are based on real life situations.

LEARNING OBJECTIVES

After reading this chapter, you will be able to:

- define case study and the critical thinking used in its development.
- describe contributory value used in paired sales analysis.
- describe the application of a gross rent multiplier in the income approach.
- define lender pressure.

CASE STUDY NO. 1 – PAIRED SALES ANALYSIS

In this case study, we will illustrate how paired sales analysis applies in a practical scenario. The **paired sales analysis** is a method of estimating the amount of adjustment for the presence or absence of any feature by pairing the sales prices of otherwise identical properties with and without that feature.

Appraiser Gayle is hired to appraise a new house in an upscale development. She began her investigation by pulling comparable sales and setting up a workfile. She then went to the site to examine the circumstances.

When performing the physical inspection, Gayle discovered that the subject property was situated at the end of a cul-de-sac. Looking from the rear of the property, the subject property definitely had an outstanding view. Comparable 1 was situated on the same cul-de-sac but was on the opposite side of the street. Because of the homes opposing it, the view was visible only from the second floor. Comparables 2 and 3 were situated in the same subdivision but located on a different street and did not have any view at all. From her physical inspection thus far, Gayle knew that the subject property indeed had a superior view to the comparables. However, she still did not know how much the view is worth or how much of an adjustment to make.

These homes were only a year to 18-months old and parts of the subdivision were still under construction. Subsequently, Gayle visited the sales office to find any recent sales that could be paired, isolating the view in order to determine what the view is worth. No such comparison could be made, but she was able to verify in the sales office that the owner of the subject property had paid a $50,000 view premium for that particular lot. By then, though, the subdivision was a year older and there was still no concrete proof of what a view was worth in this subdivision.

Gayle reviewed the data pulled at the beginning of her assignment and noticed five sales of new homes in a less expensive neighboring community on the other side of the hill—about three miles away—all on the same street. She observed that the five sales were described almost identically: approximately 2,200 square feet with all the same amenities, but there was a disparity in the prices. They ranged from $275,000 to $330,000, three of the sales clustered between $275,000 and $279,000, and the other sales were $325,000 and $330,000. They evidenced no descriptive difference in amenities, yet the price range was $55,000.

She decided to investigate the neighboring subdivision. The top level of the street was about 15 to 20 feet higher in altitude than the lower level of the street. House A sold for $325,000 and had an outstanding view from the rear yard. Houses B, C, and D on the opposite side of the street sold for $275,000, $277,500, and $279,000 respectively. They were very similar homes to House A, but they had no views because of the obstruction of the homes on the opposite side of the street. House E, situated on the corner of the upper level of the street, sold for $330,000, and had an outstanding view from both the front and rear yards.

These five properties matched up as being practically identical, except for their views. The sales prices were $55,000 apart, indicating that the view in this particular subdivision was worth approximately $55,000. Because this is a lower priced neighborhood than that of the subject property, it would be reasonable to assume that the view in the subject property's tract of homes has a contributory value of at least $55,000.

As you learned in Chapter 7, paired sales analysis can be an effective method of estimating the amount of adjustment for the presence or absence of any feature. As illustrated in this example, this was accomplished by pairing the sales prices of otherwise identical properties with or without a view. Although paired sales analysis is a theoretically sound method, it is sometimes impractical. A sufficient number of sales must be found to allow the appraiser to isolate the effect on value of the pertinent factor.

CASE STUDY NO. 2 – GROSS RENT MULTIPLIERS AND THE SALES COMPARISON APPROACH

In this case study, we will derive a gross rent multiplier (GRM) from an analysis of comparable sales. In single-family residence appraisal, the GRM is applied through the income method of valuation. Since many single-family residences are rented, the income potential may be considered in appraising the single-family home, especially when the subject property is tenant occupied.

The comparable sales are shown in the following chart. Here, we must analyze the sale properties and select a GRM to be applied to the subject property. The rent multipliers are ratios between price and rent at the time of sale, and no adjustments are necessary. The rent multipliers range from 122 to 133. The five considerations in analyzing the sale properties follow:

1. The sales should be recent. Rent multipliers may change with economic conditions.

2. The sale properties should be located in the same or equal neighborhoods as the subject property.

3. The sale properties should be reasonably similar to the subject in all essential physical elements.

4. The rent for the sale properties must be their fair market rent at the time of sale.

5. The ratio of expenses to rent should be similar for sale property and subject.

Analysis of Five Comparable Sales

Property	Monthly Rent	Sale Price	Rent Multiplier
A	$800	$104,000	130
B	$740	$94,000	127
C	$900	$110,000	122
D	$800	$106,000	133
E	$760	$100,000	132

Properties A, B, and C are comparable to the subject property in all these respects. We find that the rent for property D was established years ago and was not considered the fair market rent at the time of sale. Property E is an older sale, located in a better neighborhood than the subject property. Based on our analysis, we narrow the rent multiplier range and estimate a reasonable gross rent multiplier of 130 for the subject property. If the present rent and the economic rent for the subject property are $800 per month, we derive the value for the property as follows:

$$\$800 \times 130 = \$104,000$$

Gross rent multipliers for single-family residences, duplexes, and small apartment houses are usually expressed as a monthly multiplier factor. Multipliers applicable to large apartment houses and commercial properties are expressed on a yearly income basis. As you learned in Chapter 10, you can convert a monthly multiplier to a year factor by dividing by 12. A monthly multiplier of 130 would be the same as a yearly multiplier of 10.8.

As discussed in Chapter 10, the GRM is a reliable method of valuation only when sufficient sales data are available. As with the income approach, the gross rent for the subject property must be estimated from or substantiated by comparable rents in the area. Many investors in small residential income properties, such as duplexes and fourplexes, rely strongly on a gross rent multiplier in purchasing property.

CASE STUDY NO. 3 – THE EFFECT OF INACCURATE APPRAISALS

In this case study, we will examine the effect of inaccurate appraisals in a rising market. In the last several years, many properties were purchased with teaser rates—buyers were undercapitalized and prices were high. Foreclosures are increasing rapidly and lenders are shifting the blame to appraisers for overvaluing the properties.

This is a situation for many people across the country. Sally was renting and wanted to own her own home. The price of her condominium was $200,000. Sally was approved for 100% financing and thought she found a great deal—especially since the lender was going to give her a loan at 3% interest for the first year.

The appraiser, Pat, was hired by Sally's lender to value the home. Pat found three comparable sales and discovered that the last sale of the same floor plan sold just two months prior for $185,000. Pat recognized the $15,000 difference, but decided to "hit the mark" and valued the condominium at $200,000—the price the lender needed to fund Sally's loan. Pat figured the market was appreciating at a rate that could justify the $15,000 difference.

Though the lender did not directly pressure Pat, because this particular lender frequently hired him for appraisal assignments, Pat did not want to jeopardize his working relationship with the lender by turning in an appraisal report with a value that was considerably lower.

Sally's loan funded and the transaction closed. After one year, Sally was shocked to learn that her total payments had increased. The rate on her mortgage rose 5.9% per year—which was market rate. Sally began to fall behind on her mortgage payments and the lender filed a notice of default on her property. She considered selling the unit, but the real estate market had cooled and a local REALTOR® indicated the unit was now worth $180,000—$20,000 less than Sally paid for the home.

This case study shows what can happen when there is a rush to buy property in a seemingly rising market. As an appraiser, you need to review the purchase documents as mandated in USPAP Standards Rule 1-5 and analyze the financing to see if it is resulting in higher purchase prices than the market data will support.

In this example, the buyer thought she was buying the condominium for a market-value price. In reality, she paid top dollar. What would have happened if the appraiser had been a bit more conservative and had refused to "hit the number" to meet lender expectations? Unfortunately, lender pressure is common in the appraisal business. **Lender pressure** means to pressure (directly or indirectly) an appraiser to value a property at a certain amount. Though appraisers do not bear the primary responsibility for bad loans, accurate appraisals can certainly lessen the severity of the problem.

CASE STUDY NO. 4 – RECONCILIATION: WEIGHING THE CHOICES

In this case study, we will look at reconciling the values indicated by the three approaches, and decide which approach will receive the most weight.

Teri is appraising a single-family residence in a neighborhood near a college. Because of the need for student housing, many similar properties in the area are used as rentals. Because of the nature of this type of tenancy, the neighborhood is in decline. It suffers from excessive deferred maintenance as well as negative external influences, such as noise pollution, due to its proximity to the college campus.

From the sales comparison approach, Teri estimates the subject's value at $251,000. From the cost approach, she arrives at an estimate of $260,500, and from the income approach $255,800.

Based on the information provided above, Teri sees a range of value from $251,000 to $260,500. This range of $9,500 is relatively narrow considering all of the factors that affect the subject and its neighborhood. Teri's next step is to analyze and weigh these three value determinates and arrive at a single value conclusion that is supported by them. She should be comfortable with any conclusion reached that falls in the range of the three estimates—from $251,000 to $260,500. In addition, the final value may reflect one approach's estimate exactly, or may be a hybrid of two or three of them.

Teri knows that because of the age of the subject property and its excessive deferred maintenance, her calculation of accrued depreciation may not be the most accurate. She also knows that the cost approach tends to flank the higher end of the value range. Therefore, she decides to give the cost approach the least amount of weight.

In her analysis of the result based on the sales comparison approach, Teri recognizes that while this approach is typically the best indication of value for this type of property, in this instance, the neighborhood is in serious decline. Therefore, the sales comparison approach may lose some of its credibility. That said, she is still convinced that the value derived from her comparison analysis reflects current market value of the subject property. She double-checks her comparables and determines that all of the properties used in her sales comparison analysis are legitimately comparable to the subject and none needs extensive adjustments.

Finally, Teri reviews the income approach to value and carefully reexamines all of the information and data used in arriving at her conclusion. She determines that this approach seems to be a strong indicator of value and gives it the most weight. This is because her analysis of the neighborhood revealed several similar rental houses. The rentals are all on a month-to-month basis and are all very competitive. Therefore, they are representative of current market rent.

Teri's final analysis comes down to a value somewhere in between the sales comparison value of $251,000 and the income value of $255,800. She could choose one of the values and use it as the final value estimate for the property, but this does not satisfy her. She determines that the income estimate receives the strongest consideration, but cannot completely discount the sales comparison estimate because it is typically the best indicator of value for single-family detached residences. Teri finally reconciles that the market value for this type of property in this neighborhood is $255,000. She chose to round the income estimate figure down instead of rounding up, which she would typically do in most other circumstances, to account for the influences and disparity from the comparison analysis.

An appraiser should round the final value estimate to the nearest thousand to emphasize the fact that it is indeed an estimate. If Teri were to become too finite in her estimation, say by stating the final value at $254,654, it would be too exact for the marketplace.

An appraiser must judge and weigh the data that leads to each value conclusion. As you learned in Chapter 13, the term weight is often used by appraisers. **Weight** implies judging the importance, influence, or authority of the specific data being considered. Throughout the appraisal process, you will correlate and weigh data to form conclusions.

SUMMARY

A **case study** is an analysis of a real-life problem that may occur in any discipline including, but not limited to, the appraisal profession. It defines the problem and discusses the way to arrive at applicable solutions.

Appraisers must use **critical thinking** and carefully examine the data they receive and verify all information.

Four scenarios were examined in this chapter. They are summarized as: 1) using a paired sales analysis in order to estimate the amount of an adjustment, 2) deriving a gross rent multiplier from an analysis of comparable sales, 3) examining the effect of inaccurate appraisals in a rising market, and 4) reconciling the values indicated by the three approaches, and deciding which approach will receive the most weight.

CHAPTER 14 REVIEW EXERCISES

MATCHING EXERCISE

Instructions: Write the letter of the matching term on the blank line before its definition. Answers are in Appendix A.

Terms

A. case study

B. critical thinking

C. deferred maintenance

D. gross rent multiplier (GRM)

E. paired sales analysis

F. teaser rates

G. reconciliation

H. weight

Definitions

1. _____ The analysis of a real-life problem, which defines the problem and discusses applicable solutions

2. _____ A careful, precise analysis or examination of the facts

3. _____ An effective method of estimating the amount of adjustment for the presence or absence of any feature

4. _____ A reliable method of valuation only when sufficient sales data are available

5. _____ Implies judging the importance, influence, or authority of the specific data being considered

MULTIPLE CHOICE QUESTIONS

Instructions: Circle your response and go to Appendix A to read the complete explanation for each question.

1. The analysis of a real life problem, designed usually for training purposes, is called a(n):
    a. opinion report.
    b. database.
    c. case study.
    d. reconciliation.

2. The careful, precise analysis or examination of the facts is known as:
    a. interrogation.
    b. critical thinking.
    c. investigation.
    d. problem solving.

3. In Case Study No. 1, appraiser Gayle identified the _____ of the view in the subject property's tract of homes.
    a. net value
    b. contributory value
    c. superiority
    d. absence

4. In single-family residence appraisal, the GRM is applied through which of the following methods of valuation?
    a. Income
    b. Cost
    c. Sales Comparison
    d. All of the above

5. Directly or indirectly pressuring an appraiser to estimate a property's value at a certain amount is known as:
    a. consideration.
    b. foreclosure.
    c. reconciliation.
    d. lender pressure.

APPENDIX A: ANSWER KEY

Chapter 1 – Characteristics of Property and Value

Answers - Matching Exercise

1. Q	6. V	11. K	16. D
2. S	7. N	12. T	17. Z
3. C	8. E	13. O	18. F
4. R	9. J	14. G	19. X
5. A	10. W	15. H	20. M

Answers - Multiple Choice Questions

1. **(d)** Property is anything that is capable of being owned and gained lawfully. **Page 2**

2. **(b)** Airspace is considered real property to a reasonable height. **Page 3**

3. **(b)** The five tests to determine a fixture are method of attachment, adaptation of the article, relationship of the parties, intention, and agreement of the parties. **Pages 5–6**

4. **(a)** A fixture may remain personal property if all parties are informed. **Page 6**

5. **(a)** In legal terms, intellectual property (IP) is a general term for various legal rights, which attach to certain types of information, ideas, or other intangibles. **Page 7**

6. **(b)** The major difference between condemnation under the power of eminent domain and condemnation under police power is that in the former, the public (or condemnor) must pay fair market value for the property that is to be acquired for public use. There is no payment involved in condemnation under police power. **Page 10**

7. **(c)** When there is a conflict between a public (governmental) restriction on the construction or development of a home or lot and a private deed restriction on such construction or development, the one that is the most restrictive holds. **Page 12**

8. **(d)** Most private real property in most states is subject to real estate taxation. Exempt properties may include those of certain religious, charitable, educational, and non-profit organizations. **Page 10**

9. **(b)** Value always has to be expressed in terms of cash, terms equivalent to cash, or some other precisely revealed terms. For an appraiser, value is not a fact—it is a qualified opinion. **Page 13**

10. **(c)** Price is the amount asked, offered, or paid for a property. Once stated, price is a fact—whether it is publicly disclosed or retained in private. **Page 13**

11. **(d)** The four elements of value can be remembered by the mnemonic DUST—Demand, Utility, Scarcity, and Transferability. **Pages 13–14**

12. **(b)** Functional utility is the combined factors of usefulness with desirability. **Page 14**

13. **(a)** USPAP defines market value as the most probable price which a property should bring in a competitive and open market under all conditions requisite to a fair sale, with the buyer and seller, each acting prudently, knowledgeably, and assuming the price is not affected by undue stimulus. **Page 23**

14. **(b)** An arm's-length transaction, such as a sale of property, is one in which all parties involved are acting in their own self-interest and are under no undue influence or pressure from other parties. **Page 23**

15. **(a)** Investment value represents the value of a specific property to a particular investor. As used in appraisal assignments, investment value is not market value, but is value to an individual. **Page 24**

Chapter 2 – Valuation Principles

Answers - Matching Exercise

1. Y	6. K	11. M	16. O
2. P	7. C	12. S	17. F
3. E	8. B	13. A	18. X
4. N	9. Z	14. R	19. D
5. U	10. V	15. L	20. Q

Answers - Multiple Choice Questions

1. **(c)** Highest and best use is the use, from among reasonably probable and adequately supported alternative uses, that is physically possible, legally permitted, economically feasible, and maximally productive. The use providing the maximum return on investment should be determined. **Page 34**

2. **(b)** The principle of consistent use requires that land and improvements be appraised on the basis of the same use. **Page 37**

3. **(b)** Increasing supply or decreasing demand will reduce the price in the market. Reducing supply or increasing demand will raise the price in the market. **Page 38**

4. **(d)** Reduced to its simplest form, the principle of supply and demand must include an analysis of population growth, the buyer's ability to pay, and the relative scarcity of available land. **Page 38**

5. **(d)**   Property values tend to be set by the price of substitute properties that have similar amenities. When several similar or commensurate properties are available, the one with the lowest price attracts the greatest demand and widest distribution. **Page 39**

6. **(a)**   The principle of anticipation is most obvious and easy to measure in the case of income-producing property. Virtually all multiple residential, industrial, professional, and commercial properties are purchased with the vision of future economic returns. **Page 40**

7. **(c)**   The four stages, although not always distinct, can best be described as: (1) development, (2) stability, (3) decline, and (4) revitalization. **Page 42**

8. **(c)**   Progression and regression only affect properties of the same type. Sam's mansion is clearly defiant of the principle of conformity, which holds that maximum value results when properties in a neighborhood are relatively similar in size, style, quality, use, and/or type. **Pages 45–47**

9. **(d)**   The principle of progression states that the worth of a lesser-valued residence tends to be enhanced by association with higher-valued residences in the same area. **Page 47**

10. **(c)**   Typically, the principle of competition follows three steps: (1) market demand generates profits, (2) profits generate competition, and (3) competition stabilizes profits. **Page 48**

11. **(a)**   The principle of contribution calculates the worth of a particular component in terms of its contribution to the value of the whole property, or an item's worth is calculated as the amount that its absence would detract from the value of the whole. **Page 49**

12. **(b)**   The principle of contribution emphasizes that cost is not necessarily equal to value. **Page 50**

13. **(a)**   The principle of increasing and decreasing returns is the idea that successive increments of one or more agents of production added to fixed amounts of other agents will enhance income, in dollars, benefits, or amenities, at an increasing rate until a maximum return is reached. **Pages 50–51**

14. **(d)**   Surplus productivity is the income generated by a project after the four agents of production have been paid. **Page 51**

15. **(b)**   The economic principle of opportunity cost recognizes competing investments, usually in different industries, that may have a greater return. This is the competition between different types of investment. **Page 53**

Chapter 3 – Property Rights: Identification

Answers - Matching Exercise

1. A	6. S	11. L	16. X
2. E	7. Y	12. U	17. B
3. N	8. H	13. C	18. D
4. R	9. G	14. P	19. V
5. J	10. O	15. Q	20. Z

Answers - Multiple Choice Questions

1. **(d)**   The bundle of rights consists of all legal rights that are attached to the ownership of real property. The bundle of rights includes the right to use, possess, transfer, encumber, and the enjoyment of real property. **Page 62**

2. **(d)**   An estate in fee, also known as a fee or fee simple estate is the most complete form of ownership. **Page 64**

3. **(b)**   If a seller imposes qualifications or conditions that the buyer must do or not do, this is known as a fee simple qualified or fee simple defeasible estate. The conditions are classified as a condition subsequent or a condition precedent. **Page 65**

4. **(c)**   An estate for years is one type of leasehold estate. Other types of leasehold estates are an estate at will, estate from period to period, and estate at sufferance. **Page 66**

5. **(a)**   The estate from period to period, also known as periodic tenancy, is perhaps the most common type of lease or rental agreement for residential use. This typical month-to-month tenancy requires 30-days notice to quit. **Page 67**

6. **(b)**   A partial interest is an interest in real estate that represents less than the fee simple estate. Some examples of partial interests are ownership in common interest developments (such as condominium ownership) and leasehold interests. **Page 67**

7. **(b)**   Concurrent ownership has several forms such as tenancy in common, joint tenancy, community property, tenancy by the entirety, and tenancy in partnership. **Page 68**

8. **(c)**   Tenancy in common allows two or more people to hold unequal percentages. Each co-owner has an undivided interest, which means that each owner has a certain equitable interest in the property, but has the right to use the whole property. **Page 68**

9. **(b)** Time, title, interest, and possession are four unities of a joint tenancy. If properly formed, a joint tenancy creates a right of survivorship. The right of survivorship means that if one of the joint tenants dies, the surviving joint tenant automatically becomes sole owner of the property. **Page 68**

10. **(d)** Tenancy is a mode or method of ownership or holding title to property. **Page 69**

11. **(a)** Leases are generally classified by the type of real estate, the length of term, or the method of payment. **Page 70**

12. **(d)** Generally, a condominium consists of a separate fee interest in a particular specific space (the unit), plus an undivided interest in all common or public areas of the development. Each unit owner has a deed, separate financing, and pays the property taxes for his or her unit. **Page 71**

13. **(a)** In an undivided interest, the land itself is not divided—just the ownership. The buyer receives an undivided interest in a parcel of land as a tenant in common with all the other owners. **Pages 72–74**

14. **(a)** Both mobile homes and manufactured homes are factory built. A mobile home is a factory-built home manufactured prior to June 15, 1976. Manufactured homes are homes built in a factory after June 15, 1976 and must conform to the U.S. government's Manufactured Home Construction and Safety Standards (HUD code). **Pages 74–75**

15. **(b)** Time-share ownership is popular in resorts and other desirable areas where people like to vacation but do not need the right of possession the rest of the time. **Page 75**

Chapter 4 – Property Inspection: Site

Answers - Matching Exercise

1. Z	6. A	11. G	16. T
2. Q	7. J	12. H	17. S
3. R	8. P	13. X	18. D
4. V	9. W	14. I	19. F
5. B	10. N	15. K	20. U

Answers - Multiple Choice Questions

1. **(d)** Analysis and valuation of the site must sometimes be made separately from analysis of the improvements for several reasons, including when the existing improvements do not represent the highest and best use of the land. **Page 84**

2. **(b)** When appraising a property, an appraiser first has to determine highest and best use. **Page 85**

3. **(c)** Although other physical attributes contribute to value, location is certainly the most important factor. **Page 85**

4. **(a)** Legal documents do not report the usable area of the site, which is more important than gross area. Usable area is the portion of the site that is suitable for building. **Page 88**

5. **(a)** Buyers usually pay a premium for a cul-de-sac location. Many families with young children prefer cul-de-sac lots because they offer more seclusion and safety than other lots. **Page 88**

6. **(b)** Interior lot value is usually the benchmark from which other lots are valued, primarily because most lots are interior lots. **Page 89**

7. **(c)** The percentage or steepness of slope of a residential lot is very important in determining value. A lot that is moderately sloping or rolling has a steepness of 10 – 15%. **Page 90**

8. **(d)** An appraiser has to determine if the excess land is usable or not. It is a mistake to assume that a sizable adjustment is needed. **Page 92**

9. **(c)** In some cases, a qualified appraiser can estimate the cost of providing drainage facilities. The opinion of an engineer or other drainage expert is often needed. **Page 93**

10. **(d)** Sometimes the level or elevation of the ground has to be changed or altered using bladed machines that literally scrape the earth in a process known as grading. **Page 94**

11. **(b)** Residences with south-facing backyards suffer less sun damage to the paint on the front of the structure. Since the front is usually more extensively decorated and more carefully maintained than the back, less maintenance means less expense. **Page 95**

12. **(c)** A retaining wall is an on-site improvement. While aspects of the other choices, such as utilities, exist on site—because they originate off-site—they are classified as off-site factors. **Page 94**

13. **(b)** Electricity is generally available even in the most remote area of the country. Private and public electrical utilities have supplied the U.S. with an electrical system second to none. **Page 98**

14. **(d)** The requirements for installing a septic tank system generally include all of these choices. **Page 100**

15. **(d)** The impact of close proximity to nuclear power plants or hazardous waste disposal sites is generally obvious by lack of sales in the area, coupled with extremely depressed sales of those properties that do sell. **Page 102**

Chapter 5 – Property Inspection: Improvements

Answers - Matching Exercise

1. I	6. R	11. N	16. Q
2. V	7. B	12. M	17. O
3. T	8. G	13. A	18. Z
4. L	9. U	14. H	19. J
5. D	10. S	15. C	20. F

Answers - Multiple Choice Questions

1. **(b)** An appraiser's inspection of a residence usually has two main parts: the exterior inspection and interior inspection. **Page 110**

2. **(c)** Basic common sense in room and access layout provides maximum livability. A bedroom directly off a dining room or kitchen is considered undesirable. **Page 112**

3. **(b)** No national standard exists which defines a room. The generally accepted rule is to include those spaces that are effectively divided as separate rooms and to exclude bathrooms. **Page 113**

4. **(c)** The foundation or substructure of a home has two purposes: (1) it supports the entire building, and (2) it transfers the weight of the building to the ground. **Page 113**

5. **(d)** A floating slab is composed of one section for the floor and another for the foundation wall, each poured separately. An expansion joint separates the two parts. **Page 114**

6. **(a)** In areas that are free from wood-destroying pests such as termites, wood can be an excellent foundation material. In fact, wood is still the most popular, versatile material for residential framing. **Page 115**

7. **(a)** There is more variety of materials for roof construction than for any other component of a residence. **Page 116**

8. **(d)** Size for the interior of the home is reported in terms of gross living area (GLA), which is the total amount of finished, above ground habitable space. In most cases, attics, crawlspaces, and basements are unfinished and do not count in the GLA measurement. **Page 120**

9. **(b)** Flooring in good condition and of certain materials, like finished wood or marble, can certainly add value to a home. **Page 120**

10. **(d)** The interior wall material most often used in residential construction is drywall—also called sheetrock, plasterboard, or gypsum board. **Page 121**

11. **(c)** Newer homes have a 220-volt system, controlled by an electrical service panel with circuit breakers. Older houses have a fuse box system. An appraiser should be able to identify a 220-volt or 240-volt wiring set-up (as noted by three-wire service entrance) for newer homes. **Page 123**

12. **(c)** Many states have implemented additional laws requiring that smoke detectors be installed or upgraded at the time of sale, regardless of the age of the home. **Page 125**

13. **(d)** Energy efficiency features are becoming more and more important. In addition to insulation and windows, certain appliances and use of solar energy can also add to the energy efficiency of a home. **Pages 126–127**

14. **(a)** Unlike garages, carports are not enclosed. **Page 128**

15. **(b)** Sometimes the contributory value of site improvements does not equal the cost of building the improvement. For example, swimming pools contribute to the overall value of a home, but the contributory value is generally less than the expense of building the pool itself. **Page 134**

Chapter 6 – Sales Comparison Approach

Answers - Matching Exercise

1. Q	5. D	9. T	13. H
2. E	6. O	10. N	14. L
3. R	7. K	11. A	15. J
4. G	8. F	12. P	

Answers - Multiple Choice Questions

1. **(d)** The sales comparison approach is most applicable when there are a sufficient number of verifiable sales that are bought and sold on a regular basis. It is the most important approach for appraising single-family homes, condominiums, smaller multi-family residences, and vacant land. **Page 146**

2. **(b)** The Scope of Work Rule has three basic parts: (1) the problem to be solved has to be identified, (2) the appraiser needs to determine and perform the scope of work necessary to develop credible assignment results, and (3) the appraiser needs to discuss the scope of work in his or her report. **Page 148**

3. **(c)** Substitution states that a buyer should not pay more for a property than the cost of a substitute property of equal utility and desirability. **Page 149**

4. **(b)** The first step is collecting market data. The appraiser has to research the market for information on actual sales, listings, offers to purchase, and properties in contract. These properties should be homogeneous to the subject. **Page 150**

5. **(c)** The sales comparison approach has a systematic procedure: (1) collect market data, (2) select market data, (3) verification of data, (4) apply adjustments, and (5) reconcile adjusted comparable property values. **Pages 150–151**

6. **(d)** When collecting market data, the appraiser considers: (1) the characteristics of the subject property, (2) the area to be searched for sales, (3) the time period to be investigated for sales, and (4) the sources to be used to find sales. **Page 151**

7. **(c)** Assessment data is normally not used as it has reliability problems and assessments can be a function of law—not necessarily value. **Pages 152–153**

8. **(b)** The highest and best use of a property is the main factor determining its value. One of the simplest ways to check highest and best use is to see if there is a difference in zoning. **Page 158**

9. **(d)** The appraiser needs to make the arrangement in terms of the units of comparison that are appropriate for the particular assignment, the appraisal problem, and the nature and characteristics of the property that is appraised. **Page 159**

10. **(a)** Primary verification includes talking to someone who is or was involved in the transaction. Buyers, sellers, and/or real estate agents should be interviewed to make sure the conditions of sale match those used in the definition of value. **Page 161**

11. **(a)** USPAP indicates that the appraiser has to indicate his or her level of inspection. The inspection can be no physical inspection, a drive-by exterior only inspection, or a full interior-exterior inspection. The appraiser must be able to achieve a credible result. **Page 162**

12. **(a)** Adjustments are not normally made for elements less than 1% of the sales price of the comparable sale, as the market data is not precise enough to permit the appraiser to discern minor differences in value amounts. **Page 164**

13. **(c)** The amount of the gross adjustment is determined by adding all individual adjustments, without regard to whether they are positive or negative adjustments. Fannie Mae states that this percentage should not exceed 25% of the sales price of the comparable. **Page 165**

14. **(d)** Fannie Mae states that a single line item adjustment should not exceed 10% of the sales price of the comparable. In this problem, the adjustment for physical differences equals 12%. Keep in mind that this is not a steadfast rule—it is a guideline. The appraiser can still make the adjustment, even if it exceeds the 10% guideline for a single line item, as long as market data supports it. **Page 165**

15. **(a)** If the appraisal is for a federally related transaction, then the appraiser has to use a self-contained or summary report. The restricted use report can only have one intended user, and as such, is not suitable for federally related transactions. **Page 166**

Chapter 7 – Measurement of Adjustments

Answers - Matching Exercise

1. K	5. P	9. N	13. M
2. L	6. O	10. T	14. C
3. E	7. A	11. I	15. F
4. D	8. B	12. G	

Answers - Multiple Choice Questions

1. **(c)** The goal of the sales comparison approach is to select the market sales that are most homogeneous to the subject property. These sales are the most similar and are the ones that buyers and sellers consider when using the principle of substitution. **Page 176**

2. **(b)** When adjusting for financing, appraisers typically adjust for cash equivalency. The cash equivalency technique is a procedure in which the sales prices of comparable properties selling with atypical financing are adjusted to reflect financing that is typical in a market. **Page 179**

3. **(d)** All of the factors mentioned can affect location. A change in zoning from residential to commercial, the affect of road noise and the perception that buyers do not want to be under high tension wires all result in location adjustments. **Pages 181–182**

4. **(b)** To convert this to a monthly percentage, the appraiser will divide the yearly percentage by twelve (the total number of months in a year) and then multiply this by the number of months. Calculation: $0.05 \div 12 = 0.00417$; $0.00417 \times 9 = 0.0375$ (3.75%); $\$375,000 \times 3.75\% = \$14,062.50$ ($\$14,100$ rounded) adjustment value. **Page 189**

5. **(b)** In the sales comparison approach, the appraiser uses quantitative and/or qualitative analysis to derive an opinion of value. The two techniques can be used separately or in combination. **Page 185**

6. **(d)** Adjustments may be made using any of the three methods: (1) as a dollar amount, (2) as a percentage of the sales price, and (3) using pluses and minuses. **Page 196**

7. **(a)** If the adjustments are made strictly on a dollar basis, the sequence in which adjustments are made is unimportant. **Page 197**

8. **(c)** When applied properly, the sequence of adjustment reveals that the proper adjusted value of this particular comparable is $468,300 (rounded). **Page 199**

```
                        Sequence 1
         Sales Price                    $450,000
         Financing                ×          1.03
                                        $436,500
         Market Conditions        ×          1.05
                                        $458,325
         Physical Characteristics  +      $10,000
                                        $468,325
```

9. **(b)** Adjustments are always made to the comparables. The appraiser cannot adjust the value of the subject property because the value of the subject is unknown. In this example, features that are superior to those of the subject property require a negative adjustment. **Page 201**

10. **(c)** Paired sales analysis identifies the amount of an adjustment when at least two sales are found that are virtually identical in all aspects but one. The one differing item between the sales equals the difference in value between the two properties. For the pool, the difference between Sale 1 and Sale 2 equals the value of a pool in this neighborhood. $435,000 − $400,000 = $35,000. **Pages 200–202**

11. **(b)** The difference between Sale 1 and Sale 3 equals the value of an extra garage space. $400,000 − $390,000 = $10,000. **Pages 200–202**

12. **(c)** To determine the value of the subject, select any one of the comparables and apply the proper adjustment to it. Select the comparable that is most similar to the subject. In this case, either Sale 2 or 3 would work. If we use Sale 2, the only difference is that the comparable has a three-car garage and the subject does not. To account for the difference, subtract $10,000 (value of the garage) from the comparable, answering the question, "What would the comparable sell for if it had the same garage space as the subject?" If you select any of the other two comparables and apply the adjustments correctly, you will arrive at the same conclusion. **Pages 200–202**

13. **(b)** The difference between the sales prices is $20,000. Divide that figure by the original price ($225,000) to calculate the total percentage the market has increased (.088 or 9%) over the original sales price. Rounding this figure, property values are increasing at approximately 9% per year. **Page 189**

14. **(a)** Linear regression is a specific type of correlation that is often used by appraisers to determine how one or more independent variables affect a dependent variable. Regression is a statistical analysis assessing the association between two variables. **Page 190**

15. **(d)** The problem with using multiple regression is that all sales in an area are usually factored into the analysis, not just the sales that are comparable to the subject. Less than arm's-length transactions and fraudulent sales often get included in these analytical models. Obviously, these non-market based transactions can distort the results obtained from a multiple regression analysis. **Page 191**

Chapter 8 – Finance and Cash Equivalency

Answers - Matching Exercise

1. D	6. L	11. N	16. T
2. X	7. F	12. J	17. P
3. H	8. U	13. W	18. Z
4. S	9. Y	14. M	19. O
5. V	10. K	15. B	20. R

Answers - Multiple Choice Questions

1. **(a)** The Fed regulates the flow of money in the marketplace indirectly through its member banks by controlling their reserve requirements and discount rates. **Page 214**

2. **(d)** Lenders receive income from finance charges such as loan origination fees and discount points. Also, they obtain reoccurring income through interest payments for loans that are kept as part of the bank's portfolio and service fees for collecting payments from the borrower. **Page 215**

3. **(d)** Savings and loan institutions, mortgage brokers, and commercial banks in the primary market can serve as potential clients for an appraiser. **Page 216**

4. **(a)** A direct lender lends its own funds and handles the entire loan process from origination to funding. **Page 217**

5. **(a)** Fannie Mae operates in the secondary mortgage market and develops appraisal guidelines that help to standardize the appraisal process in the lending industry. **Pages 218–219**

6. **(c)** Chapter 3 of Fannie Mae's guidelines discusses special considerations that should be given to properties with unusual features. **Page 219**

7. **(a)** Freddie Mac aids in the purchasing, securitizing, and investing in home mortgages. It also provides homeowners and renters with lower housing costs and better access to home financing. However, Freddie Mac does not guarantee the payment of the loans it purchases. **Page 219**

8. **(d)** A fully-amortized note is the most common type of loan with institutional lenders. Interest is charged on the outstanding principal balance at the rate and term agreed upon by the lender and borrower in a loan. **Page 220**

9. **(b)** A common type of fully amortized note is a fixed rate mortgage (FRM). This type of loan consists of regular, periodic payments of both interest and principal, which pay off the debt completely by the end of the term. These types of loans are available for 40 years, 30 years, 20 years, 15 years, and even 10 years. **Page 220**

10. **(d)** Rates for an adjustable rate mortgage (ARM) are based upon some economic indicator such as Treasury bill rates, LIBOR, or some other index. **Page 221**

11. **(c)** With a reverse annuity mortgage, the lender makes payments to the homeowner. The payments are based upon the equity the homeowner has remaining in the property that is given as security for the loan. Reverse annuity mortgages allow senior citizens to supplement fixed income and enjoy life more with the extra income. **Page 222**

12. **(b)** A home equity line of credit (HELOC) is a type of second lien that taps into a property owner's equity and creates a revolving credit line. HELOCs are often used to finance home improvement projects. **Page 222**

13. **(a)** An acceleration clause gives the lender the right to call the loan due and demand repayment immediately on occurrence of a specific event **Page 226**

14. **(c)** The loan-to-value ratio (LTV) is the ratio of debt to the value of the property. In this example, $330,000 ÷ .80 = $412,500. **Page 227**

15. **(b)** Non-conforming loans do not meet the standards of Fannie Mae and Freddie Mac—these include jumbo loans and subprime loans. **Page 228**

Chapter 9 – Income Approach: Analysis of Income and Expenses

Answers - Matching Exercise

1. N	6. U	11. E	16. X
2. G	7. F	12. R	17. D
3. O	8. H	13. S	18. B
4. P	9. I	14. L	19. V
5. M	10. Y	15. Z	20. T

Answers - Multiple Choice Questions

1. **(c)** The income approach is applicable to property in which future benefits are measured by the expected net income to the owner. If a property's ability to produce income is an important factor to potential buyers, then this approach is the best indicator of value. **Page 240**

2. **(b)** The first step in applying the income approach is estimating potential gross income (PGI). The simplest income to calculate is the potential gross income, which is the maximum income a property could generate. **Page 247**

3. **(c)** Most appraisals of leased properties are actually appraisals of the leased fee estate. The owner's fee estate becomes a leased fee estate when a property is leased. **Page 243**

4. **(d)** If a tenant and landlord share expenses in accordance to the provisions of the lease, it becomes a modified gross lease. **Page 244**

5. **(d)** A triple net lease (NNN)—also known as a net-net-net lease or absolute net lease—indicates the tenant is paying rent and virtually all of the expenses. **Page 244**

6. **(b)** Economic (market) rent is what a leased property would be expected to rent for under current market conditions if the property were vacant and available for rent. Market rent should be estimated for all living units, including manager and janitor's units, even if the rent is not actually being collected. **Page 248**

7. **(c)** Service income includes receipts from laundry facilities, vending machines, and selling of utility services to tenants. **Page 247**

8. **(d)** Typically, the economic (market) rent is capitalized at normal rates and the amount of the excess rent that exceeds economic rent is capitalized at a higher rate because of the risk that it may not continue throughout the economic life of the property. **Page 248**

9. **(a)** A rental survey is an analysis of competitive rents. If it is practical, the rental survey should cover only those apartments in the general area that are of similar age and construction. **Page 248**

10. **(a)** Effective gross income is the amount of income remaining after vacancy and collection losses are deducted from gross income. **Page 251**

11. **(b)** The vacancy and collection loss allowance is not estimated solely on conditions existing at the date of appraisal, but reflects the expected vacancy and collection loss over an extended time. Any apartment house should experience some vacancy and rent loss. The allowance is considered in relation to the prevailing economic rent, not the existing contract rent. **Page 251**

12. **(c)** To calculate net operating income (NOI), an appraiser deducts operating expenses from effective gross income (EGI). **Page 252**

13. **(b)** Fixed expenses are operating costs that are more or less permanent and that vary little from year to year regardless of occupancy. Property taxes, along with insurance and license fees, are considered as fixed expenses. **Page 252**

14. **(d)** Replacement reserves are funds set aside by the property owner to pay for the replacement of certain building components and fixtures that periodically wear out in a property. Reserves for replacement cover everything from new roofs, appliances, paint, carpet, drapes, and included furniture. **Page 256**

15. **(d)** Owner's operating statements generally do not accurately depict vacancy and collection losses and do not allocate funds for replacements. **Page 260**

Chapter 10 – Income Approach: Multipliers

Answers - Matching Exercise

1. B
2. I
3. H
4. G
5. F
6. K
7. J
8. E
9. D

Answers - Multiple Choice Questions

1. **(c)** The process of estimating the present worth of a property based on its anticipated income is called capitalization. **Page 269**

2. **(b)** The gross rent multiplier (GRM) is often applied when appraising single-family residences used as rental property, as well as smaller income-producing properties such as duplex and fourplex units. The gross income multiplier (GIM), on the other hand, is generally reserved for larger income-producing and commercial properties. **Page 269**

3. **(c)** GRM = Value ÷ Gross Rent (GR) **Page 271**

4. **(b)** This is found by multiplying the PGI by the vacancy and collection loss or $80,000 × .05 = $4,000. **Pages 275–276**

5. **(c)** The EGI is calculated by taking the PGI and subtracting the vacancy and collection loss or $80,000 − $4,000 = $76,000. **Pages 275–276**

6. **(c)** PGIM = Value ÷ PGI **Page 275**

7. **(b)** Apply the formula mentioned in the previous question and the result is 5. $400,000 ÷ $80,000 = 5.0. **Page 276**

8. **(a)** $400,000 ÷ $76,000 = 5.26 **Pages 275–276**

9. **(c)** Sales price equals the EGIM times the effective annual income. EGIM = Sales price/effective gross income. $600,000 ÷ $50,000 = 12. **Pages 275–276**

10. **(a)** Sales price equals the EGIM times the effective annual income. The effective annual income equals the sales price/EGIM or $575,000 ÷ 10. **Pages 275–276**

11. **(d)** This is straight multiplication: $56,410 × 9.75 = $550,000 (rounded). **Pages 275–276**

12. **(b)** To solve this part, the appraiser has to divide the annual income by 12 or $45,000 ÷ 12 = $3,750. **Pages 275–276**

13. **(d)** Unlike the question above, we do not use a factor of 12 to divide anything. We divide the sales price by the effective monthly income or $495,000 by $3,750 and the result is 132, which is the effective gross income multiplier on a monthly basis. **Pages 275–276**

14. **(c)** To perform this calculation, you have to divide the effective income by 12 and then divide the sale price by this amount. $60,526 ÷ 12 = $5,044. $575,000 ÷ 5,044 = 114 (rounded). **Pages 275–276**

15. **(d)** The five EGIMs are:

Comp 1	12
Comp 2	10
Comp 3	9.75
Comp 4	11
Comp 5	9.5
Total	52.25

Mean = 52.25 ÷ 5 = 10.45 **Pages 275–276**

Chapter 11 – Income Approach: Capitalization

Answers - Matching Exercise

1. E	6. P	11. T	16. F
2. V	7. B	12. L	17. J
3. U	8. N	13. Z	18. S
4. R	9. H	14. W	19. X
5. Q	10. Y	15. G	20. A

Answers - Multiple Choice Questions

1. **(c)** The process of estimating the present worth of a property based on its anticipated income is capitalization, which is used to convert income to value. **Page 284**

2. **(a)** The return or profit from an investment is also known as the yield. The return of investment is the recapture or conversion of the investment. **Pages 284–285**

3. **(a)** Conversion is not one of the seven characteristics to consider when evaluating an investment. The seven characteristics are: (1) reliability of net income, (2) liquidity, (3) burden of management, (4) probability of increase or decrease in value, (5) taxation, (6) hypothecation, and (7) leverage. **Pages 286–287**

4. **(d)** Being able to use a capital asset, such as real estate, as collateral for borrowing money is known as hypothecation. **Page 287**

5. **(c)** To determine a property's value, use the following equation.
NOI ÷ cap rate = value. **Page 286**

6. **(b)** To determine a property's cap rate, use the following equation.
NOI ÷ value = cap rate. **Page 285**

7. **(b)** A low capitalization rate results in a higher value and more secure income. The investment is not as risky with a low cap rate as it would be with a high rate. **Page 287**

8. **(a)** Band of investment is a method of estimating interest and capitalization rates, based on a weighted average of the mortgage interest rate (or other cost of borrowed funds) and the rate of return on equity required. **Page 294**

9. **(b)** To determine the weighted component for the land, multiply the land percentage of NOI (55%) by its corresponding cap rate (.065) and the result is .0358. The rounding is not done here, it occurs after the two weighted components are added together. **Page 296**

10. **(c)** This is similar to the question above, but here the building percentage of the NOI (45%) is multiplied by the building cap rate (.075) and the result is .0338. **Page 296**

11. **(c)** The capitalization rate is determined by adding the two weighted components together. This yields .0696, which is rounded to .07 or 7%. The appraiser rounds the rates at this step, not in the table. **Page 296**

12. **(d)** The value is determined by dividing the NOI by the OAR (cap rate). Thus $200,000 is divided by .07 which yields $2,857,000 which is rounded to $2,860,000. **Page 286**

13. **(b)** This answer is determined by subtracting the NOI attributable to the improvements ($67,500) from the total NOI ($250,000). $250,000 – $67,500 = $182,500. **Page 303**

14. **(b)** The value of the land is determined by dividing the NOI attributable to the land ($182,500) by the land cap rate (.08). This yields $2,281,250 which is rounded to $2,280,000. **Page 303**

15. **(c)** This is the easiest part of the problem as all the appraiser has to do is add the improvement value to the land value. $750,000 + $2,280,000 = $3,030,000. **Page 303**

Chapter 12 – Introduction to the Financial Calculator

Answers - Matching Exercise

1. Q	6. O	11. G	16. A
2. T	7. B	12. I	17. R
3. K	8. E	13. H	18. P
4. D	9. F	14. L	19. S
5. C	10. J	15. U	20. V

Answers - Multiple Choice Questions

1. **(b)** This problem is solved using the following key sequence. 35 [ENTER]; 37 [X]. **Page 323**

2. **(a)** The RPN becomes advantageous when the appraiser is performing several calculations in one sequence. The key sequence to solve this problem is 20 [ENTER], 320 [X], 5 [X], 7 [÷]. **Page 324**

3. **(c)** To exchange registers, you need to use the exchange key, [x$^>$ $_<$y]. **Pages 324–325**

4. **(d)** The f function key is used to set the decimal place. For 4 places you key in f 4. **Page 325**

5. **(a)** When you use scientific notation for large numbers, you move the decimal point until there is only one number to the left (not counting zero). This is called the mantissa. You then key in the number of spaces you move the decimal point. Therefore, "a" is the only answer that meets this criterion. **Page 329**

6. **(c)** Since this is an annual payment, you do not convert the years into payment periods and you do not convert the interest rate into a monthly basis. The key sequence to solve this problem is: 100,000 [PV]; 8.75 [i]; 25 [n]; [PMT]. **Page 330**

7. **(d)** The g function key is the proper one to use for this conversion. It becomes a matter of whether to go for the "b" foil or to think that with a 20-year loan, you have to key in 20. **Page 331**

8. **(c)** The display uses the two zeros after the decimal point here, but you have to actually key the numbers and keys in to know for sure. **Page 331**

9. **(b)** The g function key is the proper one to use for this conversion. **Page 331**

10. **(b)** The answers for (b) and (c) are very similar, except that (c), although true is not the answer to the question. The display indication does not show percentage signs or express percentages. **Page 331**

11. **(b)** To get the payment amount correct, you have to input the loan term for the whole loan correctly (see question 7 above) and you have to input the interest rate properly. If everything is inputted properly, all you have to do is hit the [PMT] key and the correct answer will appear. **Page 331**

12. **(a)** If the input items are all correctly keyed in, the solution to the loan balance after five years is straightforward for the keys commands are given in the table. **Page 332**

13. **(c)** The keystrokes to solve this fairly simple problem are: 43,560 [STO] 6. Then we enter the square footage: 280,000 [ENTER]; recall 43,560 from register 6, [RCL] 6 and then we divide (÷). Store this result in 1. [STO] 1. **Pages 326–327**

14. **(b)** Enter the square footage: 620,000 [ENTER]; we then recall 43,560 from whichever register we put it, [RCL] 6 and then we divide (÷). Let's store this result in 2. [STO] 2. **Pages 326–327**

15. **(d)** We did not solve for the third parcel, so answer "a" is just for the first two parcels. The keystrokes to solve for the third parcel are: 430,000 [ENTER]; [RCL] 6; divide (÷) and the result is 9.87. To this we add what is stored in the other two registers; [RCL] 1 [+]; [RCL] 2 [+] which gives us the correct answer. **Pages 326–327**

Chapter 13 – Reconciliation

Answers - Matching Exercise

1. I	5. J	9. G	13. S
2. H	6. D	10. L	14. O
3. B	7. E	11. N	15. P
4. R	8. F	12. A	

Answers - Multiple Choice Questions

1. **(a)** In reconciliation, the appraiser considers the appropriateness of each of the three approaches to the subject, the quality of available data, and the amount of judgmental adjustment required to reach each estimate. The final opinion of value is the result of the reconciliation, but it is not a criterion to conduct the reconciliation. **Page 347**

2. **(b)** Type of property being appraised, data available, and intended use of appraisal are the three factors used to form the guidelines for judging each of the approaches in reconciling a final value estimate. **Page 349**

3. **(d)** The data available to the appraiser is probably the most important aspect of reconciliation. Regardless of which approach is most applicable to a particular type of property, if adequate data is not available, a reliable value estimate cannot be developed using that approach. **Page 349**

4. **(a)** Once an appraiser has reconciled the individual approaches to value, he or she then prepares for final reconciliation by re-evaluating the entire appraisal. Re-evaluation is the review of the entire appraisal in which the appraiser makes sure that the data available and the analytical techniques and logic applied have led to consistent judgments. **Page 352**

5. **(d)** The sales comparison and cost approach are the most appropriate methods of valuing a single-family home. As the age of the house increases, the validity of the cost approach decreases because of the difficulty of estimating depreciation. In this case, because the home is a newer home, both approaches should be considered. **Page 349**

6. **(b)** Standard 2 of USPAP stresses the importance of not misleading the reader. **Page 354**

7. **(a)** All of the data analysis in the world is useless if the appraiser does not use proper judgment. Judgment is used in reconciliation more than any other part of the appraisal process. **Page 354**

8. **(b)** Commonly known as the average, the mean is calculated by adding the average prices or numeric values of a statistical sample and dividing that by the number of values in the sample. In this example, add the variates together and divide by five (the number of variates). The result is $164,720 ($164,700 rounded). **Page 357**

9. **(c)** The median equals the middle value in a statistical sample. The median home price in an area is the price that is midway between the least expensive and most expensive homes sold. In this example, $162,500 is the number that is midway between the least and the most expensive. **Page 357**

10. **(a)** The mode equals the most frequently occurring price or value in a statistical sample. In this example, $159,000 occurs twice. When analyzing comparable sales, the most frequently occurring sales price definitely warrants consideration. **Page 358**

11. **(b)** An appraiser should round the final value estimate to emphasize the fact that it is indeed an estimate. **Page 359**

12. **(d)** A complete workfile must be developed and maintained in accordance with the provisions of USPAP. An appraiser should always keep his or her workfiles in case he or she must revisit the appraisal or defend his or her appraisal. **Page 361**

13. **(a)** The choice of report type goes back to the beginning, when the problem was defined. The client's needs are identified and the type of report is selected to meet those needs. **Page 362**

14. **(b)** The Self-Contained Appraisal Report, also called a narrative report, is the most detailed of the three types of reports. The report is exactly what the name implies, a complete rendering of the entire appraisal process. **Page 363**

15. **(d)** Restricted Use Appraisal Report is the briefest presentation of an appraisal and contains the least detail. The amount of detail in the report depends upon the client's needs and the problem being addressed by the appraisal. **Page 363**

Chapter 14 – Case Studies

Answers - Matching Exercise

1. A
2. B
3. E
4. D
5. H

Answers - Multiple Choice Questions

1. **(c)** A case study is the analysis of a real-life problem and is designed usually for training purposes. **Page 371**

2. **(b)** A professional appraiser should be a critical thinker and a good listener. Critical thinking is the careful, precise analysis or examination of the facts. **Page 371**

3. **(b)** Because this is a lower priced neighborhood than that of the subject property, it would be reasonable to assume that the view in the subject property's tract of homes has a contributory value of at least $55,000. **Page 373**

4. **(a)** In single-family residence appraisal, the GRM is applied through the income method of valuation. **Pages 373–374**

5. **(d)** Lender pressure is directly or indirectly pressuring an appraiser to estimate a property's value at a certain amount. **Page 376**

GLOSSARY

A

absorption analysis
A study of the number of units of residential or nonresidential property that can be sold or leased over a given period of time in a defined location.

absorption period
The estimated time period required to sell, lease, place in use, or trade the subject property in its marketing area at prevailing prices or rental rates.

abstraction method
See extraction method.

abut
To border on, touch, as contiguous lots along a border or with a projecting part.

abutter's rights
The reasonable right to light, air, and visibility that a property enjoys from another.

access right
The right of an owner to have ingress to and egress from owner's property over adjoining property.

accession
An addition to property through the efforts of man or by natural forces.

accessory building
A building separate from the main structure on a property.

accretion
Accession by natural forces, e.g., alluvium.

accrued depreciation
Depreciation that has already occurred. It is the difference between the cost to replace the property and the property's current market value.

acquisition appraisal
A market value appraisal of property condemned or otherwise acquired for public use, to establish the compensation to be paid to the owner.

actual age
The number of years elapsed since a structure's construction. Also called physical age, real age, or chronological age.

actual depreciation
The depreciation occurring as a result of physical, functional, or economic forces, causing loss in value to a building.

adjacent
Lying near, close, contiguous, neighboring, bordering, or juxtaposed.

adjoining
In contact with, abutting on, or lying next to, especially in actual contact along a line.

adjustment
In the sales comparison approach, a dollar or percentage amount that is added to or subtracted from the sale price of a comparable property, to account for a feature that the property has or does not have which differentiates it from the subject property.

adjustment grid
Lists important items affecting value such as site area, location, design and appeal, quality, condition, gross building area, basement area, room count, view, age, amenities, etc. Also known as a matrix.

adjustment guidelines
Per Fannie Mae, state that a single line item adjustment should not exceed 10% of the sales price of the comparable.

administration expense
The cost of direct management and services related to the management of property.

Advisory Opinions
The Appraisal Standards Board (ASB) issues Advisory Opinions to illustrate the applicability of USPAP in specific situations and offers advice for the resolution of appraisal issues and problems.

aesthetic value
Relating to beauty, rather than to functional considerations.

aesthetic zoning
Regulates the appearance of buildings in the area.

A-frame roof
A roof whose two sides slope upward at a steep pitch and meet at the top.

age/life method
A method of computing accrued depreciation in which the cost of a building is depreciated at a fixed annual percentage rate. This is the method most frequently used by residential appraisers. Also known as the straight-line method.

agents of production
Land, labor, capital, and management. See principle of increasing and decreasing returns and principle of surplus productivity.

air rights
The rights in real property for the reasonable use of the air space above the surface of the land.

airspace
The interior area which an apartment, office, or condominium occupies. Airspace is considered real property to a reasonable height. For example, an owner or developer of condominiums may sell the airspace as real property.

allocation method
The allocation of the appraised total value between land and improvements. Allocation may be made using a ratio comparing building value to the total price (or value).

allowance for vacancy and collection losses
The percentage of potential gross income that will be lost due to vacant units, collection losses, or both.

amenities
Features that add value to a property.

amenity value
That value, difficult to measure in monetary terms, that is attributable to a property because of pleasant surroundings, such as a pretty view, quiet area, or ideal climate.

annuity method
A method of capitalization that treats income from real property as a fixed, regular return on an investment. For the annuity method to be applied the lessee must be reliable and the lease must be long term.

appraisal
An unbiased estimate or opinion of the property value on a given date.

appraisal process
An orderly systematic method to arrive at an estimate of value.

appraisal report
A written statement in which an appraiser gives his or her opinion of value.

appraisal review
The review of an appraiser's analysis, research, and conclusions by another appraiser.

Appraisal Standards Board (ASB)
Part of The Appraisal Foundation, the ASB develops, interprets, and amends USPAP.

appraised value
An appraiser's estimate of the amount of a particular value, such as assessed value, insurable value, or market value, based on the particular assignment.

appraiser
A person qualified by education, training, and experience who is hired to estimate the value of real and personal property based on experience, judgment, facts, and use of formal appraisal processes.

Appraiser Qualification Board (AQB)
Part of The Appraisal Foundation and responsible for establishing minimum requirements for licensed and certified appraisers and for licensing and certifying examinations.

appreciation
An increase in the worth or value of property over time.

approaches to value
Any of the following three methods used to estimate the value of real estate: sales comparison approach, cost approach, and income capitalization approach.

area
The space or size of a surface that is defined by a set of boundaries.

arm's-length transaction
A transaction, such as a sale of property, in which all parties involved are acting in their own self-interest and are under no undue influence or pressure from other parties.

aseptic system
The clean water system.

assemblage
The process of putting several smaller, less valuable lots together under a single ownership.

assessed value
Value placed on land and buildings by a public tax assessor as a basis for use in levying annual real estate taxes.

assessment roll
A list of all taxable property showing the assessed value of each parcel, establishing the tax base.

assessor
The official who has the responsibility of determining assessed values.

association agreement
Set of conditions and restrictions applying to all properties in a planned unit development, condominium, or other community project.

attached housing
Any number of houses or other dwellings, which are physically attached to one another.

automated valuation models (AVM)
Computer software programs that analyze data using automated systems, such as regression analysis and/or so-called artificial intelligence.

average deviation
In statistics, the measure of how far the average variate differs from the mean of all variates.

avigation easement
An easement over private property near an airport that limits the height of structures and trees in order to keep the take off and landing paths of airports clear.

avulsion
A sudden and perceptible loss of land by the action of water, as by a sudden change in the course of a river.

band of investment technique
Method of estimating interest and capitalization rates, based on a weighted average of the mortgage interest rate (or other cost of borrowed funds) and the rate of return on equity required.

bargain and sale deed
Any deed that recites a consideration and purports to convey the real estate.

baseline
A survey line running east and west, used as a reference when mapping land.

basement
A building's lowest story, which is partially or entirely below ground.

bearing wall
A wall or partition that supports a part of a building, usually a roof or floor above.

benchmark
Definite identification characteristics familiar to the appraiser and relied upon in his or her further analysis of a property. A location indicated on a durable marker by surveyors.

betterment
The enhanced value of real property from improvements.

bias
A preference or inclination that precludes an appraiser's impartiality, independence, or objectivity in an assignment.

blighted area
A district affected by extensive or numerous detrimental influences that have caused real property values to seriously decline.

blockbusting
The unscrupulous practice of inducing panic selling of homes at prices below market value, particularly by exploiting neighborhoods in which the racial makeup is or appears to be changing.

book depreciation
An accounting concept referring to an allowance taken to provide for recovery of invested capital.

book value
The current value, for accounting purposes, of an asset expressed as original cost plus capital additions minus accumulated depreciation.

bracketing
When using the sales comparison approach, selection of market data so that the subject is contained within a range of data.

breakdown method
A method of computing depreciation in which the appraiser estimates the loss in value for each type of depreciation separately. Also known as observed condition method.

breezeway
A covered porch or passage, open on two sides and connecting house and garage or two parts of the house.

brownfield
An abandoned commercial or industrial site or under-utilized neighborhood where redevelopment is complicated by actual or perceived contamination.

buffer zone
A segment of land between two disparate municipal zones acting as a shield to keep one zone from encroaching upon the other. Often used to separate residential districts from commercial areas.

building capitalization rate
The sum of the discount and capital recapture rates for a building.

building code
Municipal ordinance that regulates the type and quality of building materials and methods of construction permitted.

building components
Parts of a building.

building residual technique
Technique of income capitalization in which the net income to the building (after deducting the income required for the land) is capitalized into an estimated value for the building.

building restrictions
Restrictions that limit the way a property can be used. They may appear in building codes or title documents.

built-ins
Cabinets or similar features built as part of the house.

bulk zoning
Controls density and prevents overcrowding. Bulk zoning regulates setbacks, building height, and percentage of open area.

buyer's market
A market containing more supply than demand.

capital
Money and/or property owned or used by a person or business to acquire goods or services.

capital assets
Assets of a permanent nature used in the production of an income, such as land, buildings, machinery, and equipment. Under income tax law, these are usually distinguished from inventory, which are assets held for sale to customers in the ordinary course of the taxpayer's trade or business.

capital gain
At resale of a capital item, the amount by which the net sale proceeds exceed the adjusted cost basis (book value).

capital improvement
Any permanent improvement made to real estate for the purpose of increasing the useful life of the property or increasing the property's value.

capital recapture
The return of an investment.

capitalization
The process that can be employed to convert income to value.

capitalization method
See income capitalization method.

capitalization rate

The rate of interest, which is considered a reasonable return on the investment, and used in the process of determining value, based upon net income. It may also be described as the yield rate that is necessary to attract the money of the average investor to a particular type of investment.

carport
A roofed space having at least one side open to the weather.

cash equivalency technique
Method of adjusting a sales price downward to reflect the increase in price due to assumption or procurement by buyers of a loan at an interest rate lower than the prevailing market rate.

central tendency
The numeric value that is suggested as a typical value in a statistical sample.

certification
A signed and dated statement included in an appraisal report that the appraiser has performed an appraisal in an unbiased and professional manner and that all assumptions and limiting conditions are set forth in the report.

Certified General Appraiser
An individual who has met specific education, experience, and examination requirements. May appraise any property.

Certified Residential Appraiser
An individual who has met specific education, experience, and examination requirements. May appraise any 1-4 unit residential properties without regard to complexity.

characteristics
Distinguishing features of a property.

chronological age
The number of years elapsed since a structure was built. Also known as actual or physical age.

client
The person who employs an agent to perform a service for a fee.

closing costs
The numerous expenses buyers and sellers normally incur in the transfer of ownership of real property.

cloud on title
A claim, encumbrance, or condition that impairs the title to real property until disproved or eliminated as, for example, through a quitclaim deed or a quiet title legal action.

code of ethics

A set of rules and principles expressing a standard of accepted conduct for a professional group and governing the relationship of members to each other and to the organization.

collateral

(1) The property subject to the security interest. (2) Anything of value a borrower pledges as security.

collection loss

A loss incurred if tenants do not pay their agreed-upon rents.

collusion

An agreement between two or more persons to defraud another of rights by the forms of law or to obtain an object forbidden by law.

color of title

That which appears to be good title but is not title in fact.

Comments

Extensions of USPAP DEFINITIONS, Rules, and Standards Rules that provide interpretation, and establish context and conditions for application.

common area

An entire common interest subdivision except the separate interests therein.

common interest development (CID)

A common-interest development combining the individual ownership of private dwellings with the shared ownership of common facilities of the entire project. The common areas are usually governed by a homeowners' association. Also known as common interest subdivision.

community

Part of a metropolitan area, a number of neighborhoods that tend toward common interests and problems.

community property

All property acquired by a husband and wife during a valid marriage (excluding certain separate property).

comparable sales (comps)

Sales that have similar characteristics to the subject property and are used for analysis in the appraisal process. Commonly called "comps", they are recently sold properties similarly situated in a similar market.

comparative market analysis (CMA)

A comparison analysis that real estate brokers use, while working with a seller, to determine an appropriate listing price for the seller's house.

comparative unit method

A method for estimating reproduction or replacement cost, using typical per unit costs for the type of construction being estimated. See square-foot method.

comparison approach

A real estate appraisal method, which compares a given property with similar or comparable surrounding properties. Also known as sales comparison approach or market comparison approach.

COMPETENCY RULE

Per USPAP, identifies requirements for experience and knowledge both when completing an appraisal and prior to accepting an appraisal assignment.

complete appraisal

The act or process of estimating value or an estimate of value, performed without invoking the Departure Rule of the Uniform Standards of Professional Appraisal Practice.

component

One of the features making up the whole property.

composite rate

A capitalization rate composed of interest and recapture in separately determined amounts.

comps

See comparable sales.

concessions

Additional value granted by a buyer or seller to entice another party to complete a transaction.

conclusion

(1) The final estimate of value, realized from facts, data, experience, and judgment, set out in an appraisal. (2) An appraiser's certified conclusion.

condemnation

The process to exercise the power of the government to take private property from an owner for the public good, paying fair market value.

conditional use

A use that does not meet the current use requirements but may be allowed by obtaining a special permit.

conditions of sale

Circumstances of the sale such as exposure time, marketing process, and buyer motivation. Unusual conditions may affect the final purchase price of a comparable sale and cause the sales price to reflect the market improperly.

condominium

A housing unit consisting of a separate fee interest in a particular specific space, plus an undivided interest in all common or public areas of the development. Each unit owner has a deed, separate financing and pays the property taxes for the unit.

Conduct

The section of the USPAP ETHICS RULE that identifies issues regarding appraisers' conduct.

Confidentiality

Per USPAP, the section of the ETHICS RULE which states that the appraiser must protect the confidential nature of the appraiser-client relationship and is obligated to obey all confidentiality and privacy laws.

conforming loans

Loans which conform to Fannie Mae guidelines, which set loan limits to a certain amount.

construction classification

A system that rates fireproofing of structures according to the relative fire resistance of the structures, taking into account the type of frame, walls, and roof. Class A is the most fireproof, descending to Class D, the least fire resistant.

contiguous

In actual contact, touching.

contingent

Conditional, uncertain, conditioned upon the occurrence or nonoccurrence of some future event.

contingent valuation methodology (CVM)

A method used to identify how a particular feature affects the value of a property by asking those who are knowledgeable about that market (other appraisers and agents) when no sales data is available.

contour

The surface configuration of land. Shown on maps as a line through points of equal elevation.

contract rent

The rent established by agreement or contract.

contributory value

Value given by appraisers to site improvements after identifying them.

conventional loan

Any loan made by lenders without any governmental guarantees (FHA-insured or VA-guaranteed).

conversion

Change from one character or use to another, as converting an apartment building to condominium use.

cooperative (co-op)

(1) A form of legal ownership with each owner holding a stated ownership percentage in the cooperative association. The association owns the land and buildings, and grants each owner the permanent right to occupy the specific dwelling unit, as well as the right to the joint use of the common areas. (2) A residential multifamily building.

coordination

As an agent of production, it is management.

corner influence

The effect on a property's value due to its location on or near a corner.

corner lot

A lot at the confluence or convergence of two streets.

cost

The expenses in money, labor, material, or sacrifices in acquiring or producing something.

cost approach

An approach to value in which a value estimate of a property is derived by estimating the replacement cost of the improvements, deducting the estimated accrued depreciation, and then adding the market value of the land. Also known as the summation method.

cost basis

Original price paid for a property.

cost index

Figure representing construction cost at a particular time in relation to construction cost at an earlier time, prepared by a cost reporting or indexing service.

cost multiplier

Regional or local factor used in adjusting published construction cost figures to estimate local costs.

cost services

Companies who collect and provide information regarding cost trends.

cost-to-cure method of depreciation

Method of estimating accrued depreciation based on the cost to cure or repair observed building defects.

courtyard home

A zero-lot-line home.

crawlspace

An unfinished accessible space below the first floor of a building with no basement.

credible

Something worthy of belief.

credit

A bookkeeping entry on the right side of an account, recording the reduction or elimination of an asset or an expense or the creation of or addition to a liability or item of equity or revenue.

cubic-foot method

Similar to the square-foot method, except that it takes height as well as area into consideration. The cubic contents of buildings are compared instead of just the square footage.

cul-de-sac lot

A lot situated at the end of a dead-end street that has a turn-around area.

cumulative zoning

Zoning laws that allow so-called higher uses (residential) to exist in lower use zones (industrial), but not vice versa.

curable depreciation

Items of physical deterioration and functional obsolescence which are economically feasible to repair or replace.

curb appeal

A phrase implying an informal valuation of a property based on observation and experience.

cut

The level building site or the space created in areas of sloping land when earth is removed. Unlike fill material, which can be unstable, a building site from a cut is generally a more solid base for structures.

cyclical movement

The sequential and recurring changes in economic activity of a business cycle, moving from prosperity through recession, depression, recovery, and back again to prosperity.

data

Information pertinent to a specific appraisal assignment. Data may be general (relating to the economic background and the region), local (relating to the city and the neighborhood), or specific (relating to the subject property and comparable properties in the market).

data services

The numerous companies engaged in the business of selling data to real estate appraisers.

data sources

Any of a variety of sources used by appraisers when collecting general, local, and specific information.

date of appraisal

The specific point in time when an appraiser designates the value of a home. Often stipulated as the date of inspection.

debit

A bookkeeping entry on the left side of an account, recording the creation of or addition to an asset or an expense or the reduction or elimination of a liability or item of equity or revenue.

debt capital

The amount borrowed by the buyer to purchase a property.

decline phase

Third phase in the cycle of a neighborhood, generally marked by delayed repairs and deterioration of buildings.

deed

A formal legal document used to transfer title from one person to another.

deed in lieu of foreclosure

A deed to real property accepted by a lender from a defaulting borrower to avoid the necessity of foreclosure proceedings by the lender.

deed of reconveyance

Document used to transfer legal title from the trustee back to the borrower after a debt secured by a trust deed has been paid to the lender.

deed of trust

A security instrument that conveys naked legal title of real property.

deed restrictions

Limitations in the deed to a property that dictate certain uses that may or may not be made of the property.

deferred maintenance

Building maintenance that has been postponed or neglected. A type of physical deterioration.

define the problem

Part of the appraisal process, includes identifying the client and other intended users, the intended use of the appraiser's opinions and conclusions, the type and definition of the value sought, and the effective date of the appraiser's opinions and conclusions.

DEFINITIONS section

The first section of USPAP containing definitions of terms specific to USPAP.

demand
The desire to possess plus the ability to buy.

demographic profile
A profile of a specific area that contains general demographic information such as employment, education, average age, average salary ranges, gender, occupation, number of children, etc.

demographics
The statistical characteristics of human population studies.

Department of Housing and Urban Development (HUD)
A federal department active in national housing programs, including but not limited to urban renewal, public housing, and FHA subsidy programs. HUD oversees FHA, FNMA, GNMA, and FMIC, among others.

Department of Veteran Affairs (VA)
Functions to guarantee loans to purchase and construct homes for eligible veterans and their spouses.

DEPARTURE RULE
This USPAP rule allows appraisers to "depart" from certain Standards Rules in particular situations. Replaced by the SCOPE OF WORK RULE in 2006 USPAP.

depreciated cost method
Method for adjusting comparable sales in which adjustments are calculated from an analysis of the depreciated replacement cost for each differentiating feature.

depreciation
(1) In appraisal, a loss in value from any cause. (2) A tax advantage of ownership of income property.

depreciation rate
The degree of lessening in value of an object or property, usually applied on an annual scale.

depression
A phase of the business cycle marked by industrial and commercial stagnation, scarcity of goods and money, low prices, and mass unemployment.

depth
Distance from the front lot line to the rear lot line.

depth table
A statistical table that may be used to estimate the value of the added depth of a lot.

detached house
A house surrounded by permanent open spaces.

deterioration
A worsening, impairment, or degeneration.

development method (land development method)
Method of vacant land valuation in which development costs and developer's profits are subtracted from estimated gross sales, resulting in a raw land value estimate.

development phase
First phase of the life cycle of a neighborhood, consisting of initial construction of improvements on vacant land.

diminished utility
A loss in the usefulness of a property resulting in a loss in property value.

direct capitalization method
Income capitalization technique in which value is estimated by dividing net operating income by the overall capitalization rate.

direct costs
All of the costs directly involved with the construction of a structure, including labor, materials, equipment, design and engineering, and subcontractors' fees.

direct lender
Lends their own funds and handles the entire loan process from origination to funding.

direct market comparison approach
See sales comparison approach.

discount rate
The interest rate that is charged by the Federal Reserve Bank to its member banks for loans.

discounted cash flow
Estimated future investment returns mathematically discounted to their present value.

distressed property
Property foreclosed on by the lender.

documents
Legal instruments, such as mortgages, contracts, deeds, options, wills, and bills of sale.

downzoning
A zone change from a high-density use to a lower density use. For example, a commercial zone to a light industrial zone.

drainage
The removal of excess surface water or groundwater from land by means of ditches or drains.

dry rot
A wood fungus that thrives in damp conditions and turns wood fibers into powder.

duress
The use of force to get agreement in accepting a contract.

easement

A non-possessory right to enter or use someone else's land for a specified purpose.

easement appurtenant

An easement that is connected to a particular property and is transferred along with that property. Each easement appurtenant involves two properties—the servient tenement and the dominant tenement.

easement in gross

An easement that is not appurtenant to any one parcel. For example, public utilities to install power lines.

ecology

The relationship between organisms and their environment.

economic age

Estimated age of a building based on its condition and usefulness.

economically feasible

Financially possible, reasonable, or likely. One of the tests of highest and best use.

economic base

The companies that provide jobs for a community or defined geographic area.

economic life

The estimated period over which a building may be profitably used. Also known as useful life.

economic obsolescence

Depreciation caused by changes in the economy that negatively affects the subject property's value.

economic rent

What a leased property would be expected to rent for under current market conditions if the property were vacant and available for rent. Also known as market rent.

economics

The science that studies the production, distribution, and consumption of wealth.

economic trend

Pattern of related changes in some aspect of the economy.

effective age

The age of a building based on its condition and usefulness. The apparent age based on the condition of the structure, instead of the chronological age.

effective date

The specific day the conclusion of value applies whether it is a present, past, or future date.

effective demand

Demand or desire coupled with purchasing power.

effective gross income (EGI)

The amount of income that remains after vacancy and credit losses are deducted from gross income.

egress

A way to exit a property.

element of comparison

Any aspect of a real estate transaction or any characteristic of the property that may affect the property's sales price.

elements of value

Four prerequisites that must be present for an object to have value: demand, utility, scarcity, and transferability.

elevation sheet

A labeled diagram or cutaway of a home detailing its features and building components, both interior and exterior.

Ellwood technique

A mortgage/equity method of capitalization, expressed in tables.

eminent domain

The right of the government to take private property from an owner, for the public good, paying fair market value.

encroachment

The unauthorized placement of permanent improvements that intrude on adjacent property owned by another.

encumbrance

An interest in real property that is held by someone who is not the property owner.

entrepreneur

One who assumes the risk and management of business.

entrepreneurial profit

A market-derived figure that represents the compensation the owner or developer expects to gain from developing the property.

entry-level home

A type of home for first-time buyers.

environment surroundings

All the external conditions and influences affecting the life and development of an organism, for example, human behavior, society.

Environmental Impact Report (EIR)

A formal report assessing the results or impact of a proposed activity or development upon the environment.

environmental obsolescence
See economic obsolescence.

equity
The difference between the market value of a home and the loan amount.

equity build-up
The gradual increase of the borrower's equity in a property caused by amortization of loan principal.

equity capital
The amount a buyer invests into a property.

equity capitalization rate
(1) Factor used to estimate the value of the equity in the band of investment method of capitalization and other mortgage and equity techniques. (2) The equity cash flow divided by the equity value.

equity investors
Investors using venture capital to take an unsecured and thus relatively risky part in an investment.

erosion
The gradual wearing away of land by natural processes.

escrow
A small and short-lived trust arrangement used to close real estate transactions.

estate
The ownership interest or claim a person has in real property. It defines the nature, degree, extent, and duration of a person's ownership in land.

estate at sufferance
A tenancy created when one is in wrongful possession of real estate even though the original possession may have been legal.

estate at will
A tenancy that may be ended by the unilateral decision of either party. There is no agreed-upon termination date, and either party must give 30 days notice before ending the tenancy.

estate for years
A leasehold estate with a definite end date. The lease must be renegotiated.

estate from period to period
A leasehold estate that does not need to be renegotiated upon each renewal.

estimate
(1) A preliminary opinion of value. (2) To appraise or determine value.

estimated remaining life
The period of time (years) it takes for improvements to become valueless.

ETHICS RULE
Per USPAP, identifies the requirements for "integrity, impartiality, objectivity, independent judgment, and ethical conduct."

evaluation
An analysis of a property and/or its attributes in which a value estimate is not required.

excess land
Surplus land beyond that which is needed to support the property's highest and best use.

excess rent
The amount by which the total contract rent exceeds market rent.

execute
(1) To perform or complete. (2) To sign.

execution sale
The forced sale of a property to satisfy a money judgment.

expansible house
Home designed for further expansion and additions in the future.

expenditures
Money laid out, disbursed, or expended.

expense ratio
See operating expense ratio.

expenses
The costs incurred in an enterprise. In appraisal, expenses are estimated on an annual basis regardless of the period in which they are incurred or paid.

expert testimony
Testimony given in a court trial by a person qualified by the court as an expert on a particular subject, for example, as an expert witness on real estate values.

expert witness
One qualified to give expert testimony in a court of law on a particular subject, such as medicine, engineering, or real estate appraising.

external obsolescence
A type of depreciation occurring because of negative influences outside of the specific property site (i.e. an airport flight pattern). See economic obsolescence.

externalities

Outside influences that may have a positive or negative effect on property value.

extraction method

A method of determining the land value of a comparable property by deducting the depreciated costs of the improvements on that property from the property's known sale price. The remaining value represents value attributable to the land. This method is a variation on the allocation method and is based on the same principles. Also known as abstraction method.

extraordinary assumption

Per USPAP, "an assumption, directly related to a specific assignment, which, if found to be false, could alter the appraiser's opinions or conclusions."

facade

The face of a building, especially the front face.

factory-built housing

Housing built in a factory instead of on site. Includes manufactured, modular, panelized, and precut homes.

fair market value

See market value.

fair rental value

See rent, economic.

feasibility study

An analysis of a proposed subject or property with emphasis on the attainable income, probable expenses, and most advantageous use and design. The purpose of such a study is to ascertain the probable success or failure of the project under consideration. A study of the cost-benefit relationship of an economic endeavor.

Federal Emergency Management Agency (FEMA)

A government agency involved with all the different aspects of emergency management from preparation to recovery and prevention.

Federal Housing Administration (FHA)

A government agency that insures private mortgage loans for financing of homes and home repairs.

federally related transaction

Any real estate transaction involving federal insurance or assistance.

fee simple absolute

An estate in fee with no restrictions on its use. It is the largest, most complete ownership recognized by law.

fee simple estate

The most complete form of ownership of real property, which can be passed by descent or by will after the owner's death. Also known as estate of inheritance or estate in fee.

fiduciary duty

The duty owed by an agent to act in the highest good faith toward the principal and not to obtain any advantage over the latter by the slightest misrepresentation, concealment, duress, or pressure.

fill

(1) Earth used to raise the existing ground level. (2) In residential real estate, base material that is borrowed from another source and is not generally as stable as a cut.

filtering

The process whereby higher priced properties become available to lower income buyers.

final value estimate

The appraiser's estimate of the defined value of the subject property, arrived at by reconciling the estimates of value, derived from the sales comparison, cost, and income approaches.

Financial Institutions Reform, Recovery, and Enforcement Act (FIRREA)

A federal law passed in 1989 to provide guidelines for the regulation of financial institutions. One part of the law requires a state license or certification for the performance of federally related real estate transactions (with de minimus exceptions).

finished area

The enclosed area in a home that is suitable for year-round use.

fire door

A door of fire-resistant material to prevent or retard the spread of fire.

firewall

A wall of fire-resistant material to prevent or retard the spread of fire.

FIRREA

See Financial Institutions Reform, Recovery, and Enforcement Act.

fiscal year

A 12-month accounting period not related to the actual calendar year.

fixed expenses

Operating costs that are more or less permanent and that vary little from year to year regardless of occupancy.

fixity of location
The physical characteristic of real estate that subjects it to the influence of its surroundings.

fixture
Personal property that has become affixed to real estate.

flag lot
A lot located so that access can be had only at the side of another lot.

flipping
Buying a property at one price and quickly selling it to another at an inflated price.

flood plain
An area that is adjacent to a river or watercourse and is subject to periodic flooding.

floor plan
A depiction of the floor layout including each room's size and connection with other rooms.

foreclosure
The legal procedure by which mortgaged property is sold to satisfy a debt when the borrower has defaulted on the loan.

form report
Written appraisal report, presented on a standardized form or checklist.

fraud
An act meant to deceive in order to get someone to part with something of value.

freehold estate
An estate in real property which continues for an indefinite period of time. It differs from a leasehold estate, which allows possession for a limited time.

frequency distribution
The arrangement of data into groups according to the frequency with which they appear in the data set.

front foot
Measurement in feet of the width of a property on the side facing the street.

frontage
The width of a property on the side facing a street.

frostline
The depth of frost penetration in the soil. Varies in different parts of the country. Footings should be placed below this depth to prevent movement.

fully amortized note
The most common type of loan with institutional lenders. Interest is charged on the outstanding principal balance at the rate and term agreed upon by the lender and borrower in a loan.

functional obsolescence
A type of depreciation stemming from poor architectural design, lack of modern facilities, out-of-date equipment, changes in styles of construction or in utility demand.

functional utility
The combined factors of usefulness with desirability.

future benefits
The anticipated benefits the present owner will receive from the property in the future.

future interest
An interest in real property that will take effect at a future time.

future value
The estimated lump-sum value of money or property at a date in the future.

gable roof
A roof with two sides sloping upward and meeting at the top.

gambrel roof
A curb roof, having a steep lower slope with a flatter upper slope above.

garage
A building or enclosure primarily designed or used for motor vehicles.

general warranty deed
A deed which conveys not only all the grantor's interests in and title to the property to the grantee, but also warrants that if the title is defective or has a cloud, the grantee may hold the grantor liable.

gentrification
A form of revitalization that occurs when run down properties are renovated or rehabilitated.

geodetic survey
A U.S. government survey generally used in identifying government lands and coastal areas.

gift deed
Used to make a gift of property to a grantee, usually a close friend or relative.

going concern value

The value existing in an established business property compared with the value of selling the real estate and other assets of a concern whose business is not yet established. The term takes into account the goodwill and earning capacity of a business.

goodwill

An intangible, but salable, asset of a business derived from the expectation of continued public patronage.

Government National Mortgage Association (GNMA)

An agency of HUD, called Ginnie Mae, that functions in the secondary mortgage market.

government survey system

See rectangular survey system.

grade

Ground level at the perimeter of the building.

grading

A process used when the level or elevation of the ground has to be changed or altered using bladed machines that scrape the earth.

graduated lease

A long-term lease that provides for adjustments in the rental rate on the basis of some future determination.

graphic analysis

A technique used to identify and measure adjustments to the sale prices of comparable properties.

grandfather clause

A legal clause that keeps a law from being retroactive. For example, a grandfather clause in a zoning law would allow the continuation of a previously legal use even if the new zoning law does not permit such use.

grant deed

A deed in which the grantor warrants that he or she has not previously conveyed the property being granted, has not encumbered the property except as disclosed, and will convey to the grantee any title he or she may acquire afterwards.

gross building area (GBA)

All enclosed floor areas, as measured along a building's outside perimeter.

gross income

Total income from property before any expenses are deducted.

gross income multiplier (GIM)

A figure which, when multiplied by the annual gross income, will equal the property's market value. The amount of the GIM must be obtained from recent comparable sales since it varies with specific properties and areas.

gross leasable area

Total space designed for occupancy and exclusive use of tenants, measured from outside wall surfaces to the center of shared interior walls.

gross lease

A lease agreement in which the tenant pays an agreed-upon sum as rent and the landlord pays any other expenses such as taxes, maintenance, or insurance. Also known as a flat, fixed, or straight lease.

gross living area (GLA)

The total finished, habitable, above-grade space, measured along the building's outside perimeter. This generally excludes garages and screened patios or porches ("Florida rooms").

gross rent

Income (calculated annually or monthly) received from rental units before any expenses are deducted.

gross rent multiplier (GRM)

A figure which, when multiplied by the monthly rental income, will equal the property's market value. The amount of the GRM must be obtained from recent comparable sales since it varies with specific properties and areas.

ground lease

A lease of land only on which the lessee usually owns the building or is required to build as specified by the lease. Such leases are usually long-term net leases.

ground rent

Earnings of improved property credited to earnings of the ground itself after allowance has been made for earnings of improvements.

hidden amenities

Assets of a property that contribute to its value, but are not readily apparent. Examples might include upgraded or premium building materials.

highest and best use (HBU)

The use, from among reasonably probable and adequately supported alternative uses, that is physically possible, legally permitted, economically feasible, and maximally productive. This is the starting point for appraisal.

hip roof

A roof with four sides sloping upward to meet at a ridge.

historic cost

Cost of a property at the time it was constructed or purchased.

holding period
The length of time the property will be used as an investment.

homogeneous
Of the same kind or nature.

house
A single-family detached residence.

houseboat
Essentially a barge designed and equipped for use as a dwelling.

HUD
See Department of Housing and Urban Development.

HUD-1 Statement
A standardized, itemized list, published by the U.S. Department of Housing and Urban Development (HUD), of all anticipated CLOSING COSTS connected with a particular property purchase.

hypothetical condition
Defined in USPAP as "that which is contrary to what exists but is supposed for the purpose of analysis."

improved value
A value placed upon a property when proposed improvements have been completed.

improvements
Additions made to property to enhance value or extend useful life. This term is typically used to refer to buildings and other structures that are permanently attached to the land.

incentive zoning
Allows a developer to exceed the limitations set by a zoning law if the developer agrees to fulfill conditions specified in the law.

income approach
An appraisal method that estimates the present worth of future benefits from ownership of a property to determine that property's value. Also known as income capitalization approach.

income capitalization method
Method for estimating depreciation by comparing the subject's capitalized value to its replacement cost new or by determining loss in rental income attributable to a depreciated item and applying a gross rent multiplier to that figure.

income forecast
Gross or net income estimate.

income property
Property that is purchased for its income-producing capabilities.

income stream
Actual or estimated flow of net earnings over time.

increment
An increase. Most frequently used to refer to the increase of value of land that accompanies population growth and increasing wealth in the community. The term unearned increment is used in this connection, since values are supposed to have increased without effort on the part of the owner.

incurable depreciation
Building defects or problems that would cost more to repair than the anticipated value increase from such repair.

index method
Method for estimating construction costs that adjusts the original costs to the current cost level by a multiplier obtained from a published cost index.

indicated value
Value estimate calculated or produced by an appraisal approach.

indirect costs
All of the time and money costs involved in a construction project that are not directly involved with construction itself. Examples are loan fees, interest, legal fees, and marketing costs.

industrial property
Land and/or improvements adapted for industrial use.

inflation
The increase in the general price level of goods and services.

inspection
The examination of a property, its buildings or other amenities.

instrument
A formal legal document such as a contract, deed, or will.

insurable value
The highest reasonable value that can be placed on property for insurance purposes.

intangible property
Property that lacks a physical form.

intangible value
That value attributable to a property that is difficult to determine precisely.

intellectual property (IP)
A general term for various legal rights, which attach to certain types of information, ideas, or other intangibles.

intended users
Per USPAP, parties intending to use an appraisal.

interest
(1) The charge for the use of money. (2) A legal share of ownership in property.

interest rate
The percentage of interest charged on the principal.

interim use
A short-term and temporary use of a property until it is ready for a more productive highest and best use. Occurs when the highest and best use is expected to change.

interior lot
A lot situated so that its boundaries touch no more than five lots. Generally, it is surrounded by three lots.

internal rate of return
The rate of return generated by an investment over the holding period, considering all future benefits, and discounting them to equal the present value.

intrinsic value
The value inherent in the property itself.

inverse condemnation
An action brought by a private party to force the government to pay just compensation for diminishing the value or use of his or her property.

investment property
Property purchased for expected future return.

investment value
The value of a particular property to a particular investor.

joint appraisal
An appraisal made by two or more appraisers working together.

joint tenancy
A type of ownership interest in which two or more parties own real property as co-owners, with the right of survivorship.

jumbo loans
Loans that exceed the maximum loan limit set by Fannie Mae and Freddie Mac.

junior mortgage
A mortgage recorded subsequently to another mortgage on the same property or made subordinate by agreement to a later-recorded mortgage.

jurisdiction
(1) The authority by which judicial officers take cognizance of and decide causes. (2) The power to hear and determine a cause.

JURISDICTIONAL EXCEPTION RULE
Part of USPAP, preserves the remainder of USPAP if one portion is contrary to a jurisdiction's law or public policy.

just compensation
Fair and reasonable payment due to a private property owner when his or her property is condemned under eminent domain.

key lot
A lot situated so that it is surrounded by the backyards of other lots.

labor
As an agent of production, it is the cost of all operating expenses and wages except management costs.

land
The surface of the earth including airspace, surface rights, mineral rights, and water rights.

land capitalization rate
The rate of return in investment and return of investment for the land only.

land residual technique
Income capitalization technique in which the net income remaining to the land (after income attributable to the building has been deducted) is capitalized into an estimate of value for the land.

landlocked
Property surrounded by other property with no access to a public road or street.

landlord
One who rents property to another. The lessor under a lease.

landscaping
The art of arranging plants, rocks, and lumber around the outside of a property for aesthetic or practical purposes, such as to prevent erosion or provide parking areas.

latent defects
Any defect in a property which is not readily apparent, but which has an impact on the value. Structural damage or termite infestation would be examples of latent defects.

lateral support
The support the soil of an adjoining owner gives to a neighbor's land.

lean-to
A temporary structure for protection from the elements.

lease
A contract between landlord (owner/lessor) and tenant (lessee) which gives the tenant an interest in the property. Also known as a rental agreement.

leased-fee estate
The property owner's interest in the leased property.

leasehold estate
The tenant's interest in the leased property during the term of the lease. This type of estate only has value if the agreed-on rent is less than the market rent. Also known as a less-than-freehold estate.

leasehold value
Market value of the excess of economic rent over contract rent

legal description
A land description recognized by law which can be used to locate a particular piece of property. Lot, block, and tract, government survey, and metes and bounds are types of legal descriptions.

legally permitted
Land uses that are allowed under current zoning and other land use regulations. One of the tests of highest and best use.

lender pressure
A lender directly or indirectly pressuring an appraiser to estimate a property's value at a certain amount.

lessee
Tenant or renter.

lessor
The person (landlord or property owner) who signs the lease to give possession and use to the tenant.

less-than-freehold estate
See leasehold estate.

lien
A claim on the property of another for the payment of a debt. A type of encumbrance.

life estate
An estate that is limited in duration to the life of its owner or the life of another designated person.

limited appraisal
An appraisal developed under and resulting from invoking USPAP's Departure Rule.

linear regression
Statistical technique used to calculate adjustment value or estimate sales price.

liquid assets
Assets that can be promptly converted into cash.

liquidation value
The value that can be received from the marketplace when the property has to be sold immediately.

liquidity
Holdings in or the ability to convert assets to cash or its equivalent. The ease with which a person is able to pay maturing obligations.

littoral
Land bordering a lake, ocean, or sea—as opposed to land bordering a stream or river (running water).

living units
A house or portion thereof providing complete living facilities for one family, including provisions for living, sleeping, eating, cooking, and sanitation.

loan closing
When all conditions have been met, the loan officer authorizes the recording of the trust deed or mortgage.

loan-to-value ratio (LTV)
The ratio of debt to the value of the property.

location
The site, setting, or position of a property or object in relation to other properties or objects.

locational obsolescence
Depreciation caused by the physical location of the subject property and its proximity to a negative influence. See external obsolescence.

long-lived
Structural components that need replacement infrequently, and sometimes never.

lot
A plot of ground.

lot, block, and tract system
A type of legal description that is created when developers divide parcels of land into lots. Each lot in a subdivision is indentified by number, as is the block in which it is located, and each lot and block is in a referenced tract. Also known as lot and block system, subdivision system, or recorded map system.

M

maintenance expenses
Costs incurred for day-to-day-upkeep, such as management, employee wages and benefits, fuel, utility services, decorating, and repairs.

management
The section of USPAP that discusses the disclosure of certain fees and commissions, identifies prohibited compensation arrangements, and discusses certain prohibited advertising and solicitation issues.

mansard roof
A roof with four sides sloping upward but stopping short of meeting, so that the top of the roof is flat.

margin of security
The difference between the amount of the mortgage loan(s) and the appraised value of the property.

manufactured home
A home built in a factory after June 15, 1976 which must conform to the U.S. government's Manufactured Home Construction and Safety Standards.

marginal land
Land whose value has been diminished due to some internal defect or external condition. In most cases, the cost to correct the flaw or condition is as much or more than the expected return from the property.

marital property
A general term for property owned by married people. Forms of ownership vary from state-to-state.

market
A place or condition suitable for selling and buying.

marketable title
Title that a reasonable purchaser, informed as to the facts and their legal importance and acting with reasonable care, would be willing, and ought, to accept.

market analysis
To identify, research, and analyze the particular market in which the appraised property operates.

market area
A geographic area in which similar property types compete for potential buyers or customers.

market exposure
Making a reasonable number of potential buyers of a property aware that the property is available.

market extraction
(1) General term for collecting information from the market. (2) Method of estimating depreciation in which building values abstracted from sales are compared to current costs new.

market price
The price paid regardless of pressures, motives, or intelligence.

market rent
The rent a property should bring in the open market as determined by current rents on comparable properties.

market segmentation
The process of identifying and analyzing submarkets within larger markets.

market value
The price a property would bring if freely offered on the open market, with both a willing buyer and a willing seller. Also known as objective value or value in exchange.

mass appraisal
Appraising more than one property using standard computerized techniques (statistical analysis, regression, automated valuation models, etc.).

master plan
A city or county's overall plan for physical development.

matched pair method
See paired sales method.

matrix
See adjustment grid.

mature phase
Second phase in the cycle of a neighborhood, marked by the stability of the existing buildings and occupants.

maximally productive
The property use that produces the greatest return on investment. One of the tests of highest and best use.

mean
A measure of central tendency which is calculated by adding the average prices or numeric values of a statistical sample and dividing that by the number of values in the sample. Also known as the average.

median
A measure of central tendency that equals the middle value in a statistical sample. The middle value in a statistical sample.

metes and bounds
A type of legal description that delineates boundaries and measures distances between landmarks to identify property.

mile
A linear measurement of distance. Equals 5,280 feet.

mill
Equals one-thousandth of a dollar and is numerically expressed as $0.001

millage rate
Expresses the property tax rate in terms of tenths of a cent per dollar of property value. The rate varies from district to district and county to county.

mineral rights
The legal interest in the valuable items found below the surface of a property (i.e., gold and coal).

minimum rent
The fixed minimum rent amount paid under a percentage lease. Also known as base rent.

minor
All persons under 18 years of age.

misplaced improvements
Improvements on land that do not conform to the most profitable use of the site.

mobile home
A factory-built home manufactured prior to June 15, 1976, constructed on a chassis and wheels, and designed for permanent or semi-attachment to land.

mode
A measure of central tendency that equals the most frequently occurring price or value in a statistical sample.

modified age/life method
A method of calculating depreciation. Curable physical and functional items of accrued depreciation are identified. The cost to cure all these items is deducted from the reproduction or replacement cost of the improvements. The ratio derived from the age/life method is then multiplied by the remaining cost to arrive at an estimate of accrued depreciation from all other causes.

modified gross lease
Tenant and landlord share expenses in accordance to the provisions of the lease.

modular home
Building composed of modules constructed on an assembly line in a factory.

monument
A fixed landmark used in a metes and bounds land description.

moratorium
The temporary suspension, usually by statute, of the enforcement of liability of debt.

mortgage
A legal document used as security for a debt. The mortgage is the instrument which secures the promissory note.

mortgage constant or mortgage capitalization rate (RM)
The capitalization rate of the debt. It is the ratio of annual debt service to the principal amount of the mortgage loan.

mortgage yield
The amount received or returned from an investment expressed as a percentage.

multiple listing service (MLS)
A cooperative listing service conducted by a group of brokers (usually members of a real estate association) to provide an inventory of all available properties in an area.

multiple regression analysis
A statistical technique for estimating a particular variable, such as probable sales price, using more than one other known variable.

multiplier
A number that, when multiplied by the income, gives an estimate of value. Also known as gross income multiplier or gross rent multiplier.

narrative appraisal report
A detailed, formal written report of the appraisal and the value conclusion.

negative cash flow
When monies will flow from the investor toward the investment.

negative easement
Prohibits a property owner from doing something on his or her estate because of the effect it would have on the dominant estate.

neighborhood
An area whose occupants and users share some common ties or characteristics. A neighborhood may be defined by physical boundaries, a change in land use, or intangible factors like school district boundaries.

neighborhood life-cycle
The process of neighborhood change, including four phases of change: development, maturity, decline, and renaissance.

net income
Gross annual income, less income lost due to vacancies and uncollectible rents, less all operating expenses.

net income ratio (NIR)
Net income divided by the effective gross income.

net lease
The tenant pays an agreed-upon sum as rent, plus certain agreed upon expenses per month (e.g., taxes and insurance).

net operating income (NOI)
The income remaining after deducting operating expenses from effective gross income.

net operating income ratio
The ratio between the net operating income of a property and its effective gross income (EGI).

net worth
The surplus of assets over liabilities.

non-conforming building
An existing building that does not conform to the latest building or zoning codes.

non-conforming loan
A loan that does not meet the standards of Fannie Mae and Freddie Mac. Jumbo loans and sub-prime loans are types of non-conforming loans.

non-conforming use
Legal use of property that was established and maintained at the time of its original construction but no longer conforms to the current zoning law.

non-economic highest and best use
A type of highest and best use that focuses on contribution to the community and community developmental goals rather than income-production.

nuisance value
The value reflected in the price that a buyer would be willing to pay to eliminate an objectionable situation.

observed condition method
See breakdown method.

observed conditions
The condition of a property, determined by observation.

obsolescence
Loss in value due to reduced desirability and usefulness of a structure because its design and construction became obsolete or due to factors outside the property itself. May be functional or economic.

occupancy
An act of taking or holding possession of an owned thing.

occupancy rate
The percentage of total rental units occupied and producing income.

off-site improvements
Improvements not directly on the site that add to the site's utility.

off-street parking
Designated parking spaces associated with a particular building or other structure that are not located on public streets.

on-site improvements
Buildings, structures or other amenities that are erected on a property and contribute to its value.

open housing law
A law passed by Congress in April 1968 that prohibits discrimination in the sale of real estate because of race, color, or religion of buyers.

operating expense ratio
Relationship of a property's expenses to income, found by dividing total operating expenses by effective gross income.

operating expenses
Expenses required to run a property (i.e., to maintain its income). Includes fixed, variable, and reserves for replacement.

operating statement
Written record of a property's gross income, expenses, and resultant net income for a given period of time.

optimum use
See highest and best use.

oral report
An appraisal report that is communicated to the client verbally, rather than in writing.

orientation
The placement of a building on its lot in relation to exposure to sun, prevailing wind, traffic, and accessibility from the street.

overage rent
The amount paid over and above the base rent, under a percentage lease.

overall rate
A capitalization rate that measures income attributable to both land and improvements, that is, to the whole property.

over-improvement
An improvement which is not the highest and best use for the site on which it is placed by reason of excess size or cost. Also called superadequacy.

ownership
(1) The right of one or more persons to possess and use property to the exclusion of all others. (2) A collection of rights to the use and enjoyment of property.

ownership in severalty
Property owned by one person or entity.

paired sales analysis
A method of estimating the amount of adjustment for the presence or absence of any feature by pairing the sales prices of otherwise identical properties with and without that feature. Also known as paired data set analysis, matched pairs analysis, and direct market method.

panelized home
A type of factory-built housing. A panelized home arrives at the construction site in small units, usually as completed walls with all the wiring and plumbing intact.

par value
Market value, nominal value.

parameter
A statistical term for a single number or attribute of the individual things, persons, or other entities in a population.

parcel
(1) A tract or an extended area of land. (2) A part, as in a certain piece of land is part and parcel of another piece.

parcel map
Map showing a parcel of land that will be subdivided into less than five parcels or units, and shows land boundaries, streets, and parcel numbers.

partial interest
An interest in real estate that represents less than the fee simple estate (i.e., a leased fee or leasehold estate).

partial taking
The process by which a governmental agency acquires only a portion of a property through condemnation.

partition action
A court action to divide a property held by co-owners.

party wall
A wall erected on the line between two adjoining properties that are under different ownership, for the use at both properties.

percentage adjustment
Type of sales adjustment in which the estimated difference between the comparable sale and the subject is first calculated as a percentage of the sale price of the comparable, and then applied as an upward or downward adjustment to the price.

percentage lease
A type of lease in which the tenant pays a percentage of gross monthly receipts in addition to a base rent.

percolation
The draining or permeating of water through soil.

personal property
Anything movable that is not real property.

physical deterioration
Depreciation that comes from wear and tear, negligent care, damage by dry rot or termites, or severe changes in temperature. Also known as deferred maintenance.

physical life
The length of time a structure can be considered habitable, without regard to its economic use.

physically possible
A use for the property that is not prevented by any physical issues such as poor access, steep topography, or unusable soil. The first test for highest and best use.

planned development
A planning and zoning term describing land not subject to conventional zoning to permit clustering of residences or other characteristics of the project which differ from normal zoning.

planning commission
An agency of local government charged with planning the development, redevelopment, or preservation of an area.

plat
An illustration, plan, or map of a plot of ground or a town site.

plat map
Map of a subdivision indicating the location and boundaries of individual lots.

plottage
The value added by combining two or more parcels together into one large parcel.

plottage increment
The appreciation in unit value created by joining smaller ownerships into one large single ownership.

plottage value
The increase in value brought about by the combining of two or more parcels of land with the result that the total value of the combined parcels in the "after" situation exceeds the value of the sum of the individual parcels in the "before" situation.

point of beginning
Starting place for a legal description of land using the metes and bounds method.

point estimate of value
The final value indication reported as a single dollar amount.

police power
The power of the state to enact laws within constitutional limits to promote the order, safety, health, morals, and general welfare of our society.

population
(1) The total number of people inhabiting a specific area. (2) In statistics, the entire set of data from which a statistical sample is drawn.

positive cash flow
When income generated by the property flows toward the owner.

potential gross income
A property's total potential income from all sources during a specified period of time.

potential value
The value that can reasonably be foreseen in the future.

precut home
A type of factory-built housing. A precut home is like a house in a box. All the materials are delivered to the construction site unassembled, but precut to fit exactly in place.

prefabricated
Any building or portion thereof, which is manufactured and assembled off site, then erected on a property.

pride of ownership
The pride of the owner in his or her property, reflected in the care and maintenance of the property.

primary mortgage market
The term for the market made up of lenders who make mortgage loans by lending directly to borrowers.

prime rate
The rate the bank charges its strongest customers (those with the highest credit ratings), is heavily influenced by the discount rate.

principal
(1) In a real estate transaction, the one who hires the broker to represent him or her in the sale of the property. (2) The amount of money borrowed.

principal meridian
One of 35 north and south survey lines established and defined as part of the U.S. government survey system.

principle(s) of:
anticipation
States that value is created by the anticipation of benefits derived in the future.

balance
States that the greatest value of a property will occur when the type and size of the improvements are proportional to each other as well as to the land.

change
Holds that it is the future, not the past, which is of prime importance in estimating value. Real estate values are constantly changed by environmental, economic, political, and social forces.

competition
States that real estate values are affected by supply and demand because of competition. Typically follows three steps: (1) market demand generates profits, (2) profits generate competition, and (3) competition stabilizes profits.

conformity
States that maximum value results when properties in a neighborhood are relatively similar in size, style, quality, use, and/or type.

consistent use
Requires that land and improvements be appraised on the basis of the same use.

contribution
Calculates the worth of a particular component in terms of its contribution to the value of the whole property, or an item's worth is calculated as the amount that its absence would detract from the value of the whole.

increasing and decreasing returns
The idea that income and other benefits available from real estate may be increased by adding capital improvements only up to the point of balance in the agents of production, beyond which the increase in value tends to be less than the increase in costs. Also known as law of increasing and decreasing returns.

opportunity cost

The economic principle that recognizes competing investments, usually in different industries, that may have a greater return.

progression

States that the worth of a lesser valued residence tends to be enhanced by association with higher valued residences in the same area.

regression

States that higher-valued properties tend to suffer when placed in close proximity with lower-valued properties.

substitution

Affirms that the maximum value of a property tends to be set by the cost of acquiring an equally desirable and valuable substitute property, assuming no cost delay is encountered in making the substitution. The foundation for the appraisal process.

supply and demand

States that market value is affected by the intersection of supply and demand forces in the market as of the appraisal date. Prices and rent levels tend to increase when demand is greater than supply and tend to decrease when supply exceeds demand.

surplus productivity

States that the net income that remains after the ownership expenses of labor, capital, and management have been paid is surplus income that is attributable to the land. This is also known as land rent and is used as the basis for the residual land valuation techniques.

private restrictions

Created at the time of sale or in the general plan of a subdivision.

pro rata

According to a certain percentage or proportion of a whole.

profits

The excess of returns over expenditures in a given transaction or series of transactions. Also, the excess of income over expenditure, as in a business, during a given period of time.

progress payments

Scheduled, periodic, and partial payment of construction loan funds to a builder as each construction stage is completed.

promissory note

The evidence of the debt, which states the amount of the money borrowed and the terms of repayment.

property

Anything that may be owned and gained lawfully.

property residual technique

A method of value estimation by capitalizing the income to the whole property.

proprietary lease

The lease used in co-op apartment buildings.

proration

Adjustments of interest, taxes, and insurance, etc., on a pro rata basis as of the closing or an agreed-upon date.

public record

A document disclosing all-important facts about the property.

qualitative analysis

Compares data on properties to obtain relative comparisons between properties in the same market.

quantitative analysis

Compares data on properties to obtain results that are then applied to other properties in the same market.

quantity survey method

The most in-depth and detailed method used to estimate reproduction or replacement cost. This method requires a detailed estimate of all labor and materials used in the components of a building. Items such as overhead, insurance, and contractor's profit are added to direct costs of building. This method is time consuming but very accurate.

quitclaim deed

Transfers any interest the grantor may have at the time the deed is signed with no warranties of clear title.

radon

Colorless, odorless, gas that is a carcinogen detected by a spectrometer.

range of value

The difference between the highest and lowest variant.

rate

(1) A fixed ratio, proportion. (2) A charge, payment, or price fixed according to a ratio, scale, or standard. (3) To appraise or assess value for tax assessment purposes.

ratio

Fixed or approximate relation, as between things, in number, quantity, degree, rate, or proportion.

ratio capitalization

Describes any capitalization method that uses the typical ratio of income to value to convert projected income into a value estimate for the property (or property component) under appraisal. Includes direct capitalization, as well as land, building, and equity residual capitalization methods when sales price-income ratios are used.

real estate

An identified parcel or tract of land, including any improvements.

Real Estate Settlement Procedures Act (RESPA)

A federal law requiring the disclosure to borrowers of settlement (closing) procedures and costs by means of a pamphlet and forms prescribed by the United States Department of Housing and Urban Development.

real property

Land (air, surface, mineral, water rights), appurtenances, and anything attached, and immovable by law. Also included are the interests, benefits, and rights inherent in owning real estate, i.e., the "bundle of rights". Current usage makes the term real property synonymous with real estate.

recapture

The recovery by an owner of money invested. Known as return of investment, not to be confused with interest, which is a return on investment. Also known as capital recapture.

reconciliation

The adjustment process of weighing results of all three appraisal methods to arrive at a final estimate of the subject property's market value. Also known as correlation.

reconstructed operating statement

One that eliminates the inapplicable expense items for appraisal purposes and adjusts the remaining valid expenses, if necessary.

Record Keeping

Per USPAP, this section of the ETHICS RULE identifies the record keeping requirements appraisers must follow.

rectangular survey system

A method of specifying the location of a parcel of land using prime meridians, base lines, standard parallels, guide meridians, townships, and sections. Also known as the rectangular survey system, or the U.S. Government Section and Township Survey.

redlining

An illegal lending policy, which denies real estate loans on properties in older, changing urban areas, usually with large minority populations, because of alleged higher lending risks and without due consideration being given by the lending institution to the creditworthiness of the individual loan applicant.

refinancing

The paying-off of an existing obligation and assuming a new obligation in its place. To finance anew, or to extend or renew existing financing.

region

Generally a segment of the nation set apart from other areas by geographical boundaries.

regression analysis

Statistical technique for calculating sales price or adjustments, or for estimating probable sales prices or other variables.

rehabilitation

The restoration of a property to its former or improved condition without changing the basic design or plan.

remainder depreciation

The possible future loss in value of an improvement to real property.

remaining economic life

The number of years between the structure's estimated economic life and its effective age.

remodel

An activity designed to improve the value or desirability of a property through rebuilding, refurbishing, redecorating or adding on to it.

renaissance

Fourth phase in the cycle of a neighborhood. The transition to a new cycle through the demolition, relocation, or major renovation of existing buildings.

renovation

Renewal, repair, or restoration to life.

rent

Payment for the use of a property, generally under a lease agreement.

rent roll

Total of all scheduled rental amounts for tenant space, services, and parking.

rental income

The total of the economic, or fair, rent for each of the units.

rental survey
An analysis of competitive rents used to identify the amount of income the subject property might generate.

replacement cost
Cost of constructing a building or structure that would have a similar utility to the subject improvement, but constructed with modern materials and according to current standards, design, and layout.

replacement reserves
Funds set aside by the property owner to pay for the replacement of certain building components and fixtures that periodically wear out. Also known as reserves for replacement.

replacement value
The amount of money required to replace any improvements that have been lost to fire, flood, wind, or other natural disasters.

reproduction cost
The current cost of building a replica of the subject structure, using similar quality materials.

residential lease
A lease used for single-family homes and duplexes.

RESPA
See Real Estate Settlement Procedures Act.

Restricted Use Appraisal Report
This is the briefest presentation of an appraisal and contains the least detail. Also known as restricted use because the client is the only intended user of the report.

restriction
A limitation placed on the use of property. A restriction may be placed by a private owner, a developer, or the government.

retaining walls
Walls constructed to hold back soil and prevent erosion.

retrospective appraisal
An appraisal that looks at the value of a property at a point of time in the past.

return of investment
Recapture or conversion of the investment in real estate to cash or other valuable assets.

return on investment
The interest earned by an investor on an investment. Also known as return or yield.

reversion
The right to future possession or enjoyment by a person, or the person's heirs, creating the proceeding estate.

reversionary interest
A future interest. For example, the right of a landlord to reclaim the property at the end of the lease.

right-of-way
A right of passage on, over, or under another person's land.

riparian rights
The rights of a landowner whose land is next to a natural watercourse to reasonable use of whatever water flows past the property.

risk analysis
A study made, usually by a lender, of the various factors that might affect the repayment of a loan.

risk rating
A process used by the lender to decide on the soundness of making a loan and to reduce all the various factors affecting the repayment of the loan to a qualified rating of some kind.

room
Space that is enclosed or set apart by a partition.

rounding
Expressing an amount as an approximate number.

row house
A single-family residence, much like a townhouse, with side-walls that are common with adjoining row houses. Differs from a townhouse in that the tandem garage and utility area usually occupy the ground floor or basement level and there are generally no common areas of ownership.

RULES
The five rules in USPAP: the ETHICS RULE, the COMPETENCY RULE, the DEPARTURE RULE (or SCOPE OF WORK RULE), the JURISDICTIONAL EXCEPTION RULE, and the SUPPLEMENTAL STANDARDS RULE.

rural
An area outside of an established urban area or metropolitan district.

R-value
A rating that measures how well insulation resists heat.

sale-leaseback-buyback
A sale and leaseback transaction in which the leaseholder has the option to buy back the original property after a specified period of time.

sale-resale analysis
A method for determining adjustment or depreciation amounts that is useful when a property sells and is resold in a relatively short period of time. Assuming both sales are arm's-length, open market transactions, and assuming that there have been no significant changes to the property during the time between the two sales, the difference in price could be a basis for a time adjustment.

sales price
The actual price that a buyer pays for a property.

salvage value
(1) For income tax purposes, the anticipated fair market value of the property at the end of its useful life. (2) The value imputable to a house, structure, or object if it were to be moved to another location.

sample
A defined group within the whole that appraisers work with when analyzing statistical data.

sandwich lease
A lease agreement in which a tenant sublets the property to another person, thus creating a sublessor-sublessee relationship.

scarcity
A lack of supply of some type of real property resulting in increased value when demand exceeds supply.

scheduled rent
Rent paid by agreement between lessor and lessee. Also known as contract rent.

scope of work
The type and extent of research done and the type and extent of analysis applied.

scrap value
The value imputable to components of a structure, such as lumber, copper, roofing materials, or bricks, if they are removed from the existing premises for use elsewhere.

secondary mortgage market
The market involved in the buying and selling of existing mortgage loans from the primary mortgage market or from each other.

section
An area of land that is one square mile, 640 acres, or 1/36 of a township.

Self-Contained Appraisal Report
Contains the most detailed information. Self-contained means that everything the user of the report needs to fully understand it is contained within the report.

seller's market
The market condition in which demand exceeds supply.

semi-detached house
A house with one side a party or lot-line wall.

sentimental value
The value imputable to a property because of a close personal interest or relationship by the owner or potential owner.

separate property
Property owned by a married person in his or her own right outside of the community interest including property acquired by the spouse before marriage or by gift or inheritance.

septic system
The waste removal system.

septic tank
A watertight sewage-settling tank designed to accommodate liquid and solid waste.

service income
Includes receipts from laundry facilities, vending machines, and selling of utility services to tenants.

setback
The distance a building must be set back from the lot line. It is usually a front, back, or side setback.

setback line
A line set by an ordinance that determines how close to a property line a structure can be erected or installed.

setback ordinance
An ordinance requiring improvements built on property to be a specified distance from the property line, street, or curb.

severance damage
In eminent domain actions, the damage to the remainder of a property resulting from a part take of the whole property and the construction of the improvements as proposed.

shed roof
A lean-to type roof with one sloping side and one vertical side meeting at a ridge.

shopping center, regional
A large shopping center with 250,000 to 1,000,000 square feet of store area and serving 200,000 or more people.

short-lived
Structural components that are expected to be replaced or repaired on a consistent basis throughout the life of the structure.

significant digits
Those that go from the first numeral on the left over to the last numeral on the right that is not a zero.

single-family residence
Any improvement used as a dwelling for one related family group.

sinking fund
A fund set aside from a property's income which, with accrued interest, will eventually pay for replacement of the improvements.

site
(1) Land that has been prepared for use with grading, utilities, and access. (2) The position, situation, or location of a piece of land in a neighborhood.

skylight
An opaque window in the roof.

slab-on-grade
A type of foundation in which the structure sits directly on the ground. Monolithic slabs, floating slabs, screeded slabs, and post-tensioned slabs are all types of slab-on-grade foundations.

slum area
An area of generally run-down, overcrowded residences, usually multiple-family, whose inhabitants are usually economically deprived.

solar panels
Gather the sun's heat for use in a solar water heater, solar heating system, and even as a source of electricity in the residence.

special flood hazard area
Flood-prone area identified by FEMA. If the subject property is within a flood hazard zone, it needs to be noted in the appraisal report.

special warranty deed
A deed in which the grantor warrants or guarantees the title only against defects arising during the grantor's ownership of the property and not against defects existing before the time of the grantor's ownership.

special-purpose property
Property that has unique usage requirements, such as a church or a museum, making it difficult to convert to other uses.

square foot cost
The cost per square foot of area of land or a building found by dividing the number of square feet of area into the total cost of the structure or land.

special-use permit
See conditional-use permit.

square-foot method
A method for calculating reproduction or replacement cost by multiplying the cost per square foot by the building's area in square feet. The most common method used by appraisers and real estate agents to estimate the cost of construction.

squatter's rights
The right of use and enjoyment by reason of a long and uncontested possession of a parcel of real property.

stable phase
Second phase in the cycle a neighborhood, marked by stability of the existing buildings and occupants.

standard depth
The most typical lot depth in the neighborhood.

standard deviation
A measure of the extent of variability in a sample, that is, whether the observations are clustered near the mean or scattered throughout the range.

Standards Rules
A series of rules within USPAP that specify what the appraiser must do.

Statements on Appraisal Standards
Part of USPAP, they clarify, interpret, explain, or elaborate on a Rule or Standard.

statistics
The science of collecting, classifying, and interpreting information based on the number of things.

stigmatized property
Property which buyers or tenants may avoid for reasons which are unrelated to its physical conditions or features. Also known as psychologically impacted property.

straight lease
Lease agreement in which rent is a fixed amount that stays the same over the entire lease term.

straight-line method
See economic age/life method.

structure
Anything constructed or erected from an assembly of materials (for example, a house or garage).

subdivision
A tract of land divided by the owner into building lots and streets by a recorded subdivision plat.

subdivision development method
A method of valuing land used for subdivision development. Also known as the land development method.

subdivision system
See lot, block, and tract system.

subject property
The property that is being appraised.

subjective value
Value based on personal reasons.

sublease
A lease given by a lessee.

sub-marginal land
Land from which the return or income falls short of paying all expenses.

subprime loans
loans that do not meet the borrower credit requirements of Fannie Mae and Freddie Mac. Also known as "B" and "C" paper loans as opposed to "A" paper conforming loans.

substructure
Refers to all the below grade improvements.

subsurface
That which lies below the surface.

subsurface rights
Rights in property (oil, water, minerals) found below the surface.

Summary Appraisal Report
The most commonly used report option. It fulfills the minimum requirements for lenders to process their loans.

summation method
Establishes a safe rate for an investment and adds or subtracts from this basic rate according to the proper interest rate for the subject property. Another name for the cost approach to estimating value.

superadequacy
A feature that is too large or of a higher quality than needed for a property. Also known as an over-improvement.

superstructure
Refers to all the above-grade improvements.

supply
The total amount of a given type of property for sale or lease, at various prices, at any given point in time.

surface rights
The rights to use the surface of land, including the right to drill or mine through the surface when subsurface rights are involved.

survey
The process by which a parcel of land is measured and its area is ascertained.

tangible property
Property that has a physical form. Physical objects and/or the rights thereto.

tax rate
The ratio of the tax to the tax base. The rate to be applied to assessed value of real property, which determines the amount of ad valorem tax to be paid.

tenancy by the entirety
The joint ownership, recognized in some states, of property acquired by husband and wife during marriage. On the death of one spouse the survivor becomes the owner of the property.

tenancy in common
When two or more persons, whose interests are not necessarily equal, are owners of undivided interests in a single estate.

tenancy in partnership
Ownership by two or more persons who form a partnership for business purposes.

tenant
The party who has legal possession and use of real property belonging to another.

The Appraisal Foundation
An entity created by the appraisal profession to regulate its own industry. Empowered by the Financial Institutions Reform, Recovery, and Enforcement Act of 1989 to set minimum standards and qualifications for performing appraisals in federally related financial transactions.

tidelands
Lands that are covered and uncovered by the ebb and flow of the tide.

time adjustment
A term usually applied to adjustments made because of changing market conditions.

time value of money
The financial principle that a dollar in the present is worth more than a promised dollar in the future because of the present dollar's interest earning capability.

time-share
A real estate development in which a buyer can purchase the exclusive right to occupy a unit for a specified period each year.

T-intersection lot
A lot that is fronted head-on by a street.

title
Evidence that the owner of land is in lawful possession.

title plant
The storage facility of a title company in which it has accumulated complete title records of properties in its area.

topography
Nature of the surface of land.

townhouse
One of a row of houses usually of the same or similar design with common side walls or with a very narrow space between adjacent side walls. Also known as a row house.

township
Used in the government survey system, an area six miles by six miles (36 square miles) described by its location relative to the intersection of the baseline and meridian.

tract
A piece of land in an unimproved state – it does not have utilities, sewer lines, etc.

trade fixture
An item of personal property, such as a shelf, cash register, room partition or wall mirror, used to conduct a business.

Trainee License
In some states, this is the beginning level of appraisal license. The education, experience, and exam requirements to obtain a trainee license vary widely by state. Trainees must be supervised.

transferability
The ability to transfer ownership of an item from one person or entity to another.

transition
Change in use, such as farm to residential to commercial.

trend
A particular direction of movement.

trend analysis
Analysis that uses an arrangement of statistical data in accordance with its time of occurrence, usually over a period of years.

trust deed
See deed of trust.

turnkey costs
Costs that include all of the charges to the consumer, not just the costs to the developer or builder.

under-improvement
An improvement which, because of a deficiency in size or cost, is not the highest and best use of the site.

underwriting
Insuring something against loss.

unearned increment
An increase in real estate value that comes about from forces outside the control of the owner(s), such as a favorable shift in population.

unfinished areas
The areas of a home that do not have flooring, insulation, etc., that is similar to the rest of the house.

Uniform Residential Appraisal Report (URAR)
An example of a summary report. It is probably the most widely used form.

Uniform Standards of Professional Appraisal Practice (USPAP)
A set of standards and ethics, originally developed by nine appraisal associations to guide members in the development and reporting of appraisals. Now developed, published, interpreted, and amended by the Appraisal Standards Board of the Appraisal Foundation.

unimproved
Not improved, as not used, tilled, cultivated, or built upon.

unit
(1) A single object. (2) A standard of measure by which other quantities are evaluated.

unit cost
The cost in money of a standard quantity (for example, a square foot or a cubic yard) of a particular item.

unit-in-place method
A method of determining reproduction or replacement cost. Also known as the segregated cost method.

unit-of-comparison adjustment
Sales analysis tool, wherein the sales prices of the comparables are converted to price per physical or economic unit that is found to be closely related to selling price or value.

unit of measurement
The particular measurement being used. The two most commonly used are square foot (area) and cubic foot (volume).

urban property
City property.

urban sprawl

The unplanned and often haphazard growth of an urban area into adjoining areas.

usable area

That portion of the gross area of a site that can be built on or developed. Also known as useful area.

useful life

See economic life.

utility

The ability of a property to satisfy a need or desire, such as for shelter or income.

vacancy factor

The percentage of a building's space that is unrented over a given period.

vacancy loss

Loss of potential income because of a vacant unit.

vacant land

Land or site that is unimproved and that does not have any structures.

valuation

The process of estimating value.

value

The present and future anticipated enjoyment or profit from the ownership of property. Also known as worth.

value conclusion

See final value estimate.

value in exchange

See market value.

value-in-use

(1) The subjective value of an item or object to a particular user. (2) The value of a property under a given use. Also known as use value.

variable expenses

Operating expenses that vary with occupancy level or intensity of use of a property (e.g., utility costs and maintenance).

variance

An exception granted to existing zoning regulations for special reasons.

verification

An inquiry into the circumstances surrounding and affecting a sale.

warranty deed

A deed used to transfer title to property, guaranteeing that the title is clear and the grantor has the right to transfer it.

waste

The destruction, or material alteration of, or injury to, premises by a tenant.

water rights

(1) The right to draw water from a water course. (2) The right to use water, as water on a lake, for recreation.

water table

The depth below the land surface at which water is found.

wear and tear

Depreciation of an asset due to ordinary usage.

workfile

Appraiser's records that contain all the documentation necessary to support the appraiser's analyses, opinions, and conclusions conveyed in the appraisal report.

xeriscape

A patented name for landscaping that conserves water by using a wide variety of plants appropriate for the natural environment.

yield

The interest earned by an investor on an investment (or by a bank on the money it has loaned). Also known as return or profit.

yield capitalization

A method that discounts future benefits at appropriate yield rates, producing a value that reflects the income pattern, value change, and yield-rate characteristics of the investment.

yield rate

The yield expressed as a percentage of the total investment. Also known as rate of return.

zero lot line

A municipal zoning category wherein a building or other fixture may abut the property line.

zeroscaping

The use of rock and hardscape with only a few sparse plants to create low water landscaping.

zone

An area subject to certain restrictions or restraints.

zoning

The regulation of structures and uses of property within selected districts.

zoning law

Type of law used to execute master plans and control the mix of properties in a particular area.

zoning variance

An exemption from a zoning ordinance or regulation permitting a structure or use that would not otherwise be allowed.

INDEX